Changing Sustainability Norms through Communication Processes

CORPORATIONS, GLOBALISATION AND THE LAW

Series Editor: Janet Dine, *Director, Centre for Commercial Law Studies, Queen Mary, University of London, UK*

This uniquely positioned monograph series aims to draw together high quality research work from established and younger scholars on what is an intriguing and under-researched area of the law. The books will offer insights into a variety of legal issues that concern corporations operating on the global stage, including interaction with the World Trade Organization (WTO), international financial institutions and nation states, in both developing and developed countries. While the underlying foundation of the series will be that of company law, broadly-defined, authors are encouraged to take an approach that draws on the work of other social sciences, such as politics, economics and development studies and to offer an international or comparative perspective where appropriate. Specific topics to be considered will include corporate governance, corporate responsibility, taxation and criminal liability, amongst others. The series will undoubtedly offer an important contribution to legal thinking and to the wider globalisation debate.

Titles in the series include:

Secured Credit and the Harmonisation of Law
The UNCITRAL Experience
Gerard McCormack

A Legal Framework for Emerging Business Models
Dynamic Networks as Collaborative Contracts
Emily M. Weitzenboeck

Directors' Duties and Shareholder Litigation in the Wake of the Financial Crisis
Edited by Joan Loughrey

Governance of Distressed Firms
David Milman

The Nature of Corporate Governance
The Significance of National Cultural Identity
Janet Dine and Marios Koutsias

Corporate Social Responsibility in Contemporary China
Jingchen Zhao

Corporate Social Responsibility, Private Law and Global Supply Chains
Andreas Rühmkorf

Enhancing Firm Sustainability Through Governance
The Relational Corporate Governance Approach
Francesco de Zwart

Human Rights and Corporate Wrongs
Closing the Governance Gap
Simon Baughen

Changing Sustainability Norms through Communication Processes
The Emergence of the Business and Human Rights Regime as Transnational Law
Karin Buhmann

Changing Sustainability Norms through Communication Processes

The Emergence of the Business and Human Rights Regime as Transnational Law

Karin Buhmann

Professor of Business and Human Rights, Copenhagen Business School, Denmark

CORPORATIONS, GLOBALISATION AND THE LAW

Cheltenham, UK • Northampton, MA, USA

© Karin Buhmann 2017

All rights reserved. No part of this publication may be reproduced, stored in a retrieval system or transmitted in any form or by any means, electronic, mechanical or photocopying, recording, or otherwise without the prior permission of the publisher.

Published by
Edward Elgar Publishing Limited
The Lypiatts
15 Lansdown Road
Cheltenham
Glos GL50 2JA
UK

Edward Elgar Publishing, Inc.
William Pratt House
9 Dewey Court
Northampton
Massachusetts 01060
USA

A catalogue record for this book
is available from the British Library

Library of Congress Control Number: 2017947104

This book is available electronically in the Elgaronline
Law subject collection
DOI 10.4337/9781786431653

ISBN 978 1 78643 164 6 (cased)
ISBN 978 1 78643 165 3 (eBook)

Typeset by Servis Filmsetting Ltd, Stockport, Cheshire
Printed and bound in Great Britain by TJ International Ltd, Padstow

For Nicholas

Contents

List of figures	x
Acknowledgements	xi
List of abbreviations	xiii
Table of documents and instruments	xv

PART I   SETTING THE STAGE

1   Introduction 3
   1.1   What this book is about 3
   1.2   Why business and human rights is significant for understanding multi-stakeholder regulation on private-sector impact on society 6
   1.3   Approach, methodology and cases 14
   1.4   Structure of the book 38
2   The context: the CSR discourse and its relation to law, human rights and social sustainability 40
   2.1   CSR and law 40
   2.2   Public policy interests, CSR and human rights 59
   2.3   International human rights law, CSR and business: Normativity for business action and business interest in governments protecting human rights 68
   2.4   The relevance of international soft law for CSR and business and human rights 70
   2.5   Developing norms on business impact on society: Civil society and business participation 74
3   Argumentative strategies, discourse and system-specific rationality 79
   3.1   System-specific rationality and communication in reflexive law 79
   3.2   Discourse and multi-stakeholder communication on CSR and BHR normativity 85

viii *Changing sustainability norms through communication processes*

PART II DISCURSIVE CONSTRUCTION OF BUSINESS RESPONSIBILITIES FOR CSR

4 Two steps forward, one back – more than once: Developing normative guidance for business on human rights in a CSR context   105
   4.1 From moral acting to legal action: direct and indirect human rights concerns   106
   4.2 Initial steps towards intergovernmental normative guidance: UN, OECD and ILO   111
   4.3 The Draft Norms on the Responsibilities of Transnational Corporations and other Business Enterprises with regard to human rights   116
   4.4 The United Nations Global Compact   131
   4.5 The European Multi-Stakeholder Forum on CSR   142
   4.6 The CSR Alliance   164
   4.7 Summing up   168
5 From incremental steps to emerging regime   173
   5.1 From the Draft Norms to the resolution establishing the SRSG mandate   176
   5.2 First mandate year: From establishment of mandate to 2006 ('Interim') report   186
   5.3 Second mandate year: From 'Interim' report to 2007 report   202
   5.4 Third mandate year: From 2007 report to UN Framework   226
   5.5 Clarification of 'complicity' and 'sphere of influence': Rejecting 'sphere of influence' and introducing human rights due diligence   243
   5.6 From the UN Framework to the UNGPs   252
   5.7 Arguing the outputs of the SRSG terms into acceptance   256

PART III ARGUING FOR CHANGE

6 Argumentative strategies   269
   6.1 Introduction   269
   6.2 Power, discourse and communication in system-specific logics   271
   6.3 Playing on system-specific interests: Stabilising and de-stabilising argumentative strategies   285
   6.4 Specificity   309
   6.5 Towards the BHR regime   312

7	Conclusion	315
	7.1 Summing up on analysis and findings	315
	7.2 The emergence of the BHR regime: Background, institutionalisation, and break-through	320
	7.3 Perspectives for the future evolution of sustainability norms	325
	7.4 Theory implications	327
	7.5 Implications for practitioners	329

Bibliography 332
Index 365

Figures

1.1	Basic model for text analysis	33
3.1	General model of relations and reaction for analysis of system-specific interest-based arguments	92
3.2	Basic triangular model	94
3.3	Triangular model for NGO statement on supply chain in SRSG consultation (example)	95
4.1	UN Draft Norms: Model of relations and reaction for analysis of system-specific interest-based arguments	130
4.2	UN Global Compact: Model of relations and reaction for analysis of system-specific interest-based arguments	141
4.3	EU MSF: Model of relations and reaction for analysis of establishment of MSF and system-specific interest-based arguments in discursive construction of CSR normativity	162
4.4	CSR Alliance: Model of relations and reaction for analysis of system-specific interest-based arguments for establishment of CSR Alliance	167
5.1	SRSG process: Model of relations and reaction for analysis of system-specific interest-based communication for discursive construction of business responsibilities for human rights	259
5.2	SRSG process – 2005–2008 term – mandate point (c): Model of relations and reactions for analysis of system-specific interest-based communication in discursive construction of business responsibilities for human rights: 'complicity', 'sphere of influence' and human rights due diligence	263
6.1	The SRSG's argumentative strategy for human rights due diligence (company audience)	296
6.2	Arguing why businesses should commit to the Global Compact	299

Acknowledgements

Several institutions and individuals made this book possible through their assistance and support.

First and foremost, most of the research on which the book builds on was made possible by a grant from the Danish Research Council for the Social Sciences for the research project 'The legal character of CSR (Corporate Social Responsibility): reflections between CSR and Public International Law, and implications for corporate regulation' (2006–2010). I am also grateful to the Research Council for its grant for the collaborative research project 'Ny styrings- og retsformer i Multi-Level Governance: Statens rolle mellem international, transnational, national og sub-national styring af bæredygtigt skovbrug' ('New forms of governance and law in Multi-Level Governance: the role of the State in international, transnational, national and sub-national governance of sustainable forestry') (2010–2013), which also contributed to research informing this book. By enabling my host institutions to reduce my teaching load the grants provided for extended periods of coherent time for research and writing, which allowed me to develop the analysis on which part of this book draws.

For institutional hosting, my thanks go to the Department of Management, Society and Communication at Copenhagen Business School (CBS), where parts of the said research projects were developed into this book; to the Department of Society and Globalisation at Roskilde University where the research idea was conceived and the initial years of work carried out; the Institute for Food and Resource Economics at the University of Copenhagen, where some of the research was carried out; and the Department of Communication, Business and Information Technologies at Roskilde University where the research was finalised. For inspiring short term research stays in 2007, 2009–10 and 2013, I am grateful to the Danish Institute for Human Rights, Columbia Law School in New York City and the School of Law at the University of Nottingham. I wish to extend my thanks to Hans Otto Sano, Benjamin Liebman and Mary Footer, respectively, for making those visits possible.

While working on the research on which this book draws I have benefitted from views, advice and friendly critique from a large number of colleagues and experts in very diverse academic or practice-oriented environments. For the fruitful discussions and encouragement, I would like in particular to thank Annali Kristiansen, Anne Lise Kjær, Beate Sjåfjell, Ben Cashore, Bettina Lemann Kristiansen, Cedric Ryngaert, David Kinley, David Monciardini, Errol Meidinger, Håkan Hydén, Inger-Johanne Sand, Jacob Dahl Rendtorff, Jan Wouters, Jette Steen Knudsen, Johanna Alkan Olsson, Jørgen Dalberg-Larsen, Linda Nielsen, Knud Sinding, Lynn Roseberry, Mary Footer, Margaret Jungk, Mette Morsing, Michael Addo, Nicola Jägers, Nils Åkerstrøm Andersen, Radu Mares, Rass Holdgaard, Steen Thomsen, Surya Deva, and Sune Skadegaard Thorsen, as well as colleagues at the departments and institutions that employed and hosted me during the work that led to this book.

I wish to also extend my gratitude to research librarians, financial and secretarial staff and supportive heads of departments at the institutions where I was employed during my work feeding into this book.

Moreover, I have been fortunate to have informative conversations with Professor John (G.) Ruggie in his capacity as the United Nations Secretary General's Special Representative on Business and Human Rights and with members of his team, especially Lend Wendland and Vanessa Zimmermann. Conversations with Søren Mandrup Petersen and Ursula Wynhofen at the UN Global Compact, and with Genevieve Besse and Dominique Bé at the European Commission and the European Social Funds, respectively, also contributed valuable information. I also wish to acknowledge the participation and engagement by Professor Gunther Teubner at a workshop on reflexive law held in Copenhagen in November 2007, funded under the grant from the Danish Research Council for the Social Sciences noted above.

Further thanks go to my editor Laura Mann at Edward Elgar for her support and patience, to Jacqueline Tedaldi for very useful comments and for doing a wonderful job editing the text and references, and to the Governing Responsible Business (GRB) research environment at CBS for financial support for language and text editing.

Last but not least, I wish to thank my son Nicholas for his patience and understanding when I was working strange hours, physically absent or, maybe even more demanding, simply mentally absent with my mind preoccupied by the research that informed this book and much of my other work during part of his childhood and much of his adolescence.

Copenhagen, March 2017
Karin Buhmann

Abbreviations

BHR	Business and Human Rights
BIAC	Business and Industry Advisory Committee
BLIHR	Business Leaders Initiative for Human Rights
CDA	Critical Discourse Analysis
CEEP	European Centre of Employers and Enterprises providing Public Services and Services of general interest
CSR	Corporate Social Responsibility
CSR Europe	European Business Network for Corporate Social Responsibility
Draft (UN) Norms	Norms on the Responsibilities of Transnational Corporations and Other Business Enterprises with regard to Human Rights
ECHR	European Convention on Human Rights
ECtHR	European Court of Human Rights
ECOSOC	United Nations Economic and Social Council
ESC	European Society Charter
ESG	Environment, Social and Governance
ETUC	European Trade Union Confederation
EU	European Union
FIDH	The International Federation for Human Rights
FSC	Forest Stewardship Council
GRI	Global Reporting Initiative
ICC	International Chamber of Commerce
ICCPR	International Covenant on Civil and Political Rights
ICEM	International Federation of Chemical, Energy, Mine and General Workers' Union
ICESCR	International Covenant on Economic, Social and Cultural Rights
ICFTU	International Confederation of Free Trade Unions
ICJ	International Commission of Jurists
ICMM	International Council on Mining and Metals
IGO	Intergovernmental Organisation

ILO	International Labour Organisation
IOE	International Organisation of Employers
ISO	International Organization for Standardization
MDG	Millennium Development Goals
MNC	Multinational Corporation
MSF	European Commission's Multi-Stakeholder Forum on CSR
NGO	Non-governmental organisation
OECD	Organisation for Economic Development and Cooperation
OHCHR	Office of the High Commissioner for Human Rights
PEFC	Programme for the Endorsement of Forest Certification
PRI	Principles for Responsible Investment
SDG	Sustainable Development Goals
SME	Small and Medium-sized Enterprises
SR	Social Responsibility
SRI	Socially responsible investment
SRSG	Special Representative of the UN Secretary-General on Business and Human Rights
TFEU	Treaty on the Functioning of the European Union
TNC	Transnational Corporation
TUAC	Trade Union Advisory Committee to the OECD
UDHR	Universal Declaration of Human Rights
UN	United Nations
UNCITRAL	UN Commission on International Trade Law
UNDP	United Nations Development Programme
UNEP	United Nations Environment Programme
UNGP, UNGPs	United Nations Guiding Principles on Business and Human Rights
UNICE	Union of Industrial and Employers' Confederations of Europe (now BusinessEurope)
WBCSD	World Business Council of Sustainable Development
WHO	World Health Organisation

Table of documents and instruments: International and national law and policy instruments, CSR and BHR instruments, organisation documents and stakeholder statements

INTERNATIONAL INSTRUMENTS (HARD LAW, SOFT LAW, POLICY INSTRUMENTS)

Council of Europe
European Convention on Human Rights (ECHR) 145, 155
European Social Charter, Council of Europe (1961), ETS No. 35 .... 145, 150, 152, 155
European Social Charter (Revised), Council of Europe (1996), ETS No. 163 .... 145, 150, 152, 155

European Union (EU)
Commission of the European Communities (2001) Promoting a European Framework for Corporate Social Responsibility COM(2001)366 .... 50, 144, 145, 146, 147, 148, 303
Commission of the European Communities (2002) Corporate Social Responsibility: A business contribution to sustainable development COM(2002)347 ...... 49, 144, 145, 148–150, 303, 306
Commission of the European Communities (2006) Communication from the Commission to the European Parliament, the Council and the European Economic and Social Committee: Implementing the Partnership for Growth and Jobs 144, 145, 165, 170, 303, 306, 324
Annex.... 165, 166, 170, 171, 270, 306
Directive 2014/95/EU Non-Financial Reporting, OJ 2014 L 330 .... 47, 57, 211, 265
European Commission (2011) Communication on a renewed EU Strategy 2011–14 for Corporate Social Responsibility 265, 325
European Parliament (1999) Resolution on EU standards for European enterprises operating in developing countries: towards a European Code of Conduct, OJ C 104/180, EP Resolution A4-0508/98, adopted on 15 January 143
European Parliament (1999) Resolution on the Communication from the Commission to the Council on the trading system and

internationally recognised labour standards (COM(96)0402 – C4048896), A4-0423/98, adopted on 13 January, OJ 1999 C104/63, 14 April.................................... 143, 144
Lisbon Goals (Council of the European Union (2000) Presidency conclusions, Lisbon European Council, 23 and 24 March 2000). 144, 145, 146, 166, 167
Regulation (EC) No 2173/2005 of 20 December 2005 on the establishment of a FLEGT licensing scheme for imports of timber into the European Community, EU doc. OJ 2005 L 347/1 47
Regulation (EU) 995/2010 of 20th October 2010 Timber Regulation – obligations of operators who place timber and timber products on the market, EU doc. OJ 2010 L 295/23......................................47, 53
Transparency Directive (2013/50/EU)... 47
Treaty on the Functioning of the European Union, TFEU, 2009 (Lisbon Treaty)............................145

International Labour Organisation (ILO)
ILO Constitution, adopted by the Peace Conference April 1919, 15 UNTS 40........................114
ILO Convention No. 29, Forced Labour Convention (1930) 39 UNTS 55.............................9, 68, 99
ILO Convention No. 87, Freedom of Association and Protection of the Right to Organise Convention (1949) 68 UNTS 17 ....9, 68, 99
ILO Convention No. 98, Right to Organise and Collective Bargaining Convention (1949) 96 UNTS 257 ....9, 68, 99

ILO Convention No. 100, Equal Remuneration Convention (1951) 165 UNTS 303..........9, 68, 99
ILO Convention No. 105, Abolition of Forced Labour Convention (1957) 320 UNTS 291 ....6, 68, 99
ILO Convention No. 111, Discrimination (Employment and Occupation) Convention (1958) 362 UNTS 31 ....9, 68, 99
ILO Convention No. 138, Minimum Age Convention (1973) 1015 UNTS 297........9, 68, 99
ILO Convention No. 182, Worst Forms of Child Labour Convention (1999) 2133 UNTS 161............................9, 68, 99
ILO Declaration on Fundamental Principles and Rights at Work (1988), 37 ILM 1233 ... 73, 112, 113, 132, 136, 149, 155, 156, 171, 217, 302
Art 2...113
ILO Fundamental conventions 143, 148, 149, 150, 151, 152, 155, 169, 174, 241, 261, 279, 281, 287, 298, 302, 313, 314, 320
ILO Tripartite Declaration of Principles concerning Multinational Enterprises and Social Policy (MNE Declaration, 1977).....35, 42, 73, 112, 113, 114, 115, 119, 121, 129, 143, 144, 155, 156, 179, 188, 217, 279, 290

United Nations (UN)
Commission on Human Rights (2006) Interim report of the Special Representative of the Secretary-General on the issue of human rights and transnational corporations and other business enterprises, UN Doc. E/CN.4/2006/97, 22 February 194, 293
Framework Convention on Climate Change 1992 75

Table of documents and instruments xvii

Human Rights Council (2008)
Corporations and human
rights: a survey of the scope
and patterns of alleged
corporate-related human
rights abuse, UN Doc. A/
HRC/8/5/Add.2, 23 May 234
Human Rights Council (2008)
Clarifying the concepts of
"Sphere of Influence" and
"Complicity", UN Doc. A/
HRC/8/16, 15 May 234, 295
Human Rights Council (2008)
Mandate of the Special
Representative of the
Secretary-General on the issue
of human rights and
transnational corporations
and other business enterprises,
Human Rights Council
Resolution, 8/7June 242, 252
Human Rights Council (2009)
Business and human rights:
Towards operationalizing the
"protect, respect and remedy"
framework, Report of the
Special Representative of the
Secretary-General on the issue
of human rights and
transnational corporations
and other business enterprise,
UN Doc. A/HRC/11/13, 22
April..254
Human Rights Council (2010)
Business and human rights:
Further steps toward the
operationalization of the
"protect, respect and remedy'
framework', Report of the
Special Representative of the
Secretary-General on the issue
of human rights and
transnational corporations
and other business enterprises,
John Ruggie, UN Doc. A/
HRC/14/27, 9 April 254
Human Rights Council (2014)
Elaboration of an
international legally binding
instrument on transnational

corporations and other
business enterprises with
respect to human rights, UN
Doc. A/HRC/RES/26/9, 14
July...88, 262
International Bill of Human
Rights (UDHR, ICESCR,
ICCPR)......................... 9, 155, 165,
174, 241, 281, 298, 313, 314, 320
International Covenant on
Economic, Social and Cultural
Rights (ICESCR)......9, 143, 145, 155
International Covenant on Civil
and Political Rights (ICCPR)........ 9,
143, 155
K. Annan (1999), Address of
Secretary-General Kofi Annan
to the World Economic
Forum in Davos, Switzerland,
31 January.......................... 134, 139,
284, 286, 287, 298
Paris Climate Change Accord
2015 ....4, 13, 325, 326
Rio Declaration on Environment
and Development, UN Doc.
A/CONF.151/26 (Vol. I), 12
August 1992 .... 42, 121, 132, 136
Rome Statute of the
International Criminal Court,
adopted by the UN General
Assembly on 17 July1998, UN
Doc. A/Conf.183/9 ....22, 222
Sustainable Development Goals
(SDGs).......................... 13, 15, 326
Treaty on the Non-Proliferation
of Nuclear Weapons..................... 11
UN Charter (1945), UNTS 993....... 97,
198, 204, 298, 301, 321
Preamble 15
Art 1...135
Art 71... 17
UN Commission on Human
Rights (2005) Human rights
and transnational
corporations and other
business enterprises
(resolution)...................174, 183, 244
UN Commission on Human
Rights (2006) Interim report
of the Special Representative

of the Secretary-General on the issue of human rights and transnational corporations and other business enterprises, UN Doc. E/CN.4/2006/97, 22 February 2006(SRSG 2006 (Interim) Report) 186–202
UN Convention against Corruption, UN Doc. A/58/422, 31 October 2003 132
UN Convention on the Rights of Persons with Disabilities, December 2006............................150
UN Declaration of the Right to Development (1986), UN Doc. A/RES/41/218, 4 December.................................... 72
UN Declaration on the Rights of Indigenous Peoples, UN Doc. A/61/L.67, 13 September 2007 .... 73, 231
UN Draft Code of Conduct on Transnational Corporations. Development and International Economic Cooperation: Transnational Corporations, UN Doc. E/1990/ 94, 12 June 1990 ....8, 73, 111, 112, 114, 115, 116, 131, 170, 251
UN 'Protect, Respect and Remedy' Framework (UN Framework), Report of the Special Representative of the Secretary General on the issue of human rights and transnational corporations and other business enterprises, John Ruggie, UN Doc. A/HRC/8/5, 7 April 2008..........6–9, 10, 11, 12, 13, 20, 25, 35, 36, 38, 39, 40, 42, 45, 47, 48, 53, 58, 68, 88, 89, 95, 96, 101, 102, 105, 106, 123, 124, 125, 126, 145, 168, 171, 172, 173, 174, 175, 176–226, 228, 229, 231, 232, 233–243, 244, 246, 247, 248, 249, 251, 252–256, 260, 261, 262, 264, 265, 270, 271, 275, 276, 280, 281, 282, 284, 285, 288–298, 303, 304, 306, 307, 308, 309, 312, 313, 314, 316, 318, 319, 320, 321, 322, 324, 325, 328, 329, 331

UN General Assembly, Towards global partnerships: Resolution adopted by the General Assembly, UN Doc. A/RES/55/215, passed 21 December 2000......................73, 137
UN General Assembly, Towards global partnerships: Resolution adopted by the General Assembly, UN Doc. A/RES/56/76, passed 11 December 2001......................73, 137
UN General Assembly, Towards global partnerships: Resolution adopted by the General Assembly, UN Doc. A/RES/58/129, 19 December 2003 ....73, 137
UN General Assembly, Towards global partnerships: Resolution adopted by the General Assembly [on the report of the Second Committee (A/60/495 and Corr.1)], UN Doc. A/RES/60/215/, 29 March 2006 (passed 22 December 2005)...73, 137
UN Global Compact 15, 19, 20, 34, 36, 39, 42, 44, 51, 52, 63, 73, 96, 102, 105, 106, 113, 118, 119, 123, 128, 129, 131–142, 146, 147, 150, 155, 156, 159, 163, 171, 179, 192, 244, 250, 270, 278, 279, 283, 284, 285, 286, 287, 293, 297, 298–302, 303, 304, 308, 312, 313, 316, 318, 322, 324, 329
Principles 1–2, Human rights 131, 278, 323
Principle 2 123
Principles 3–6, Labour rights......113, 131, 278, 323
Principle 3 223
Principles 7–9, Environment.......131, 278
Principle 10, Anti-corruption 132, 278
UN Guiding Principles (UNGPs), Human Rights

Table of documents and instruments   xix

Council (2011) Guiding
 Principles on Business and
 Human Rights: Implementing
 the United Nations 'Protect,
 Respect, Remedy' Framework,
 Report of the Special
 Representative of the
 Secretary-General on the issue
 of human rights and
 transnational corporations
 and other business enterprises.
 UN Doc. A/HRC/17/31, 21
 March 6–9, 11, 12, 13,
   20, 35, 49, 57, 88, 96, 105, 106, 115,
   123, 124, 172, 173, 174, 175, 184,
   204, 211, 223, 243, 251, 252–256,
   260, 261, 262, 265, 271, 275, 276,
   280, 281, 282, 289, 298, 312, 313,
     314, 319, 320, 321, 325, 326
UN High Commissioner for
 Human Rights/Commission
 on Human Rights (2005)
 Report on Human Rights and
 the extractive industry, 10–11
 November, UN Doc. E/
 CN.4/2006/92, 19 December 189,
                                          245
UN High Commissioner for
 Human Rights/Commission
 on Human Rights (2007)
 Report on Human Rights and
 the Financial Sector, 16
 February, UN Doc. A/
 HRC/4/99, 6 March 215
UN Human Rights Council
 (2007) Business and Human
 Rights: Mapping international
 standards of responsibility
 and accountability for
 corporate acts, Report of the
 SRSG on the issue of human
 rights and transnational
 corporations and other
 business enterprises (SRSG
 2007 Report), UN Doc. A/
 HRC/4/35, 9 February 202–243,
                                          314
UN Millennium Declaration 42, 121
UN Millennium Development
 Goals (MDG) 195

UN Sub-Commission on
 Prevention of Discrimination
 and Protection of Minorities
 (1995) The realization of
 Economic, Social and Cultural
 Rights: The relationship
 between the enjoyment of
 human rights, in particular,
 international labour and trade
 union rights, and the working
 methods and activities of
 transnational corporations,
 UN Doc. E/CN.4/
 Sub.2/1995/11, 24 July 116
UN Sub-Commission on
 Prevention of Discrimination
 and Protection of Minorities
 (1996) The impact of the
 activities and working
 methods of Transnational
 Corporations on the full
 enjoyment of human rights, in
 particular Economic, Social
 and Cultural Rights and the
 Rights to Development,
 Bearing in mind existing
 international guidelines, rules
 and standards relating to the
 subject matter, UN Doc. E/
 CN.4/Sub.2/196/12, 2 July 117
UN Sub-Commission on
 Prevention of Discrimination
 and Protection of Minorities
 (1998) The realization of
 Economic, Social and Cultural
 Rights: The Question of
 Transnational Corporations,
 UN Doc. E/CN.4/Sub.2/198/6,
 10 June 117
UN Sub-Commission on the
 Promotion and Protection of
 Human Rights (1998)
 Resolution, 1998/8, 20 August
 1998 117
UN Sub-Commission on the
 Promotion and Protection of
 Human Rights (2003) Norms
 on the Responsibilities of
 Transnational Corporations
 and Other Business

Enterprises with regard to
Human Rights, UN Doc. E/
CN.4/Sub.2/2003/12/Rev.2
(Draft Norms)..........8, 19, 20, 34, 35,
    36, 38, 39, 73, 96, 102, 105, 116–
    131, 132, 133, 134, 137, 146, 168,
    169, 170, 173, 175, 176–185, 186,
    187, 191, 196, 198, 200, 204, 205,
    208, 210, 211, 218, 222, 231, 233,
    233, 239, 244, 245, 246, 248, 254,
    273, 276, 278, 280, 282, 284, 285,
    288–298, 302, 306, 307, 308, 318,
        319, 321, 322, 327, 328
Preamble 42, 121, 122
Universal Declaration on
    Human Rights (UDHR) 8,
    9, 10, 68, 71, 99, 121, 122, 132,
    136, 155, 156, 171, 195, 298, 302
World Summit on Sustainable
    Development, Plan of
    Implementation,
    Johannesburg (2002) 42, 63, 121

**Organisation for Economic
Collaboration and Development
(OECD)**
OECD Declaration on
    International Investment and
    Multinational Enterprises...........112,
        113, 114
OECD Guidelines for
    Multinational Enterprises.......35, 42,
    112, 113, 114, 115, 119, 121, 128,
    129, 143, 144, 147, 148, 149, 150,
    152, 155, 156, 159, 169, 179, 188,
    217, 229, 234, 240, 265, 279, 287,
        290, 325

Other
Maastricht Guidelines on
    Violations of Economic,
    Social and Cultural Rights 187

NATIONAL LEGISLATION

China
Labour Contract Law 2007 56

Denmark
Act on Financial Statements
    2008 63

India
Companies Act, 2013 revision.......... 45
    Art 135(5)................................... 47,
        57

United States
Alien Torts Statute, 28 U.S.C. §
    1350 (Alien Torts Claims Act)....110,
        111, 193
Dodd-Frank Wall Street Reform
    Act 2010
    s 1502 47
    s 1504 47
Lacey Act, 16 U.S.C. § 3371–
    3378 47

CSR AND BHR INSTRUMENTS (PRIVATE, PUBLIC AND HYBRID)

Equator Principles 108
EU CSR Alliance (2006–08) 35,
    36, 39, 42, 96, 105, 164–168, 169,
    170, 276, 278, 279, 280, 283, 285,
    287, 302–306, 307, 308, 312, 313,
        316, 318, 322, 324, 329
EU Multi-stakeholder Forum
    (MSF) on CSR 34, 35, 36,
    39, 42, 96, 105, 106, 142–164, 165,
    166, 191, 208, 209, 276, 277, 278,
    279, 280, 283, 284, 285, 286, 287,
    298, 302–306, 307, 308, 311, 312,
    313, 316, 318, 319, 322, 327, 328,
        329, 331
Forest Stewardship Council
    (FSC), Principles.......................... 51
Global Reporting Initiative, GRI 48,
        51
ISO 26000 Social Responsibility
    (SR) Guidance Standard............. 41,
        51, 325
Kimberley Process 207, 217

Table of documents and instruments xxi

SA8000 (Social Accountability
  International) 51
Principles for Responsible
  Investment (PRI) 63,
      108
Programme for the Endorsement
  of Forest Certification
  (PEFC) 51–52
OECD Declaration on
  International Investment and
  Multinational Enterprises 112,
      113, 114
OECD Guidelines for
  Multinational Enterprises 35,
      42, 112, 113, 114, 115, 119, 121,
      128, 129, 143, 144, 147, 148, 149,
      150, 152, 155, 156, 159, 169, 179,
      188, 217, 229, 234, 240, 265, 279,
      287, 290, 325
Voluntary Principles on Business
  and Human Rights 207, 217
UN Framework: UN Protect,
  Respect and Remedy
  Framework, Report of the
  Special Representative of the
  Secretary General on the issue
  of human rights and
  transnational corporations
  and other business enterprises,
  John Ruggie, UN Doc. A/
  HRC/8/5, 7 April 2008 6–9,
      10, 11, 12, 13, 20, 25, 35, 36, 38, 39,
      40, 42, 45, 47, 48, 53, 58, 68, 88, 89,
      95, 96, 101, 102, 105, 106, 123, 124,
      125, 126, 145, 168, 171, 172, 173,
      174, 175, 176–226, 228, 229, 231,
      232, 233–243, 244, 246, 247, 248,
      249, 251, 252–256, 260, 261, 262,
      264, 265, 270, 271, 275, 276, 280,
      281, 282, 284, 285, 288–298, 303,
      304, 306, 307, 308, 309, 312, 313,
      314, 316, 318, 319, 320, 321, 322,
      324, 325, 328, 329, 331
UN Global Compact 15, 19,
      20, 34, 36, 39, 42, 44, 51, 52, 63, 73,
      96, 102, 105, 106, 113, 118, 119,
      123, 128, 129, 131–142, 146, 147,
      150, 155, 156, 159, 163, 171, 179,
      192, 244, 250, 270, 278, 279, 283,
      284, 285, 286, 287, 293, 297,
      298–302, 303, 304, 308, 312, 313,
      316, 318, 322, 324, 329
Principles 1–2, Human rights 131,
      278, 323
Principle 2 123
Principles 3–6, Labour rights 113,
      131, 278, 323
Principle 3 223
Principles 7–9, Environment 131,
      278
Principle 10, Anti-corruption 132,
      278
UN Guiding Principles
  (UNGPs), Human Rights
  Council (2011) Guiding
  Principles on Business and
  Human Rights: Implementing
  the United Nations 'Protect,
  Respect, Remedy' Framework,
  Report of the Special
  Representative of the
  Secretary-General on the issue
  of human rights and
  transnational corporations
  and other business enterprises.
  UN Doc. A/HRC/17/31, 21
  March 6–9, 11, 12, 13,
      20, 35, 49, 57, 88, 96, 105, 106, 115,
      123, 124, 172, 173, 174, 175, 184,
      204, 211, 223, 243, 251, 252–256,
      260, 261, 262, 265, 271, 275, 276,
      280, 281, 282, 289, 298, 312, 313,
      314, 319, 320, 321, 325, 326

ORGANISATIONAL DOCUMENTS AND STAKEHOLDER STATEMENTS

Amnesty International (2005)
  Letter to Professor John
  Ruggie, AI ref UN 260–2005,
  16 September 187–188, 291
Amnesty International (2006)
  Letter to John Ruggie, 27
  April 247
Amnesty International (2005)
  Statement, UN Commission

on Human Rights: The UN's chief guardian of human rights? January 178, 179, 290
Amnesty International (2005) Statement, UN Commission on Human Rights: Amnesty International welcomes new UN mechanism on Business and Human Rights, April.... 182, 186
Asian civil society statement to UN Special Representative on transnational business and human rights at the Asia Regional Consultation, Bangkok, Thailand, 27 June 2006 211
CIDSE – Développement et la Solidarité, (2008) Submission to the Special Representative of the United Nations Secretary-General on Business and Human Rights: Recommendations to reduce the risk of human right violations and improve access to justice, February 228, 258, 309
Clean Clothes Campaign (2007) Letter to John Ruggie, Amsterdam, 23 March 228, 258, 309
ESCR-Net Corporate Accountability Working Group (2005) Joint NGO submission: Consultation on human rights and the extractive industry, final version 9 December 190, 191, 290
FIDH (2006) 'Position paper: Comments to the interim report of the Special Representative of the Secretary-General on the issue of Human Rights and Transnational Corporations and other business enterprises, February 22, 2006', 15 March ...203– 204, 205, 225, 246
Forest Peoples Programme and Tebtebba Foundation (2006), Indigenous Peoples' rights, extractive industries and transnational and other enterprises: A submission to the Special Representative of the Secretary-General on human rights and transnational corporations and other business enterprises, 29 December 203
Human Rights Watch and others (2006) Joint NGO letter in Response to Interim Report 1 205
Interfaith Center for Corporate Responsibility (2006) Letter to John Ruggie, 6 February 191, 212, 291
Interfaith Center on Corporate Responsibility (2006) Letter to John Ruggie, 10 October 213
International Chamber of Commerce and International Organisation of Employers (2003), Joint views of ICC and the IOE on the draft Norms on the Responsibilities of Transnational Corporations and Other Business Enterprises with regard to Human Rights 289
International Commission of Jurists (2005) Corporate Accountability, International human rights law and the United Nations, Geneva, 9 June 187, 250
International Council on Mining and Metals (ICCM) (2006) Submission to UN Secretary General's Special Representative on Human Rights and Business: Clarity and consensus on legitimate human rights responsibilities for companies could accelerate progress, March 2006 .... 207, 208, 213
International Council on Mining and Metals (ICMM) (2006) Second submission to UN Secretary General's Special

Representative on Human
Rights and Business: Mining
and Human Rights: How the
UN SRSG can help spread
good practice and tackle
critical issues, October 208, 209
International Network for
Economic, Social and Cultural
Rights (2007) Letter to John
Ruggie, 5 September 230
International Network for
Economic, Social & Cultural
Rights (2007) Letter to John
Ruggie, Joint NGO letter on
work of the mandate, 10
October 229, 309
IOE, ICC, BIAC (2006) Business
and human rights: The role of
business in weak governance
zones: Business proposals for
effective ways of addressing
dilemma situations in weak
governance zones, Geneva,
December 2006 .... 209, 210,
211, 225, 247, 250, 254, 257, 259,
284

PART I

Setting the stage

1. Introduction

This chapter first introduces the topic and objective of the book, explaining the importance of understanding how arguments made in negotiations on new sustainability norms can promote acceptance of change in a context of divergent interests, and how this knowledge is of benefit to civil society, businesses and public organisations with a concern for sustainability (1.1). The chapter proceeds to explaining why the emergent Business and Human Rights (BHR) regime is an important and relevant case for understanding such a multi-stakeholder regulatory process with competing and often conflicting interests among participants in the regulatory process and the stakeholders whom those participants represent (1.2). Next, it sets out the approach and methodology undertaken for the analysis of the discursive construction of sustainability related norms in five case studies (1.3), explaining the pragmatic approach that draws on socio-legal regulatory theory and systems thinking on how change may be communicated into acceptance, combines this with discourse analysis developed in a political science context, and also considers theory on argumentative stabilising and de-stabilising strategies developed in linguistic communication science. The five case studies, body of empirical data and coding of texts are introduced. Finally, the structure of the book is set out (1.4).

1.1 WHAT THIS BOOK IS ABOUT

The current concern with social, environmental and climate-change related sustainability has been accompanied by calls on private organisations to reduce adverse impacts and enhance their positive impacts on society. Business organisations, in particular, are expected to change their actions to avoid adverse impacts, but also other societal actors like local governments and private non-for-profit organisations are called upon to consider the implications of their actions on society. With the call for change of actions comes a need for norms to guide such change. In addition to private codes of conduct and guidance on sustainability, civil society and business organisations rely on national governments and international organisations, especially the United Nations (UN) to deliver normative directives in the form of soft law (non-binding guidance) or hard law (binding rules). A series of efforts to develop new international law or policy on climate change or social sustainability issues shows that political support, which governments may give to international organisations like the UN to regulate such problems in a manner that draws on their authority and power and may evolve into hard law, is not easily forthcoming or uniform. A diversity of interests at stake often complicates the process of developing norms and reaching agreement.

When we think about normative directives for private or public organisations for actions that conform to global sustainability needs, the focus is often on the substantive content of the rule as such: in other words, what are organisations encouraged or required to do? However, that normative substance is a result of the road that led to the agreed rule, whether soft or hard. In a context marked by interests of different business organisations and sectors, different civil society organisations with diverse focus issues, and various national or local governments with diverging interests, developing norms of conduct becomes a process of negotiation in which participants often have regard for their own interests. The bumpy road to the 2015 Paris Climate Change Accord is a case in point, but in no way unique. Similar concerns can be raised for many other fields. For example, due to differentiated interests global supply chains for timber products apply public, private or hybrid sustainability-related schemes that are not fully aligned within the sector.

Sustainability challenges are likely to remain pressing in the short, medium and longer term, even with the not unlikely potential to expand to extra-terrestrial resource exploitation as resources on this planet are being depleted. For global society to agree on norms of conduct without wasting valuable time, there is a need to understand *how* norms on sustainability issues are negotiated and how stalemates that have marked many such effort in the past can be broken. This book responds to that need by undertaking an analysis of the discursive construction of detailed normative guidance for businesses and states in regard to business responsibilities on human rights, and the argumentative strategies applied in that context. Spurred by a combination of the general Corporate Social Responsibility (CSR) movement and concerns with adverse business impacts on human rights, a process undertaken under the UN between 2005 and 2011 resulted in what is emerging as an autonomous specialised regime within the general international law regime. Set apart from the conventional state-centrist regime of international human rights law, the BHR regime formally recognises that business organisations have responsibilities in regards to standards of conduct developed under international law. Even if so far on a soft law basis, this is a major novelty, which forms part of the output of the process and confirms the significance of the process that lead to that result.

To understand how this came about, this book analyses the multi-stakeholder process leading to the emergent BHR regime, as well as other multi-stakeholder processes that were initiated around the same time by international organisations to develop normative guidance on business responsibilities for human rights or on CSR with a strong human rights element. Recognising that arguments are a major part of what convinces participants in a process of negotiation to agree or what inhibits agreement, the focus is on the content of the debates that took place to develop normative guidance.

In the longer term, an expanded recognition of the private sector as having international responsibilities could have considerable and highly interesting potential. Such recognition and resulting normative directives could involve businesses more actively in responding to transnational sustainability challenges. This underscores the pertinence of understanding and learning from the discursive process that led to a breakthrough in the field of business and human rights, a social sustainability field that until the early 2000s was marked by a stalemate. In revising or updating the conception of relevant actors and their roles in terms of both output and process, the construction of business responsibilities for human rights offers insights for other emergent issue-specific regimes. That applies in particular to those that relate to the division of rights and obligations between and across public and private actors in a global world with increased competition for resources and increased awareness of the consequences of such competition.

Accordingly, the analysis also has regard to the *argumentative strategies* framing the specific arguments made in the construction of the BHR regime and related multi-stakeholder processes. It considers how particular types of arguments can promote or inhibit acceptance of normative change with other participants by either speaking to the interests and logic of those participants, or not doing so. Such knowledge can help participants in future processes of developing, negotiating and agreeing on normative guidance in the sustainability field to develop convincing arguments and effective argumentative strategies. Regardless of whether such processes occur at the international, national or local level or aim at developing public, private or public-private (hybrid) norms, these insights will be of benefit to civil society organisations, businesses, governments, intergovernmental organisations or other parties with an interest in sustainability.

1.2 WHY BUSINESS AND HUMAN RIGHTS IS SIGNIFICANT FOR UNDERSTANDING MULTI-STAKEHOLDER REGULATION ON PRIVATE-SECTOR IMPACT ON SOCIETY

1.2.1 Breaking a Stalemate in Sustainability Regulation: The UN Framework and the UN Guiding Principles

A milestone was reached when in 2008 and 2011 the UN Human Rights Council adopted normative directives for both states and businesses to prevent, manage and remedy adverse impacts on human rights caused by businesses. The first breakthrough in the previous stalemate was reached with the UN 'Protect, Respect and Remedy' Framework (UN Framework),[1] which the Human Rights Council adopted in 2008. In 2011 the UN Guiding Principles (UNGPs)[2] followed, spelling the general normative directives introduced in the UN Framework into detailed operational steps. Both came about through processes that led to broad agreement in the UN Human Rights Council and support from non-state actors from the camps of civil society as well as business. These processes were discursive in debating, shaping and eventually reaching agreement on concepts that were not well defined, in particular the normative idea of what responsibilities the business sector has for human rights, and the implications of that overall concept and its sub-elements. Clarifying the role of the private sector in a field generally marked by state obligations was a major point of contention in the discursive process.

Entitled a 'policy framework' and developed by an expert at the request of the UN Secretary-General, the UN Framework broke ground in three major ways: *First,* the fact that the document became adopted – in the language of the Human Rights Council, 'welcomed' – was significant because preceding UN efforts on the regulation of business responsibilities for human rights had failed to achieve similar agreement. *Second,* the

---

[1] Human Rights Council (2008) 'Protect, respect and remedy: A framework for business and human rights', Report of the Special Representative of the Secretary-General on the issue of human rights and transnational corporations and other business enterprises, John Ruggie, UN Doc. A/HRC/8/5, 7 April 2008 (Hereafter abbreviated UN Framework).

[2] Human Rights Council (2011) 'Guiding Principles on Business and Human Rights: Implementing the United Nations "Protect, Respect, Remedy" Framework', Report of the Special Representative of the Secretary-General on the issue of human rights and transnational corporations and other business enterprises. UN Doc. A/HRC/17/31, 21 March 2011 (Hereafter abbreviated UNGP).

idea of businesses having responsibilities for human rights assumes that these private non-state actors have duties that under international law are normally seen to pertain to governments and other public organisations. The adoption of the UN Framework entailed an explicit recognition by the normally state-centrist UN that non-state actors must consider their impact on human rights, act in such a way as not to cause harm, and must be prepared to be held accountable for adverse impacts, whether such accountability is in front of courts of law or through the market. *Third*, the process through which the UN Framework was developed was unusual and innovative for UN human rights rule-making and potentially beyond, because it explicitly involved the business sector along with other non-state actors in the evolution of a new set of norms. While non-state actors are often involved in UN human rights rule-making, they normally participate as rights-holders or representatives of actual or potential victims. Civil society provided important input to shape the process. However, interestingly and by contrast to conventional international human rights law-making, business organisations were involved too and played a role in developing the normative result. The outcome of this process was a settling, at least in part, of the previously contentious issues of what business responsibilities for human rights entailed, and whether businesses have such responsibilities at all. This involved a discursive process in the construction of an idea that at the outset was fluid. As will be explained below, much of this was due to the idea of business responsibilities for human rights emerging on a backdrop of the CSR discourse. CSR, too, had been subject to a discursive construction in public-private multi-stakeholder processes under the UN and the European Union (EU) that had been vibrant but also complicated in the years prior to the agreement on the UN Framework.

At the outset, both the concepts of CSR and business responsibilities for human rights were what discourse scholars refer to as 'floating signifiers', elaborated in Chapter 3 (3.2.1). Closely connected with this and in the process of branching off into a discourse of its own, the emergent BHR regime evolved partly within the discursive struggles and outcomes of processes to define or 'fix' the meaning of CSR. The evolution of the BHR regime also reached back to previous efforts within the UN to set norms of conduct for transnational corporations (TNCs),[3] both with regard to

---

[3] The terms Transnational Corporations (TNC) and Multinational Corporations (MNC) are used interchangeably by the international organisations that play a role in emergent rule-making for sustainable business conduct. The Organisation for Economic Development and Cooperation (OECD) and International Labour Organization (ILO) prefer 'MNC' while the UN prefers

their societal impacts (through an almost 20-year process to draft a Code of Conduct for TNCs[4] that was begun in the 1970s), and more specifically on human rights (through the process leading to the so-called Draft UN Norms on Business and Human Rights, or 'Draft Norms').[5]

Hence, it is relevant to look at the process that led to the UN Framework and UNGPs in order to understand why the breakthrough occurred and how the foundations for agreement on a previously contentious issue were created. These are the central questions guiding this book.

At only 30 pages, the relative brevity of the UN Framework for treating a complex topic was due to formal UN requirements. Similar to other UN human rights texts, such as the Universal Declaration on Human Rights (UDHR), such brevity invites elaboration. Accordingly, in 2011 the UN Framework was followed by the UNGPs. Responding to a request from the Human Rights Council for an operationalisation of the UN Framework, the UNGPs explain in more detail how states and businesses should act in order to honour their legal obligations and, in the case of businesses, also social expectations with regard to adverse human rights impacts caused by businesses. Like the UN Framework, the UNGPs are limited to a 30-page document. For both, a series of much more extensive sub-reports and other documents add additional information.

The UN Framework develops a structure of three 'pillars': (1) the State Duty to *Protect*, (2) the Corporate Responsibility to *Respect*, and (3) for both states and businesses to provide Access to *Remedy*. This normative structuring takes its point of departure in international human rights law, which has primarily been concerned with the three-pronged obligation of governments to respect human rights (observe rights, such as the freedom of speech), protect human rights (against violations) and fulfil human rights (providing for health services, education, etc.). For pragmatic reasons governed by the aim of reaching agreement on a partial solution

---

'TNC' for referring to an economic entity or group operating in more than one country. See J. Wouters, and A. Chané (2013) 'Multinational corporations in international law', Working Paper No. 129, Leuven: Leuven Centre for Global Governance Studies, at 2–3.

[4] Draft Code of Conduct on Transnational Corporations. *Development and International Economic Cooperation: Transnational Corporations*, UN Doc. E/1990/94, 12 June 1990; see also P. Lansing and A. Rosaria (1991) 'An analysis of the United Nations proposed Code of Conduct for Transnational Corporations', 14(4) *World Competition* 35–50.

[5] Sub-Commission on the Promotion and Protection of Human Rights (2003) 'Norms on the Responsibilities of Transnational Corporations and Other Business Enterprises with regard to Human Rights', UN Doc. E/CN.4/Sub.2/2003/12/Rev.2 (hereinafter Draft Norms).

rather than seeking to solve all problems at the risk of no agreement at all,[6] the UN Framework limits the corporate responsibility to *respect* human rights, that is, to a so-called negative responsibility to 'do no harm'. While the UN Framework did not develop normative guidance for how the private sector may contribute to the fulfilment of human rights, it also did not rule out that companies can contribute to the delivery of public goods of a human rights nature. The UNGPs build upon the three Pillars set out by the UN Framework.

Neither the UN Framework nor the UNGPs establish new human rights. Rather, they explain the implications for businesses and governments of already existing human rights, with a particular focus on adverse business impacts. Both documents refer to the International Bill of Human Rights and the International Labour Organisation's (ILO) fundamental labour conventions as the minimum standards that should inform business responsibilities for human rights. The former comprises of the UDHR, the International Covenant on Economic, Social and Cultural Rights (ICESCR) and the International Covenant on Civil and Political Rights (ICCPR). The latter comprise of eight ILO treaties on so-called core labour rights, that is the abolition of slavery and forced labour; the elimination of child labour; the protection of labour unions and the right to organise and engage in collective negotiation; and freedom from discrimination in the work place.

1.2.2 Business and Human Rights as an Emergent Regime

The processes towards the UN Framework and the UNGPs can be considered transnational law-making, because they included public and private actors in regulating issues that are essentially public policy concerns. Transnational law is a field that merges elements of conventional public (international, regional, and sometimes even national) law and conventional private law as well as new forms of law- and rule-making.[7] Transnationalisation of law is

---

[6] J. G. Ruggie (2013) *Just Business: Multinational Corporations and Human Rights*, New York: W. W. Norton & Co; J. G. Ruggie (2016) 'Hierarchy or ecosystem? Regulating human rights risks of Multinational Enterprises.' Forthcoming in C. Rodriguez-Garavito (ed.) *Business and Human Rights: Beyond the End of the Beginning*, available at SSRN: http://ssrn.com/abstract=2776690 (accessed 29 September 2016); see also K. Buhmann (2012) 'The Development of the "UN Framework": A pragmatic process towards a pragmatic output'. In R. Mares (ed.) *The UN Guiding Principles on Business and Human Rights: Foundations and Implementation*. Martinus Nijhoff Publishers, pp. 85–105.

[7] P. Zumbansen (2012) 'Transnational law, Evolving'. In J. Smits (ed.) *Elgar Encyclopedia of Comparative Law*, Cheltenham UK, Northampton MA, USA:

partly a result of the fact that markets have internationalised while governments remain by definition bound by their borders.

While human rights from the philosophical perspective may be considered moral obligations for everyone, a juridification[8] of human rights that has occurred in national and international law during the past centuries establishes the respect, protection and fulfilment of human rights as obligations of states. This is clear from the UDHR and the large number of international and regional human rights treaties that have been developed during the twentieth century. Even so, the UDHR's reference to 'all actors in society' in its preamble (a policy introduction) has been taken by companies with a commitment to social responsibility as an invitation to the private sector to commit to human rights. Yet the wording was not originally intended to apply to businesses.[9] At the time when the UDHR was developed from 1945 to 1948, it was largely unfathomable that businesses would attain the political and economic power that they came to have during the second half of the twentieth century.

According to the so-called horizontality doctrine, which has been developed in international human rights law, states' obligation to protect human rights goes beyond protecting individuals against harm caused by state agencies. It also includes the protection of individuals against human rights abuse caused by non-state actors, such as businesses. While the full extent of the implications of the horizontality doctrine remain debated,[10] the core of the doctrine informed the UN Framework with regard to the state duty to protect human rights.

From the perspective of international law, the protection of human rights is an obligation of states. Moreover, the fulfilment of social, economic or cultural human rights, such as providing for access to health services or to primary schooling, is a governmental obligation under

---

Edward Elgar, 2nd ed., pp. 898–925; H. K. Koh (1997) 'Why do nations obey international law? (Review essay),' 106(8) *The Yale Law Journal* 2599–659, at 2626–7.

[8] The term 'juridification' refers to an expansion of law into fields beyond law. It entails a legal framing of societal phenomena (such as social expectations of companies), a proliferation of law into other fields of practice or science (such as politics or ethics), or an increased regulation by law of social actors or processes. See further K. Buhmann (2016) 'Public regulators and CSR: The "Social Licence to Operate" in recent United Nations instruments on Business and Human Rights and the juridification of CSR', 136(4) *Journal of Business Ethics* pp. 699–714 with references at section 5.

[9] L. Henkin (1999) 'The Universal Declaration at 50 and the challenge of global markets', 25 *Brooklyn Journal of International Law* pp. 17–25, at 24–5.

[10] J. H. Knox (2008) 'Horizontal human rights law', 102 *American Journal of International Law* pp. 1–47.

international human rights law. However, from the political or political-economic perspective, many and especially social and economic human rights correspond to public policy objectives, *e.g.* in regard to health and education or an increasing enhancement of occupational health and safety and general working conditions. Involving businesses in developing norms of conduct to that end therefore amounts to involving businesses in a process with the aim of contributing to the solution of public policy objectives. This accords with the understanding of transnational law that as explained Professor Harold Koh may appear to be private, but is fundamentally public in character, represented by such fields as human rights, labour, environmental and public health law.[11]

Accordingly, the adoption of the UN Framework and subsequently of the UNGPs indicates a major shift in the idea of what types of actors carry responsibilities for human rights. The shift brought about the emergence of a new legal regime, which recognises businesses as having explicit responsibilities under international law, despite their status as so-called for-profit non-state actors. Even if those responsibilities are currently framed in policy and soft law documents, they refer explicitly to international legal standards in international human rights and labour law, which were originally developed and adopted as obligations for states. The recognition of businesses as bearers of international responsibilities, even on a soft law (guiding) basis, is a major change in the way that bearers of international obligations are perceived.

An international regime may be defined as a set of implicit or explicit principles, norms, rules, and decision-making procedures[12] around which actor expectations converge.[13] In the past, treaty-related normative developments such as the prevention of nuclear proliferation have been defined as emergent autonomous regimes.[14] In international relations studies,

---

[11] H. K. Koh (2002) 'Opening remarks: Transnational legal process illuminated'. In M. Likosky (ed.) *Transnational Legal Processes: Globalisation and Power Disparities*, Colchester: Butterworths, pp. 327–32, at 331.

[12] Krasner defines norms as standards of conduct in terms of rights and obligations, and rules and procedures as instructions for action and practices of making and realising collective choices (see S. D. Krasner (1982) 'Structural causes and regime consequences: regime as intervening variables', 36(2) *International Organization* pp. 185–205, at 186). This work applies rule with a broader meaning, *e.g.* 'rule-making' and 'law-making' are used interchangeably.

[13] S. D. Krasner (1982) 'Structural causes and regime consequences: regime as intervening variables', 36(2) *International Organization* pp. 185–205, at 186.

[14] A. Hasenclever, P. Maye and V. Rittberger (1997) *Theories of International Regimes*, Cambridge: Cambridge University Press, at 9, referring to the Treaty on the Non-Proliferation of Nuclear Weapons.

regimes are forms of cooperation that exist despite the restrictions that they place on involved actors.[15] Convergence on a regime is attractive despite such restrictions, because it offers order in place of anarchy.[16] The evolution of the conventional state-centrist human rights regime, which evolved based on ethics, political philosophy and national law and which became codified in international law during the twentieth century, is a case in point. This human rights regime limits each state's power vis-à-vis individuals within its jurisdiction, but on balance, the international human rights regime contributes to global order by reducing abuse of power that threatens peace and co-existence.

Like studies of international law and international relations in general, regime theory takes a state-centric point of departure. It may be expanded to issue-specific cooperation involving non-state actors where the extension to such actors is generated by the difference between the existing lack of order and the order offered by the regime.[17] The normative convergence that evolved with the support of non-state actors, states and international organisations in 2008 and 2011 for the UN Framework and UNGPs, respectively, represents an example of such an emergent regime. This emergent Business and Human Rights (increasingly in the literature referred to as 'BHR') regime breaks off from conventional state-centrist human rights by explicitly recognising for-profit non-state actors as bearers of specifically defined responsibilities, and also by in practice including them in the rule-making process. Eventually, this may come to innovate conventional international law, but currently, we are witnessing a new development that is still taking shape and is doing so because it is occurring in a singular field within international law.

The explicit focus on actions of non-state actors that often occur across the borders of home and host states, brings a transnational character to the emergent BHR regime. Indeed, in addition to being an emergent specialised regime in international law, the BHR field represents a transnational regime in terms of both the actors involved in the collaborative regulatory process, and in the normative outcome of that process. Being UN driven, it also exemplifies that the UN as an international organisation and in its rule-making is able to adapt to the growth of transnational interaction, impacts and concerns.

This is significant far beyond the human rights field. The impact that

---

[15] N. Seppala (2009) 'Business and the International Human Rights Regime: A comparison of UN initiatives', 87 *Journal of Business Ethics* pp. 401–17.
[16] Seppala (n 15).
[17] Ibid.

businesses have on human rights has formed a major element in the 'social' or 'people' dimension of the normative idea of CSR for years and the interface between the role of the public and the private sectors in regard to sustainability. International sustainability policies increasingly integrate the role of businesses in solving global sustainability problems (evidenced by the 2015 Sustainable Development Goals (SDGs)), but turning policy agreement into directives for implementation continues to encounter challenges (such as the Paris Climate Change Accord as well as the SDGs). As evidenced by the complex journey towards the Paris Accord, even the process of reaching agreement on a global concern as acute as climate change encounters difficulties, in part because of the numerous and often conflicting interests at stake between governments and the private sector, and even within those. The process towards the emergent BHR regime too suffered from such conflicts, which as it will be described below brought it close to a complete standstill before a major turn-around occurred that led to the UN Framework and UNGPs.

1.2.3 The Significance of the Emergent BHR Regime for Insights on Regulating Sustainability Through Discursive Processes Involving Multiple Interests

Centred from within the UN and already agreed international human rights law but explicitly extending it to non-state actors, the BHR regime offers concreteness that the emergent transnational climate change regime lacks.[18] The evolution of agreed normative directives that explicitly assign a role for the private sector in regard to a core policy concern of nation states and of the international society – such as human rights – is a novelty that offers potentially significant insights for other policy areas and international regulation of transnational policy concerns. The significance is further underscored due to the need to take account of or handle jurisdictional limitations of nation states against the fact that human rights or other sustainability-related impacts caused by transnational businesses often occur outside the home states of companies.

This makes it pertinent to understand how the issue of business responsibilities for human rights, which at the outset suffered from lack of agreement and support, was discursively constructed into a normative idea that

---

[18] E. Calliari, A. D'Aprile and M. Davide (2016) 'Paris Agreement: Strengths and weaknesses behind a diplomatic success', *Review of Environment, Energy and Economics,* May 2016; K. W. Abbott (2014) 'Strengthening the transnational regime complex for climate change', 3(1) *Transnational Environmental Law* pp. 1–32.

enjoyed agreement, and more particularly what lessons this may hold for future negotiations on norms of conduct in fields with highly divided conflicts of interests. This book provides insights for those concerned with the evolution of norms of conduct that govern business impact on society in order to limit adverse impact, or promote positive impact. This pro-active and preventative approach by no means excludes the parallel existence of re-active and punitive measures. However, because sustainability impacts are often hard to fully remedy, prevention is preferable so as to avoid the need for a cure that is often incomplete. With a particular focus on moving the agenda forward through agreement from state and non-state actors on new norms of conduct, new understanding on strategies for promoting change based on normative directives or regulated self-regulation is relevant to civil society, businesses committed to sustainability, public regulators, academics and others with a concern in promoting sustainable business action. It will help these actors structure arguments and negotiation processes so as to have maximum influence and stimulate change in business organisations in support of sustainability and necessary changes of conduct.

1.3 APPROACH, METHODOLOGY AND CASES

1.3.1 A Pragmatic Approach to an Interdisciplinary Topic

As noted above, there is a close connection between CSR and BHR discourses. An analysis of how BHR has branched off into an autonomous discourse and an emergent regime will need to consider issues and processes that are related to the broader 'People, Planet and Profit' aspects of the CSR concept as well as the more specific social (or 'People') aspects inherent in BHR. Much CSR and BHR action has been spurred by civil society actions, sometimes complemented by media campaigns or market expectations. Thus, the development of CSR and BHR normativity for economic actors and even beyond these is pluricentric, engaging a range of organisations or actors in a de-facto role as norm-setters, even though they do not belong to traditional centres of law-makers.

The analysis here is grounded in a pragmatic approach to the development of norms of conduct relating to business impact on society within a broader context of global economic integration, sustainability, and continuous dynamic change in the political, economic, informational and regulatory conditions framing public regulation of private sector activity. A pragmatic approach is both a necessity and an effect of the point of departure being taken in a regulatory process that involved non-state actors in the evolution of norms of conduct for business within a context framed by international law and the UN as the world's largest international organisation charged with ensuring peace and promoting social progress, human rights and better standards of life.[19] According to the doctrinal conception of for-profit non-state actors (that is, businesses) in international law, business has little or no role – neither in terms of obligations, nor in terms of law-making. This accords neither with the enormous economic and political power that the private sector has obtained since the middle of the twentieth century, nor with the capacity of business to both contribute to society and cause societal harm, which leads to societal expectations that business enterprises take responsibility for their impacts and act both to do no harm and to do more good.[20] Finally, the idea that business enterprises do not have a place in international law-making is not in accordance with how much sustainability related rule-making at both international and regional level has in fact taken to include business.[21] Pragmatism, as a scholarly approach, allows for recognising observable facts even if these differ from doctrine, and to lend inspiration from methods and theories from other sciences. A pragmatic approach, therefore, is particularly well suited for a study of fields such as business responsibilities for human rights and transnational multi-stakeholder law-making, which both involve non-state actors and particularly business in ways that jump the borders of international law doctrine, and which transgress the boundaries of academic disciplines like organisational studies, law and political science by engaging or calling upon application of neighbouring disciplines. This has been aptly phrased by socio-legal theorist David Trubek as 'crossing a number of boundaries which are often carefully policed'.[22] Pragmatic studies bring forth new knowledge by doing precisely that.

Without necessarily using the term 'pragmatism', legal pragmatists are

---

[19] *United Nations Charter* (1945), UNTS 993, preamble.

[20] The 2015 update of the website and of the communication strategy of the UN Global Compact testifies to this. Originally based on ten principles, all guiding businesses to prevent or reduce harm in the issue areas of human rights, labour, environment and anti-corruption, the Compact's website and communication in 2015 and onwards has engaged actively the 17 Sustainable Development Goals (SDGs) with a broad message to business to do more good for society by contributing to the implementation of the SDGs.

[21] See K. Buhmann (2018) *Power, Procedure, Participation and Legitimacy in Global Sustainability Norms: a Theory of Collaboratory Regulation,* Routledge.

[22] D. M. Trubek (2004) 'Human rights, transnational private law litigation and corporate accountability'. In C. Joerges, I.-J. Sand and G. Teubner (eds) *Transnational Governance and Constitutionalism,* Oxford: Hart, pp. 321–5, at 322.

concerned with the usefulness or expediency of a practice or approach,[23] its practical applicability, effects and results, rather than with doctrine.[24] A pragmatic approach focuses on solving problems of reality rather than delving into abstract conflicts based in theory. In a legal context, a pragmatic approach entails arguments or analysis, which stress the usefulness or expediency of particular actions or legal institutions.[25] Moreover, it entails the application of relevant theories and methods in order to analyse problems found in societal reality (as opposed to theory), and it produces knowledge of practical applicability. A pragmatic approach also allows a departure from earlier theories and doctrines, such as on forms of law, duty-holding subjects or participation in international law-making, in favour of dealing with problems that are observed in the current context of societal reality. Pragmatism allows for recognition of theory complementarity, and for the application of a combination of approaches in complementary synergy.[26] Accordingly, legal pragmatism permits the integration and application of theories from other (social) sciences, such as political science theory, as this may help identifying, understanding and analysing legal problems, their backgrounds, and solutions.[27] Along lines shared by critical discourse analysts, pragmatic theory also recognises that language has a decisive role in the construction of perceptions of problems and reality.[28]

The choice of a pragmatic approach is anchored in the fact that conditions of society are subject to continuous change. This challenges regulatory strategies to adapt so that they may respond to the current conditions at any point of time. Thus, while businesses and civil society, being non-state actors, do not have a formal role in international law-making, the role that such non-state actors have taken or been given in recent decades' efforts to grapple with social, environmental and climate change threats prove that in practice, non-state actors play crucial roles. These roles are obvious in the implementation of political goals and legal agreements. However, the necessity to involve businesses in the implemen-

---

[23] B. Von Eyben (2004) *Juridisk Ordbog*, Copenhagen: Thomson Gad Jura: definition of 'pragmatisk'.
[24] J. Dalberg-Larsen (2001) *Pragmatisk retsteori*, Copenhagen: Jurist- og Økonomforbundets Forlag, at 13.
[25] B. Z. Tamanaha (1997) *Realistic Socio-Legal Theory: Pragmatism and a Social Theory of Law*, Oxford: Oxford University Press; Dalberg-Larsen, ibid., at 13–14, 21–2, 37.
[26] Tamanaha, ibid., at 58–59.
[27] Dalberg-Larsen, (n 24) at pp. 103–11, 140–41.
[28] Ibid., at 24–5.

tation and the expert role of civil society have led to a growth of formal and informal inclusion of these actors also in the processes to develop policy and international law.[29] Many civil society groups, notably non-governmental organisations (NGOs), but also some business associations enjoy consultative status with the UN,[30] and some have done so for a long time. However, the political role and influence in some cases go beyond strictly 'consultative'. With regard to NGOs, this has been observed in the environmental sphere,[31] whereas business influence has been considerable in relation to business enterprises' social impacts.[32]

This study adopts a pragmatic legal approach within the broad field of socio-legal studies.[33] Socio-legal studies encompass a group of disciplines that apply a social science perspective to the study of law.[34] In accordance with the legal pragmatist approach, the theoretical framework in here (explained in section 1.3.2.2) has regard to regulatory strategy and communication. It draws in part on legal theory, but also applies discourse theory and textual analysis from political science, as well as argumentative strategy theory developed in business communication/organisational studies.

At the foundational level, the study is grounded in a conviction of the need for international law to adapt in order to respond to the emerging power of the private sector. This necessitates a pragmatic renewal in terms of how the regulatory process takes account of the expertise of civil society,

---

[29] M. A. Hajer. (1995) *The Politics of Environmental Discourse: Ecological Modernization and the Policy Process*, New York: Clarendon Press – Oxford; B. Arts (2001/2003) 'The impact of environmental NGOs in international conventions'. In B. Arts, M. Noortmann and B. Reinalda (eds) *Non-state Actors in International Relations*, Hants: Ashgate, pp. 195–210.

[30] This is possible under art 71 of the UN Charter, which empowers the UN Economic and Social Council (ECOSOC) to 'make suitable arrangements for consultation with non-governmental organisations which are concerned with matters within its competence'.

[31] A. Kolk (2001/2013) 'Multinational enterprises and international climate policy'. In Arts, Noortmann and Reinalda (n 29), pp. 211–5; Arts (n 29).

[32] D. Kinderman (2013) 'Corporate social responsibility in the EU, 1993–2013: Institutional ambiguity, economic crises, business legitimacy and bureaucratic politics', 51(4) *JCMS: Journal of Common Market Studies* pp. 701–20; K. Buhmann (2012) 'Reflexive regulation of CSR: A case study of public-policy interests in EU public-private regulation of CSR', *International and Comparative Corporate Law Journal* pp. 38–76, and below in discussions of the Draft Norms and EU MSF.

[33] Tamanaha (n 25) at 2, 7.

[34] Studies of responsive law and autopoietic law (see further below) are also socio-legal studies, due to their combinations of theories of law and its relation to society, see Tamanaha, ibid., at 19 with references.

the political and economic power of business, and the claims of both to participation in law-making pertaining to business impact on society. At the same time, the study is based on a strong belief in the capacity of law – in terms of both legal theory and specific fields of legal practice and law-making, especially international law – to provide institutionally sustainable solutions to pressing societal and global problems. Unfolding such capacity is feasible, provided openness to societal change reflected in legal scholarship and theory-based legal practices, and a willingness to adapt in order for international law theory and practice to respond to such change.

Accordingly, the current study's approach to international law is process oriented. As described by Professor Rosalyn Higgins, international law can be considered as a process of dynamic adaptation to political, economic and other changes rather than as an unchanging system of actors and rules. In here, process and norms connect not just in the study of specific cases but also to inform a quest for understanding processes through which state-centrist international human rights law as a set of norms of conduct relates to and feeds into broader sets of norms on business impact on society. In a broader perspective this has implications for international and transnational law-making to address global concerns that involve companies in both their cause and solution.

The study approaches both BHR and CSR from the perspective of public regulation and public-private co-regulation as modalities to induce self-regulation in companies. This perspective differs from the company perspective taken by many CSR studies, including those that have been conducted within other social sciences than law. It also differs from the more squarely cut private law or international law approaches taken by many law-based studies of CSR or BHR.

Issues related to BHR as well as the field of CSR and their regulation transgress the boundaries of legal sub-areas normally seen to be distinct: international law and national law, public law and private law. Even emerging regulation of CSR initiated at intergovernmental level builds on a plurality of sources of CSR-normativity, encompassing private regulation and codes, international law, national law, as well as a plurality of modalities of regulation, some of which include non-state actors not normally seen at the tables where international law, even international soft law, is made.

A few international business organisations, such as the International Chamber of Commerce (ICC), hold consultative status with the UN. Generally, however, companies have not previously been seen as partners to regulatory initiatives within the fields of human and labour rights except through representative organisations of employers within the ILO's tri-partite structure or through representatives in specific trade- or business-related international regulatory initiatives designed to promote international trade rather than regulate business conduct.

In line with the pragmatic approach, the study not only draws on other social science approaches but adapts these to use in the context of the focus on the discursive construction of business responsibilities for human rights, leading to the emergent BHR regime. In line with the process-oriented law-making focus, for empirical data the study draws on processes of developing normative directives related to businesses' social impact on society.

In this, the pragmatic and process focus on international law also informs the empirical basis for the study, meaning that unlike many other studies of law, this one is not based on an analysis of case law or decisions by authorities. Case law relating to BHR and CSR is (so far) found mainly in specific national jurisdictions, especially in so-called Common Law countries (the United States, the United Kingdom and state members of the Commonwealth of Nations (formerly the British Commonwealth)). That limited and culturally specific basis somewhat reduces its applicability to events occurring in so-called Civil Law jurisdictions, especially if there is no connection to Common Law states. As many of the world's countries, including socialist states, are Civil Law jurisdictions, the significance of this should not be overlooked.

In sum, a pragmatic approach is relevant in a context like the current one, because it allows for an analysis of facts that are observable and have legal relevance although they do not build on conventional legal method of gathering empirical data, and for an analysis combining theory developed inside as well as outside of the field of law. A combination of theories makes sense precisely because it is useful for analysing observable phenomena that are not contained within singular academic fields or sub-fields, and for understanding how normative evolution occurs in a multi-stakeholder process that needs to span diverse and frequently not aligned concerns.

1.3.2 Methodology

1.3.2.1 Case studies
Case studies provide empirical basis for the analysis and offer real-life examples of the complexity surrounding the discursive construction of sustainability normativity. Five selected cases are subjected to analysis by application of a combination of discourse analysis and socio-legal theory.

The ten-year period from 1998 to 2008 witnessed the emergence of the UN Global Compact in 1999, the failure of the Draft UN Norms on

Business Responsibilities for Human Rights in 2003, the relative success of two EU initiatives – the 2002–04 EU Multi-Stakeholder Forum (MSF) on CSR and the CSR Alliance, launched in 2006 – in developing guidance on CSR, but also a relative failure of these EU initiatives of giving a strong role to human rights in such guidance, and finally in 2008 the ground-breaking adoption by the UN Human Rights Council of the UN Framework on Business and Human Rights. Led by Professor John Ruggie in his capacity as the UN Secretary-General's Special Representative on Business and Human Rights, commonly referred to as 'SRSG', the process towards the UN Framework is hereafter referred to as the SRSG process. The UN Framework formed the basis for the UNGPs, and the adoption of both paved the way for negotiations currently taking place for an international treaty on business and human rights. With a particular focus on the processes leading to the normative outputs, the empirical case studies applied in this work comprise of the Draft UN Norms, the UN Global Compact, the SRSG process, the EU MSF, and the EU's CSR Alliance.

The key empirical part is a detailed study on the SRSG process that led to the UN Framework and UNGPs. Selected for the reasons set out below (section 1.3.2.4), the other cases provide a backdrop for the analysis of the SRSG process. Some of those were less successful in delivering agreement on the normative product of a regulatory process, or in delivering comprehensive norms of conduct that set directives for business with regard to their societal impact, in particular with regard to human rights. The Draft UN Norms is an example of less successful efforts at developing such norms. (As explained in Chapter 2, it was also not the first failure of the UN to develop norms of conduct for TNCs with regard to human rights, among other issues.) The UN Global Compact, which was developed and launched around the same time, was relatively more successful but contrary to the Draft Norms was explicitly described in terms intended to avoid the initiative being seen to be a legal instrument. Debates and outcomes of efforts by the EU, a regional organisation with policies to promote sustainable conduct by EU-based enterprises in regard to their activities and impacts outside their home region, also place the discourse and argumentative strategy that led to the current emergent BHR regime into perspective. The EU initiatives were not a general failure in terms of being CSR initiatives, but the processes did not deliver on the original ambitions to develop strong normative guidance and for this to be detailed in regard to human rights. By comparing discursive and argumentative strategies across these examples of constructing normative guidance on CSR with a particular focus on business and human rights, it is possible to identify what led to failures and success.

1.3.2.2 Theoretical framework: International and reflexive law, autopoiesis, discourse theory, and stabilising/de-stabilising arguments

It was noted above that the theoretical framework for the study in line with the pragmatic approach draws on legal science theory as well as discourse theory and argumentative strategy theory. This section explains the theories in more detail.

International law, including *international human rights law* sets the outer framework for the analysis, as it defines the formal role of non-state actors in law-making and the inclusion of non-state actors in practice in relation to both policy- and law-making. This also speaks to the need, observed above in the discussion of the need for pragmatic renewal, for international law and its processes to adapt to changes in the political, economic and other external conditions, in order for international law to deliver solutions to societal problems. The socio-legal theory of *reflexive law* with a particular emphasis on communication and the role of arguments offers part of the theoretical framework for the analysis of the discursive construction of norms, which took place in the multi-stakeholder processes that make up the five case studies. The polycentric aspects of the construction of CSR and BHR normativity call for a theoretical framework that allows for analysis of multi-stakeholder debates in processes for defining economic actors' social responsibility and developing normative directives. Applied within the theoretical regulatory framework of reflexive law, *discourse analysis* provides a method for such analysis the purposes of the present analysis. Finally, the theory on *stabilising and de-stabilising arguments* allows for performing an analysis of the internal complexity of an argument that aims at promoting (or preventing) a course towards normative change with participants in a multi-stakeholder regulatory process.

1.3.2.2.1 International law and international human rights law: state duties, doctrine, and horizontal obligations to protect International law is founded on theories that emerged in the sixteenth century and onwards, spurred by a desire to create a legal order for states' interaction in times of war and peace. As a result, the international law regime is fundamentally concerned with states: states are the makers of international law; they are the primary subjects of international law, both in terms of being rights-holders and duty bearers; and where accountability does arise in international law and under its institutions, it normally affects states and not individuals. Legal accountability modalities at the international level are limited, and where institutions to assess accountability do exist, sanctions are also often limited (partly as a result of the fact that international law is based on and evolves through states adopting rules pertaining to themselves and other states: the ambition for a state to set up strong accountability modalities that it might fall prey to itself is limited). The international criminal law regime is an exception, but also only emergent and limited to specific, very serious, actions recognised to be genocide, war crimes or crimes against humanity. Under this specialised international law regime, which dates to the Nuremberg and Tokyo processes following World War II and during the twentieth century evolved into the International Criminal Court[35] and tribunals related to international crimes that have occurred in specific countries in specific contexts (e.g., in Yugoslavia during the civil war of the 1990s), individuals may be prosecuted. However, this does not extend to businesses, despite these being considered individuals (so-called legal persons) in some jurisdictions.

Another specialised regime, international human rights law differs from general international law by establishing rights for individuals (against their state). Where general international law establishes rights and duties for states, international human rights law establishes rights for individuals, and duties for their states.[36] In view of the diversity of human rights – civil, cultural, economic, political and social – states' obligations for human rights comprise the duty to respect human rights (e.g., rights of freedom of expression and assembly), the duty to protect human rights (against violation by the state, e.g. through discrimination or torture by state agents), and the duty to fulfil human rights (e.g., by providing access to education and health services). According to the horizontality doctrine (mentioned in 1.2.2.), human rights obligations not only apply to the vertical relationship between a state and individuals but also to horizontal relationships within a state, for example between an individual and a corporation.[37] The horizontality doctrine does not neglect the role of states: governments must protect individuals against human rights violations by other individuals and ensure enforcement.[38] As we shall see in the following, this doctrine has come to play an important role in the emergent business and human rights regime, as it informs the idea of the state's duty to protect individuals against human rights abuse caused by companies. As we shall also see, this only emerged gradually, partly because the ways

---

[35] Rome Statute of the International Criminal Court, adopted by the UN General Assembly on 17 July1998, UN Doc. A/Conf.183/9.

[36] See e.g., D. L. Shelton (2014) *Advanced Introduction to International Human Rights Law*. Cheltenham, UK, Northampton, MA, USA: Edward Elgar.

[37] N. Jägers (2002) *Corporate Human Rights Obligations: In Search of Accountability*, Antwerp: Intersentia, esp. at 10, 32–7, 40–45.

[38] On the horizontality doctrine particularly in relation to business and human rights, see discussion in Knox (n 10).

in which international human rights law differs from general international law are not well-known by all, nor is there full agreement on the extent of states' obligations to protect against horizontal human rights abuse.

In international law as in other fields of law, *lex lata* refers to the way the law currently is according to existing legal doctrine, whereas *lex ferenda* refers to how the law should be changed, according to the views of the person(s) or organisation(s) who make that statement. A *lex ferenda* proposal seeks to change the current doctrine. A proposal to establish binding (hard law) international duties for businesses under international human rights law is a *lex ferenda* proposal, because it aims to change the current doctrinal perception that human rights obligations are only binding duties for states. A proposal to develop non-binding specific norms on the responsibility for business in regard to human rights in a text to be adopted as a formal soft law text by an intergovernmental body with the competence to do so is also a *lex ferenda* proposal, for the same reasons. An elaboration of the obligations for states to protect human rights against abuse caused by businesses is doctrinal, referring to the specialised human rights law doctrine on the state duty to protect, which includes obligations for states to legislate and engage in other relevant activities to ensure the effective implementation and protection of the human rights in question. However, those that are not aware of that specialised doctrine or wish to contest it may counter the proposal as conflicting with doctrine, or as being a *lex ferenda* proposal. Such contestation may be a result of the horizontality doctrine still being subject to debates on its extent and implications for states as well as non-state actors.

1.3.2.2.2 Reflexive law and autopoiesis in communication for normative change The theory of reflexive law belongs to a group of socio-legal theories concerned with instrumental regulation, that is, how law may be deployed as a regulatory strategy to induce change, without harm necessarily having occurred. The focus is primarily proactive, looking to change conduct with specific actors in society in order to prevent harm. Thus, the approach of reflexive law differs from the re-active enforcement approach that is often associated with institutional law.[39] Indeed, reflexive law builds strongly on communication as a modality for inducing normative change, and in doing so is informed by systems theory rather than institutional theories. It is the communicative aspect that gives reflexive law

---

[39] On the law's preference for enforcement, see G. Berger-Walliser and P. Shrivastava (2015) 'Beyond compliance: Sustainable development, business, and Pro-active Law', 46(2) *Georgia International Law Journal* pp. 417–75.

relevance for the analysis of how norms of conduct for sustainable business conduct may be 'talked' into acceptance through a discursive process; and therefore, why that instrumental regulatory theory is a relevant part of the theoretical framework for the current study.

As explained in detail in Chapter 3, reflexive law theory, proposed by Gunther Teubner,[40] draws on a combination of the system-theory of Niklas Luhmann[41] and the discourse ethics of Jürgen Habermas,[42] which was later expanded into Habermas' theory on legitimate law-making.[43] Reflexive law has been thoroughly addressed in socio-legal theory and applied in practice in several contexts of national or transnational regulation of sustainability related issues.[44] Based on a combination of habermasian emphasis on citizens' participation in law-making and systems-thinking that recognises the significance of the core rationality that distinguishes diverse functions in society,[45] reflexive law theory focuses on multi-stakeholder law-making on issues marked by competing or often conflicting interests. Drawing on the theory of autopoiesis,

---

[40] See especially G. Teubner (1983) 'Substantive and reflective elements in modern law', 17(2) *Law and Society Review* pp. 239–85; G. Teubner (1984) 'Autopoiesis in Law and Society: A Rejoinder to Blankenburg', 18(2) *Law and Society Review* pp. 291–301; G. Teubner (ed.) (1986) *Dilemmas of Law in the Welfare State,* Berlin and New York: Walter de Gruyter.

[41] See for the current purposes especially N. Luhmann (1986) 'The self-reproduction of law and its limits'. In G. Teubner (ed.) *ibid.*, pp. 111–27; N. Luhmann (1992) 'The coding of the legal system'. In G. Teubner and A. Febbrajo (ed.) *European Yearbook in the Sociology of Law: State, Law and Economy as Autopoietic Systems: Regulation and Autonomy in a New Perspective,* Milano: Guiffre Publishers, pp. 146–86.

[42] J. Habermas (1981) *Theorie des kommunikatives Handelns,* Frankfurt am Main: Suhrkamp.

[43] J. Habermas (1996) *Between Facts and Norms: Contributions to a Discourse Theory of Law and Democracy,* translated by William Rehg. Cambridge: Polity Press/Blackwell.

[44] For example, E. W. Orts (1995) 'Reflexive environmental law', 89(4) *Northwestern University Law Review* pp. 1229–340; E. W. Orts (1995) 'A reflexive model of environmental regulation', 5(4) *Business Ethics Quarterly* pp. 779–94; R. Rogowski and T. Wilthagen (eds) (1994) *Reflexive Labour Law: Studies in Industrial Relations and Employment Regulation,* Deventer and Boston: Kluwer Law and Taxation Publishers; D. Hess (1999) 'Social Reporting: A reflexive law approach to corporate social responsiveness', 25(1) *Journal of Corporation Law* pp. 41–84; I.-J. Sand (1996) *Styring av kompleksitet: Rettslige former for statlig rammestyring og desentralisert statsforvaltning,* Bergen: Fagbokforlaget Vigmostad & Bjørke; K. Buhmann (2009) 'Regulating Corporate Social and Human Rights Responsibilities at the UN plane: Institutionalising new forms of law and law-making approaches?', 78(1) *Nordic Journal of International Law* pp. 1–52.

[45] See below Chapter 3 and K. Buhmann (n 44).

reflexive law theory posits that it is possible to induce organisational self-regulation and acceptance of a need for normative change through exchanges that engage the rationality (or logic) of the actor with whom change is desired. According to this socio-legal theory, new norms related, for example, to business impact on society can be created in a communicative process in which external stakeholders stimulate organisational change with others by sharing views on needs, concerns and demands. This occurs by stakeholders communicating in ways that resonate with the logic of the audiences by speaking directly to the implications for their core concerns – such as, in the case of business, making profits or suffering losses. As elaborated in Chapter 3, within social science, autopoiesis explains change in organisations as a result of adaptation to external pressure. Such pressure can induce change when it resonates with the rationality on which the organisation builds in terms of its core function in society. For example, for businesses, making a profit is necessary in order to remain solvent and meet shareholder expectations (regardless of its commitment to social sustainability needs, it will not be able to go on if it fails economically). Its rationality therefore turns on making a profit or suffering a loss, and it will respond to pressure that activates that logic.

Due to its complex theory basis, reflexive law is sometimes thought to be highly theoretical or abstract. However, socio-legal and pragmatic legal scholars have demonstrated that the application of reflexive law can be concrete, focused and deliver results of direct application to future regulation.[46] This book follows in those steps by taking a point of departure in selected cases of multi-stakeholder rule-making involving both public organisations and private organisations. Within this context it observes and analyses the manner in which participants in such processes use specific types of arguments with the aim of obtaining their desired normative outputs, which would either entail normative change in business conduct, or uphold a *status quo* situation marked by more limited normative expectations and guidance or directives for business conduct.

Among the case studies, most can be defined as examples of reflexive law either due to their explicit organisation (the Global Compact process, the EU's MSF and CSR Alliance) or due to the way in which they came to operate (the SRSG process). However, the theory of autopoiesis and the role

---

[46] Hess (n 44); W. E. Scheuerman (2001) 'Reflexive law and the challenges of globalization', 9(1) *The Journal of Political Philosophy* pp. 81–102; E. W. Orts (1995) 'A reflexive model of environmental regulation'; J. Dalberg-Larsen (2008) Selvregulering og miljøret. In *Miljøretlige emner: Festskrift til Ellen Margrethe Basse*, Copenhagen: Jurist- og Økonomforbundets Forlag, pp. 297–313; J. Dalberg-Larsen (1991) *Ret, styring og selvforvaltning*. Aarhus: Juridisk Bogformidling.

played by system-specific rationality in arguments also contributes to understanding argumentative strategies that were decisive for the outcome of the process towards the Draft Norms, which was neither set up nor effectively operated as a reflexive law process. Indeed, this is a key point of the current work and the theoretical insights that it provides for the creation of new sustainability norms: the application of autopoiesis offers a highly practice-oriented basis for understanding how an argument may promote acceptance of normative change with other participants in a regulatory process; and how an argument may (sometimes against its own intention) prevent change.

1.3.2.2.3 Discourse theory Discourse theory and discourse analysis offer a way to identify and read texts to understand how their positions and arguments impact on social constructs, such as CSR, specific norms of conduct, or perceptions of accepted conduct, such as in regard to business impact on human rights. For the current study, discourse theory adds theoretical and informing perspective to the analysis of the struggles between participants in a reflexive law forum to set the meaning of value-laden ideas such as CSR and BHR. Recognised to be applicable to processes related to the social construction of policies, norms, and normative concepts, discourse theory has been applied to understand the evolution of norms of conduct in contexts of international[47] and EU law,[48] as well as argumentative strategies of lawyers[49] and judges,[50] and the communication of CSR by companies to stakeholders.[51] In various ways, they all resemble the context for application in the current study. Studies based on discourse analysis have indicated that certain CSR-relevant practices, such as voluntary adoption of social and environmental reporting, may form part of a strategy to resist pressure for other forms of accountability by attempting to project an argument that there are no conflicts between business practice and societal interest for sustainability (and therefore no need for authorities to regulate).[52] Research

---

[47] D. Kennedy (1987) 'The sources of international law', 2(1) *American University Journal of Law & Policy* pp. 1–96.

[48] R. Holdgaard (2005) 'Classic external relations law of the European Community: Doctrines and discourses'. Ph.D. thesis, 1 edn, Museum Tusculanum, Copenhagen.

[49] M.-L. Staffe (2008) *Retsretorik*, Copenhagen: Thomson Reuters.

[50] Holdgaard (n 48).

[51] J. M. Conley and C. A. Williams (2005) 'Engage, embed and embellish: Theory versus practice in the Corporate Social Responsibility Movement', 31(1) *Journal of Corporation Law* pp. 1–38.

[52] Spence, C. (2007) 'Social and environmental reporting and hegemonic discourse', 20(6) *Accounting, Auditing & Accountability Journal* pp. 855–82, at 859–60 with references.

suggests that discourse may serve in processes of network building, enrolling allies and overcoming dissent in order to achieve particular aims.[53] Other studies demonstrate that corporate scandals may affect regulatory processes.[54] This illustrates that discourse analysis may be instrumental for providing understanding of whether and how discourses or sub-discourses form parts of strategies to avoid (conventional) legal regulation, as well as to inform regulatory language and discourses arguing for legislative and regulatory change.

Knowledge, power and hegemony (dominance) are key features in discourse analysis. Discourse analysis is not concerned with diagnosing statements as true or false, but with analysing patterns in statements and discourses and determining results from discursive struggles to achieve hegemony in construction of concepts and knowledge.[55] The application of discourse analysis in social science is in part related to the preoccupation with change as a social process that occupies much institutional, political and sociological research.[56] In legal science, an interest in understanding change and mechanisms that drive processes of change is shared not only by socio-legal scholars, but also by scholars with an interest in the application of law, particularly in or by courts.[57]

Joined by a common concern with power, power relations and their role (and use) to shape society through language or other statements, discourse theory comes in a number of forms and approaches. The French school represented by Michel Foucault, Ernesto Laclau and Chantal Mouffe and others, comprises rather abstract theories, which are concerned with

---

[53] S. Cuganesan, C. Boedker and J. Guthrie (2007) 'Enrolling discourse consumers to affect material intellectual capital practice', 20(6) *Accounting, Auditing and Accountability Journal* pp. 883–911.

[54] R. Khalifa, N. Sharma, C. Humphrey and K. Robson (2007) 'Discourse and audit change: Transformations in methodology in the professional audit field', 20(6) *Accounting, Auditing and Accountability Journal* pp. 825–54, esp. at 826–30 and 839 with references.

[55] M. W. Jørgensen and L. Phillips (1999) *Diskursanalyse som teori og metode*. Frederiksberg: Samfundslitteratur/ Roskilde University Press, especially at 31; compare on the application of discourse theory where law, politics and economics overlap in the processes of constructing new terms or defining their normative implications, O. Wæver (2001) Europæisk sikkerhed og integration: en analyse af franske og tyske diskurser om state, nation og Europa. In T. B. Dyrberg and A. D. Hansen (eds) *Diskursteorien på arbejde*, Roskilde: Roskilde Universitetsforlag, pp. 279–317, at 284–5.

[56] N. Å. Andersen (2003) *Discursive Analytical Strategies – Understanding Foucault, Koselleck, Laclau, Luhmann*, Bristol: Policy Press, at IX; Holdgaard (n 48) at 335.

[57] See for example, Holdgaard ibid., at 320, 323; Staffe (n 49).

power at a general level related to particular groups, organisations, etc. Through discourse, the way we use language therefore is constitutive of social reality. For example, the corporation as a legal entity may be talked into reality through language.[58] The critical discourse analysis (CDA) school represented by Norman Fairclough and other primarily English or Germanic culture scholars offers theories that turn on specific analysis of texts focusing on words, signs, conversations and their use. Different varieties of discourse theory are often applied in combination. Laclau and Mouffe's discourse theory recognises power as constitutive in a productive sense as well as a modality for one group's obtaining of hegemony over others. Its authors see power as a societal constitutive factor, and discourse as constitutive of power. Set at a relatively high level of abstraction, their approach seeks to map discourses that exist in a society at a particular time or regarding a particular societal topic. That theory is often combined with other, less abstract, approaches, such as Norman Fairclough's textual analysis.[59] For the purposes of the current study, discourse theory is applied in a way which links abstract and concrete approaches, drawing on Laclau and Mouffe's emphasis on discourse as a way to obtain or preserve power, and Fairclough's approach to analysing text to understand how discourse creates and shapes power.

Discourses are communicative events in a broad sense. They are institutionalised ways of using speech and other linguistic elements in determining and consolidating action. As a particular discourse is typically about power in a specific context, discourses, in general, exercise power by transmitting (institutionalised) knowledge, influencing individual and collective action and shaping society,[60] for example through the construction and fixation of specific concepts. Antagonistic relations arise, for example between companies and NGOs in relation to CSR normativity and expectations. This instigates discursive struggles to obtain influence in constructing meaning within a discourse or two conflicting discourses.[61] The successful actor will see its interests protected or promoted through

---

[58] E. Laclau and C. Mouffe (1985) *Hegemony and Socialist Strategy: Towards a Radical Democratic Politics*, London: Verso, esp. Ch. 3; Spence (n 52) at 858–9; Jørgensen and Phillips (n 55) at 29.

[59] Jørgensen and Phillips ibid., at 30.

[60] S. Jäger (2001) Discourse and knowledge: theoretical and methodological aspects of a critical discourse and dispositive analysis. In R. Wodak, and M. Meyer (eds.) *Methods of Critical Discourse Analysis,* London: Sage Publications, pp. 32–62, at 34 with references.

[61] See for example, T. A. Van Dijk (1997) 'Discourse as interaction in society'. In T. A. van Dijk (ed.) *Discourse as Social Interaction*, London: Sage Publications, pp. 1–37, at 28.

the settled meaning of the concept. By achieving dominance in this respect, hegemony is obtained.

Discourse analysis is based on the assumption that words and communicative events do not reflect an already established reality but constitute it. It also assumes that discursive patterns are maintained or changed through discursive practices.[62] As a result, discourse analysis offers a way to critically assess and uncover the way that language constructs and changes (parts of) the world. Examples include relationships between institutions and their clients, the construction of particular phenomena, such as concepts of the environment or sustainability, national identities and particular minorities' culture.[63]

CDA, including Fairclough's approach, aims to assess and illuminate how power relations are constructed and reproduced through discursive practices. Relations between men and women or between social classes are typical examples of such power relations. For the current purposes, this connects to power relations between social actors involved in multistakeholder processes to develop norms of conduct, including the construction of social responsibility expected of such actors. Moreover, the main power issue relates to the implications for involved actors that may result from the prospective norms of conduct that they are negotiating. In other words: are these norms likely to increase or decrease their current power or stabilise it? From the systems thinking perspective introduced above, companies will be concerned with implications for their ability to generate profits or manage risks to their profit-making; whereas public policy-makers will be concerned with their ability to be seen as effective in developing policy and law related to public policy objectives. NGOs will be concerned with their own effectiveness in making an imprint on policy and law in accordance with the aims of their constituencies (e.g., to promote environmental sustainability, decrease adverse business impacts on human rights, or promote active business contributions to the delivery of social goods). The interests at stake are considerable for political system representations, such as (inter-)governmental organisation and NGOs, economic system representations such as companies, and for the international legal system as a relevant and efficient mode of regulation of current global sustainability concerns.

The textual analysis of Norman Fairclough functions as a bridge between the power analysis according to the approach of Laclau and Mouffe, and the discursive and argumentative strategy deployed in a

---

[62] Jørgensen and Phillips (n 55) at 21.
[63] Ibid., at 9; Hajer (n 29).

reflexive regulatory process, which ideally invokes the rationality of other stakeholders in order to stimulate normative change with them. Fairclough's approach has its focus on analysing text as a medium for constructing and reproducing power relations through discourse, in line with the general approach of CDA, which considers specific use of language, actors, mode, vocabulary and argumentation to be important elements for the purpose of analysis. For example, an analysis may consider the form of argumentation, argumentative strategies, logic and composition of text, style, and references to science.[64] Seeing language this way therefore provides an operational mode for analysis of the construction of normativity through texts produced and presented in the context of the five case studies. CDA considers text to be intertextual and interdiscursive, that is, constituted by (and constitutive of) other utterances (such as statements) and surrounding discourses.[65] Thus, analysis of a text gains from considering the larger context of that text, in terms of related statements and the discursive environment. Like pragmatic legal theory, CDA recognises interdisciplinary work.[66] The interdisciplinary aspect means that CDA acknowledges the significance of contextual features, such as political and ideological components, in analysis of discourse.[67] Critical discourse theory does not insist on one particular way of collecting data. Data collection may be on-going rather than completed before analysis is begun. It may also employ methods belonging to other fields of theory than the one which frames a study at the overall level.[68] As critical discourse analysis is often undertaken on the basis of a large body of text, it is recognised that a complete analysis of the text body may not be possible.[69]

Whereas Laclau and Mouffe are interested in the construction of power through discourse in the abstract sense, Fairclough's theory-based method

---

[64] On the linguistic orientation of CDA, see e.g., M. Meyer (2001) 'Between theory, method, and politics: positioning of the approaches to CDA'. In R. Wodak, and M. Meyer (eds) *Methods of Critical Discourse Analysis*, London: Sage, pp. 14–31, at 25 with references; Jäger (n 60).

[65] See further L. Chouliaraki (2001) 'Refleksivitet og senmoderne identitet: et studie i mediediskurs'. In T. B. Dyrberg, A. D. Hansen and J. Torfing (eds) *Diskursteorien på arbejde*, Frederiksberg: Roskilde Universitetsforlag, pp. 247–78, at 252.

[66] R. Wodak (2001) 'What CDA is about – a summary of its history, important concepts and its developments'. In R Wodak and Meyer (n 64) at 11; R. Wodak (2001) 'The discourse-historical approach'. ibid., pp. 6–94, at 64.

[67] Meyer (n 64) at 15.

[68] Ibid., at 23–4 with references.

[69] Ibid., at 26–7 with references; T. A. Van Dijk (2001) 'Multidisciplinary CDA: a plea for diversity'. In Wodak and Meyer (n 64) pp. 95–119.

for discourse analysis is inherently focused on the specific text. It is concerned with linguistic features of a specific statement or 'communicative event'; with intertextuality, placing the text in a context of discursive practices; and social practices with an emphasis on the emergence of new orders of discourse, struggles over normativity, attempts at control, and resistance against regimes of power.[70] In accordance with the generally flexible approach to discourse analysis, scholarly studies often adapt Fairclough's method to fit the texts and topics subject to analysis. Such adaptation is also made in the current study, as explained in the following.

The analysis draws on Fairclough's method in terms of the attention paid to language (with written text as a medium) as a modality for constituting or attempting to constitute change as a social practice in a wider social context. Due to the large body of text that forms the empirical materials, for the current study statements in the text material have been analysed based on a limited set of criteria (coding as explained below). This has allowed for an analysis of how linguistic elements in the text have contributed to constructing the understanding of business responsibilities for human rights within in the context formed by the five multi-stakeholder regulatory processes that form the case studies. The analysis leans on Fairclough's recognition of textual study of linguistic elements of texts produced and presented as elements in a particular discourse that seeks to construct particular perceptions of the world to bring about change. It does not go into details of the linguistic features as would a 'true' faircloughian discourse analysis.[71] The analysis in this work therefore is Fairclough-*inspired,* in keeping with the pragmatic approach outlined above and the flexibility recognised in general discourse theory for its application and adaptation to various types of texts and studies.

As social practice also contains non-discursive elements, Fairclough holds that the discourse analysis should be supplemented by other

---

[70] J. Blommaert and C. Bulcaen (2000) 'Critical Discourse Analysis', 29 *Annual Review of Anthropology*, pp. 447–66, at 449.

[71] A 'true' faircloughian analysis of internal relations of a text would provide a detailed analysis of the linguistic elements and relations of a text. It considers its semantic relations (relations between words and longer expressions, elements of clauses, and clauses and sentences), its grammatical relations, its vocabulary relations (patterns of how words or expressions co-occur, e.g. a particular noun that co-occurs with various prepositions or other compositions), and phonological relations (intonation, rhythm graphics). It would also consider the genre of a text (or texts) in a more detailed way than done in the current study. (N. Fairclough (2003) *Analysing Discourse: Textual Analysis for Social Research.* New York: Routledge, at 36–7).

theory.[72] For the current study legal theory, in particular reflexive law theory, provides the supplementary theory for analysis, and to put the discursive elements into perspective. The theoretical foundations for these points are also elaborated in Chapter 3.

1.3.2.2.4 Stabilising and de-stabilising arguments The theory of stabilising and de-stabilising argumentative strategies helps explain how arguments can stimulate acceptance of normative change by invoking the threat of disturbance inherent in the core rationality of an actor or organisation (e.g., for a business: an economic loss), and pitting it against its opposite by suggesting, sometimes paradoxically, the stability that may be gained by shifting stances and adopting normative change that meets the environment's needs and therefore their rationalities.

As noted, the main contribution of reflexive law in the context of the discourse analysis is the former's use of autopoiesis for examining how an argument may promote or prevent acceptance of normative change. The theory of stabilising and de-stabilising argumentative strategies, which has been developed with a linguistic focus to communication in a business context, adds to this with a view to a nuanced textual analysis. In the current context, following the general analysis of interest-based discursive communication for the construction of norms on business social responsibilities, it is relevant to examine how an argumentative strategy may play on the interests of the recipient for that purpose. For example, the argument may explain how the preservation of the recipient's interest (stabilisation) may in fact be obtained through acceptance of change (de-stabilisation). This serves to examine and demonstrate how the strength of an argument can be enhanced by strategically structuring it to speak to the interests of an audience (recipient), and how the opposite may be the case if the argument is structured mainly around the interests of the speaker (transmitter). Based on the interests that they want to protect and promote, discourse participants may seek to stabilise or destabilise the role to be played by international human rights law as a normative source for CSR based on their interests. Some will use conservative *stabilising strategies* to argue that human rights are obligations for states, and therefore should not be transferred onto companies as obligations or even expectations. Others will employ *destabilising* strategies, seeking to argue that CSR should be normatively informed by or even hinged upon international human rights law.

---

[72] Jørgensen and Phillips (n 55) at 82.

1.3.2.2.5 Delimitation and reservations Where power is at stake, power disparities may significantly distort a process and its outputs. That, too, applies to regulatory processes with a high degree of exchanges between participants. That power issue is highly significant for the legitimacy of a regulatory process and its outcome. In particular, privileged access to those who establish and/or act upon the output of the regulatory process, or privileged knowledge of the broader context in which that forum may be significant in that context. Such factors have been recognised in the literature on, for example, reflexive law as a method for multi-stakeholder rule-making.[73] A detailed treatment of how to manage power disparities in these contexts goes beyond the current work. The topic has been addressed in other work by this author,[74] which complements this book.

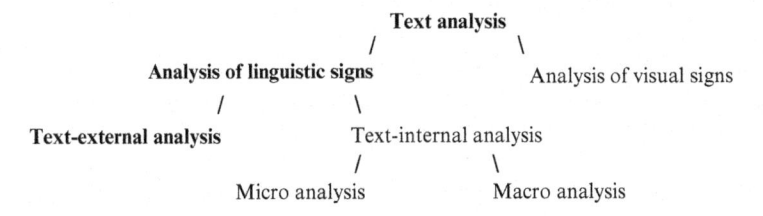

```
                        Text analysis
                         /        \
        Analysis of linguistic signs      Analysis of visual signs
             /        \
  Text-external analysis    Text-internal analysis
                            /        \
                    Micro analysis    Macro analysis
```

Source: Adapted from Ditlevsen *et al.* 2007, at 67.

Figure 1.1   Basic model for text analysis

1.3.2.3   Determination of textual focus for analysis

The textual focus for the analysis is marked by bold in Figure 1.1 above. The figure draws on a basic model for text analysis developed in a business school academic environment for communication through texts based on special knowledge or concerns, and often addressing an audience with different knowledge or concerns. The model lists the main elements of a text (linguistic signs, visual signs) on which an analysis may focus and the approaches (internal, external), which an analysis may take. For the current purposes, we focus on the linguistic signs and text-external analysis (elaborated below).

Text-external analysis comprises elements outside the text, such as the transmitter (sender), recipient (audience), context, function and contextual theme. For our purposes, the transmitter and recipient are important for the appreciation of the discursive strategy and particularly the usage of

---

[73] See, e.g., Sand (n 44).
[74] See Buhmann ((2018), n 21).

system-specific language and other text-internal elements. The text function is also important. The (intended) function relates to the objective of a text and therefore influences the discursive structure and argument. For example, the function may be assertive, directive or affective. A directive function may be binding or non-binding. A text seeking to affect the recipient may have a *stabilising or de-stabilising function*. These functions seek to affect the recipient's emotional attitude towards an issue. A text with a stabilising function seeks to influence recipients to accept a particular issue or situation. A text with a de-stabilising function seeks to influence the recipient to change the matter that the text relates to. These functions are related to the objectives of discursive struggles to affect acceptance or change of conceptions of corporate responsibility for impact on society, CSR normativity and the role of human rights law for norms on business conduct.

Text-internal micro-analysis comprises specific words, syntax, sentence structure, metaphors and related elements. *Text-internal macro-analysis* considers the structure of the text, themes, use of pronouns, tempus etc. Text-internal elements are not specifically addressed in the analysis in this work.

The analysis of text complements the discourse analysis of arguments that seek to activate the core rationality of recipients (audiences) by enabling an analysis of a complementary argumentative strategy of deploying stabilising or de-stabilising strategies.[75]

1.3.2.4 Empirical data: case selection and coding of text

As explained in 1.3.2.1, the book draws on five case studies. This section explains the reasons for the selection of the case studies and how the texts were coded for the analysis.

The multi-stakeholder regulatory initiatives that serve as case studies were all launched by intergovernmental organisations and all aimed to develop normative guidance for business: the process towards the Draft Norms, which entailed a UN project to develop normative guidance on business and human rights and the decision by the UN Commission on Human Rights on the proposed Draft Norms (1998–2004);[76] the process of developing and obtaining agreement on the principles of the UN Global Compact (1999–2000);[77] the European Commission's MSF on CSR and

---

[75] M. G. Ditlevsen, J. Engberg, P. Kastberg and M. Nielsen (2007) *Sprog på arbejde: Kommunikation i faglige tekster*. Frederiksberg: Forlaget Samfundslitteratur, pp. 65–103.
[76] Draft Norms.
[77] UN Global Compact, available at http://www.unglobalcompact.org/ (last accessed 30 December 2016).

its main normative output, a process that was launched with the objective of developing a European Framework for CSR (2002–04);[78] the launch of the EU's CSR Alliance and its major normative output (2006–08); and finally the main case study: the SRSG process on Business and Human Rights 2005–11, which resulted in the UN Framework in 2008 and in 2011 the UNGPs, which were adopted by the UN Human Rights Council.

The case studies were selected on the following basis: The SRSG process is the main case study, because it delivered the break-through in terms of broad multi-stakeholder agreement on normative guidance on business responsibilities for human rights. The four other cases, addressed in Chapter 4 in order to set the backdrop for the analysis of the SRSG process in Chapter 5, occurred in the years just prior to the launch of the SRSG process and its first output, the UN Framework. Those four regulatory processes were selected as cases because all embodied an element of multi-stakeholder consultation or dialogue; because all had a strong (if not necessarily exclusive) focus on human rights; and because they represent a diversity of results in terms of contents of the normative guidance and whether it was formally adopted or launched. Two of the processes that form the case studies addressed in Chapter 4 were launched by the UN; the two others by the EU. As the SRSG process was a UN initiative, other initiatives launched by the UN for related purposes are relevant to place the SRSG process and its outcome into perspective. The EU cases have been selected because the EU is also an intergovernmental organisation, and as such unusual both in being a host region to many TNCs (which are registered in EU Member States) and in launching initiatives, in its capacity as an intergovernmental organisation with a market focus, to develop normative guidance for TNCs.

Because they had varying results in terms of their outputs and the acceptance of those outputs to be launched formally as guidance for companies, the Draft Norms, UN Global Compact, EU MSF and CSR Alliance processes therefore place the SRSG process into a broader context of the political, economic and legal issues and concerns of the time. Other efforts at major normative guidance texts for TNCs by intergovernmental organisations, such as the UN's efforts to develop a Code of Conduct for TNCs, OECD Guidelines for Multinational Enterprises, and ILO Declarations setting guidance for on TNCs, precede the SRSG

---

[78] European Multistakeholder Forum on CSR (2004) *Final Results and Recommendations*, 29 June 2004 ('Final Report'), http://forum.europa.eu.int/irc/empl/csr_eu_multi_stakeholder_forum/info/data/en/CSR%20Forum%20final%20report.pdf (last accessed 12 March 2013, website has been removed).

process by more than two decades as they go back to the 1970s. They also form part of the backdrop (and are introduced in Chapter 4 prior to the case studies) but are not as relevant to place the SRSG process into the context of the time as the four recent case studies.

The text body of 153 texts is comprised of reports, written statements, or written summaries of oral statements made by participants in the processes that form the case studies. For the identification of texts, official websites of the initiatives or their host organisations have been used to the extent possible.[79]

Coding was done according to whether the statement expressed a political, an economic or a legal system rationality (or more of these at one time). The code of a statement therefore does not necessarily reflect the actor's own functional sub-system, but rather, the rationality deployed by the statement. This informed the analysis by providing information on whether and how actors from different functional sub-systems deployed rationality different from their own, and therefore mainly communicated (or sought to communicate) with stakeholders with similar views or objectives, or mimicked codes from other sub-systems in order to cause perturbation within the system of the pertinent code (the recipient system). The analysis in the empirical Chapters 4 to 6 draws on the full body of 153 statements, reports and other written utterances. Due to space limitations, explicit reference is not made to all the texts that were analysed.[80]

---

[79] These official websites of the initiatives have been used: The SRSG process: Business and Human Rights Resource Centre, *UN Secretary-General's Special Representative on business and human rights*, available at: https://business-human rights.org/en/un-secretary-generals-special-representative-on-business-human-right s; The Draft Norms: reports from sessional meetings of the Working Group on the working methods and activities of transnational corporations, available on the internet through their UN document identification name ('UN Doc.' indicated in references in Chapter 4); The UN Global Compact, available at http://www.unglobalcompact.org/; The EU MultiStakeholder Forum (2002–04): *The EU MSF homepage* through the EU Commission's website at http://circa.europa.eu/irc/empl/csr_eu_multi_stakeholder_forum/info/data/en/csr%20ems%20forum.htm (last accessed 12 March 2013, website has been removed); CSR Alliance: Not one single website, but information at the website of the EU Commission DG Enterprise and Industry at http://ec.europa.eu/enterprise/policies/sustainable-busi ness/corporate-social-responsibility/european-alliance/index_en.htm (last accessed 12 March 2013, website has been removed), CSR Europe at http://www.csreurope.org/pages/en/alliance.html (last accessed 12 March 2013, website has been removed), and BusinessEurope at https://www.businesseurope.eu/european-alliance-csr (last accessed 30 December 2016).

[80] For more details on the texts and to consult all texts and code markings, see K. Buhmann (2014) *Normative Discourses and Public-Private Regulatory*

1.3.2.5 Genres

A genre is not only a particular type of text, but a process of producing, distributing or consuming text. A genre may be a form of communication between organisations, such as governments or business organisations, and individuals. Genres may be identified with various degrees of abstraction – from the very general, 'all-encompassing' pre-genre to the very concrete. Genres are important because a genre has or may have a regulating capacity, associated with an institution's activity to manage social practices of other institutions or networks.[81] For example, the outcome of an activity and its significance for participants as well as consequences for the future process are managed to some extent by the way the report or summary is written.

The general genre of the texts that serve as data for this study is non-fiction. The context is political with a general objective of shaping CSR-normativity. The specific situation within the overall context may be a multi-stakeholder meeting organised by the SRSG, a meeting under the EU MSF, a reporting session for the SRSG to the Human Rights Council, or the UN General Assembly's adoption of a resolution on the UN Global Compact in the textual context of partnerships with the private sector.

Within the overall context, a number of sub-genres occur. Because of the political context and its specific objective, a uniting feature of the sub-genres is that the content seeks to affect the construction of a particular concept. Depending on transmitter, transmitter's objective, audience (recipient) and relational context, several sub-genres are in operation. These aspects all influence the style and form of a text to present its contents. For example, the language of a report addressing the UN Human Rights Council will typically be aligned with the international and human rights law oriented work and insight of the Council. A report addressing the Human Rights Council will keep to the form required for such reports (for example, for the reports from the SRSG, a 30-page limit, and a particular structure that is common for reports from mandate holders under the Council), and a resolution passed by the UN General Assembly will be in the particular style of such resolutions. The main sub-genres of texts produced in the context of the cases are:

Strategies for Construction of CSR Normativity: Towards a Method for Above-National Public-Private Regulation of Business Social Responsibilities. Copenhagen: Multivers, in particular the Annex.

[81] Fairclough (n 71) *Analysing discourse,* at 32, 70–75, 124, 216; N. Fairclough (1995) *Critical Discourse Analysis: The Critical Study of Language,* London [u.a.] Longman, at 126; N. Fairclough (1992) *Discourse and Social Change,* Cambridge: Polity Press, at 9.

- Political documents are texts from public bodies with a political mandate that allows them to require or suggest certain action by other bodies, for example, resolutions from the European Parliament. They may take the form of underlying analytical or elaborative documents (e.g., analytical reports of the European Parliament).
- Policy documents are prepared by an organisation charged with setting out policy, including to encourage and institutionalise public regulation, public-private co-regulation and private self-regulation. Examples include the SRSG's *Protect, Respect and Remedy* report and the EU Commission's Green Paper on CSR. Some policy documents among those included in the current analysis may have soft law aspects or effects.
- Consultation documents are prepared or presented as part of a consultative or multi-stakeholder reflexive law process. NGO or business organisations' statements are typically submitted in such documents.

Some other genres play a minor or indirect role. These are in particular:

- Legal texts may be in form of treaties, declarations, recommendations or drafts in similar style, such as the Draft Norms. UN General Assembly resolutions are soft law albeit sometimes with strong political contents.
- Other reports or analyses include analyses by academics or researched reports by NGOs or intergovernmental organisations, etc.
- Media articles, such as articles from CSR oriented media, typically express a view of the author or media, but may also relay views of interviewees.

In the analysis, the particular genre of a text will be indicated only where this is found to be of specific use for the appreciation of the text, its linguistic elements or its discursive style.

1.4 STRUCTURE OF THE BOOK

Part I sets the stage through the introduction (Chapter 1), and explains the context for the discursive struggles on constructing the meaning and normative implications of CSR and BHR, which took place during the case study processes (Chapter 2). Additionally, it presents the theoretical framework for the study in detail (Chapter 3). Part II looks at the evolution of business responsibilities for human rights based on the empirical analysis, focusing on the discursive struggles and arguments that took place in the background cases: the Draft Norms, the Global Compact, the EU's MSF and CSR Alliance (Chapter 4), and the main case: the SRSG process (Chapter 5). Part III performs a comparative analysis of the argumentative strategies relative to the processes and their outputs. Based on that analysis and a synthesis, insights are drawn up on the particular argumentative strategies that were decisive in defining the outcomes of the discursive struggles, identifying what elements led to the turn-around that resulted in the emergence of the BHR regime (Chapter 6). The final chapter concludes by developing implications for practice as well as theory, offering insights for effective structuring of argumentative strategies and negotiations to develop agreement around new soft or hard law framing norms on sustainable conduct (Chapter 7).

2. The context: the CSR discourse and its relation to law, human rights and social sustainability

Chapter 2 provides the contextual background for understanding CSR, the normative role of human right in CSR, and the emergence of BHR as an autonomous discourse and emergent regime. It sets out concerns for public regulators and businesses that inform and feed into debates and power struggles in the construction of normativity on these. Section 2.1 clarifies the state of the art in regard to CSR understandings and the role of law, describes the voluntary/mandatory dichotomy, and sets out the implications for the concerns involved by participants on the discursive construction of CSR normativity and normative guidance on business responsibilities for human rights. Section 2.2 describes the relationship between CSR and human rights in regard to public policy perspective and the advantages that business involvement in the provision, implementation and respect of human rights offers to governments and intergovernmental organisations. Section 2.3 focuses on the role of human rights in CSR, describing this from the business perspective. Section 2.4 describes the relevance of international soft law as normative guidance for businesses with regard to their social impacts. Finally, section 2.5 considers non-state actor participation and activism in international law-making. It deals with business and civil society participation, referring to theory perspectives on the significance of such participation and methods of non-state actors for influencing regulatory processes for norms on sustainability issues in line with their interests with a particular regard to human rights.

2.1 CSR AND LAW

With the solidification of the BHR regime, the discourse on business and human rights is increasingly taking on an autonomous character, distinct from the CSR discourse. The UN Framework helped clarify that BHR differs from CSR by not just referring to responsibilities for businesses, but also to obligations for states. Moreover, whereas the CSR discourse tends to have a preference for voluntary action (even if such action is in recent years not infrequently shaped by law, whether hard, soft or smart-mix regulation), BHR refers to hard law (binding requirements) as well as soft law (guidance or recommendations).[1] Still, business responsibilities for human rights continue to also be discussed in more explicit CSR-contexts in which human rights remain one issue among others under CSR (or just Social Responsibility or 'SR', as in the case of the ISO 26000 Social Responsibility Guidance Standard) as an umbrella term. Even more importantly for the current purposes, much of the political debate across civil society, intergovernmental organisations, business and other organisations that led to what is today BHR was spurred by a broader concern with business impacts on society and encompassed with the broader CSR discourse. To appreciate how the evolution of the BHR regime evolved discursively and in terms of argumentative strategies, it is necessary to first place the debate on business impacts on human rights within the CSR context. It is also necessary to place the debate within the focus on how companies can contribute to public policy objectives. Whether related to the capacity of businesses to do harm, or their capacity to do good by helping public authorities deliver services and task in regard to health, education, etc., the role that businesses may play for the implementation of public policy objectives has also marked a considerable part of the evolution of CSR and social sustainability in recent years. That issue has come to inform both private CSR action and public organisations' efforts to shape such action through policy, incentives, guidance and mandatory requirements. As will be seen, human rights are in the background of many of these social sustainability oriented measures. This background role has contributed to building the importance of social sustainability in CSR, which has been a significant driver of the push for what today amounts to an autonomous concept of BHR and an emergent regime.

Among the case studies addressed in this work, some were launched within a CSR context rather than an explicit human rights context. Even so, they had considerable focus on human rights, and the normative role of

---

[1] K. Buhmann (2016) 'Juridifying corporate social responsibility through public law: assessing coherence and inconsistencies against UN guidance on Business and Human Rights', 11(3) *International and Comparative Corporate Law Journal* pp. 194–228; K. Buhmann (2006) 'Corporate social responsibility: What role for law? Some aspects of law and CSR', 6(2) *Corporate Governance: The International Journal of Business in Society* pp. 188–202; A. Ramasatry (2015) 'Corporate Social Responsibility versus Business and Human Rights: Bridging the gap between responsibility and accountability', 14 *Journal of Human Rights* pp. 137–59.

international human rights law played a strong role in the process of developing the normative outputs. This applies to the UN Global Compact and EU's MSF on CSR and the CSR Alliance. Despite its explicit focus on human rights, the SRSG process was also set in a context of corporate responsibilities closely related to the conception of CSR at the time. Indeed, this spurred parts of the construction of normativity that occurred through the SRSG process. Even the Draft Norms, with an explicit human rights orientation, referred extensively in the preamble to a series of instruments that are generally seen as having broad CSR relevance rather than being specifically on human rights.[2] Thus, CSR plays a role for the case studies and throughout this analysis and its identification of argumentative strategies that contributed to the emergence of the BHR regime.

2.1.1 Understanding CSR and its Relation to Sustainability

CSR is a dynamic and open term, which continues to undergo change in regard to its substantive contents and application. During the years when the processes analysed in this book occurred, CSR was the term used for what towards 2020 is increasingly referred to as corporate sustainability. While the 'corporate sustainability' term obviously clearly signals the emphasis on sustainability, social and environmental sustainability are also key elements in CSR.

Although neither scholars nor practitioners agree on a single definition of CSR,[3] there is a general consensus that CSR is the idea that compa-

---

[2] For example, the Draft Norms' preamble referred to the Rio Declaration, the Plan of Implementation of from the World Summit on Sustainable Development (Johannesburg) and the UN Millennium Declaration, as well as, *i.a.*, ILO's Tripartite Declaration of Principles concerning Multinational Enterprises and Social Policy and the OECD Guidelines for Multinational Enterprises.

[3] On the debate on defining CSR, see for example T. Devinney (2009) 'Is the socially responsible corporate a myth? The good, the bad, and the ugly of Corporate Social Responsibility', *Academy of Management Perspectives*, May 2009, pp. 44–56; A. Crane, D. Matten and L. J. Spence (2008) *Corporate Social Responsibility*, New York: Routledge, at 4–7; A. Crane, A. McWilliams, D. Matten, J. Moon and D. Siegel (2008) The Corporate Social Responsibility Agenda. In A. Crane, *et al.* (eds.) *The Oxford Handbook of Corporate Social Responsibility*, Oxford: Oxford University Press, pp. 3–18; P. Newell and J. G. Frynas (2007) 'Beyond CSR? Business, poverty and social justice: An introduction', 28(4) *Third World Quarterly* pp. 669–81, at 673; R. V. Aguilera, D. E. Rupp, C. A. Williams, and J. Ganapathi (2007) 'Putting the S back in corporate social responsibility: A multilevel theory of social change in organisations', 32(2) *Academy of Management Review* pp. 836–63; M; Hopkins (2006) 'Commentary: What is Corporate Social Responsibility all about?', 6 *Journal of Public Affairs*, August–November 2006,

nies take or should take responsibility for their social and environmental impact. In practice, this means that companies take action to mitigate or prevent negative social and environmental impact or to maximise positive impact, generally beyond obligations following from directly applicable statutory law and beyond the economic obligations they have to their owners.

The dynamic and internally complex character of CSR[4] means that the term tends to escape precise definitions in favour of broader and more fluid understandings. The fact that CSR is also an umbrella term[5] and overlaps or is synonymous with some other conceptions of relations between business and society (such as in the current decades's 'sustainability') contributes to this fluidity. Moreover, defining or just describing what CSR is does not become less complex when the phenomenon is addressed in a public-private regulation context.[6] While the idea that companies contribute to societal objectives is an integrated part of CSR, what exactly companies must or should do for this has been a major challenge for practitioners and scholars alike. From a political science perspective, Edward Epstein in 1989 noted that CSR entails that 'business organizations have societal obligations which transcend economic functions of producing and distributing scarce goods and services and generating a satisfactory level of profits for their shareholders'.[7]

Not only is the literature marked by a variety of CSR definitions. Definitions of CSR employed by various business organisations, NGOs and (inter-)governmental organisations are as diverse as the many definitions that have been suggested by scholars over the past decades. The dynamic character of CSR is evidenced by the fact that organisations

---

pp. 298–306. For a general overview, see F. G. A. De Bakker, P. Groenewegen and F. Den Hond (2005) 'A bibliometric analysis of 30 years of research and theory on Corporate Social Responsibility and Corporate Social Performance', 44(3) *Business and Society*, pp. 283–316.

[4] D. Matten and J. Moon (2008) '"Implicit" and "Explicit" CSR: A conceptual framework for a comparative understanding of corporate social responsibility', 33(2) *Academy of Management Review* pp. 404–24, at 406–7.

[5] M. Blowfield and J. G. Frynas (2005) 'Setting new agendas: critical perspectives on Corporate Social Responsibility in the developing world', 81(3) *International Affairs* pp. 499–513, at 503.

[6] J. Fairbrass (2011) 'Exploring corporate social responsibility policy in the European Union: A discursive institutionalist analysis', 49(5) *JCMS: Journal of Common Market Studies* pp. 949–70, esp. at 952–4.

[7] E. M. Epstein (1989) 'Business ethics, corporate good citizenship and the corporate social policy process: A view from the United States', 8(8) *Journal of Business Ethics* pp. 583–95, at 585.

change their CSR definitions over time,[8] and that in recent years, climate concerns and responsible handling of greenhouse gas emissions have been added to the general understanding of CSR.

Complicating any quest to develop a uniform definition, understandings of CSR practices differ somewhat between regions. Whereas corporate philanthropy has been and remains a relatively prominent part of the conception of CSR in the United States and in some parts of Asia, in Europe CSR is generally perceived as corporate practice directly related to the employees of the company, its community, suppliers or customers.[9] Somewhat simplified, the former is mainly about the way profit is spent, whereas the latter is mainly about the way profit is made. Moreover, the idea that CSR as 'voluntary' business action should or must be de-linked from public regulation has been challenged

---

[8] For example, the World Business Council of Sustainable Development (WBCSD) in 1998 referred to CSR as 'the continuing commitment by business to behave ethically and contribute to economic development while improving the quality of life of the workforce and their families as well as of the local community and society at large'. In 2002, this definition was changed to 'the commitment of business to contribute to sustainable economic development, working with employees, their families, the local community and society at large to improve their quality of life'. (Blowfield and Frynas (n 5) at 501). Notably the WBCSD definition at the WBCSD's website in January 2013 and June 2009 like the 2002 definition referred only to 'economic development', not 'sustainable economic development'. During 2011–14 'ESG' (Environment, Social and Governance) issues were prominent on the WBCSD's website rather than CSR, whereas since 2016 climate change mitigation has been a core element on the WBCSD's website and its sustainability focus.

[9] On the regional differentiation of what is understood by the term CSR as philanthropy and charity (US and Asia), or as some sort of standard based initiative in an effort to go beyond those standards (Europe), see also Crane, A. et al. (n 3) at 4–7 and Matten and Moon (n 4); and compare the discussion on the American approach to CSR as philanthropy and employee voluntarism and the EU tendency towards global standards, environment and product safety in G. F. David, M. V. N. Whitman and M. N. Zald (2006) 'The responsibility paradox: Multinational firms and global Corporate Social Responsibility', University of Michigan, Michigan Ross School of Business Working Paper Series, Working Paper No. 1031, April 2006. For Africa, the tendency seems to be a mixture, with some TNCs and other foreign registered companies providing charity services (in some cases under UN Global Compact Partnerships) and African national CSR discourses and some National Human Rights Institutions pressing for a standards-informed approach to CSR, see W. Kimathi (2010) 'Corporate Social Responsibility in Africa: A fig leaf or a new development path worth pursuing?' In K. Buhmann, L. Roseberry and M. Morsing (eds) *Corporate Social and Human Rights Responsibilities: Global Legal and Management Perspectives,* London: Palgrave Macmillan, pp. 129–43.

by recent tendencies in several countries and regions for governments to establish specific CSR requirements on firms.[10] Since the adoption of the UN Framework, the explicit BHR connection between the public and private sectors has fuelled the growth of similar tendencies in Europe, building on what was already occurring particularly in some Nordic countries.[11]

It follows from the above that a precise definition of CSR in terms of the substantive issues covered by the term does not exist. Nor is such a definition necessarily desirable. Arguably, the dynamic character of CSR may be precisely what is needed for the private sector to become conscious of society's expectations, and for understandings of these expectations to accommodate evolving issues, which require the attention and action of the private sector at any given point of time and under specific geographic, economic or other conditions. The dynamic character of CSR may also be an impetus for an evolving expansion leading to a gradual hardening of soft norms. This may provide public regulation of corporate behaviour with higher private sector support than what would otherwise have been the case. The tendency with national law-makers to promulgate CSR reporting requirements over the past years with the acceptance of companies and their organisation is a case in point.[12]

CSR has often been argued or thought to be distinct from law, typically understood at least to encompass specific legal requirements on a company. This was the case, for example, with the first EU definition

---

[10] J.-P. Gond, N. Kang and J. Moon (2011) 'The government of self-regulation: on the comparative dynamics of corporate social responsibility', 40(4) *Economy and Society* pp. 640–71; see also the mandatory CSR clause introduced in India with the 2013 revision of the India Companies Act (The Gazette of India, New Delhi, the 30th August, 2013) requiring large companies to set aside 2 per cent of their profit for CSR; and for China, see Buhmann, K. (forthcoming) 'Social transformation and normative change through CSR standards? China's engagement with international labour law in guidance for firms' social impact', *NAVEIN REET: Nordic Journal of Law and Social Research*.

[11] Buhmann (2016, n 1); K. Buhmann (2013) 'The Danish CSR reporting requirement as reflexive law: Employing CSR as a modality to promote public policy', 24(2) *European Business Law Review* pp. 187–216; M. Gjølberg (2010) 'Varieties of corporate social responsibility (CSR): CSR meets the "Nordic Model"', 4 *Regulation & Governance* pp. 203–29.

[12] See, e.g., Gjølberg, ibid.; K. Buhmann (2015) 'Defying territorial limitations: Regulating business conduct extraterritorially through establishing obligations in EU law and national law'. In J. L. Cernic and T. Van Ho (eds) *Human Rights and Business: Direct Corporate Accountability for Human Rights*. The Hague: Wolf Legal Publishers, pp. 179–228.

of CSR,[13] which applied from 2001 until a new definition introduced in mid-2011 changed the official EU understanding of CSR to 'the responsibility of enterprises for their impacts on society'.[14] However, even before that change, notions of compliance, law, and regulation in general were not distinct from the concept. A few examples demonstrate the span of issues and forms of regulation covered in various understandings of CSR, showing that the role of law is certainly not insignificant for companies to navigate the fluid expectations entailed in CSR. Already in 1979, organisational studies professor Archie Carroll defined CSR as having legal as well as economic and ethical aspects.[15] Carroll has expanded on this later, and together with Mark S. Schwartz in 2003 recognised that the legal dimension of CSR relates not just to the letter of the law, but also sometimes the 'spirit' (or intention) of the law.[16] From this perspective, in order to claim to be socially responsible a company must not only stay in business economically, engage in ethical 'do-gooding', and observe the law. It must also avoid exploiting or benefiting from governance gaps, for example where the company's observance of the law in the books on working hours or occupational health and safety requirements is not adequately monitored or enforced by local authorities; or where local regulations on minimum wages are inadequate for a decent standard of living because the local regulations have not been sufficiently updated. Under such circumstances the company must observe the spirit of the law by observing the formal health and safety requirements and paying a salary that offers employees the intended standard of living.

Michael Blowfield and Jedrzej G. Frynas observe that CSR refers to

---

[13] Commission of the European Communities (2001) *Promoting a European Framework for Corporate Social Responsibility,* COM(2001)366, para. 8; Commission of the European Communities (2002) *Corporate Social Responsibility: A business contribution to sustainable development.* COM(2002)347, at 3 and 5; Commission of the European Communities (2006) *Communication from the Commission to the European Parliament, the Council and the European Economic and Social Committee: Implementing the Partnership for Growth and Jobs: Making Europe a Pole of Excellence on CSR,* COM (2006)136.final.

[14] European Commission (2011) *A renewed EU Strategy 2011–2014 for Corporate Social Responsibility,* Communication from the Commission to the European Parliament, the Council, the European Economic and Social Committee and the Committee of the Regions, Brussels, 25.10.2011, EU Doc. COM(2011)681, section 3.1.

[15] A. B. Carroll (1999) 'Corporate Social Responsibility: Evolution of a definitional construct', 39(3) *Business & Society Review* pp. 264–95.

[16] M. S. Schwartz and A. B. Carroll (2003) 'Corporate Social Responsibility: A three-domain approach', 13(4) *Business Ethics Quarterly* pp. 503–30.

theories and practices, which recognise that 'companies have a responsibility for their impact on society and the natural environment, sometimes beyond legal compliance and the liability of individuals'.[17] Jennifer Zerk, who has a background in law, integrates a compliance element into her understanding of CSR. To Zerk, CSR refers to 'the notion that each business enterprise, as a member of society, has a responsibility to operate ethically and in accordance with its legal obligation and to strive to minimise any adverse effects of its operations and activities on the environment, society and human health'.[18] In several Asian countries and increasingly in Europe and elsewhere, CSR is becoming subject to governmental regulation setting out obligations for companies, whether in the form of mandatory 'philanthropy' as in India, mandatory reporting as in the EU and certain European countries,[19] or the disclosure of supplying practices and supply chains, as required both in the EU and the US with regard to specific goods like timber[20] or 'conflict minerals'[21] or concession payments.[22] However, much of this juridification of CSR through public law has occurred in response to the evolution of the BHR regime since the adoption of the UN Framework, or been spurred by normative developments

---

[17] Blowfield and Frynas (n 5) at 503.

[18] J. A. Zerk (2006) *Multinationals and Corporate Social Responsibility: Limitations and Opportunities in International Law*. Cambridge: Cambridge University Press.

[19] The India Companies Act (The Gazette of India, New Delhi, 30 August, 2013), art. 135(5); Directive 2014/95/EU of the European Parliament and of the Council of 22 October 2015 amending Directive 2013/34/EU as regards disclosure of non-financial and diversity information by certain large undertakings and groups, EU doc. OJ 2014 L 330.

[20] For the US, see the United States Lacey Act, 16 U.S.C. § 3371–3378; for Europe, see Council Regulation (EC) No 2173/2005 of 20 December 2005 on the establishment of a FLEGT licensing scheme for imports of timber into the European Community, EU doc. OJ 2005 L 347/1; Regulation (EU) 995/2010 of the European Parliament and of the Council of 20th October 2010 laying down the obligations of operators who place timber and timber products on the market, EU doc. OJ 2010 L 295/23; see also on timber-related human rights issues K. Buhmann and I. Nathan (2013) 'Plentiful forests, happy people? The EU's FLEGT approach and its impact on human rights and private forestry sustainability schemes', 4(2) *Nordic Environmental Law Journal* pp. 53–82.

[21] See s. 1502 of the Dodd-Frank Wall Street Reform Act of 2010, United States Congress, *Dodd-Frank Wall Street Reform and Consumer Protection Act* (2010 – H.R. 4173), available at https://www.govtrack.us/congress/bills/111/hr4173 (last accessed on 22 December 2016).

[22] Ibid., s. 1504. The EU Transparency Directive (2013/50/EU) requires the disclosure of payments made to governments by both listed and large, non-listed companies active in the extractive industry or in the logging of primary forests.

that have taken place as a result of that process.[23] At the time when the evolution of the BHR regime took off, CSR was still largely understood and argued to be 'voluntary' in the sense of being disconnected from legal requirements. This was the case in several initiatives that preceded the process towards the UN Framework, as will be elaborated below in this chapter and in Chapter 4. Chapters 5 and 6 explain that the shift leading to the turn-around in relation to acceptance of business responsibilities for human rights was to a significant extent due to discursive and argumentative strategies that combined the public and the private dimensions of a plurality of forms of regulation. As will be shown, this succeeded in convincing business managers that paying attention to underlying legal norms is meaningful for businesses and their managers in order to understand and deliver on social expectations related to business impact on society, whether presented as CSR, as sustainability, or in other related terms.

Although one specific substantive definition of CSR does not exist, and although CSR is much more than human rights, the private sector's responsibility for its impact on human rights is seen by many actors as part of CSR. Partly due to the political sensitivity of human rights in some states, partly perhaps because human rights remain primarily obligations of states, corporate responsibilities for human rights and labour rights are often referred to as 'social issues' in CSR instruments or strategies. This was reflected in the so-called 'Triple Bottom Line: People, Planet, Profit' proposed by sustainable management expert John Elkington in 1998,[24] which spurred voluntary CSR-reporting in many companies in Europe and beyond. The human and labour rights informed understanding of social sustainability issues as part of CSR remains obvious in the widely used CSR reporting tool Global Reporting Initiative (GRI) as well as in CSR policies and strategies of many companies.

As will also be elaborated in Chapters 5 and 6, the work of the SRSG came to fork off the understanding of business and human rights in a direction which emphasises state obligations under international human rights law (to protect individuals against abuse by other individuals), but also retains business responsibilities of a more moral type ('social expectations'). The distinction between CSR and what is increasingly referred to as BHR began to crystallise with the work of the SRSG in the later part

---

[23] See further K. Buhmann (2016) 'Public regulators and CSR: The "Social Licence to Operate" in recent United Nations instruments on Business and Human Rights and the juridification of CSR', 136(4) *Journal of Business Ethics* pp. 699–714.

[24] J. Elkington (1998) *Cannibals with Forks: The Triple Bottom Line of 21st Century Business*, Gabriola Island BC: New Society Publishers.

of his first term (2005–08). At the same time, BHR is coming to influence CSR understanding and guidance. Under the influence of the outputs of the SRSG process, the EU revised its definition of CSR. The previous definition[25] emphasised the voluntary element in CSR; the 2011 definition excludes any explicit reference to voluntary action.[26] The change was introduced to ensure alignment with the UNGPs, which recognise that the state duty to protect entails explicit government action, such as legislation to promote the corporate respect of human rights.

2.1.2 The Uneasy Relationship Between CSR and Law: The Voluntary-Mandatory Dichotomy

The understanding of CSR as 'voluntary' was prevalent in the late 1990s and early 2000s, and therefore the time when much of the discursive construction of business responsibilities for human rights analysed in this work took place. Just as there is no commonly applied definition of CSR, there is also no specific understanding of what exactly 'voluntary' means with regard to CSR. Various definitions and discussions, however, indicate that 'voluntary' in the CSR context implies that CSR is to act beyond compliance with law.[27] This came out, for example, in the EU's definition of CSR from 2001 up to the change in 2011. During that time, CSR was officially defined by the EU as 'behaviour by businesses over and above legal requirements, voluntarily adopted because businesses deem it to be in their long-term interest',[28] on a backdrop of a reference

---

[25] The EU Commission's first CSR Communication described CSR as 'a concept whereby companies integrate social and environmental concerns in their business operations and in their interaction with their stakeholders on a voluntary basis' (Commission of the European Communities (2002) *Corporate Social Responsibility*, at 5).

[26] European Commission (2011) *A renewed EU Strategy 2011–2014 for Corporate Social Responsibility*, section 3.1.

[27] See also F. Wettstein (2009) 'Beyond voluntariness, beyond CSR: Making a case for human rights and justice', 114(1) *Business and Society Review* pp. 125–52, esp. at 125–42; D. McBarnet (2008) 'Corporate social responsibility beyond law, through law, for law: the new corporate accountability'. In D. McBarnet, A. Voiculescu and T. Campbell (eds) *The New Corporate Accountability: Corporate Social Responsibility and the Law*, Cambridge: Cambridge University Press, pp. 9–58; and J. Moon and D. Vogel (2008) 'Corporate Social Responsibility, government, and civil society'. In A. Crane, A. McWilliams, D. Matten, J. Moon and D. S. Siegel (eds) *The Oxford Handbook of Corporate Social Responsibility*, Oxford: Oxford University Press, pp. 302–23.

[28] Commission of the European Communities (2002) *Corporate Social Responsibility*, at 5.

to CSR definitions generally entailing an idea of companies 'acting on a voluntary basis', 'going beyond compliance', or 'going beyond basic legal compliance'.[29] This CSR definition assumes a positivist understanding of law, seeing 'law' as specific hard law requirements that must be complied with and can be enforced. A positivist approach to law typically excludes soft law guidance instruments or socio-legal approaches that recognise instrumental legal approaches to promote change, which do not necessarily count on hard law or judiciary enforcement. As already observed there is a lot more to 'law' than simply mandatory requirements and enforcement, based on hard law. The positivist approach to law in CSR therefore, arguably, adopts an amputated conception of what law is. It is not surprising that such a conception leads to confusion in companies and among business associations on how they should respond to a continually growing range of guidance instruments that refer to international law on human or labour rights as guiding for companies, or how they should understand and relate to initiatives by public regulators to formally define CSR normativity or even develop 'normative frameworks' for CSR, as the EU tried to do through the MSF. Arguably, that confusion as well as some business resistance to defining norms on CSR might have been reduced if a broader conception of law had been applied. In accordance with the argumentative strategy that was later applied by the SRSG during the second half of his first mandate and much of the second, as explained in Chapter 5, this might have highlighted the benefits for businesses of looking to normative guidance in soft law. The positivist idea that saw law as a limitation for business informed much corporate resistance to CSR normativity and specifically to norms on business responsibilities for human rights during the processes analysed in Chapter 4.

Indeed, in the CSR context, 'voluntary' is typically contrasted to 'mandatory', and as we shall see below, this was very much the case in the discursive struggles that shaped BHR within a context of CSR. The implication of 'voluntary' as opposed to 'mandatory' is that CSR is an action not required by public law. Understandings of CSR in organisational scholarship, such as the 'implicit'/'explicit' characterisation of CSR developed by Matten and Moon,[30] suggests that even where organisational theory recognises that public law is not without significance to CSR, this literature has been going to some lengths to present CSR as separate from

---

[29] Commission of the European Communities (2001) *Promoting a European Framework for Corporate Social Responsibility*, paras. 20–21.
[30] Matten and Moon (n 4).

basic compliance with legal requirements applying to a specific organisational entity. By 'explicit CSR' Matten and Moon refer to corporate policies that assume and articulate responsibility for some societal interests. Explicit CSR normally comprises 'voluntary programs and strategies by corporations which combine social and business value'. Moreover, explicit CSR 'rests on corporate discretion rather than reflecting either governmental authority or broader formal or informal institutions'. 'Implicit CSR' 'consists of values, norms and rules which result in (often codified or mandatory) requirements for corporations to address stakeholder issues and which define proper obligations of corporate actors in collective rather than individual terms'.[31] An alternative approach might have recognised that in particular implicit CSR often occurs in response to public soft, reflexive or mixed forms of regulation and not infrequently arises in response to policy or other forms of directives that occur in the shadow of the law. The shadow of the law refers to the implicit power of policymakers and public regulators to introduce mandatory requirements, if organisational self-regulation is not seen to be adequate for public policy purposes.

As apparent above, the dichotomy that has characterised much of the CSR discourse assumes that 'mandatory' is distinguished from 'voluntary' by a presence or absence of public law and coercion related to the non-observance of such law. It therefore also assumes a positivistic approach to law, according to which legal obligation implies effective coercive sanctions other than sanctions imposed or induced by other economic actors.

However, as evidenced by the normative sources informing such CSR schemes of global application as the UN Global Compact Principles,[32] GRI,[33] SA8000,[34] ISO 26000,[35] the principles of the Forest Stewardship Council (FSC)[36] and the Programme for the Endorsement of Forestry

---

[31] Ibid., at 410–12.

[32] UN Global Compact, 'The ten principles of the UN Global Compact', available at: https://www.unglobalcompact.org/what-is-gc/mission/principles (last accessed 5 January 2017).

[33] Global Reporting Initiative, available at: https://www.globalreporting.org/Pages/default.aspx (last accessed 5 January 2017).

[34] Social Accountability International, available at: http://www.sa-intl.org/index.cfm?fuseaction=Page.ViewPage&PageID=937 (last accessed 5 January 2017).

[35] ISO (2010) *ISO 26000 – Social Responsibility,* http://www.iso.org/iso/iso_catalogue/management_standards/social_responsibility.htm (last accessed 5 January 2017).

[36] Forest Stewardship Council, available at: https://ic.fsc.org/en (last accessed 5 January 2017).

Certification (PEFC),[37] instruments and standards of public international law serve as normative guidance for much CSR action. And as evidenced by media stories on child labour, forced labour, excessive working hours and unpaid overtime as well as occupational health and safety, lethal substances and environmental damage[38] the ideals represented by, for example, international labour law and international environmental law also inform social expectations of business in relation to their impact on society. The assertion that CSR is 'voluntary' therefore also assumes that the pertinent international law instruments and standards are perceived – and the international legal order construed – to not establish obligations for companies. To companies that prefer minimal legal constraint and who build on CSR as 'voluntary' as a marketing parameter ('do-gooding'), a construction of international law as not creating obligations for companies may therefore be significant from a (short-termist) focus on economic freedom for profit-making. Such considerations can be observed in several statements made by business organisations in the processes of constructing CSR with regard to social or human rights impacts noted in Chapter 4, as well as in the first stages of the SRSG process, described in Chapter 5.

Overall, the dichotomy between mandatory and voluntary action has played a prominent role in recent decades' efforts to define corporate responsibilities for social and human rights. After it was launched, the UN Global Compact Office took great care to describe the initiative as not being a regulatory instrument.[39] The dichotomy has, however, also been described by business practitioners as both unfruitful and having slowed down progress in developing normative consensus and guidelines.[40]

---

[37] Programme for the Endorsement of Forest Certification (PEFC), available at http://www.pefc.org/ (last accessed 5 January 2017).

[38] For example, Reuters (2016) *Maersk to scrap ships at certain Alang sites, NGO dismayed*, 12 February 2016, http://in.reuters.com/article/maersk-shipping-alang-idINKCN0VL1VZ (last accessed 9 January 2017); C. Digges (2016) *Danish shipping giant caught beaching ships in India and Bangladesh*, retrieved from http://bellona.org/news/industrial-pollution/2016-10-danish-shipping-giant-caught-beaching-ships-in-india-and-bangladesh (9 January 2017); Danwatch (2016), *Maersk scraps ships at dangerous shipyards in India*, 13 October 2016, retrieved from https://www.danwatch.dk/en/nyhed/maersk-scraps-ships-at-dangerous-shipyards-in-india/ (9 January 2017).

[39] J. G. Ruggie (2002) 'The theory and practice of learning networks'. Reprinted in M. McIntosh, S. Waddock and G. Kell (eds.) *Learning to Talk: Corporate Citizenship and the Development of the UN Global Compact*, Sheffield, Greenleaf Publishing, pp. 32–41, at 35.

[40] G. Chandler (2008) Business and human rights – A personal Account from the front line, *Ethical Corporation*, 11 February 2008, compare Zanitelli, L. M. (2011) 'Corporations and Human Rights: The debate between volun-

In practice, law works in many more ways than through state coercion. For example, and highly relevant in the CSR context, law frequently works through incentives and rewards (such as tax breaks in some states, publicly funded financial support in others, reduced fees for governmental inspection or certification of CSR relevant concerns, such as occupational health and certificates, or as introduced with the 2010 EU 'Illegal Timber' regulation,[41] privileged access to the EU market for legality certified tropical timber). Moreover, in international law, the effectiveness of coercive sanctions is recognised to be vague and often non-existent, due to the absence of coercive institutions in many fields of international law. Still, international law is recognised to be law.[42]

It is the fact that obligation and duty build on something else than coercion (or fear of legal sanctions) that drives much current CSR development. From the early days of the CSR movement, the non-coercion-based conviction has played a strong role in motivating consumers, civil society and investors to expect companies to observe human rights even though international human rights law does not apply directly to companies. An acceptance that obligation and duty do not depend on coercive institutions has allowed recent work under the UN in the field of business and human rights to deliver results, particularly through the process that led to the UN Framework. The absence of effective coercive institutions for enforcement in international law also matters in this context. When enforcement is weak, the role it plays to prevent harm is reduced. As described by Thomas Franck, this calls for international law being developed in such a way that it obtains a strong inherent 'compliance pull'.[43] Arguably, a similar point can be made about CSR regulation, whether public or private. Because legal enforcement modalities are typically weak, it is significant that norms are such as to prevent harm from occurring and that they do so by inspiring compliance by their very existence. This means

---

tarists and obligationists and the undermining effect of sanctions', 8(15) *SUR International Journal on Human Rights* pp. 35–54.

[41] Regulation (EU) 995/2010 of the European Parliament and of the Council (n 20). During the drafting process, the (then draft) Regulation was referred to as the 'Due Diligence Regulation', it is now referred as the 'Timber Regulation'.

[42] For example, while H.L.A. Hart emphasised the significance of obligation and duty in law, he recognised that these features are not opposed to the presence of a non-coercive element. Hart rejected the idea that legal obligation requires the existence of organised sanctions or the imposition of sanction or punishment for disobedience (H. L. A. Hart (1961) *The Concept of Laws*, Oxford: Oxford University Press, at 217–18).

[43] T. M. Franck (1990) *The Power of Legitimacy Among Nations*, Oxford: Oxford University Press.

that the difference between whether something is mandatory or voluntary is not significant, because the pull towards compliance is not dependent on an *ex-post* facto sanction or enforcement. Rather, it has to rely on an *ex-ante* inherent conviction about what type of action is acceptable or not.

In his oft-cited 1979 article on CSR, Archie B. Carroll noted that '(t)he social responsibility of business encompasses the economic, legal, ethical, and discretionary expectations that society has of organizations at a given point in time'.[44] In Carroll's understanding of CSR, those four categories are not mutually exclusive, nor are they intended to portray a continuum with economic concerns on the one end and social concerns on the other. According to Carroll, *economic responsibilities* constitute the first and foremost social responsibility of business. The business institution is the basic economic unit in our society. As such, a company has responsibility to produce goods and services that society wants and to sell them at a profit. This economic obligation is the basis on which other business roles rest. *Legal responsibilities* are understood as business' fulfilment of its economic mission within the framework of legal requirements. These are 'the ground rules – the laws and regulations – under which business is expected to operate'. *Ethical responsibilities* are additional behaviour and activities that are not necessarily codified into law, but nevertheless expected of business by society's members. These are expectations 'over and above legal requirements'. Ethical responsibilities are 'ill defined' and 'consequently among the most difficult for business to deal with'. *Discretionary* (or *volitional*) *responsibilities* are different from ethical responsibilities in that society has no clear-cut message about them for business. Often philanthropic, these activities are purely voluntary, left to individual judgment and choice, and 'the decision to assume them is guided only by a business's desire to engage in social roles not mandated, not required by law, and not even generally expected by businesses in an ethical sense'.[45]

Carroll's 1979 definition of CSR assumes a positivist approach to law according to which social responsibilities of business include compliance with law in the narrow sense of directly applicable legal obligations (statutory or judge-made law). But interestingly, it includes this as part of CSR – rather than exclude it, as the EU's definitions between 2001 and 2011 did. Carroll's 'CSR Pyramid', which he presented in a 1991 article also includes legal responsibility, understood as obeying the law.[46] In that

---

[44] A. B. Carroll (1979) 'A three-dimensional conceptual model of corporate performance', 4(4) *The Academy of Management Review* pp. 497–505, at 500.
[45] Ibid., at 500 (all quotes in this paragraph).
[46] A. B. Carroll (1991) 'The Pyramid of Corporate Social Responsibility:

article, Carroll summarised his view of CSR to mean that '[t]he CSR firm should strive to make a profit, obey the law, be ethical, and be a good corporate citizen'.[47] In 1999, Carroll traced the evolution of the CSR construct beginning in the 1950s, which to him marks the modern era of CSR. Carroll identified an evolving (and solidifying) social contract between business and society, with society increasingly expecting business to take social responsibility for tasks beyond immediate business profit-seeking practices. Among common characteristics of definitions of CSR emerging from the 1999 overview, is a general perception of CSR as more than compliance with minimal requirements in national law.[48] Thus, there is a social expectation that companies not only comply with law, but also go beyond this.

In the 2003 article with Mark S. Schwartz, Carroll introduced a three-domain approach developed partly in response to weaknesses of the 1979 definition and the 1991 pyramid.[49] One of the major points of the 2003 article is an elaboration of the 'legal domain' to go beyond simple legal compliance and include action undertaken in order to avoid civil litigation and in anticipation of (new) law.[50] In addition, compliance was elaborated to comprise three forms: 'passive' (the idea that a company does what it wants and just happens to be acting within the boundaries of the law, i.e., no specific intention to comply with the law), 'restrictive' (the idea that the legal system limits, constrains or modifies otherwise intended behaviour in a restrictive fashion, in order for the actor to stay within the boundaries of legal compliance), and 'opportunistic' (when a company takes advantage of loopholes in legislation, in many cases complying with the letter of the law, but not the spirit of the law; or chooses to place operations in a particular jurisdiction because its weaker legal standards are favourable to the company's objectives).[51]

Both research and practice suggest that Schwartz and Carroll's ideas

---

Toward the moral management of organizational stakeholder', *Business Horizons,* July/August, pp. 39–48.

[47] Ibid., at 43.

[48] Carroll (n 15). It should be noted that the article is based mainly on US literature on CSR. Another basic uniting feature emerging from Carroll's 1999 overview of CSR definitions is the idea that CSR need not conflict with a firm's economic (profit-oriented) considerations.

[49] Schwartz, and Carroll (n 16).

[50] Compare Rendtorff, J. D. (2007) *Virksomhedsetik: En grundbog i organisation og ansvar,* Frederiksberg: Forlaget Samfundslitteratur, at 114, who based on a reading of some of Carroll's articles states that the legal aspect of CSR goes beyond immediate compliance to include 'the spirit of the law'.

[51] Schwartz and Carroll (n 16).

on the role of law as informing 'compliance' in a wide sense touch a note that corresponds to reality in an increasingly CSR conscious world. Opportunistic compliance is of particular relevance in an (international) human rights and labour law context. Low labour law standards or enforcement gaps in many low-wage countries make it possible for companies elsewhere to outsource production to such countries and claim to engage in CSR, while in fact only complying with the requirements of host country laws or going minimally beyond these.[52] Research suggests that the category of anticipation of potential regulation (the effect of the proactive role of 'the shadow of the law') is also of high practical relevance in a number of contexts. In other words, a company may act in a particular way to pre-empt new or amended law and therefore to uphold the idea of voluntary action.[53] Historically, at least in some parts of Europe, much CSR has in fact been motivated by efforts by company managers to demonstrate their CSR approaches as viable alternatives to emerging or increased welfare-state law prescribing duties for managers.[54]

---

[52] Numerous reports on TNCs' production in or supplying from low wage countries with international labour standards or enforcement below the requirements of international labour law, not to mention labour standards of host countries, indicate that opportunistic compliance by CSR conscious companies takes place based on economic considerations. Consider for example sport shoe producer Nike's production in Vietnam in the 1990s, and sourcing or outsourcing of apparel from Bangladesh and other countries in South Asia by US and European textile companies, including Disney and H&M. Consider also the submissions of the US Chamber of Commerce and the European Chamber of Commerce to the government of the People's Republic of China at the occasion of that government's drafting of the 2007 Labour Contract Law. The foreign Chambers of Commerce indicated that strengthening of workers' contractual rights, in particular to not be laid off from day to day, could result in US and European companies shifting production from China to other countries in the region with less stringent protection of workers (see e.g., K. Buhmann (2007) Vestlig dobbeltmoral i Kina, *Politiken,* 7 July 2007).

[53] See for example, D. Hess and D. E. Warren (2008) 'The meaning and meaningfulness of corporate social initiatives', 113(2) *Business and Society Review* pp. 163–97, with references; A. Héritier and D. Lehmkuhl (2008) 'The shadow of hierarchy and new modes of governance: Sectoral governance and democratic government', 28(1) *Journal of Public Policy*, pp. 1–17; C. A. Adams, (2002) 'Internal organisational factors influencing corporate social and ethical reporting beyond current theorising', 15 *Accounting Auditing & Accountability Journal* pp. 223–50; D. P. Angel and M. T. Rock (2004) 'Global standards and the environmental performance of industry', WPG 04-13, Oxford: Oxford University, School of Geography and the Environment, pp. 19–24.

[54] See the discussion in A. Roepstorff (2010) *CSR: Virksomheders sociale ansvar som begreb og praksis,* Copenhagen: Hans Reitzels Forlag.

As evidenced by Carroll's evolving CSR scholarship and publications, the distinction between CSR and law is not categorical, but blurred. In practice, at least since the later 1990s CSR has been subject to a variety of forms of governmental encouragement and regulation, ranging from the very soft to hard regulation through legislation mandating compliance with specific standards of conduct. Applying these in 'intelligent' combinations aimed at promoting corporate responsibility through different and complementary measures has come to be recognised as 'smart regulation'.[55] The term was deployed in 2011 by the UNGPs, which observe that states may deploy a smart mix of measures, comprising national and international, mandatory and voluntary elements, to foster business respect for human rights.[56] Measures increasingly applied by governments in relation to CSR, such as governmental guidance for due diligence or even due diligence requirements (such as were proposed in France in 2016),[57] tax-breaks or governmental salary subsidies (which require a legal basis),[58] mandatory CSR-reporting on non-financial reporting such as that introduced by the EU for large firms with effect from 2016/2017,[59] or even the Indian requirement that large companies spend at least 2 per cent of their profits every year on CSR[60] can be regarded are examples of smart regulation. Combined in various forms (or 'mixes') they may be mutually complementary, and ideally jointly raising the bar for corporate contributions to society and the manner in which they manage their adverse impacts. Smart-mix regulation is obviously context-specific, and knowledge on what regulatory mixes are particularly apt to smartly promote the intended objectives is still work in progress.

---

[55] Compare D. Kinderman (2016) 'Time for a reality check: is business willing to support a smart mix of complementary regulation in private governance?', 35(1) *Policy and Society* pp. 29–41.

[56] UNGP, at 3, Commentary.

[57] Proposition de loi relative au devoir de vigilance des sociétés mères et des entreprises donneuses d'ordre ('Loi Vigilance'), https://www.senat.fr/dossier-legislatif/ppl14-376.html.

[58] In Denmark, the government had already in 1998 introduced salary subsidies for companies employing individuals who are unable to obtain or handle employment on ordinary terms due to physical, mental or social conditions. Danish companies have referred to their inclusion of workers on governmentally subsidised 'flex job schemes' as CSR (Brejning, J. (2012) *Corporate Social Responsibility and the Welfare State: The Historical and Contemporary Role of CSR in the Mixed Economy of Welfare*, Farnham: Ashgate).

[59] E.g., Directive 2014/95/EU of the European Parliament and of the Council of 22 October 2015 (n 19).

[60] The India Companies Act (The Gazette of India, New Delhi, 30 August, 2013), art. 135(5).

As this shows, while the dichotomy between 'mandatory' and 'voluntary' in relation to CSR generally corresponds to a distinction between coercion and non-coercion in line with the positivist conception of law, that does not mean that CSR and law are distinct. Not only do many CSR initiatives or actions build on presumptions of duty, often normatively informed by international law standards, particularly on human rights, labour standards, environment anti-corruption. That is so despite the fact that the foundational international law instruments establish obligations or soft law responsibilities for states. Moreover, some CSR initiatives and actions also build on statutory requirements on incentive measures (positive as well as negative), many of which are based in national law. Regardless of this, as the following chapters show, the alleged dichotomy between 'voluntary' and 'mandatory' has played a part in the discursive struggles on CSR normativity in or with regard to the case studies analysed in this work. The analysis in Chapters 4–6 will show that several business organisations argued strongly for CSR to remain 'voluntary', and that many NGOs argued as strongly for business impact on society to be subject to governmental or intergovernmental hard law. Yet, as the analysis also depicts, the UN Framework and the emergence of the BHR regime came about through a series of arguments and explanations that highlighted that the regulation of societal impact caused by business is not necessarily a question of either-or.

Understanding CSR or its more recent terminological concoctions like corporate sustainability, and its mechanisms, presumptions and potential can be greatly enhanced by departing from a positivist view on law in favour of a socio-legal and pragmatic perspective. That allows for wider conceptions of law and its interrelationship with other social sciences or sub-disciplines to inspire the debate and on-going evolution and implementation of CSR and private-sector roles for sustainability.

As this section has shown, CSR and law need not be distinct or opposed, and in fact are often connected. Part of the connection is made through law as coercion, part through the voluntary or non-coercive decisions of companies to act in certain ways, which in practice often draws on international law standards (such as on human or labour rights) as a normative source. As observed by Jennifer Zerk, the crucial question is not whether CSR should be 'voluntary' or 'mandatory', but what is the best regulatory response in light of a particular problem.[61] Incentives and reflexive regulatory strategies or techniques (such as reporting requirements) may encourage self-regulation, promote transparency and allow for economic or

---

[61] Zerk (n 18) at 36.

reputation sanctions imposed by economic actors and other stakeholders. To provide the context for understanding motivating factors for efforts at developing CSR norms, which have played a role in framing intergovernmental efforts at promoting business responsibilities for human rights, the subsequent section will address the relationship between CSR and public policy interests and the role played by human rights in that connection.

2.2 PUBLIC POLICY INTERESTS, CSR AND HUMAN RIGHTS

2.2.1 Beyond the 'Business Case for CSR': CSR and Public Policy Interests

Much economic, organisational and management literature on CSR is concerned with the so-called 'business case for CSR'. This 'business case' is assumed to demonstrate that CSR is justified economically, through pay-off.[62] Based on the profit-gaining motive that a company has as an economic actor, the 'business case' idea refers to an assumption that a company's engagement in CSR is to the economic advantage of the company because resources spent support a specific business need. Even when aligned with the concept of strategic CSR and combined private-public sector benefit through the creation of 'shared value',[63] at an overall level the 'business case' approach is that a company's socially motivated dispersal of funds on workers, the community or other 'stakeholders'

---

[62] See, for example, D. J. Vogel (2005) 'Is there a market for virtue? The business case for Corporate Social Responsibility', 47(4) *California Management Review* pp. 19–45; J. D. Margolis and J. P. Walsh (2003) 'Misery loves companies: Rethinking social initiatives by companies', 48(2) *Administrative Science Quarterly* pp. 268–305; J. D. Margolis and J. P. Walsh (2001) *People and Profits? – the Search for a Link between a Company's Social and Financial Performance*, Mahwah, New Jersey: Erlbaum; M. Orlitzky, F. L. Schmidt and S. L. Rynes (2003) 'Corporate social and financial performance: A meta-analysis', 24(3) *Organization Studies* pp. 403–41; T. Fox (2004) 'Corporate Social Responsibility and development: In search of an agenda', 47(3) *Development* pp. 29–36; L. Burke and J. M. Logsdon (1996) 'How Corporate Social Responsibility pays off', 29(4) *Long Range Planning* pp. 495–502; and for an overview of literature and stances, M. L. Barnett (2007) 'Stakeholder influence capacity and the variability of financial returns to corporate social responsibility', 32(3) *Academy of Management Review* pp. 794–816.
[63] M. Porter and M. Kramer (2011) 'Creating Shared Value', January/February *Harvard Business Review*.

rather than shareholders benefits the company's economic gains in the long term.

However, CSR also has major relevance from the public policy perspective. Whereas the 'business case' builds on the business rationality or logic of making a profit and sustaining the company in terms of its reputation, recruitment opportunities and customers and general business opportunities, from the public policy perspective CSR may contribute to fulfilling governmental objectives (such as on environment and human rights, nationally and internationally); legal obligations (such as those that national governments have under international environmental, labour or human rights law); or delivering goods that are fundamentally public tasks, not only often defined as national policy objectives but also in many cases prescribed as obligations for states under international or regional human rights law (such as vocational training, employment opportunities, and access to education and health services). This connects to the public policy rationality or logic of power, because delivering on policies and fulfilling public expectations on access to public goods signals effective public government that cares for citizens and provides for their needs.[64] This helps promote legitimacy with their constituencies and uphold governmental power.

Similarly, CSR relates to the rationality of intergovernmental organisations, in particular of the UN, which is charged with promoting socio-economic growth in accordance with human rights, and organisations like the ILO or the World Health Organisation (WHO) that are associated with the UN. Just as the business case is about the benefits that a company may derive from CSR, from the public policy perspective governments and intergovernmental organisations have an interest in CSR as a modality to contribute to fulfilling social and environmental public policy objectives. In particular, CSR activities by a company acting in host states or in their relations with suppliers or other business relations offer governments in the company's home state options to see their policies implemented outside their jurisdiction and their own policy sphere. This helps explain why governments are so eager to try to promote CSR and shape CSR activities in the private sector by regulatory measures, including smart-mix regulation. In view of the impact on society and the enormous economic

---

[64] Elsewhere, I have referred to this as 'the government case' for CSR (K. Buhmann (2013) 'Recognising a "Government case for CSR": Public policy objectives' impact on Global Governance through institutionalisation of CSR and business access to rule-making at intergovernmental level'. In S. D. Benedetto, and S. Marra (eds) *Legitimacy and Efficiency in Global Economic Governance*, Cambridge Scholars Publishing, pp. 210–37).

and even political power that especially TNCs have come to enjoy since the middle of the twentieth century, this is only logical. If managed carefully, the potential benefits are dual: governments may see (more of) their policies implemented and public goods delivered than they might be able to do on their own, and businesses may enhance their organisational legitimacy and social licence to operate while at the same time remaining in overall control of the specific activities through which they engage in CSR.

An appreciation of the distinction between the business concern with the 'business case' logic and the governmental rationality may provide for enhanced understanding of the interests at both international and national levels that have been driving much activity at intergovernmental level to develop CSR normativity through public-private regulation of CSR. Similarly, national hard or soft regulation to promote CSR, for example through mandatory CSR reporting or incentives such as tax breaks or CSR awards, may be understood as grounded in government rationality aiming to implement public policy. Without supplanting the obligations of national governments, companies' respect for human rights and contribution to their fulfilment may add to the efforts of national governments and complement those of intergovernmental organisations in this field. It may contribute to or build on governmental obligations to promote the respect and actual implementation of human rights at the horizontal level between employers and employees, and/or companies and communities. In this manner, companies may effectively assist governments in living up to their international obligations on human and labour rights as well as the environment.

Within their own national boundaries too, governments have an interest in companies conducting themselves in accordance with human rights, because this limits social tension, creates jobs and options for vocational training, and may provide empowerment and enhance non-discrimination and equal opportunities. Ultimately, this contributes to government funds (through employment and salary taxation) and reduces the need to spend such funds on social services for the unemployed or underemployed, court cases on discrimination, or a host of other issues.

For a number of the same reasons, intergovernmental organisations also have an interest in companies conducting themselves in a manner that conforms to social expectations on CSR, in particular those related to human rights and labour conditions. Although these reasons are transposed to the international level of the pertinent organisations' mandates or objectives, they effectively also play out in national settings, at the level of the states which created the organisations. The UN objective of achieving stability, well-being and universal respect for and promotion of human rights may not easily be accomplished in today's globalised world without the active participation of business. From a public policy perspective, governmental promotion of CSR may therefore be approached as a logical extension of the role which business has in today's world.

Governments and intergovernmental organisations basically have two complementary options to make businesses act in accordance with public policy interests. At one extreme, they may adopt legislation that requires or forbids specifically defined actions. At the other, they may implement measures that provide guidance or incentives for companies to (hopefully) self-regulate. The former has a coercive character, the latter a non-coercive character. Use of the latter often, but not always, takes place on an implicit background of authorities' competence to introduce binding legislative requirements if the non-coercive measures do not result in intended effects. In the case of the UN or other international organisations for which law-making requires a majority of member states to specifically support the measure, the non-coercive regulatory approach provides an alternative modality for shaping business conduct. When such modalities can be implemented through administrative measures (as was the case for the UN Global Compact initially) they may be particularly appealing for issues which cannot or are not likely to be able to generate sufficient support among states in their capacity as the law-makers in international law. CSR may be an avenue, among others, to involve companies in the practical implementation of UN goals related to human rights, labour rights, environment and other issues. As CSR is transnational in scope and outlook, particularly in relation to company activities that affect UN goals negatively or positively, and as governmental interests in CSR vary between states, CSR measures may stand a better chance to be promoted through non-coercive approaches that do not require an international law-making process to take place.

In the case of nation states or regional economic organisations, such as the EU, objectives such as labour market development and competitiveness combine with limitations of direct legislative powers of the organisations so that a non-coercive approach to promoting the role and contributions of companies has particular appeal. While nation states may regulate the actions of home-state-based companies extraterritorially, many refrain from doing so for political reasons and/or perhaps fear that other countries will reciprocate. The EU enjoys only limited conferred powers or shared legislative powers with Member States in relation to labour market issues. For the EU Commission, being the institution charged with the practical rolling-out of EU policy objectives, CSR has been seen as a contribution towards intra-EU policy objectives related to employment and other substantive areas, in addition to international objectives of promoting human and labour rights and environmental protection.

Indeed, CSR is increasingly being seen by public authorities as a modality for meeting societal needs and challenges. While the capacity of business to act to promote societal interests has been an issue in academia for about as long as the discussion on the legal rights of corporate managers to spend profits on social responsibility[65] (see further below), the intentional political-cum-legal use of business to promote social interests and public policy is more recent. The background to the 2008 introduction of the CSR reporting requirement in the Danish Act on Financial Statements is one particularly clear example. The legislative history demonstrates that the government and the ministerial agency charged with the drafting were driven by an aim to engage companies in CSR in order to deliver on national foreign policy objectives on improved respect for human and labour rights, anti-corruption and environmental sustainability in third countries, particularly those suffering from governance gaps.[66] From analysis of the legislative history it also becomes clear that part of the aim was to engage company action where national law does not reach, that is, in the legal, political and economic sphere of third countries. An option for companies' annual Communication on Progress reports to the UN Global Compact or Principles for Responsible Investment (PRI) to double as the report required by the Danish authorities was introduced partly in an effort by the government to encourage more companies to participate in or at least follow the principles of the Global Compact or PRI.

Many CSR concerns that arise in industrialised countries are motivated by a concern with human and labour rights issues in developing and transitional states. This is not just a concern found within private actors such as consumers and investors, but also within political and executive authorities. At the World Summit on Sustainable Development in Johannesburg in 2002, CSR was addressed by governments and intergovernmental organisations, amongst others, as a possible avenue towards reducing

---

[65] See among the numerous twentieth century academic presentations on business as an economic actor with social responsibilities, see for example H. Bowen (1953) *Social Responsibilities of the Businessman*, New York: Harper & Row; C. Kaysen (1957) 'The social significance of the modern corporation', 47(2) *American Economic Review (Papers and proceedings)* pp. 311–19; K. Davis (1960) 'Can business afford to ignore social responsibilities?', 2(3) *California Management Review* Spring, pp. 70–76; G. Goyder (1961) *The Responsible Company*, Oxford: Blackwell; P. Nonet and P. Selznick (1978) *Law and Society in Transition: Toward Responsive Law*, New York: Harper/Colophon; A. B. Carroll, (n 44); Carroll (n 46).

[66] K. Buhmann (2010) 'CSR-rapportering som refleksiv ret: Årsregnskabslovens CSR-redegørelseskrav som typeeksempel', 92(4) *Juristen* pp. 104–13; Buhmann (n 11).

poverty in emerging economies.[67] CSR has come to be seen by some governmental and multilateral financial or international collaboration institutions as providing an avenue for promoting the respect, implementation and enforcement of human rights, labour rights and protection of the environment.[68] In states that lack strong national legal and economic institutional frameworks, it is particularly important that business activities are managed so as not only to limit possible harm, but also to enhance positive impact.[69]

Many nation states have policies of promoting human and labour rights in countries in which the respect for and implementation of those rights are inadequate if compared to international law or governmental obligations. Traditionally, development cooperation and bilateral policy dialogue have been the means for implementation of foreign policy goals. For some states or regions, such as the EU, this has been complemented by trade agreements, which include labour or human rights requirements as conditionalities for trade with the EU. In this sense too, CSR complements those means: if companies undertake human rights relevant activities that go beyond the requirements of national law in host states or beyond the extent to which such law is enforced, they may effectively contribute to the implementation of the foreign policy goals of their home states to promote human rights extraterritorially.

Having established that CSR in general holds considerable potential for governments in relation to social and economic public policy objectives, the following section draws up key points on business impact on human rights in relation to public policy and the complementary advantages for governments in regard to their legal objectives and obligations.

---

[67] Compare, however, critical perspectives offered by academic observers, e.g., Kimathi (n 9); S. Jeppesen and P. Lund-Thomsen (2010) 'Introduction', 93(Supp. 2) *Journal of Business Ethics* pp. 139–42; M. Halter, and M. Arruda (2009) 'Inverting the pyramid of values? Trends in less-developed countries', 90(Supp. 3) *Journal of Business Ethics* pp. 267–75; M. Prieto-Carron, P. Lund-Thomsen, A. Chan, A. Muro and C. Bhushan (2006) 'Critical perspectives on CSR and development: What we know, what we don't know, and what we need to know', 82(5) *International Affairs* pp. 977–89; M. Blowfield (2003) 'Corporate Social Responsibility in international development: an overview and critique', 10(3) *Corporate Social Responsibility and Environmental Management* pp. 115–28; J. Bendell (2005) 'Making business work for development: Rethinking corporate social responsibility', 54 *Id21 insights* April 2005; Fox (n 62).

[68] This is the case with bilateral donors, e.g., the Danish Ministry of Foreign Affairs/Danida, as well as multilateral donors and development banks, e.g. the United Nations Development Programme (UNDP) and the World Bank.

[69] Kimathi (n 9).

2.2.2 Business Impact on Human Rights, Public Policy Interests and Legal Objectives

While there is some recognition in CSR and governance literature that private self-regulation can contribute to fulfilling public policy objectives,[70] it is less well recognised that from a public policy perspective, corporate self-regulation on human rights may be useful in its own right.[71] Yet, business action may offer important contributions to horizontal level respect or fulfilment of such rights between two or more individuals (including companies in their capacity as legal persons). While contributions of business to human rights at the horizontal level does not relieve states of their duty to protect and ensure implementation of human rights through substantive law and government action in a vertical relationship, it can make their tasks easier and provide for innovative approaches

---

[70] See for example F. Cafaggi and A. Renna (2012) 'Public and private regulation: Mapping the labyrinth'. *CEPS Working Document* No. 370, October 2012; M. Gjølberg (2009) 'The origin of corporate social responsibility: Global forces or national legacies?' 4(4) *Socio-Economic Review* pp. 605–37; Matten and Moon (n 4); A. Midttun (2008) 'Partnered governance: aligning Corporate Responsibility and public policy in the global economy', 8(4) *Corporate Governance* pp. 406–18; C. Glinski (2008) 'Bridging the gap: The legal potential of private regulation'. In O. Dilling, M. Herberg and G. Winter (eds) *Responsible Business: Self-governance and Law in Transnational Economic Transactions,* Oxford and Portland Oregon: Hart, pp. 41–66; O. Lobel (2005) 'The Renew Deal: The fall of regulation and the rise of governance in contemporary legal thought', 89 *Minnesota Law Review* pp. 7–27; D. M. Trubek and L. G. Trubek (2006) 'New governance and legal regulation: complementarity, rivalry or transformation', 13 *Columbia Journal of European Law* pp. 1–26; V. Haufler (2001) *A Public Role for the Private Sector: Industry Self-regulation in a Global Economy,* Washington D.C.: Carnegie Endowment for International Peace.

[71] Cf., however, for a view recognising private regulation as 'a form of regulation which can significantly enhance capacity for developing and implementing public-regarding norms', C. D. Scott, F. Cafaggi and L. Senden (2011) 'The conceptual and constitutional challenge of transnational private regulation', 38(1) *Journal of Law and Society* pp. 1–19, esp. at 5. See also the emergent recognition of the complementarity between the public and private sectors in the provision of public goods in A. G. Scherer, A. Rasche, G. Palazzo and Spicer, A. (2016) 'Managing for political corporate social responsibility: new challenges and directions for PCSR 2.0', 53(3) *Journal of Management Studies* pp. 273–98 (rather than the mutually exclusive role of states or the private sector assumed in some of Scherer and Palazzo's previous 'Political CSR' scholarship, e.g., A. G. Scherer and G. Palazzo (2011) 'The new political role of business in a globalized world – a review of a new perspective on CSR AND its implications for the firm, governance, and democracy', 48(4) *Journal of Management Studies* pp. 899–931).

through companies' integration of human rights into their policies, strategies and actions.

CSR holds important societal potential for human rights in two major ways: on the one hand, as a modality for minimising negative impact of business on society; on the other, as a modality for maximising positive impact of business on society. The former includes business violations or complicity in violations of human rights and business exploitation or degradation of the environment that may adversely affect human rights, for example, the local community's access to clean drinking water. The latter counts on business to contribute to general implementation of human rights. This includes issues noted above: human rights related to work, education, health services and other elements related to living conditions, but is not limited to those human rights.

CSR consciousness among companies reduces the risk that companies benefit from governance gaps or weak governance, such as weak state institutions that do not deliver on their national or international obligations in relation to human rights protection and respect. That risk entails that companies benefit from inefficient law or enforcement by producing at low costs under standards below those set by international law and often also by national legislation. Another key issue is whether and how business may contribute to implementation of human rights obligations that are, essentially, obligations of the state but, in some cases, obligations that a state is not (currently) able to meet due to limited resources.

Public-private partnerships on CSR intended to promote work-place integration, training and education not only serve social policy ends, but also contribute to implementing human rights and fulfilling human rights objectives. Although often not addressed in human rights terminology, the activities of the private sector may effectively assist governments in living up to their human rights obligations, especially with regard to equal treatment and social and economic rights of a labour-related character. Somewhat overlooked in both the CSR and the legal debate, those tasks are often closely related to governments' international obligations on social and economic human rights, ranging from the provision of education and health services to water and sanitation, vocational training and non-discriminatory employment practices.

2.2.3 Connecting the Dots: Public Policy Interests in CSR, Business Contributions to Human Rights, and Power of Public Organisations

As the above discussion has shown, CSR or corporate sustainability, public policy objectives and human rights are related in a number of ways. This makes it valuable for governments to involve business in contributing to the implementation of public goods of a social or economic human rights character. Governments have a number of modalities at their disposal for this. These include the option to adopt mandatory requirements on firms, but they also include many other forms of regulatory initiatives, which may make it attractive for business to engage in actions that effectively contribute to governmental public policy objectives on human rights, both nationally and internationally. Whether national governments or international organisations engage companies in such activities through incentives, through awards, through guidance, through reflexive-law type measures that ideally stimulate companies' internalisation of external needs and expectations, or through compliance-oriented hard law, the result will benefit the public policy organisation: it will help the organisation implement its own policies and legal obligations and be seen to effectively deliver on societal needs. As a result, engaging companies in CSR can strengthen the power of governments or international organisations, because citizens, civil society organisations and even (some) business associations will see the public organisation in question deliver on its tasks. The bottom line is that public organisations may preserve and possibly strengthen their power base, if they are effective in promoting CSR. As part of this, constructing international human rights law as part of CSR normativity benefits governments to the extent that this can increase business respect of human rights or labour standards in their international operations, because governments often do not regulate this directly. In view of the close connection between public obligations on human rights and the delivery of public goods like education and health-related services or infrastructures, the case for governments is also strong in business contributions to such public goods, even without explicit reference to international human rights law.

A connection between public policy interests, human rights and international regulation is by no means a novel development. This connection feeds on early business ethics conceptions tied to what later became international law standards against slavery, child labour, working conditions, etc. The evolution of bans on slavery and child labour that emerged in international human rights and labour law in the twentieth century reflected moral convictions that emerged from certain religious groups and professions in the nineteenth century and soon spread beyond these. The development of international human rights law as well as international labour law has also been prompted by recognition of the importance of international agreement to provide protection of the needs of individuals. The exploitation of workers, which was prevalent in industrialised states competing with each other in an already globalising market in the late 1800s and early 1900s, led to the establishment of the ILO in 1919. Its tripartite structure, encompassing not only states but also representatives of workers and employers, recognises the human as well as organisational institutional elements of labour and labour rights protection. This illustrates the close connection between moral concerns that fuel CSR concerns and the evolution of corporate sustainability, and the evolution of national and international law to protect individuals against corporate related abuse. This also underscores that CSR and law, including public international law, are not distinct and can in fact be very closely associated, travelling on complementary paths that sometimes converge.

The subsequent section addresses the interrelationship between human rights and business with a particular focus on how social expectations of acceptable business practices are informed by international human rights law and how governments' protection of human rights matters to companies.

2.3 INTERNATIONAL HUMAN RIGHTS LAW, CSR AND BUSINESS: NORMATIVITY FOR BUSINESS ACTION AND BUSINESS INTEREST IN GOVERNMENTS PROTECTING HUMAN RIGHTS

The idea that companies have responsibilities for human rights has long been an integrated part of the general CSR discourse and social expectations of business. Just as some social actors expect businesses not to pollute the environment and/or to contribute to the local community through philanthropy, some expect businesses not to take advantage of the need for employment, which leads many individuals in poor states to sell their labour for salaries below international or national legal minimum standards, or to accept working conditions below those standards. Some social actors also expect businesses not to take advantage of ineffective legal frameworks or ineffective enforcement of existing law. International human and labour rights standards have come to inform these expectations, which therefore have come to be tied to a legal framework. Although they do not apply directly to companies, international law human and labour rights standards have come to form a baseline of social expectations of businesses among many non-state actors, ranging from the individual 'ethical' or 'political' consumer or investor to civil society organisations, institutional investors, media and often also other business partners. This became formally recognised with the UN Framework's definition of the IBHR and ILO core labour standards as the minimum base line for the corporate responsibility to respect human rights, but effectively was part of the CSR reality before that.

In the course of its profit-making activity, which as noted is its core rationality, a company may affect the entire range of human rights in a number of ways. Businesses of all sizes provide employment opportunities for a large proportion of the global population. Although the creation of employment opportunities by business is not by itself CSR, employment and business activity may spin off possibilities for individuals for the realisation of some human rights. An obvious case is that sufficient salaries gained through employment may provide employees with the possibility to provide for themselves and their dependants. Conversely, businesses may also harm the human rights of employees, local communities and others directly through their own activities, and indirectly through procurement activities or cooperation with other private or public entities.

Concerns with business impacts on human rights (including core international labour rights, which are also human rights) differ from many other CSR concerns because they are intrinsically related to clearly defined obligations of states under international law to protect, respect and fulfil human rights. The duty to protect requires a state to protect individuals against human rights violations by third parties, including corporations. If the state does not introduce national legislation to implement its international human rights obligations or if it does not enforce such legislation, the state does not honour its duty to protect. If companies do not observe such national law, they may cause human rights abuse. From this perspective, companies therefore have a strong interest in governments delivering on their own human rights obligations. That is particularly the case in regard to business risks of causing adverse impacts on human rights. In other words, businesses have strong interest in governments acting actively to protect human rights against business abuse, whether authorities do so through hard law (which they typically limit to apply within their own country), soft law guidance, smart-mix regulatory modalities, or enhanced market access for overseas companies that respect certain policies related to human or labour rights standards.

Because of the economic risks to companies that may result from reputational damage or legal or financial liability in response to incidents of human rights abuse, companies in principle have an interest in governments protecting human rights regardless whether the company is opposed to the idea of governments involving businesses in the delivery of public policy tasks, or whether it supports such measures. Thus, whereas governments can have an interest in involving businesses in the implementation of certain human rights, businesses will have an interest in governments protecting human rights in such a way that they are not susceptible to business abuse. The former situation is often related to social or economic rights connected with public goods in which business may 'do good' by contributing (such as infrastructure and social services) and the latter often to adverse impacts on workers, communities and other cases in which businesses may do harm. In principle, however, both situations may involve all types of human rights.

2.4 THE RELEVANCE OF INTERNATIONAL SOFT LAW FOR CSR AND BUSINESS AND HUMAN RIGHTS

According to the general understanding developed in international law, soft law is non-binding but not devoid of legal relevance. It indicates a level of commitment that goes beyond the purely political. Soft law drafters intend it to have a legal scope as rules of conduct.[72] A growth of interest in soft law that has been taking place in recent decades includes innovation in terms of form and application. This has been spurred by political developments that have lent themselves to unconventional non-binding forms of regulation at the international stage.[73] Wellens and Borchardt explain that soft law is not only a means to explain normative phenomena of state practice, but is 'also and above all a concept which finds its raison d'être in the need to describe and define the legal effects of non-conventional instruments for the sake of the legal situations at issue and of the rights and obligations of the legal subjects involved'.[74]

In international law, the hard law/soft law distinction denotes a differentiation between legally binding law (generally treaty law and customary international law) and non-binding law, respectively. Because of the dearth of strong enforcement institutions in several areas within international law, many binding international law instruments are not enforceable at the international level. For this reason, the distinction between hard and soft law or enforceable/non-enforceable law often lacks strong significance in practice in international law.[75] This is especially the case for soft law instruments that display a clear normative intent as well as those that express a measure of law-making/'law-in-process' intent.[76] Generally

---

[72] K. C. Wellens and G. M. Borchardt (1989) 'Soft law in European Community law', 14 *European Law Review* pp. 267–321.
[73] Ibid., at 267–9.
[74] Ibid., at 269.
[75] Compare for example the reasoning C. Chinkin (2000) 'Normative development in the international legal system'. In Shelton (ed.) (2003), *Commitment and Compliance: The Role of Non-binding Norms in the International Legal System*, pp. 21–42, at 39–40.
[76] A. Boyle (2006) 'Soft law in international law-making'. In M. D. Evans (ed.)

seen to have at least a guiding effect, in international law literature it is recognised that soft law also often serves as proto-law or as precursor for later instruments of hard international law (treaties).[77] The UDHR is a prominent example of the precursory role of international soft law for later hard law (both in terms of treaty law and, for some provisions, in terms of customary international law).

According to a widely applied definition proposed by Francis Snyder, formulated in relation to EU law but applicable beyond, soft law comprises rules of conduct that, in principle, have no legally binding force but may nevertheless have practical effects.[78] In an international law context, Charney has characterised soft international norms as predetermined generalised norms of behaviour that, while not binding as law, attract compliance by the targeted members of the international community.[79] Dinah Shelton notes that soft law usually refers to any international instrument other than a treaty containing principles, norms, standards, or other statements of expected behaviour. Some soft law texts are political commitments that can lead to law.[80] In other cases, soft law is utilised because it allows for rule-making that responds to the needs of the evolving international system, both in terms of procedure and normative output.[81] Compared to hard international law, soft law allows for more active participation by non-state actors, for speedy adoption, for flexibility and for details to be filled out by technical or other institutions at administrative level.[82] Soft law instruments often reflect emerging

---

International Law, 2nd ed., Oxford: Oxford University Press, pp. 141–58, at 143; see also D. Kinley and R. Chambers (2006) 'The UN Human Rights Norms for corporations: The private implications of public international law', 6(3) *Human Rights Law Review* pp. 447–97; D. Shelton, D. (2006) International law and 'Relative Normativity'. In M. D. Evans (ed.) ibid., pp. 159–85, at 162.

[77] See e.g., F. Beveridge and S. Nott (1998) 'A hard look at soft law'. In P. Craig and C. Harlow (eds) *Lawmaking in the European Union,* London: Kluwer Law International, pp. 285–309; P.C. Szasz (1995) 'General law-making processes'. In O. Schachter and C. C. Joyner (eds.) *United Nations Legal Order,* Vol I., Cambridge: University Press, pp. 35–108; Wellens and Borchardt (n 72) at 272.

[78] F. Snyder (1994) 'Soft law and institutional practice in the European Community'. In S. D. Martin (ed.) *The Construction of Europe: Essays in Honour of Emile Noël,* Dordrecht: Kluwer, pp. 197–225, at 198.

[79] J. L. Charney (2000) 'Commentary: Compliance with international soft law'. In D. Shelton (ed.) *Commitment and Compliance: The Role of Non-Binding Norms in the International Legal System,* Oxford: Oxford University Press, pp. 115–18, at 116.

[80] Shelton (n 75) at 180.

[81] See for example Chinkin (n 75).

[82] D. Shelton (2000) 'Introduction'. In Shelton (n 76) pp. 1–18, at 10–13.

trends in the world community, which have not yet matured for hard law regulation but nevertheless constitute such a concern of the international community that various institutions and other actors engage in efforts towards regulation.[83] Soft law is often carefully negotiated and contains carefully drafted statements, intended to have normative effects despite the non-binding form.[84] Some also employ the term 'soft law' for weak or openly worded provisions in treaties,[85] underscoring the grey zone between hard and soft law.

'Soft law' in this study refers to non-binding rules or principles, i.e., non-treaty instruments or provisions with a normative intent. They are produced with an element of formal governmental or intergovernmental participation, but may be a result of multi-stakeholder regulation, involving private actors as well.

At the international stage, soft law is of obvious legal relevance. Due to its structure and close interaction with politics, law-making at the international level often encounters challenges with regard to agreement on legally binding treaty law to regulate transnational social and other concerns. Soft law offers a possibility for states and intergovernmental law-making organisations and, in some cases, other actors to 'test' the normative substance of new regulation and pave the way for sufficient political support for the adoption of hard law. Soft law offers regulatory opportunities to international organisations, which generally do not have the power to adopt binding texts although much contemporary standard-setting takes place within these organisations.[86] Soft law often reflects or results from initiatives of intergovernmental organisations or other collective bodies to promote regulation of certain societal concerns or respond to concerns raised by civil society. In these cases, soft law can be a first step towards hard regulation.[87] In other cases, soft law is preferred as a method for regulation of issues for which it has been possible to achieve a degree of political support but not enough for the adoption of a binding instrument.[88] The UN Declaration of the Right to Development (1986)[89] may be regarded an example of the latter.

---

[83] A. Cassese (2005) *International Law,* Oxford: Oxford University Press, at 196.
[84] Boyle (n 76) at 142–3.
[85] Ibid., at 149; Shelton (n 76) at 180.
[86] Shelton, ibid., at 183.
[87] See also for example Cassese (n 83) at 196; see also Boyle (n 76) at 143–7, Shelton (n 76) at 182–3.
[88] Cassese, ibid., at 196.
[89] United Nations General Assembly (1986) 'Declaration on the Right to Development: resolution adopted by the General Assembly', UN Doc. A/RES/41/218,

It is well-known that the process from the drafting of a first soft law instrument on a new topic to the possible adoption of a treaty or for the soft norms to turn into customary international law may be protracted. The UN Declaration on the Rights of Indigenous Peoples,[90] which was almost 25 years in the making, is a case in point. In other cases (such as with the Draft Code of Conduct on Transnational Corporations and the Draft Norms, both described in the following chapters), sufficient state backing for adoption of binding rules does not materialise at crucial points of time, and the new instrument not only does not make it to treaty law, but is taken off the agenda. Yet, this does not foreclose the possibility that parts of the normative substance of such instruments may become customary international law.

Developed under the auspices of international organisations, which are established by states, international soft law expresses a degree of state consent. Implicit state consent backs instruments made by intergovernmental organisations within the mandate of such organisations or in accordance with resolutions of a wider applicability, such as the resolutions of the UN General Assembly. For example, a set of UN General Assembly Resolutions on Public-Private-Partnerships were drafted and adopted to provide formal support to the UN Global Compact, initially without making direct reference to the Global Compact. The UN Global Compact and its ten principles therefore enjoy state consent, even though the initiative was organised within the executive structure of the UN.

Soft law instruments like ILO's Declaration on Principles concerning Multinational Enterprises and the Declaration on Social Policy and Principles and Rights at Work (see further Chapter 3) are frequently referred to in CSR context and serve as normative sources (for example, ILO's Declaration on Fundamental Principles and Rights at Work is the key normative source for the Global Compact's labour principles). They effectively constitute examples in an evolving chain of soft law instruments developed by intergovernmental organisations in cooperation with non-state actors in processes that do not conform with traditional state-centrist international law-making, all in an effort to reach out to companies to proactively engage them in taking responsibility for their impact on global concerns, such as labour rights in their countries of operation.

---

4 December 1986.
[90] United Nations General Assembly (2007) Declaration on the Rights of Indigenous Peoples: adopted by the General Assembly, UN Doc. A/61/L.67, 13 September 2007.

2.5 DEVELOPING NORMS ON BUSINESS IMPACT ON SOCIETY: CIVIL SOCIETY AND BUSINESS PARTICIPATION

The role of non-state actors is related to the development of CSR normativity and rule-making in several ways. Several types of non-state actors have been and are actively involved in the development of CSR normativity at intergovernmental level. In varying formal and sometimes self-positioned roles, intergovernmental organisations, non-governmental civil society organisations (sometimes referred to as 'PINGOs', i.e., Public Interest Non-Governmental Organisations, but in this study mainly referred to as NGOs), and private for-profit actors, which comprise two types, business organisations as well as individual companies have been involved in such processes. Indeed, much of the CSR discourse as well as arguments that TNCs should be made duty-bearers under international law are promoted by NGOs. While there is no questioning that normative developments on business social responsibilities have been taking place at the above-national level, these have not only or primarily been driven by the traditional actors in international law, i.e., states.

While international lawyers may tend to see NGO influence in terms of the formal consultative status of those organisations, political science studies and some socio-legal scholars have demonstrated that the role of NGOs in practice transcends the pure consultative role and includes active participation in negotiations with impact on law-making beyond the extent assumed by 'consultative' status under international organisations like the UN.[91] Studies have also demonstrated that companies and business organisations in practice have considerable influence on actual law-making through a number of channels, ranging from formal consultative status with degrees of active participation in negotiations, to defensive lobbying of states and taking the lead offensively through self-regulation that may feed into international standard setting.[92]

---

[91] For example, B. Reinalda (2001) 'Private in form, public in purpose: NGOs in international relations theory'. In B. Arts, M. Noortmann and B. Reinalda (eds) *Non-state Actors in International Relations*, Hants: Ashgate, pp. 11–40, with references; B. Arts (2001/2003) 'The impact of environmental NGOs in international conventions'; compare from a legal perspective Chinkin (n 75) esp. at 35; and specifically with regard to human rights law-making at the UN see H. Hannum (1995) 'Human rights'. In Schachter and Joyner (n 77) pp. 319–48; S. Charnovitz (1997) 'Two centuries of participation: NGOs and international governance', 18(2) *Michigan Journal of International Law* pp. 183–286.

[92] E.g., A. Kolk (2001/2003) 'Multinational enterprises and international climate policy'. In Arts, Noortmann and Reinalda (n 91); Arts (2001/2003) 'The

Studies have demonstrated that despite their lack of formal role as actual participants in international law-making, NGOs and private non-state actors play active roles in international law-making processes and intergovernmental rule-making in several ways: non-state actors possess information and expertise, which is often welcomed by intergovernmental organisations; they influence political discourse and agenda setting, law-making and other decision-making and sometimes play a part in implementation procedures; and they are part of political, policy and institutional arrangements, including some legal arrangements in the international system.[93] Moreover, research demonstrates that NGOs and business organisations employ a variety of strategies to influence international policy- and law-making. These include peaceful means such as advocacy of special interests of public importance, active use of possibilities for speaking and dialogue in consultative capacity, and lobbying or national level pressuring of states to participate in treaty-making efforts. They also include the formation of coalitions, mobilisation of, and participation in, public opinion making, data-gathering to help frame or define a problem in ways that influence the work of intergovernmental conferences, and persuasion in general, as well as less peaceful means such as violent protests.[94] Studies also indicate that NGO and business organisations are either constrained or enabled by other players as well as by contextual factors. The former includes states, private non-state organisations including companies, and intergovernmental organisations. The latter includes the distribution of resources and formalities for negotiation and participation. Findings suggest that the ability of private non-state actors to exert influence depends primarily on two factors: the quality of their interventions (in particular expert knowledge and skills), and the similarity between their demands and existing related regulatory regimes.[95] Main constraining factors include the use of a non-appropriate approach (e.g.,

---

impact of environmental NGOs in international conventions', in ibid. Compare also D. Kinley and J. Nolan (2008) 'Trading and aiding human rights in the global economy', 79(4) *Nordic Journal of Human Rights Law* pp. 353–77.

[93] M. A. Hajer (1995) *The Politics of Environmental Discourse*; B. Reinalda, B. Arts and M. Noortmann (2001/2003) 'Non-state actors in international relations: Do they matter?' In Arts, Noortmann and Reinalda (n 91) pp. 1–8.

[94] Reinalda *et al.*, ibid.

[95] For example, a study by Arts found that NGOs succeeded putting pressure on climate negotiations in relation to the 1992 Framework Convention on Climate Change by establishing a case of similarity to the existing ozone regime and government inconsistency. Governments accepted what Arts refers to as 'strong norms' in relation to ozone regulation but refused to accept such norms in relation to climate. See Arts (n 91) at 208.

a violent approach or a strongly defensive opposition), traditional bloc-politics (e.g., North-South), and the presence of like-minded but dominant states. In the latter case, governments tend to dominate the issue on their own without input from private non-state actors. Of relevance to the analysis in Chapters 4–6 of the arguments made by both business and NGOs, there are indications that a consensus-oriented approach is more enabling for influence than a confrontational approach, as is the relative strength of actors compared to others, and the political relevance of the issue at stake. There are also indications that the ability to politicise issues and mobilise support among other groups can be decisive, and that this allows NGOs to sometimes compete with powerful business interests.[96] In other cases, NGOs successfully used persuasion as a non-confrontational strategy to affect changes on the positions of states' interests.[97]

In addition to specific strategies, business organisations gain power from liaising with political elites.[98] Research indicates that companies and business associations generally favour voluntary initiatives and self-regulation to public regulation.[99] The reasons for this range from dissatisfaction with the time that intergovernmental organisations often take to decide on regulation, to the obvious, that self-regulation enables the self-regulator to decide for itself what it wants to do. However, while companies and business associations often oppose regulation at first, they may change stances and embrace (self-)regulation for strategic reasons.[100] These include perceived opportunities for strategic restyling or potential new markets, following competitors' lead for fear of missing chances for profit, or to avoid financial or publicity risks.[101] All of these resemble ideas that have been promoted by organisational CSR scholars as reasons why companies accept or adapt to social expectations on CSR.[102]

In his analysis of network-based discourse in relation to policy pro-

---

[96] B. Arts (1998) *The Political Influence of Gglobal NGOs: Case Studies on the Climate and Biodiversity Conventions*, Utrecht: International Books; Reinalda (n 91); Arts (n 92); Kolk (n 92).

[97] This was the case in negotiations to establish the International Criminal Court (N. Deitelhoff (2009) 'The discursive process of legalization: Charting islands of persuasion in the ICC case', 63(Winter) *International Organization* pp. 33–65, esp. at 56–8).

[98] Arts (n 92) at 204.

[99] Kolk (n 92) at 214.

[100] Ibid., at 222–3.

[101] Ibid.

[102] See overview in K. Buhmann, L. Roseberry, and M. Morsing (2011) 'Introduction'. In Buhmann, Roseberry and Morsing (n 9) pp. 1–22, at 15–17; and in Matten and Moon (n 4).

cesses on environment and sustainability,[103] Marten Hajer has described how discourse coalitions collaborate to construct environmental politics and gain influence on their contents. Hajer demonstrates that the idea of sustainable development, at least in the environmental context, has been developed as a struggle between various political coalitions. For many practical purposes, the actors in a particular discursive coalition differ in terms of social roles, but they are united through efforts to sustain and continually develop a particular conception and approach to sustainable development and by sharing a way of talking about the matter.[104] Discursive construction of sustainability problems to a considerable degree influences the conceptualisation of problems, solutions and social strategies for regulatory achievements.

Arguing that the key point is to establish business buy-in for the normative ideals for business conduct that public regulators wish to promote, some international law scholars have long called for an increased degree of business participation in international law-making relating to business impact on society. In 1964 in his study on the changing character of international law, Wolfgang Friedmann argued in favour of the inclusion of the business sector in international law-making intended to have implications for companies.[105] In 1983 Jonathan I. Charney made a similar argument,[106] observing that the development of rules pertaining to TNC conduct with little or no direct participation of TNC participation was detrimental to the effectiveness as well as the implementation of the rules.[107] Failure to include these business organisations in negotiations under UN or other intergovernmental organisations to produce norms for TNCs behaviour would cause TNC resistance to implementation. Moreover, it would mean that the proposed codes 'do not resolve the underlying political and economic issues, they merely convert them into legal issues'.[108] Charney argued that greater participation of TNCs might in fact strengthen the system of international law by recognising the increasing power of TNCs and reducing efforts to protect business interests through lobbying states.[109] As examples of the benefits of including

---

[103] Hajer (n 93).
[104] Ibid., at 15.
[105] W. Friedmann (1964) *The Changing Structure of International Law,* London: Stevens & Sons.
[106] J. I. Charney (1983) 'Transnational corporations and developing public international law', 32 *Duke Law Journal* pp. 748–88, at 756.
[107] Ibid.
[108] Ibid., at 754.
[109] Ibid., esp. at 775–80.

businesses in such normative endeavours, Charney referred to the ILO and OECD systems of international law-making, which involve business representatives (as well as employees' organisations) in developing norms applying to business. Indeed, as elaborated in Chapter 3, ILO and OECD in the 1970s were able to obtain agreement on international soft law instruments providing guidance for TNCs in their transnational activities that may have an impact on host societies.

Summing up, this chapter has demonstrated that the normative links between CSR and law are numerous and negate an inflexible understanding of CSR as only requirements beyond law. It has shown that the relationship between CSR and human rights offers a close connection to public policy objectives and governmental interests in companies contributing to the implementation of those objectives. It has described the significance of soft law in general and as a normative source for CSR and corporate sustainability, and has explained that non-state actors already play important roles in international law-making through expertise, lobbying and active if perhaps informal participation. Finally, it noted that international law scholars have long argued for increased formal participation of business in international law pertaining to the actions of those organisations in order to strengthen its relevance and implementation.

This raises several perspectives for the following chapters. When international law and law-making extends beyond the state-centric and becomes transnational in reaching out to the private sector in terms of duties and participation, strategies for argumentation and negotiation may need to adapt in order to speak to the new actors by using arguments that activate their rationality by communicating in their logic. In recent decades' efforts to construct norms on CSR and on business responsibilities for human rights, the complex interrelationship between public and private interests in CSR and their rationality logics have fuelled a diversity of discursive statements and arguments to promote the particular interests of involved organisations. Chapters 4 and 5 revert to these, following an elaboration in Chapter 3 of public-private regulation, the significance of the rationalities of involved organisations for communicative regulatory purposes, and discourse.

3. Argumentative strategies, discourse and system-specific rationality

Reaching back to Chapter 1 and setting out details of the theoretical foundations for the subsequent analysis, Chapter 3 elaborates on the communicative aspects of reflexive law and discourse theory, and introduces linguistic communication theory models that support the analysis of argumentative strategies. The chapter explains how these complement each other for the purpose of analysing the evolution of normativity in multi-stakeholder processes on the social responsibilities of business with a particular focus on the role of argumentative strategies for the normative outputs. Section 3.1 elaborates on communication related to the core rationality of a recipient and its functions, which is a key element in reflexive law. It explains how organisational self-regulation or acceptance of normative change may be stimulated by others who are able to communicatively activate the core interest of the organisation within which change is desired. Section 3.2 expands on discourse theory and communication in multi-stakeholder regulation. This section describes what is understood by 'floating signifiers' and how struggles for power unfold around such concepts, e.g., CSR or business responsibilities for human rights. It proceeds to textual analysis as discourse analysis. Through three figures it explains how participants in a multi-stakeholder process may invoke system-specific logics to stimulate change in recipients, and offers examples of that argumentative strategy. Finally, drawing on linguistic communication analysis the chapter elaborates on the usage of stabilising and de-stabilising arguments as an alternative argumentative strategy and explains how this may complement or reinforce the effects of arguments made in system-specific logics.

3.1 SYSTEM-SPECIFIC RATIONALITY AND COMMUNICATION IN REFLEXIVE LAW

Socio-legal theories lean towards instrumental regulation to promote normative change through appreciation of societal interests and needs and self-regulation rather than enforcement. This sets them apart from much other legal and regulatory theory, in which the focus is on enforcement through legal institutions such as fines and sentencing. First proposed in the 1980s,[1] reflexive law belongs to a group of socio-legal instrumental regulatory theories that also count responsive law,[2] responsive regulation[3] and more recently, the theory of pro-active law.[4] Reflexive law differs from these through its strong emphasis on communication as an agent for change and its operational directives for how public regulators may act to support communicative processes that aim to stimulate understanding and appreciation of societal needs and in turn promote internal normative change within, for example, a company.

Building in part on systems thinking, reflexive law considers the social system as made up by social sub-systems that are specialised to perform particular functions. For the current purposes, the most important functional sub-systems are the political system (which comprises not just formal and informal policy-makers, but also the implementing agencies of public organisations, which carry out policies), the economic system (mainly comprised of companies) and the legal system.

At the overall level, the theory of reflexive law builds on the idea that for certain purposes, regulation may better deliver on its intended objectives if details are defined by those who will be subjected to the requirements, and if developed in close coordination with those to whom those requirements matter in terms of conduct and for the protection of their interests. Reflexive law is typically thought to be well suited for addressing problems that are closely related to companies' actions, such as employment practices, and their impact on society, such as on the environment. Reflexive law was proposed as a theory for how governments may regulate in a way that actively involves societal actors in solving problems in the environmental area, employment and inequality.[5] A procedural theory for regulated self-regulation, whose normative outputs come about as a result of social actors defining detailed norms based on overall normative directives from public

---

[1] G. Teubner (1983) 'Substantive and reflective elements in modern law', 17(2) *Law and Society Review* pp. 239–85; G. Teubner (1986) 'Introduction'. In G. Teubner (ed.) *Dilemmas of Law in the Welfare state,* Walter de Gruyter: Berlin and New York, pp. 3–11.
[2] P. Nonet and P. Selznick (1978) *Law and Society in Transition Toward Responsive Law,* New York: Harper/Colophon.
[3] I. Ayres and J. Braithwaite (1992) *Responsive Regulation: Transcending the Deregulation Debate*, New York: Oxford University Press.
[4] G. Berger-Walliser and P. Shrivastava (2015) 'Beyond compliance: Sustainable development, business, and pro-active law', 46(2) *Georgia International Law Journal* pp. 417–75.
[5] Teubner (1983, n 1); Teubner (1986, n 1).

regulators, reflexive law supplements conventional law top-down law that sets out detailed normative requirements and follows up by monitoring and legal sanctions (command-control law). Reflexive law applies a different approach to developing normative standards, aiming to complement command-control law in specific issue areas and for specific actors and societal problems. Communication based on interaction between different societal actors is a key element in reflexive law's *modus operandi*. Reflexive law theory posits that authorities can establish procedural frameworks to enable stakeholders with a concern in a particular issue to interact and formulate norms based on exchanges that stimulate learning of needs and expectations held by others and, in turn, internalisation of these needs and expectations through self-regulation.[6] Such procedural forums may be physical (e.g., a multi-stakeholder meeting) or take a virtual form (e.g., an internet-based process of dialogue between a company and some of its stakeholders, such as NGOs, with a view for the company to understand about the stakeholders' perceptions of the company's impact and society and gain inputs for its sustainability report and CSR work). The approach has been taken up by governments in Europe and elsewhere in several regulatory contexts, especially in environmental law[7] and labour law including regulation of occupational health and safety.[8] In their quest to deliver

---

[6] Teubner (1983, ibid.); G. Teubner, R. Nobles and D. Schiff (2005) 'The autonomy of law: An introduction to legal autopoiesis'. In J. Penner, D. Schiff and R. Nobles (eds) *Jurisprudence*, New York: Oxford University Press, pp. 897–954.

[7] For example, E. W. Orts (1995) 'A reflexive model of environmental regulation', 5(4) *Business Ethics Quarterly* pp. 779–94; L. Farmer and G. Teubner (1994) 'Ecological self-organization'. In G. Teubner, L. Farmer and D. Murphy (eds) *Environmental Law and Ecological Responsibility: The Concept and Practice of Ecological Self-Organisation,* Chichester: John Wiley & Sons, pp. 3–13; E. Rehbinder (1992) 'Reflexive law and practice: The corporate officer for environmental protection as an example', *European Yearbook in the Sociology of Law: State, Law and Economy as Autopoietic Systems: Regulation and Autonomy in a New Perspective*, Milano: Guiffre Publisher, pp. 579–608.

[8] H. Arthurs (2008) 'Corporate self-regulation: political economy, state regulation and reflexive labour law'. In B. Bercusson and C. Estlund (eds) *Regulating Labour in the Wake of Globalisation,* Oxford and Portland, Oregon: Hart, pp. 19–35; S. Deakin and R. Hobbs (2007) 'False dawn for CSR? Shifts in regulatory policy and the response of the corporate and financial sectors in Britain', 15(1) *Corporate Governance* pp. 68–76; S. Deakin (2005) 'Social rights in a globalised economy'. In P. Alston (ed.) *Labour Rights as Human Rights*, New York: Oxford University Press, pp. 25–60; R. Rogowski (2001) 'The concept of reflexive labour law: Its theoretical background and possible applications'. In J. Priban and D. Nelken (eds.) *Law's New Boundaries: The Consequences of Legal Autopoiesis,* Aldershot: Ashgate, pp. 179–96; R. Rogowski (1994) 'Industrial relations, labour conflict resolution and reflexive labour law'. In R. Rogowski and T. Wilthagen

solutions to problems that require action by typically companies or other societal actors, reflexive law forums often take a multi-stakeholder character. Often implemented at the initiative of the executive arm of government, some are explicitly designed to be reflexive law processes, whereas others can be determined to function as reflexive law according to the theory but without being explicitly informed by that theory.[9]

Reflexive law theory assumes that a reflection takes place at three levels, entailing three different types of reflection.[10] However, for those involved at one particular level, the two other levels of reflection may not be very explicit. The analysis in this study turns on the second of these levels, which as will be seen is a result of the first level and provides input to the third level.

At the first level, public regulators or authorities engage in reflection on their own regulatory capacities, typically in terms of formal regulatory capacity or expertise to define rules with sufficient precision to target the problem at hand in the context where the problem they aim to solve affects those who encounter the problem and defines the action of those who are required to change their conduct. This process of reflection leads authorities to set up procedures (or procedural forums) to induce a second level of reflection, this time among social actors, such as civil society organisations, companies, citizens, and/or local authorities. The procedural forum establishes a setting that enables an exchange of views among the participants, allowing them to obtain insights on expectations, needs and demands of other participants. If the process adequately activates the right rationalities, this induces participants with whom change is desired to reflect upon their actions, on their (adverse) impact on society, and on needs for adopting correctives. This feeds into the third level, which takes

---

(eds) *Reflexive Labour Law: Studies in Industrial Relations and Employment Regulation,* Deventer and Boston: Kluwer Law and Taxation Publishers, pp. 53–93; Rogowski, R. and Wilthagen, T. (1994) 'Reflexive Labour Law: An Introduction', ibid.

[9] E. W. Orts (1995) 'Reflexive environmental law' 89(4) *Northwestern Law Review* pp. 1229–340; K. Buhmann (2013) 'The Danish CSR reporting requirement as reflexive law: Employing CSR as a modality to promote public policy', 24(2) *European Business Law Review* pp. 187–216.

[10] See especially Teubner (1983, n 1); G. Teubner (1986) 'After legal instrumentalism?'. In Teubner (ed., n 1) pp. 299–325; G. Teubner (1988) 'Introduction to Autopoietic law'. In G. Teubner, (ed.) *Autopoietic Law: A New Approach to Law and Society,* Berlin and New York: Walter de Gruyter, pp. 1–11; G. Teubner (1992) Social order from legislative noise, *European Yearbook in the Sociology of Law* (n 7) pp. 609–49; see also N. Luhmann (1986) 'The self-reproduction of law and its limits'. In Teubner (ed., n 1).

place within the organisation (or functional sub-system) of the participant or participants intended to change conduct.. That reflection leads to the normative output, which may have the form of self-regulation within a participant or its group (e.g., a company or sector), based on understanding and appreciation of external needs and acceptance of the changes that those needs require. The third level of reflection may also lead to a joint normative product that may support or promote self-regulation in a particular normative direction, based on participants' appreciation of external needs and demands.

The exchanges of needs and expectations which take place at the second level set in motion a process in which external needs and expectations may be internalised and reflect normatively on the self-regulation of the pertinent organisation. For example, when the objective is to induce changed norms of conduct for business, participation and dialogue with authorities and civil society offer companies an opportunity to become exposed to societal expectations on business conduct so that they may consider the normative implications for themselves. Through interaction with each other, companies are enabled to learn about and reflect on modalities for dealing with those societal expectations.

As a regulatory approach, reflexive law theory was developed for a national context. Yet many of the concerns that the theory addressed have since shifted from the national to the international level. As a general rule, international organisations have limited legal or political powers to create obligations for companies. Given its emphasis on self-regulation based on understanding of societal needs, even on a backdrop of specific normative guidance or directives from authorities, reflexive law therefore offers a regulatory modality for these organisations, whether applied on the basis of specific knowledge of the theory or on a more coincidental basis.[11]

At the second level of reflection, legal autopoiesis is a key element. In this respect, reflexive law draws on but also diverts from Niklas Luhmann's systems theory, which had been inspired by biology and knowledge of the neural system's self-reproduction and interaction with the body.[12] Biological autopoiesis is the process of cells or body organs to respond in reaction to occurrences outside themselves. This pressure

---

[11] K. Buhmann (2014) *Normative Discourses and Public-Private Regulatory Strategies for Construction of CSR Normativity: Towards a Method for Above-National Public-Private Regulation of Business Social Responsibilities.* Copenhagen: Multivers; see also Orts (n 7) 'A reflexive model of environmental regulation'; Orts, (n 9).

[12] H. Maturana, (1981) 'Autopoiesis'. In M. Zeleny (ed.) *Autopoiesis: A Theory of Living Organizations*, New York: North Holland; M. Neves (2001) 'From the

or irritation from the environment causes internal perturbation, which stimulates a change.[13]

The autopoietic aspect of reflexive law theory is important for an understanding of multi-stakeholder regulation, and the role played by arguments in stimulating change. According to reflexive law theory, autopoiesis allows parts of the social system, that is, social sub-systems such as the political, the economic and the legal system, to adapt based on 'irritants' transmitted by other social sub-systems. Such 'irritants' cause perturbation that sets in motion internal processes of change. A reflexive law process at the second level allows social sub-systems to exchange information. If this information is communicated in a manner that resonates with the rationality of the recipient, it has potential to stimulate perturbation inside the recipient sub-system. In 'digesting' the irritants, a process of internal reflection on the sub-system's impact on its surroundings ('environment') is strengthened. This may enhance acceptance of the needs or demands of the environment and induce self-regulation to meet the concerns and needs of other social sub-systems, which served as irritants.[14] With this point of departure in Luhmann's rather abstract theory, reflexive law theory as developed by Gunther Teubner takes autopoiesis to a practical level of application in suggesting that public regulators develop procedural settings that enable various stakeholders to meet (actually or virtually) to exchange views on societal needs and ensuing demands or social expectations, such as for companies to assume specific social responsibilities to reduce their adverse societal impacts. Such procedural settings are referred to as reflexive law forums in here.

To be effective, the process of developing and causing irritation in other functional sub-systems entails the use of signals or, in system theory terminology, 'binary codes' that are specific to a system and based on its core rationality. To induce the internal process of reflection (that is, the third level of the process), which is key to the generation of new norms or the acceptance of external demands, external stakeholders must activate the rationality of the recipient. Thus, to bring about irritation that in turn causes perturbation within companies, policy-makers, regulators or civil

---

autopoiesis to the allopoiesis of law', 28(2) *Journal of Law and Society* pp. 242–64; see also Teubner, G. *et al.* (n 6).

[13] Maturana, ibid.; H. Rottleuthner (1988) 'Biological metaphors in legal thought'. In G. Teubner (ed.) *Autopoietic Law: A New Approach to Law and Society,* Berlin and New York: Walter de Gruyter, pp. 97–127.

[14] G. Teubner (1993) *Law as an Autopoietic System,* Oxford: Blackwell; G. Teubner (1984) 'Autopoiesis in law and society: a rejoinder to Blankenburg', 18(2) *Law and Society Review* pp. 291–301.

society must activate the economic system rationality of profit/loss of profit or related binary codes. Conversely, if businesses activate the rationality of power/weakness or power/loss of power or legal/illegal with policy-makers or regulators, they may be able to stimulate increased policy initiatives or public regulation with these actors, or change the focus of such initiatives. Functional sub-systems basically communicate in their own rationality, but they may 'mimic' those of others.[15] The ability to do so can be crucial for stimulating change with recipients. Obviously, even within a functional sub-system, preferences on approaches towards achieving the core rationality may vary. Some companies may agree with the idea that they should assume responsibility for the impact on human rights and perceive it to be a well-justified strategy towards, for example, protecting themselves against risks of economic losses (for example as a result of reputational damage resulting from reports on child labour in the supply chain). Others may find the idea of business responsibilities for human rights or CSR in general opposed to the rationality of making profits.

Reflexive law's focus is on pro-actively shaping desired conduct and preventatively avoiding undesired conduct, rather than re-actively sanctioning undesired conduct that has occurred. It is therefore apt for purposes that embody situations in which harm is ideally fully prevented rather than remedied if it occurs, such as adverse business impact on human rights.

3.2 DISCOURSE AND MULTI-STAKEHOLDER COMMUNICATION ON CSR AND BHR NORMATIVITY

A process of constructing normativity for business impact on society drawing on statements from several social sub-systems seeking to promote and protect their own interests has a discursive element. It involves discursive struggles to influence the implications of the normative concept or concepts, which will result from each process. In other words, interaction within a reflexive law forum to create normativity takes place through discursive exchanges between participants who seek to argue their case to promote and protect their interests in ways that are intended to lead to the desired adaptation within other participating sub-systems.

A variety of interests at stake among businesses, NGOs and other civil

---

[15] Compare M. King (1996) 'Self-producing systems: implications and applications of autopoiesis by John Mingers (review article)', 23(4) *Journal of Law and Society* pp. 601–5.

society, and governments are likely to affect their reactions to efforts to develop normative guidance or requirements of CSR and business responsibilities for human rights. Discourse analysis focuses on power issues and interests, their influence on communicative processes, and how to detect this in texts or other forms of communicative events.

A particular discourse is one particular way of representing the world (or a small part of it, for example represented into a value-laden concept), and of constructing the world. Within a discourse, sub-discourses are formed when a group of articulations (statements in specific text or discursive events) take on a regular shape that allows the distinction of a commonality within that set of articulations.[16] For example, the discourse on CSR posits that companies have social responsibilities, and seeks to shape these through the construction of related concepts and defining their implications, for example the extent of business responsibilities for human rights (from none to comprehensive), whether CSR may or should be 'voluntary' or 'mandatory', or the normative role of international human rights law. Within a discourse, sub-discourses may struggle for hegemony in fixating particular elements, for example on the normative role of international law instruments in CSR normativity.

Linguistic utterances, such as speech acts and written statements, are key objects for discourse analysis.[17] The current study is based mainly on written statements that claim to represent the truth (even as part of a process to influence a normative outcome).

Discourses are often dynamic, combining with other discourses and developing into new discourses. A discourse (such as the CSR discourse) represents a reality of its own, but also feeds on past and other current discourses (such as the discourse on sustainable development), and may influence conduct and other or new discourses. For instance, the CSR discourse has influenced the development of expectations on business with regard to human right and what is emerging as an autonomous discourse

---

[16] R. Holdgaard (2005) 'Classic external relations law of the European Community: doctrines and discourses'. Ph.D. thesis, Museum Tusculanum, Copenhagen at 346 (also available as Holdgaard, Rass (2008) *Legal Reasoning and Legal Discourses: External Relations Law of the European Community*, Kluwer Law International).

[17] Speech acts and written statements comprise various types, including *representatives* (truth claims), *directives* (commands or requests), *commissives* (promises or threats), *expressives* (praise or blame) and *declaratives* (declaring war, proclaiming a constitution). The effective performance of speech acts depends on the speaker's status, institutional position, the style of language and type of event (P. Chilton and C. Schäffner (1997) 'Discourse and politics'. In T. A. van Dijk (ed.) *Discourse as Social Interaction*, London: Sage Publications, pp. 206–30, at 216, 219–21).

Argumentative strategies, discourse and system-specific rationality

on BHR. The BHR discourse, in turn, has been influencing the CSR discourse, for example in regard to the mandatory/voluntary dichotomy (as seen in the EU's 2011 change of CSR definition).

3.2.1 Floating Signifiers

According to political science informed discourse theorists Ernesto Laclau and Chantal Mouffe, language is constantly changing, subject to a struggle between its language users to provide the concepts and terms used with meaning, or to change already accepted meaning. These discursive battles are particularly strong with regard to 'floating signifiers', which are value-laden terms or concepts whose meaning is not (yet) fully settled. Different versions of their meaning have been proposed, and different actors may wish to promote particular versions of understanding or meaning that fit their interests and obtain hegemony in defining the settled meaning. The discursive battle, therefore, is a struggle between discourses for hegemony in deciding the signification ('meaning') of the floating signifier. Such hegemonic struggles are often political or ideological battles. Even when hegemony has been won through the fixation, it comes under threat for a re-definition and new hegemonic struggles.[18]

'Democracy' is often given as an example of a floating signifier. Democracy has a positive connotation in modern societies based on the rule of law and public participation. For this reason, different discourses – for example, defined by different approaches to what exactly is understood by a society based on the rule of law, or the degree and form of public participation – compete for power in a struggle of providing the fixed signification of what exactly is understood by 'democracy'. They do so in order to strengthen their positions and interests. As part of the process of establishing signification of 'democracy', different discourses engage in establishing associations between 'democracy' and other terms with a positive connotation within that discourse[19] (for example, public partici-

---

[18] E. Laclau and C. Mouffe (1985) *Hegemony and socialist strategy: Towards a Radical Democratic Politics*, London: Verso., esp. at 112–13; see also Holdgaard (n 16) at 327–8, 339–40; F. Collin (2004) *Konstruktivisme*, Frederiksberg: Samfundslitteratur – Roskilde Universitetsforlag, at 101–2; N. Å. Andersen (2003) *Discursive Analytical Strategies – Understanding Foucault, Koselleck, Laclau, Luhmann,* Bristol: Policy Press, at 50–55; M. W. Jørgensen and L. Phillips (1999) *Diskursanalyse som teori og metode,* Frederiksberg: Samfundslitteratur/Roskilde University Press, at 37–8.

[19] Andersen, ibid., at 52; Collin, ibid. at 102–3; Jørgensen and Phillips, ibid. at 37; Holdgaard, ibid. at 327–8.

pation) and establishing dissociations to terms with negative connotations (for example, rule by man (autocracy/tyranny) or rule by law, as opposed to rule of law).

In the context of the current study, Laclau and Mouffe's theory on floating signifiers helps understand the power issues and struggles that shaped discursive processes in the context of constructing CSR normativity, its partial branching off and into the BHR discourse and the further evolution of that into an emergent BHR regime. More specifically, the idea of floating signifiers provides a theoretical framework for analysing the discursive construction of CSR, BHR, and elements such as the normative role to be played by international human rights law, and the implications of 'responsibility' for the roles of states and business. At the outset of the period of time considered in this work, CSR was a concept with an unfixed meaning (and by many accounts, it still is). It may therefore be approached as a floating signifier. Similarly, the idea of business responsibilities for human rights, which has arisen more recently as a specific normative concept, is still subject to fixation. The agreement that emerged with the adoption of the UN Framework and UNGPs led to a fixation. However (and in accordance with Laclau and Mouffe's theory), that fixation soon came to be challenged: whereas the UN Framework and UNGPs in principle apply to all firms, the process towards a treaty on business and human rights looks like it may reduce the application of the potential treaty to only TNCs, excluding companies that do not operate across borders.[20]

As we have already seen in Chapter 2, a range of economic, political and legal interests are tied to current and future normative perceptions of business social responsibilities, as well as the implications of such responsibility. Various camps of interests, including networks of and across social sub-systems, therefore struggle for hegemony in fixing what is (to be) understood by CSR or more specific areas of business social responsibilities, in particular with regard to business responsibilities for human rights. Laclau and Mouffe's analytical perspective places power struggles into a context on which they may be subjected to more detailed analysis. It complements the autopoietic perspective of the usage of system-specific language by providing an entry point to understanding the construction of BHR and CSR normativity in terms of hegemonic struggles on the fixation of the normative construction of business social responsibilities within a discursive context.

To be more specific: the discourse of CSR, its constituting elements of

---

[20] Human Rights Council (2014) 'Elaboration of an international legally binding instrument on transnational corporations and other business enterprises with respect to human rights', UN Doc. A/HRC/RES/26/9, 14 July 2014.

the form of regulation and the role to be played by international (human rights) law for defining normative substance have been subject over the past decades to intense efforts between the economic, the political and parts of the legal system to define what exactly is meant or is to be meant by CSR. The same applies to business responsibilities for human rights whether seen as a part of CSR or as a specific type of business social responsibility with particular regard to human rights, which has come to be referred to as BHR. Like 'democracy', both have positive connotations, but at the time of the processes of fixing the meaning addressed in the case studies below, the exact normative substance and therefore implications of CSR and business responsibilities for human rights were of considerable current and future significance to economic actors, and to political and legal communities and civil society organisations and their constituencies. The same applied to the legal character of CSR as 'voluntary' or 'mandatory', and the normative role to be played by international human rights law. This spilled over on the form which any current or future type of public guidance or regulation on CSR and business responsibilities for human rights would take on: will CSR and/or business responsibilities for human rights be subject to clearly defined top-down regulation or to more open and flexible guidance? The case studies to which we turn in Chapters 4 and 5 show that both the substantive understanding of business social responsibilities, and the form of regulation – hard, soft, or a type of mixture, such as the 'smart mix' that the SRSG came to suggest – were subject to intense discursive struggles for hegemony between actors from different social sub-systems. With particular relation to business responsibilities for human rights, contested notions like 'spheres of influence' or 'complicity', which formed part of the mandate of the SRSG also constitute floating signifiers in their own right, as further discussed in Chapter 5 and 6.

3.2.2 Textual Analysis to Identify how Linguistic Statements Influence Discourse and Meaning

Within the overall textual approach of CDA, Norman Fairclough proposes a pragmatic, problem-oriented approach to textual analysis. Fairclough's theoretical approach allows for selection of data that may be followed by a structural analysis of the context, and on interactional analysis focusing on linguistic features undertaken within a context of interdiscursivity to compare the dominant and less dominant or resistant discursive strands.[21]

---

[21] M. Meyer, (2001) 'Between theory, method and politics: positioning of the approaches to CDA'. In R. Wodak and M. Meyer (eds) *Methods of Critical*

Fairclough's discourse theory builds on the idea that language is an integrated part of social life and that discourse constitutes social reality and is itself shaped by social practices and structures.[22]

To Fairclough, discourse contributes to the construction of social identities, social relations and systems of knowledge and meaning through discursive practice. A discursive practice covers the production and consumption of spoken and written language. Fairclough understands 'language' to refer to ordinary verbal language, consisting of words, sentences, etc. By *discourse* (in the abstract sense) Fairclough refers to language used as a social practice. *A discourse* (in the concrete sense) refers to a particular discourse,[23] for our purposes such as that on BHR.

In the view of Fairclough, a text is a social causal event.[24] Texts can bring about changes in our knowledge, beliefs, attitudes, values, etc. They may introduce, or contribute to introducing, changes in social relations and individuals' actions.[25] The analysis of this requires taking into account not only the linguistic form of the text itself, but also its meaning and context.[26] Analysis of text cannot be isolated from analysis of institutional and discursive practices in which the text is embedded, and its social consequences. Discursive practices include the production and consumption of a text, as well as interdiscursivity in drawing on existing discourses.[27]

The approach proposed by Fairclough entails identifying the social event and chain of social events, if any, that a text is part of. For our purposes, this is provided by the general societal concern with sustainable human and environmental development, societal concern with adverse impacts caused by companies, and the emergence of intergovernmentally initiated public-private regulatory forums, which seek to restrain corporate conduct through the development of CSR normativity and clarify roles and responsibilities for business impact on human rights.

By analysing intertextuality, i.e., how a text draws on elements and discourses from other texts, discourse analysis is able to show how a discourse

---

Discourse Analysis. London: Sage Publications pp. 28–9; N. Fairclough (2001) 'Critical discourse analysis as a method in social scientific research'. In ibid. pp. 121–38.

[22] N. Fairclough (2003) *Analysing Discourse: Textual Analysis for Social Research*. New York: Routledge at 2.
[23] Ibid.; Jørgensen and Phillips (n 18), at 79–80.
[24] Fairclough (n 22), at 21–38.
[25] Ibid., at 8.
[26] Ibid., at 13.
[27] Fairclough (n 21), at 4, 9; N. Fairclough and R. Wodak (1997) 'Critical discourse analysis'. In T. A. van Dijk (ed.) *Discourse as Social Interaction*, London: Sage, pp. 285–312; Jørgensen and Phillips (n 18) at 80–86.

or its use of language reflects already established meaning and therefore reproduces or seeks to reproduce or challenge established discourses or power structures. For the current purposes, examples include which types of actors may or should bear (hard law) duties or (soft law) responsibilities for human rights, or CSR as business driven and dissociated from public regulatory directives. Discourse analysis illuminates how language used in text, such as statements or reports, may change established discourses and the power structures inherent in them by combining elements from different discourses. Change in discourses mirrors change in the social and cultural environment and vice versa.[28] The inter-textual element considers how a text incorporates elements from other texts or refers to other texts.[29] This way of considering developments and change in a relationship between the text itself and texts outside it carries a certain resemblance to the autopoietic features of reflexive law according to which change in a functional sub-system takes place in reaction to 'irritants' from the environment. Some related features are found in Fairclough's ideas that a high level of interdiscursivity often indicates change, while a low level of interdiscursivity indicates that the text mainly reproduces existing discourse or social practice.

3.2.3 Discourse and Textual Analysis of Constructing Normativity in Multi-Stakeholder Regulatory Processes

Reflexive law theory and its emphasis on communication in system-specific rationality as a means to bring about change through 'irritation' causing perturbation in recipient sub-systems provides the specific linguistic linkage for the purpose of the study. This allows the textual analysis to focus on the use of system-specific rationality in statements, and on embedded system-specific interests with transmitters as well as consumption of statements and their impact on the process of construction of normative concepts. International law theory and CSR theory form part of the larger contextual framework to appreciate the discourse and embedded interests. That connects to Laclau and Mouffe's focus on fixing of floating signifiers. In combination with reflexive law, it also connects to system-specific power concerns, for example a company's concern with the impact that the end product of a regulatory process may have on the way it will be expected or required to manage human rights issues in its supply chain.

Drawing on linguistic models developed for communication through texts

---

[28] Jørgensen and Phillips ibid. at 15, 84–5.
[29] Fairclough (n 22), at 36.

addressing an audience with different knowledge and concerns than those of the transmitter,[30] the connection between reflexive law and discourse theory can be visually represented through a relational model, originally developed for language analysis. For the purpose of the current work, the model connects the relatively abstract ideas of floating signifiers, autopoiesis and reflexive law-making with the textual analysis and its focus on system-specific language. They support the discourse analysis through explicit focus on the context for texts, their production, transmission, consumption and effects, on text types and genres, and on linguistic features in the text.

Adapted to the current study, the relational model in Figure 3.1 below indicates the relationship in which the text is sent by the transmitter in the

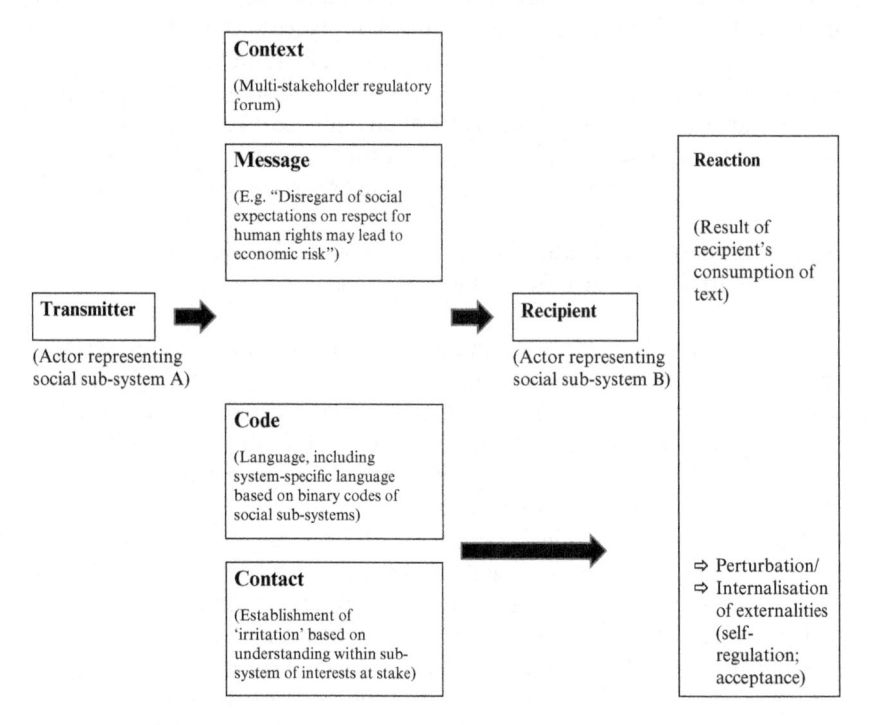

Context
(Multi-stakeholder regulatory forum)

Message		Reaction
(E.g. "Disregard of social expectations on respect for human rights may lead to economic risk")		(Result of recipient's consumption of text)

Transmitter	→	Recipient
(Actor representing social sub-system A)		(Actor representing social sub-system B)

Code
(Language, including system-specific language based on binary codes of social sub-systems)

Contact
(Establishment of 'irritation' based on understanding within sub-system of interests at stake)

⇨ Perturbation/
⇨ Internalisation of externalities (self-regulation; acceptance)

Source: Adapted and expanded from Ditlevsen *et al.* 2007: 64.

Figure 3.1 General model of relations and reaction for analysis of system-specific interest-based arguments

---

[30] M. G. Ditlevsen *et al.* (2007) *Sprog på arbejde Kommunikation i faglige tekster.* Frederiksberg: Forlaget Samfundslitteratur.

context of a reflexive regulatory forum, which provides for interaction between representatives of different social sub-systems. The transmitter seeks to convey a message to the recipient, typically a representative of another social sub-system. For example, a civil society organisation may transmit a message to a business association to the effect that if companies disregard social expectations on respect for working conditions in the supply chain, they may suffer divestment or consumer boycotts, suggesting that this may lead to economic loss. The message is transmitted by drawing on the binary code of a social sub-system, or makes an argument that activates the rationality of the recipient. (In the example above, the civil society organisation activates the economic code of profit/loss of the recipient.) If the statements are effective in activating the rationality of the recipient, the transmitter may succeed in establishing irritation upon contact.

Because autopoiesis assumes that functional sub-systems primarily communicate in their own binary codes, but may draw on (or mimic) another sub-system's codes to affect changes within the recipient, the analysis in Chapters 4–6 will seek to determine whether and how this in fact plays a part. That is, does a statement deploy the rationality of the recipient, or does it rather employ the rationality of the transmitter? What is the difference in the effect on the recipient? Does irritation arise and cause observable results in terms of the reaction, if the transmitter deploys the code of the recipient social sub-system that is likely to activate its rationality? If irritation is effective in causing perturbation within the recipient sub-system, it is more likely to stimulate changes within that system to respond to the 'irritation', that is, needs or demands from the environment. Changes within the system may take the form of self-regulation or acceptance rather than resistance to external demands. The latter may lead to collaboration rather than antagonism. Reactions have an impact on the output of the multi-stakeholder regulation process.

To different extents, the normative substance of CSR and the meaning and implication of business responsibilities for human rights were subjected to discursive struggles through the case studies. This led to varied results, evidenced by different outputs described in Chapters 4 and 5.

Fairclough's linguistic focus links to reflexive law theory's emphasis on the rationalities of recipients, represented by system-specific binary codes applied or mimicked by the political, the economic and the legal systems as social sub-system, and the strategy of inducing change through perturbation in other social sub-systems, as shown in Figure 3.1. In the analysis, faircloughian theory is adapted to a textual reading focusing on system-specific use of binary codes and their role and impact in the discursive struggle to fix 'CSR', and 'business responsibilities for human rights', and constituting elements, in particular the regulatory form as voluntary or mandatory, and the informing role played by international human rights law as a normative source.

With CSR, 'business and human rights', and the constituting elements of the regulatory form of voluntary/mandatory and the informing role of international human rights law all perceived as floating signifiers, the analysis is able to identify the way in which system-specific rationalities affected or were activated in arguments made as part of the discursive construction of these floating signifiers. This allows for identification of arguments and deployment of stabilising and de-stabilising argumentative strategies, as explained below.

Figure 3.2 below indicates system-specific language features on which the analysis will focus: text function, context and linguistic means. This model too has been developed for linguistic analysis and has been expanded in Figure 3.3 below to offer specific examples related to the analysis in here.

As an example, consider the example provided at Figure 3.3, an NGO's statement in a multi-stakeholder consultation on supply chain responsibility. Assume that the NGO specialises in human rights of workers in the textile sector with a particular focus on working conditions. The specific situation (the top of the triangle) is a meeting under a multi-stakeholder forum on CSR, with the specific meeting being convened to generate insight, and to allow stakeholders to present their views on the issue.

Situation (within context)
(e.g., meeting under multi-stakeholder consultation)

Function
(e.g., make companies respect rights)

Linguistic means
(e.g., statement)

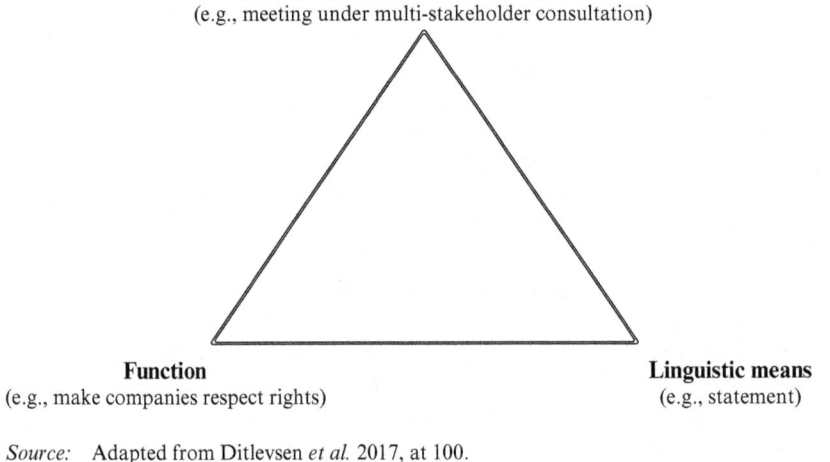

Source: Adapted from Ditlevsen *et al.* 2017, at 100.

Figure 3.2 Basic triangular model

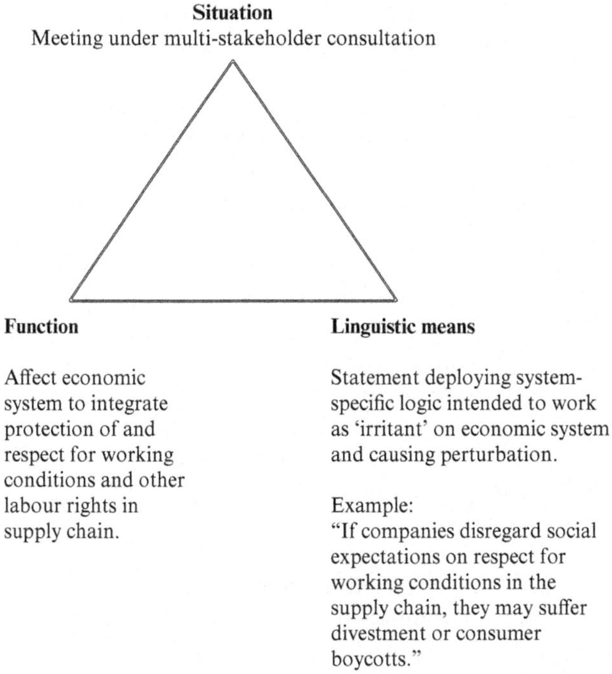

Argumentative strategies, discourse and system-specific rationality 95

Situation
Meeting under multi-stakeholder consultation

Function

Affect economic system to integrate protection of and respect for working conditions and other labour rights in supply chain.

Linguistic means

Statement deploying system-specific logic intended to work as 'irritant' on economic system and causing perturbation.

Example:
"If companies disregard social expectations on respect for working conditions in the supply chain, they may suffer divestment or consumer boycotts."

Figure 3.3   Triangular model for NGO statement on supply chain in SRSG consultation (example)

The objective and therefore intended function of the NGO's statement (left corner of the triangle) is to affect the economic system (or its representatives at the meeting, that is, companies or business associations) to incorporate the respect for working conditions and other labour rights in the textile sector. The linguistic means to do so is a statement which argues that point with a particular focus on its field of specialisation.

Figure 3.2 did not consider whether or not a message is transmitted in the code of the recipient. This was the subject of Figure 3.1. Figure 3.3 adds that aspect to Figure 3.2. Consider again the relational model introduced at Figure 3.1: for the purpose of achieving the objective of the affective function, the linguistic means may be structured in a manner assumed by the transmitter (the NGO) to support the realisation of the objective. For the purposes of the objective in this example, as represented in Figure 3.3 the NGO may decide to articulate the message in the economic system code, because this may cause perturbation with the recipient.

3.2.4 Argumentative Strategies for Construction of CSR Normativity and Business Responsibilities for Human Rights

In the following chapters, Chapter 4 will consider the UN Norms, the Global Compact and the EU MSF and CSR Alliance with a view to the statements made and the effects on the normative outputs of the discursive processes. Chapter 5 considers the SRSG process that led to the UN Framework and UNGPs. This is the main case study of the current work and therefore more detailed than the analysis in Chapter 4. The analysis in Chapter 4 of initiatives that took place in the years just prior to the SRSG process provides a backdrop for understanding how the SRSG process differed, and for a comparison of argumentative strategies. Chapter 6 proceeds to the comparative analysis with a particular emphasis on argumentative strategies that invoke system-specific codes of recipients or transmitters, the effects of this on the outputs, and the use of stabilising and de-stabilising argumentative strategies. That analytical focus is elaborated below in this section.

3.2.4.1 Activating system-specific interests

Figure 3.3 illustrates the interaction to construct CSR normativity and business responsibilities for human rights through discursive exchanges between participants deploying linguistic means seeking to protect and promote their interests in ways that will lead to the desired adaptation within other participating sub-systems. In varying constellations of participants, such interaction occurs in each of the five case studies analysed in Chapters 4–6. A range of interests are at stake for companies, civil society and governments as well as intergovernmental organisations related to an institutionalisation of CSR normativity into soft law or hard law, the normative role to be played by international human rights law, and the roles and responsibilities for states and business.[31] For example, companies which are 'CSR leaders' and have established policies and practices on CSR may welcome a hardening of CSR normativity and seek to promote it in order to strengthen their own economic interests. Other companies may prefer to maintain the status quo and, as such, will seek to promote that objective. Also, the interests of intergovernmental organisations at the administrative level that launched several of the multi-stakeholder regulatory initiatives serving as cases in this study, are not always paral-

---

[31] See further, K. Buhmann (2018) *Power, Procedure, Participation and Legitimacy In Global Sustainability Norms: A Theory of Collaboratory Regulation*, Routledge, at 34–36.

leled by the interests of individual governments. For example, for the UN Secretariat (the top executive arm within the UN), the implementation of the UN's goals as set forth in the UN Charter may be seen as calling for complementary approaches. As a result, the Secretariat may seek to involve companies through CSR and the provision of specific CSR norms to guide companies, or through BHR. Some governments, on the other hand, may perceive such moves as political or economic threats to national institutional structures or trade or investment interests, as threats to the legal make-up of the freedom of enterprise within their legal culture, or even as threats to the idea of the sovereignty of the state. For this reason, it is possible to observe several competing interests unfold in the discursive struggles to construct CSR normativity under the case studies even within a single functional sub-system. The interests at stake affect the discursive power and concerns of participants involved in the construction of business responsibilities for human rights, as discussed in Chapter 6 (6.2.) in regard to the case studies.

In his analysis of international policy processes on environment and sustainability, Marten Hajer has demonstrated that discourse analysis focusing on argumentative strategies and discourse coalitions is a valid way to shed light on the way in which sustainability related problems and proposed solutions are constructed. He demonstrates that discourse related to the construction of such problems can be seen as complex and continuous struggles over the definition and meaning of a problem, rather than as a conflict over a predefined problem with actors taking specific stances for or against. Through argumentative practices and skills, discourse actors seek to persuade each other to see the world 'in the light of the orator'[32] (or to put it in the terminology of this study: the concerns of the transmitter, even if the means to that is to activate the rationality of the recipient). Through discursive interaction, discourse actors seek to create new cognitions and new positioning, with an impact on regulation. Hajer's argumentative approach recognises that language is not only based in preconceived interests of discourse actors, but also influences the perception of interests.[33]

Hajer's approach illuminates the interaction between policy and legal regulation in relation to a topic subjected to discourse analysis. Hajer's objective is to develop insights into the way in which discourse affects politics, specifically environmental politics. As such, it touches on the iterative

---

[32] M. A. Hajer (1995) *The Politics of Environmental Discourse: Ecological Modernization and the Policy Process,* New York: Clarendon Press, Oxford at 53.
[33] Ibid., esp. Chapters 2.4 and 6.3.

development of regulation from problem conception to solutions, that is, the politics of law to the extent that law or other institutionalised solutions emanate[34] (such as new normative guidance 'fixing' the implications of international human rights law for business conduct).

Hajer demonstrates that the struggle around environmental sustainability enacts itself discursively drawing both on economic system orientated language and considerations, and governmental focus on efficiency. For the purposes of the current analysis, this underscores the mixture of social sub-system interests and use of binary codes that may be employed by discursive actors and their coalitions.

To strengthen the possibility to obtain the intended effects with recipients, discourse participants may compose their statements in language apt to affect recipients to respond positively to the interests of the transmitter. This was depicted in Figure 3.1 as well as Figure 3.3. In a reflexive regulatory forum, those representing particular social sub-systems may employ language apt to make the argument easily received, understood and internalised by recipients. In other words, legal or political system transmitters seeking to make companies or their organisations internalise sustainability-related expectations may employ economic system-specific language when expressing their expectations or demands of company conduct. This will cause irritation upon contact, and upon digestion within the economic system (and its representations, including individual companies) may lead to internalisation of the external expectations. To obtain that affect, when addressing companies, the transmitters would draw on the economic system binary code of profit/loss and related considerations, such as risks that may lead to economic losses. Similarly, economic system transmitters of a message may seek to affect changes with political system actors through employing political system-specific language or building the argument on political system considerations. Such a statement would draw on the binary code of power/no-power or power/weakness and related considerations, such as employment/no employment of the political economic system as outlined above. Those seeking to affect changes with political economic actors, such as international organisations, would address the particular combination of economic and political interests, for example employment/unemployment, or access/no access to social services. Economic actors seeking to affect the legal system and those working in a legal system capacity may employ legal system language to influence the recipient. For example, companies may build an argument seeking to construct CSR in terms of the binary code of coercion/no

---

[34] Ibid., at 22–3.

coercion in order to influence regulators or those who make reports or recommendations that serve as input for formal regulators to abstain from subjecting CSR conduct to legal requirements.

Whereas the understanding and protection of human rights may vary between national and regional legal systems, human rights are defined quite precisely in international human rights law. In addition to the UDHR, a range of UN conventions (hard law) and declarations (soft law) on human rights spell out the provisions of the UDHR. ILO's fundamental conventions[35] relate to rights, which are also recognised as human rights (the freedom from discrimination, freedom of association and right to collective negotiation, elimination of forced labour and elimination of child labour are all human rights, which are recognised to be core labour rights). Treaty bodies comprising human rights specialists develop authoritative interpretation of the specific rights set out in human rights conventions and duties connected to those rights. An institutionalisation of international human rights law as a normative source for CSR is therefore a way of 'fixing' CSR normativity, at least with regard to human rights. This would lead consumers, investors, governments and others to be able to have specific expectations of companies in relation to their social impact, regardless of whether CSR is understood to be voluntary or not. It would also provide specific guidance for companies with regard to the conduct that they should observe. At the same time, an institutionalisation of international human rights law as a normative source for CSR could open the door for an institutionalisation of other parts of international law as normative sources for CSR. For example, this could apply to environment and anti-corruption as part of CSR. The impact of this could also lead to an expansion of specific expectations of companies' conduct as well as specific guidance for companies with regard to CSR. An institutionalisation of international human rights law as a defined normative source would facilitate an institutionalisation of the role of international human rights law in regard to business responsibilities for human rights as

---

[35] ILO Convention No. 29, *Forced Labour Convention* (1930) 39 U.N.T.S. 55; Convention No. 87, *Freedom of Association and Protection of the Right to Organise Convention* (1949) 68 UNTS 17; Convention No. 98, *Right to Organise and Collective Bargaining Convention* (1949) 96 U.N.T.S. 257; Convention No. 100, *Equal Remuneration Convention* (1951) 165 U.N.T.S. 303; Convention No. 105, *Abolition of Forced Labour Convention* (1957) 320 U.N.T.S. 291; Convention No. 111, *Discrimination (Employment and Occupation) Convention* (1958) 362 U.N.T.S. 31; Convention No. 138, *Minimum Age Convention* (1973) 1015 U.N.T.S. 297; Convention No. 182, *Worst Forms of Child Labour Convention* (1999) 2133 U.N.T.S. 161.

an autonomous normative discourse. The next step in that context might be a hard institutionalisation, resulting in binding norms. Conversely, if a process to define CSR norms does not lead to an institutionalisation of human rights law for CSR, a process towards constructing business responsibilities for human rights will not be able to take its point of departure in such a normativity as already agreed.

Here too, discourse participants may draw on system-specific language of recipients to strengthen the possibility of a discursive statement to reach its functional objective. Legal or political system transmitters seeking to make companies or their organisations adopt or accept international human rights law as a normative source for CSR may employ (mimic) economic system-specific language or build an argument on the economic risks caused by disregard of social expectations of respect for ILO core labour standards. Again referring to Figure 3.1, this will cause irritation upon contact, and upon digestion within the economic system may lead to internalisation of ILO standards or an acceptance of these standards as guiding for CSR standards that result from the reflexive law forum. Economic system transmitters of a message seeking to limit the role to be played by international human rights law as a normative source for CSR may seek to affect political system representations towards that objective by employing political system-specific language or building the argument on political system considerations. Such a statement would draw on the binary code of power/no-power, or in the current context be built on the political-economic interests of the pertinent political system. Within the EU it could therefore argue in terms of employment or labour market considerations. Organisations seeking to affect the legal system and those working in a legal system capacity to abstain from formalising international human rights law as a normative source for CSR may address recipients through international law arguments on international law establishing duties for states.

3.2.4.2 Stabilising and de-stabilising argumentative strategies

An institutionalisation of CSR or business responsibilities for human rights through detailed normative guidance or even requirements of specific action means less choice for economic actors to decide whether they want to engage in social responsibility, and what type of action they want to perform, if any.

As observed above, discourse actors will seek to influence the construction of new normativity based on their interests. Some will see the intergovernmental initiatives as threats in the sense that they may lead to a hardening of CSR normativity, with spill-over effects on hard or soft requirements on companies under international law and/or under national

Argumentative strategies, discourse and system-specific rationality 101

law in home and/or host countries. These actors will seek to influence the discursive construction of CSR in the initiative in which they are involved in a way that is intended to lead to CSR being perceived as a fully voluntary matter. They will invoke the understanding that CSR is 'voluntary', and argue that any hardening of CSR requirements on companies contradicts the nature of CSR. Through such conservative *stabilising strategies*, these discourse participants seek a stabilising effect of their input into the discourse. In addition to the 'CSR as voluntary' argument, they may build their argument along a *lex lata*[36] course with a conservative approach to international law, arguing that international law is for states, and therefore cannot and should not be extended to set duties for companies.

Others will employ *de-stabilising strategies*, arguing in favour of CSR becoming less voluntary or even perhaps mandatory. These actors may also employ a *lex ferenda*[37] line of argument suggesting that international or EU law should change to establish obligations on companies to promote CSR. Such obligations could take several forms, ranging from disclosure or transparency requirements, which may be supported by economic incentives, to obligations of conduct for companies in their business relationships and for host or home states to regulate and enforce CSR related norms of conduct on companies. It may also invoke the adaptations which international law has already made with regard to legal personality of individuals, arguing that the recognition of rights and (limited) duties under international human rights and criminal law should be expanded towards recognition of duties for legal persons.

Based on the interests that they wish to protect and promote, discourse participants may also seek to stabilise or de-stabilise the role to be played by international human rights law as a normative source for CSR based on their interests in this context too. Some will use conservative *stabilising strategies* to argue that human rights are obligations for states, and therefore should not be transferred onto companies as obligations or even expectations. Others will employ *de-stabilising* strategies, seeking to argue that CSR should be normatively informed by or even hinged upon international human rights law.

In the first term of the SRSG process, two concepts mentioned in SRSG's mandate became the subject of particular discursive negotiations towards the presentation of the UN Framework: 'sphere of influence' and

---

[36] The term *lex lata* refers to 'the law as it is', that is, current law (see Chapter 1).
[37] The term *lex ferenda* refers to 'the law as it should be', that is, this invokes a proposal for changing the law from what it currently is (see Chapter 1).

'complicity', which came to function as floating signifiers in their own right. The CSR idea of responsibility beyond legal compliance filtered into the debate on business human rights responsibilities through those two concepts. Both had generated considerable contention following the dismissal of the Draft Norms by the Commission on Human Rights, augmented because they were used in the Global Compact's principles. The contention concerned the extent of responsibility in terms of the company's *sphere of influence*, and in terms of corporate *complicity* in human rights violations committed by others. At the outset, there was neither agreement from the various stakeholder groups or networks on the exact meaning of the concepts, nor any authoritative interpretation. Both relate to company responsibilities, including to suppliers' as well as host state actions. The SRSG's process of 'clarifying' and eventually fixing the relevance of the two concepts for future use in the BHR discourse offers interesting examples of use of stabilising and de-stabilising argumentative strategies, as seen in Chapter 6.

PART II

Discursive construction of business responsibilities for CSR

4. Two steps forward, one back – more than once: Developing normative guidance for business on human rights in a CSR context

Comprising Chapters 4 and 5, Part II is the empirical part of this study. These two chapters relay the processes of the case studies with regard to the discursive construction of CSR with a social and human rights focus, the general progression (and frequently also, regression) of the construction process of social responsibilities of business to be informed by international human rights law, and the deployment of system-specific logic of either the recipients or transmitters in a general sense. Opening Part III, Chapter 6 compares the findings that emerge from Chapters 4 and 5 and develops a synthesis with a particular emphasis on what led to the breakthrough that facilitated the emergence of the BHR regime.

Chapter 4 is concerned with the background to the SRSG process in terms of regulatory efforts to turn social expectations on business with regard to their impact on society into normative guidance or requirements. Chapter 4 opens by introducing nineteenth and twentieth century efforts and initiatives towards business responsibility for their social impact, with a particular emphasis on how human rights or human rights related concerns formed part of this, for example in regard to provision of housing or exploitation of human labour (section 4.1). Next it describes initiatives by intergovernmental organisations in the second half of the twentieth century to develop norms for TNC conduct, which preceded the Draft Norms process (section 4.2). It proceeds to the four case studies that offer the immediate backdrop to the analysis of the SRSG process and contribute to placing that main case study into perspective by demonstrating the antagonism that preceded the evolution of the UN Framework and UNGPs: The UN's Draft Norms (section 4.3), the UN Global Compact (section 4.4), the European Multi-Stakeholder Forum on CSR (section 4.5), and the European CSR Alliance (section 4.6). Finally, section 4.7 draws together the main insights from this chapter.

The five multi-stakeholder regulatory processes that form the case studies in this book all occurred within a period of less than 15 years. In a chronological perspective, the UN Norms resulted from a regulatory process initiated in 1998, were presented to the Commission on Human Rights in 2003 and debated in 2004; the UN Global Compact was developed 1999–2000; the EU MSF took place 2002–04; and the CSR Alliance was launched in 2006. The discursive evolution is addressed in this chapter. Chapter 5 deals with the evolution of the BHR regime through the SRSG process that took place between 2005 and 2011 and delivered the UN Framework in 2008 and the UNGPs in 2011. Even as these initiatives to some extent relate to or even fed off each other, they also occurred on a backdrop of previous efforts to develop normative guidance for businesses with regard to their impact on human rights, which responded to early pressure for institutionalising moral views on acceptable business conduct into international law. Some of these were successful, others less so, and in this way form part of the backdrop for the evolution of the BHR regime and its ground-breaking character. Yet, even preceding those steps, various actors had been engaging in activities to reduce adverse business impacts or contribute to societal needs, with an emphasis on issues that today would be framed as social, economic or other human rights. This chapter opens by introducing those efforts from a historical perspective relating to the nineteenth and twentieth centuries. It proceeds to efforts in the second half of the twentieth century at developing international law to reduce adverse business impacts or human rights, including labour rights, preceding the five case studies but also providing part of the backdrop to the evolution of the BHR regime. Thereafter, it moves to the four UN and EU case studies, which are presented and discussed in the chronological order listed above.

4.1 FROM MORAL ACTING TO LEGAL ACTION: DIRECT AND INDIRECT HUMAN RIGHTS CONCERNS

Although dating back to the 1930s,[1] the term CSR only entered the business and social science vocabulary strongly in the late 1990s. However, neither the idea that the private sector has social responsibilities nor the term corporate social responsibility are new. Indeed, corporate social

---

[1] A. A. Berle, Jr. (1931) 'Corporate powers as powers in trust', 44(7) *Harvard Law Review* pp. 1049–74; E. M. Dodd, Jr. (1932) 'For whom are corporate managers trustees?', 45(7) *Harvard Law Review* pp. 1145–63.

responsibility has been around both in terms of societal perceptions of proper corporate behaviour, and in terms of legal thinking from at least the late nineteenth century. From the outset, both aspects have displayed a clear link to what is or has become human rights normativity, relating to the full spectrum of civil, cultural, economic, political and social rights. In several cases, what began as a morally based conviction that business should 'do no harm' signalled a concern with a social problem or practice that later came to be regulated by human rights law.

Beginning at least at the time of the early industrial revolution, some owners and managers of large as well as smaller companies engaged in activities that would now be considered CSR or corporate contributions to social sustainability. These activities were related to employee relations and accommodation, health and community services, and the company's relation to external society based on perceptions of a duty not to harm others or exploit those in need. Today, many would refer to such activities as relating to labour right and contributing to access to social human rights of housing and access to health services.

Investment in companies involved in slavery or in the weapons industry was avoided by the Quakers (a religious group engaging in industrial and economic activity) in the US in the 1800s.[2] The ban on slavery, which became a fact in international labour law in the early twentieth century and in international human rights law in the mid-twentieth century after being introduced in national law in several states in the preceding century, is one of the strongest examples of how moral convictions of what type of action is acceptable or not, are transformed into law.

In the 1960s and early 1970s, socially concerned corporations or investors in some countries took to limiting investments in companies involved in the war in Vietnam, and in the 1980s in South African corporations in order to avoid support to the Apartheid regime.[3] These were reactions to practices that took human lives arbitrarily or discriminated on the basis of race. Socially responsible investment (SRI) is part of the broader field of corporate sustainability.[4] Its connections with human rights continue to be strong, as evidenced in the early twenty-first century by institutional

---

[2] E. Sjöström (2004) *Investment Stewardship: Actors and Methods for Socially And Environmentally Responsible Investments*, Copenhagen: The Nordic Partnership, at 12.

[3] Ibid.

[4] S. Zadek, M. Merme and R. Samans (2005) *Mainstreaming Responsible Investment,* World Economic Forum Global Corporate Citizen Initiative in cooperation with Accountability, January 2005; GES Investment Services (2005) *Nordic Sustainability Index II,* Copenhagen: Nordic Council of Ministers: TemaNord 2005,

investors' policies and decisions on divestment from companies whose activities may contribute to human rights abuse.[5]

From the outset, corporate efforts to contribute to responding to social needs have been linked not only to civil and political rights, but also to economic, social and cultural rights. Family-owned companies in the nineteenth and early twentieth century provided for health care services, education, housing, and pension schemes for employees and their families.[6] With the development of the welfare state in Europe during the twentieth century, the state gradually took over many of the social tasks, which socially responsibly inclined owners and managers had provided. Many of those tasks are today codified into states' economic or social human rights obligations. In the US, which has traditionally lacked a similar structure of governmentally provided health care and pension schemes and higher education, some companies continued to provide relatively extensively for these services in addition to other types of community service, as well as affirmative action programmes to counteract race- and gender-based discrimination.[7]

Partly as a result of growing welfare and human rights orientation in the West during the twentieth century, companies came to be seen as having social functions that exceeded the maximisation of owners' economic interests. An increasing number of stakeholders began to make demands on companies to assume social responsibility with the rights of workers a major issue,[8] again highlighting the interest of stakeholders on company impacts on human rights.

---

at 534; see also S. Vallentin (2002) *Pensionsinvesteringer, etik og offentlighed – en systemteoretisk analyse af offentlig meningsdannelse,* Copenhagen: Samfundslitteratur.

[5] E.g., Equator Principles, available at: www.equator-principles.com/; and the Principles for Responsible Investment, available at www.unpri.org (last accessed 27 December 2016).

[6] M. Rostgaard (2000) Patriarkalisme og industriledelse i Danmark ca. 1880–1910. In M. Rostgaard, and M. F. Wagner (eds) *Lederskab i dansk industri og samfund 1880–1960,* Aalborg: Aalborg University Press; G.F. David et al. (2006) 'The responsibility paradox'; see also A. Roepstorff (2010) *CSR: Virksomheders sociale ansvar som begreb og praksis,* at 29–38.

[7] David et al., ibid.

[8] See e.g., P. Selznick (1992) *The moral Community: Social Theory and the Promise of Community,* Berkeley: The University of California Press, at 350; T. Wilthagen (1994) 'Reflexive rationality in the regulation of occupational safety and health'. In R. Rogowski and T. Wilthagen (eds) *Reflexive Labour Law: Studies in Industrial Relations and Employment Regulation,* Deventer and Boston: Kluwer Law and Taxation Publishers, pp. 345–76, at 372–3; E. M. Epstein, (1998) 'Business ethics and Corporate Social Policy', 37(1) *Business & Society Review* pp. 7–39, at 15–21.

Since the 1960s and 1970s, attention to international law as a modality to realise the political objectives held by civil society, governments and even some companies has grown. The 1970s saw efforts to regulate companies to take responsibility and to be held accountable for their impact on human rights and the environment. Following a period of emphasis on deregulation and corporate rights in the 1980s, the 1990s saw renewed NGO and media concern with the negative social effects of globalisation.[9] Towards the turn of the millennium, it became increasingly clear that an imbalance between the trade rights of TNCs and their duties not to exploit governance gaps gave rise to human rights violations by business, especially TNCs: trade rights were not sufficiently balanced by duties not to exploit weak labour laws, weak enforcement and other types of bad governance in the interest of economic gains. The debate on corporate roles and responsibilities gradually shifted from acceptance of companies as social actors to a discussion of the appropriate institutions and institutional level for legal regulation of the private sector's impact on society. Legal regulation of companies, especially TNCs, was no longer seen to be solely a matter between contractual partners, but rather an issue requiring the attention of regulators at national, supranational and international levels.[10] Just like the development of international labour law started out at the turn of the nineteenth century into the twentieth as a measure to create basic levels of protection of workers so as to discourage employers and states from competing for profit generation and investment by applying the lowest standards,[11] the CSR movement shifted its focus to the international level of regulation in a combined concern with avoiding protectionism and to 'raise the bar' of social and environmental production standards.

At the end of the 1980s and during the 1990s, societal attention on business impact on the environment and, sometimes, related involvement with or complicity in human rights violations grew. This was spurred by specific events such as the Brent Spar and Nigeria Ogoni-land incidents

---

[9] J. Nolan (2005) 'The United Nation's compact with business: hindering or helping the protection of human rights?' 24(2) *University of Queensland Law Journal* pp. 445–66.

[10] For a detailed discussion, see L. C. Backer (2006) 'Multinational Corporations, transnational law: The United Nations' Norms on the Responsibilities of Transnational Corporations as a harbinger of Corporate Social Responsibility in international law', 37(Winter) *Columbia Human Rights Law Review* pp. 287–389, at 310–17.

[11] J. -M. Servais (2014) *International Labour Law*, Wolters Kluwer, pp. 21–5.

(both involving oil company Shell),[12] and by increased information flows on global inequality and sub-standard working conditions in emerging economies. Factors contributing to civil society concern with the social impact of business included the prevalence of child labour in some exporting industries in poor countries.

Particular attention was drawn to Asia, where large quantities of apparel and textiles sold on the global market were produced. Reports of substandard working conditions at apparel and textile facilities in Vietnam, Bangladesh and Indonesia, which supplied to buyers elsewhere all led to consumer concerns and pressure on investors and states to cease activities that might support abusive regimes.[13] Several TNCs, including Nike, Reebok, Nestlé and Shell, were the targets of boycott campaigns organised by NGOs in response to the alleged negative impact on the environment and on human rights or labour rights that was associated with the actions of these corporations and their productions and sourcing practices.[14] At the end of the nineteenth century, the US Alien Torts Statute,[15] a centuries old US legal statute saw a revival as a way to sue companies for violations of international law on human and labour rights. Some of these involved allegations of corporate complicity in human rights violations by authori-

---

[12] For a detailed presentation of the Nigeria issue and discussion of the conflict, see T. Lambooy (2010) *Corporate Social Responsibility: Legal and Semi-Legal Frameworks Supporting CSR – Developments 2000–2010 and Case Studies*, Groningen: Groningen University, at 385–433.

[13] D. L. Spar and L. T. La Mure (2003) 'The Power of Activism: Assessing the Impact of NGOs on Global Business', 45(3) *California Management Review* pp. 78–101.

[14] See for example J. Bendell (2004) 'Barricades and boardrooms: A contemporary history of the corporate accountability movement'. Technology, Business and Society Programme Paper Number 13. United Nations Research Institute for Social Development; M. Hernandez (2004) 'Institutionalising global standards of responsible corporate citizenship: Assessing the role of the UN Global Compact'. In M. McIntosh, S. Waddock and G. Kell (eds) *Learning to Talk: Corporate Citizenship and the Development of the UN Global Compact*, Sheffield: Greenleaf Publishing, pp. 114–28, at 114; case studies of ABB, Premier Oil and Levi Strauss & Co in J. Hepker and A. Newton (eds) (2004) *The Business and Human Rights Management Report: A study of eight companies and their approaches to human rights policy and management system development*. Ethical Corporation, November; C. F. Hillemans (2003) 'UN Norms on the responsibilities of transnational corporations and other business enterprises with regard to human rights', 4(1) *German Law Journal* pp.1065–80, at 1067; K. Schoenberger (2002) *Levi's Children: Coming to Terms with Human Rights in the Global Market Place*, New York: Atlantic Monthly Press.

[15] Alien Torts Statute, 28 U.S.C. § 1350 (also referred to as the Alien Torts Claims Act).

ties in relation to natural resource extraction in Asia or Africa by TNCs headquartered in the US or Europe.[16] US Supreme Court rulings have since meant a reduction in the application of the statute.

As this shows, concerns that today would be referred to as human rights issues have long been an issue for social movements to reduce socially adverse business impact and for certain businesses in their efforts to contribute to fulfilling the needs of employees and local communities. In parallel to many initiatives to develop private codes for TNCs, international organisations sought to develop normative guidance in international law, mainly international soft law. These processes and their outcomes, which occurred according to the conventional law-making approach of international organisations with limited stakeholder participation, are the topic of the next section.

4.2 INITIAL STEPS TOWARDS INTERGOVERNMENTAL NORMATIVE GUIDANCE: UN, OECD AND ILO

The first major attempt by an international organisation to formulate a Code of Conduct for transnational corporations was initiated in the 1970s by the UN.[17] In 1973 the UN Economic and Social Council (ECOSOC) appointed a so-called Group of Eminent Persons to study the impact of TNCs on economic development and international relations, and to advise the UN on this issue. This group presented its recommendations in 1974. The recommendations included the establishment of a permanent Commission on Transnational Corporations and a Centre on TNCs, which was to study the feasibility of producing a multilateral agreement on TNCs.[18] The draft 'agreement' later came to be referred to as a UN Code of Conduct on Transnational Corporations. If it had been adopted, the

---

[16] See J. A. Zerk (2006) *Multinationals and Corporate Social Responsibility: Limitations and Opportunities in International Law,* Cambridge: Cambridge University Press, at 207–15 for an account of some of the major cases relating to human rights. Since the so-called Kiobel ruling by the US Supreme Court in 2013, the application of the Alien Torts Statute to such cases has become limited.

[17] Established by the Economic and Social Council under resolution 1913 (LVII) of 5 December 1974.

[18] United Nations Intellectual History Project (2009) *The UN and Transnational Corporations,* Ralph Bunche Institute for International Studies, Briefing Note No. 17, July 2009; see further T. Sagafi-Nejad in collaboration with J. H. Dunning (2008) *The UN and Transnational Corporations: From Code of Conduct to the Global Compact,* Indiana University Press.

draft text[19] that was agreed on in the late 1980s would have defined duties for TNCs to respect host countries' development goals, observe their domestic law, respect fundamental human rights, and observe consumer and environmental protection objectives.[20] However, two decades after it was begun the project towards the UN Code of Conduct was abandoned in the beginning of the 1990s, partly due to opposition and divergence of investment-related interests among certain governments.[21]

Efforts by the OECD and ILO were more successful. Beginning around the same time as the UN's Code of Conduct project, the OECD developed and in 1976 adopted the first version of the OECD Guidelines for Multinational Corporations. Similarly, the ILO developed and in 1977 adopted the ILO Tripartite Declaration of Principles concerning Multinational Enterprises and Social Policy,[22] followed in 1998 by the ILO Declaration on Fundamental Principles and Rights at Work.[23]

The OECD Guidelines for Multinational Enterprises are an Annex to an OECD Declaration on International Investment and Multinational Enterprises.[24] Like other soft law instruments, the Guidelines are non-

---

[19] Draft Code of Conduct on Transnational Corporations. Last version of the proposed draft code: *Development and International Economic Cooperation: Transnational Corporations*, UN Doc. E/1990/94, 12 June 1990.

[20] For discussions of the Draft Code of Conduct and its human rights aspects, see A. E. Mayer (2009) 'Human rights as a dimension of CSR: The blurred lines between legal and non-legal categories', 88 *Journal of Business Ethics* pp. 561–77; P. Redmond (2003) Transnational enterprise and human rights: Options for standard setting and compliance. 37 *Int'l Lawyer*, pp. 69–102; Hillemans (n 14); Bendell (n 14) at 12–13; P. O'Reilly and S. Tickell (1999) 'TNCs and social issues in the developing world'. In M. K. Addo (ed.) *Human Rights Standards and the Responsibility of Transnational Corporations*, The Hague: Kluwer Law International, pp.273–87, at 274; P. Lansing and A. Rosaria (1991) 'An analysis of the United Nations proposed Code of Conduct for Transnational Corporations', 14(4) *World Competition* pp. 35–50.

[21] Sagafi-Nejad with Dunning (n 18).

[22] ILO (1977) Tripartite Declaration of Principles concerning Multinational Enterprises and Social Policy (MNE Declaration), originally adopted in 1977 by the ILO Governing Body, available at: http://www.ilo.org/empent/Publications/WCMS_094386/lang--en/index.htm (last accessed 27 December 2016).

[23] ILO (1998) Declaration of Fundamental Principles and Rights at Work adopted by the International Labour Conference, 86th session, Geneva, June 1998, 37 I.L.M. 1233, http://www.ilo.org/public/english/standards/decl/declaration/text/ (last accessed 27 December 2016).

[24] OECD (2011) Declaration on International Investment and Multinational Enterprises, available at: http://www.oecd.org/daf/inv/investment-policy/oecddeclarationoninternationalinvestmentandmultinationalenterprises.htm (last accessed 20 November 2016).

binding. However, somewhat unusually for an international instrument, they actually address themselves to companies, albeit through states: the Guidelines are recommendations from governments to companies operating *in* or *out of* adhering states.[25] The Investment Declaration, which like the Guidelines was first adopted in 1976, is a policy commitment by adhering governments to provide an open and transparent environment for international investment and encourage the positive contributions that multinational enterprises can make to economic and social progress. The OECD Guidelines were developed in response to a concern among industrialised states (many of whom were OECD members) that actual or potential political or other interference by TNCs in developing host states in the context of investments that were to be promoted with the Declaration, might lead host states to impose restrictions on the rights of foreign investors. The Guidelines were therefore intended to provide home state guidance for TNCs incorporated in OECD member states as to their conduct in such other states.

ILO's 1977 Tripartite Declaration was conceived as an effort to realign TNCs' activities with host state policy objectives and workers' interests. The Tripartite Declaration encourages TNCs to comply with ILO social policy Conventions and Recommendations, even where the host state is not bound by these or does not enforce them. The ILO's 1998 Declaration on Fundamental Principles and Rights at Work ('ILO 1998 Declaration') refers to the core labour principles of freedom of association and collective bargaining, non-discrimination in employment, abolition of forced labour and elimination of child labour. It declares that all ILO members – whether or not they have ratified the ILO conventions on those principles – have an obligation arising as a consequence of their ILO membership.[26] The implicit message for businesses was that they should respect international core labour standards, regardless of whether a host state has ratified the specific conventions in question. Accordingly, this Declaration is a strong invitation to businesses to self-regulate. It came to be invoked by the UN Global Compact precisely for this purpose, as the Declaration informs the Global Compact's Principles 3–6 on labour rights.

In addition to the various global political issues that emerged as obstacles during the two decades of the UN's Code of Conduct project, a possible explanation for the success of the OECD Guidelines and ILO Declarations as compared to the UN's project may be sought in some

---

[25] The Guidelines are open to accession by non-OECD states.
[26] ILO (1998) (n 23) art. 2.

factors that set the OECD and ILO instruments and organisations apart from the proposed Code of Conduct as well as from the UN as an organisation. The Code of Conduct aimed to encompass TNC impact on society broadly; and the UN is a global organisation with a broad and not specialised mandate. Nor does the UN have a particular focus on economic activity of private actors; rather, as an international organisation its focus is on states and state conduct. As a first and ambitious effort by that global organisation to develop normative guidance for TNCs, the Code of Conduct may have been too broad in its coverage and out of focus with the UN's objectives to gain the necessary support to move ahead in the 1970s when the OECD and ILO more successfully acted on similar issues. By contrast, OECD's Guidelines and ILO's 1977 Declaration have a more limited focus within a specific field of economic activity, which in both cases is closely related to the specialised charge of each organisation. They establish rather general recommendations for states, which are related to commitments that states had already assumed under the issuing organisations (under the OECD Guidelines, an investment declaration;[27] under the ILO Declarations, states' obligations under the ILO Constitution[28] and for many states also the specialised fundamental labour conventions). For business enterprises, they offer guidance worded in rather general terms, and not legally binding obligations.

Moreover, the OECD's Guidelines and the ILO's Declaration were developed in settings that include stakeholders, including business representatives, and therefore the actors to whom the recommendations or guidance are essentially addressed. The ILO's foundational tripartite structure ensures that not only states but also representatives of workers' and employers' organisations take part in the elaboration of all hard and soft law instruments, including declarations. In the case of the OECD, a close cooperation with advisory committees representing business[29] and workers[30] ensures an institutionalised degree of a tripartite collabora-

---

[27] Countries adhering to the Guidelines make a binding commitment to implement them in accordance with the Decision of the OECD Council on the OECD Guidelines for Multinational Enterprises. Furthermore, matters covered by the Guidelines may also be the subject of national law and international commitments.

[28] Constitution of the International Labour Organization, adopted by the Peace Conference in April of 1919, established the International Labour Organization (ILO), 15 UNTS 40.

[29] The Business and Industry Advisory Committee to the OECD (BIAC), established in 1962.

[30] The Trade Union Advisory Committee to the OECD (TUAC), established in 1948.

tion. Both organisations have a specific focus, making the binding legal instruments and soft law guidance that they issue relatively targeted as compared to the scope of the Draft UN Code of Conduct. In the case of the ILO, all instruments are related specifically to labour rights. In the case of the OECD Guidelines, initially the focus was on international investment-related economic activities by (typically large) enterprises that were transnational. (As a result of regular revisions, most particularly the 2011 revision that aimed to align the Guidelines with the UNGPs, the scope of types of economic activities and businesses covered by the Guidelines has been expanded. Again, this has been negotiated by member states with the collaboration of industry and workers' representatives.) In addition, the OECD Guidelines as well as the ILO Declaration were negotiated and agreed to over a relatively short span of time. They were therefore not caught in extended political debates on the role of states and businesses, whereas the process of the Draft UN Code of Conduct spanned almost two decades of major changes, in this respect during a period that witnessed considerable shifts in North-South and East-West politics. Additionally, the pressure on the UN to adopt a Code of Conduct for TNCs was reduced with the adoption – only a few years after the Code of Conduct was launched – of the ILO's Tripartite Declaration and OECD's Guidelines, both of which address TNC impacts on society.

As this shows, intergovernmental efforts had been underway since the middle of the second half of the twentieth century to develop normative guidance for TNCs with regard to their social impact, especially when operating outside home states. As also shown, the first effort by the UN was not successful in becoming adopted, whereas efforts launched by specialised international organisations (OECD and ILO) with a full or partial focus on economic operations and an institutionalised process for a broad multi-stakeholder process became adopted. The way these specialised organisations develop new legal instruments includes not only governments but also labour organisations, which represent the actual or potential victims of TNC abuse of labour, as well as representatives for employers and, therefore, business organisations. As a result, the processes offer opportunities for dialogue among participants, which approximate or function according to the *modus operandi* of reflexive law, enabling an exchange of views, needs and demands to stimulate acceptance of new norms and contributions to joint rule-making, also by business organisations that were targeted as duty-bearers by the new norms of conduct.

The remaining sections in this chapter proceed to the next steps in intergovernmental efforts to formulate normative guidance for TNC, which also form four of the five empirical studies for the analysis in here. The first of these was the process that resulted in the Draft Norms. With a particular human rights focus, this process emerged in the second half of the 1990s, soon after the UN's Code of Conduct project had been abandoned.

4.3 THE DRAFT NORMS ON THE RESPONSIBILITIES OF TRANSNATIONAL CORPORATIONS AND OTHER BUSINESS ENTERPRISES WITH REGARD TO HUMAN RIGHTS

4.3.1 Origin and Evolution of the Draft Norms

In several reports prepared in the second half of the 1990s, the UN Human Rights Commission's Sub-Commission on Prevention of Discrimination and Protection of Minorities addressed the impact of TNCs on the enjoyment of human rights, labour rights and the right to development. The Sub-Committee[31] was an expert body under the UN Human Rights Committee, which was composed of politically appointed representatives from 53 UN Member States.

A 1995 report observed that TNCs were assuming power resembling that of states and that as a corollary, TNCs should share a responsibility for development and human rights, especially in poor states.[32] A 1996 report proposed regulating companies internationally through corporate governance, but with a public international law regulatory focus. The report observed that while businesses may actively contribute to economic and social development, including labour relations, human rights, environmental protection and technology transfer, they also have the capacity to infringe on human rights. On that basis, the report argued that it was

---

[31] The Sub-Commission was a subsidiary body of the UN Commission on Human Rights. It comprised 26 human rights experts from around the globe. Its mandate included human rights standard-setting and preparing studies of current human rights issues in all parts of the world. The Sub-Commission was initially subsumed under the auspices of the UN Human Rights Council, which was established on 3 April 2006 by the UN General Assembly as a replacement to the Commission on Human Rights. The Human Rights Council decided to terminate the mandate of the Sub-Commission after the Council's 58th session (2006).

[32] Sub-Commission on Prevention of Discrimination and Protection of Minorities (1995) The realization of Economic, Social and Cultural Rights: The relationship between the enjoyment of human rights, in particular, international labour and trade union rights, and the working methods and activities of transnational corporations, UN Doc. E/CN.4/Sub.2/1995/11 (24 July 1995).

necessary to establish a uniform system applicable across borders in order to avoid the exploitation of weak governance or economic differences between states by TNCs or other powerful non-state economic actors.[33] Taking that argument further, in a 1998 report the Sub-Commission argued that economic non-state actors must be regulated by public international law in order to reduce their negative impacts.[34]

Following this, in 1998 a working group set up under the UN Sub-Commission on the Promotion and Protection of Human Rights under the UN Human Rights Commission began a process to develop a document that in an advanced draft came to be entitled Norms on Human Rights Responsibilities of Transnational Corporations and other Business Enterprises.[35] The Draft Norms were never formally adopted by the Human Rights Commission, but the debate that evolved within and between civil society, business organisations, media and other stakeholders is evidence of highly differentiated and antagonistic views on the normative idea of business responsibilities for human rights, and whether or not this should be regulated by international law.

The background to the Draft Norms reflects an increasing acknowledgement within the UN human rights system of the relevance of addressing the role and impact of the private sector with regard to human rights. The ground had been prepared by various studies, including the Sub-Commission reports noted above. The points that were on the working group's agenda and those brought up by stakeholders involved in the process illustrate the major issues at stake.

The working group that prepared the Draft Norms was established in 1999 with a mandate to examine the working methods and activities of transnational corporations.[36] Adopted with a human rights focus, the

---

[33] Sub-Commission on Prevention of Discrimination and Protection of Minorities (1996) The impact of the activities and working methods of Transnational Corporations on the full enjoyment of human rights, in particular Economic, Social and Cultural Rights and the Rights to Development, Bearing in mind existing international guidelines, rules and standards relating to the subject-matter, UN Doc. E/CN.4/Sub.2/196/12, 2 July 1996.

[34] Sub-Commission on Prevention of Discrimination and Protection of Minorities (1998) The realization of Economic, Social and Cultural Rights: The Question of Transnational Corporations, UN Doc. E/CN.4/Sub.2/198/6, 10 June 1998.

[35] Sub-Commission on the Promotion and Protection of Human Rights (2003) Norms on the Responsibilities of Transnational Corporations and Other Business Enterprises with regard to Human Rights, UN Doc. E/CN.4/Sub.2/2003/12/Rev.2.

[36] Sub-Commission on the Promotion and Protection of Human Rights (1998) Resolution, 1998/8, 20 August 1998. The drafting history of the Norms has

working group's agenda focused on activities of transnational corporations, including their effects 'on the enjoyment of civil, cultural, economic, political and social rights, including the right to development, the right to a healthy environment and the right to peace'.[37] It included to assess of how existing human rights standards apply to activities of TNCs; to collect and analyse existing standards and international, NGO and other standard-setting activities; to prepare a collection of international, regional and bilateral investment agreements to analyse their compatibility with human rights; and finally to develop recommendations. The growth of power of business enterprises, the argument that "with power comes responsibility", and weakening power of the state vis-à-vis increasingly stronger corporations were all listed as parts of the rationale for prospective principles or code of conduct.[38]

Indeed, the initial aim was to formulate recommendations in the form of a code of conduct for corporations[39] that was to be a general guidance document of a soft law character. Gradually this developed into the much more ambitious aim of formulating a text that might develop into a binding instrument,[40] that is, an international treaty. Apparently, the shift came about because the working group felt that the experience of the Global Compact during its first years of operation proved that voluntary initiatives were insufficient to have the necessary normative effect on corporate behaviour.[41] An innovation in how international law instruments are named, the term 'Norms' was adopted by the working group in early 2002.[42] The working group member who had the main role in drafting the Norms has referred to the text as 'amount[ing] to more than aspirational statements of

---

been described in detail in D. Weissbrodt and M. Kruger (2003) 'Norms on the Responsibilities of Transnational Corporations and Other Business Enterprises with Regard to Human Rights', 97(4) *American Journal of International Law* pp. 901–22. See also Backer (n 10) at 321–7; and Hillemans (n 14).

[37] Report of the sessional working group on the working methods and activities of transnational corporations, 1st session, UN Doc. E/CN.4/Sub.2/1999/9, para. 9.

[38] Report of the sessional working group on the working methods and activities of transnational corporations, 2nd session, UN Doc. E/CN.4/Sub.2/2000/12, para. 26; Report of the sessional working group on the working methods and activities of transnational corporations, 3rd session, UN Doc. E/CN.4/Sub.2/2001/9, preamble.

[39] Report of the sessional working group, 1st session (n 37).

[40] Report of the sessional working group, 2nd session (n 38); Report of the sessional working group 3rd session (n 38); Report of the sessional working group on the working methods and activities of transnational corporations, 4th session, UN Doc. E/CN.4/Sub.2/2002/13; see also Weissbrodt and Kruger (n 36).

[41] Hillemans (n 14) at 1069.

[42] Report of the sessional working group, 4th session (n 40), para. 14.

desired conduct', '[going] beyond the voluntary guidelines found in the UN Global Compact, the ILO Tripartite Declaration, and the OECD Guidelines for Multinational Enterprises'.[43] Members of the Sub-Commission provided input for the Draft Norms through working papers that discussed such issues as the balance between rights of TNCs under international trade law and obligations of states under international human rights law, and the potential positive and negative effects of TNC activities on individual human rights such as the right to employment, the right to health and access to drinking water. They also discussed the state duty to protect against third-party violations of human rights, the state duty to fulfil human rights, and procedures for international and national monitoring of state compliance with their human rights obligations and duty to protect.[44]

The binding or non-binding form of regulation of the prospective Norms was an issue throughout the drafting process, as was the general future form of regulation of business with regard to human rights. At several meetings, the working group debated what might be the most effective form of implementation of the standards, and whether the standards were to be legally binding. Some members of the working group argued in favour of a legally binding code of conduct. Others suggested the preparation of a soft law declaration, which might form the basis for drafting a treaty.[45] Several NGOs argued in favour of a legally binding instrument.[46] While some business organisations welcomed the prospects of human rights guidance,[47] others did not welcome the idea of specifically defined business responsibilities for human rights, let alone a binding text.[48]

---

[43] Weissbrodt and Kruger (n 36) at 913; compare also D. Weissbrodt (2006) 'UN perspectives on "Business and humanitarian and human rights obligations",' ASIL Proceedings: Proceedings of the 100th Annual Meeting, March 29–April 1 2006, Washington DC, at 135–9.

[44] A. Eide (2001) 'Corporations, states and human rights: A note on responsibilities and procedures for implementation and compliance', Commission on Human Rights, Sub-Commission on the Promotion and Protection of Human Rights, UN Doc. E/CN.4/Sub.2/2001/WG.2/WP.2; E.-H. Guissé (2001) 'The realization of economic, social and cultural rights: The question of transnational corporations', Commission on Human Rights, Sub-Commission on the Promotion and Protection of Human Rights, UN Doc. E/DN.4/Sub.2/2001/WG.2/WP.3.

[45] Report of the sessional working group, 2nd session (n 38), paras 37–38.

[46] Ibid., para. 52.

[47] D. Kinley, J. Nolan and N. Zerial (2007) 'The politics of corporate social responsibility: Reflections on the United Nations Human Rights Norms for Corporations', 25(1) *Company and Securities Law Journal* pp. 30–43; see also the discussion in Nolan (n 9).

[48] B. Hearne (2004) 'Proposed UN Norms on human rights: Is business opposition justified?', *Ethical Corporation,* 22 March 2004.

The diversity of stances is also evident in reports from the Working Group. The report from the Working Group's second session meeting noted that '[t]he most effective implementation would be for companies to take on the standards as a matter of their own business practice',[49] thus indicating a preference for soft and self-regulatory approaches. Later meetings favoured hard law implementation mechanisms, such as enforcement in national courts or mandatory annual non-financial reports of companies.[50] At that time, a hard law approach was also adopted by members of the working group and in comments from the Sub-Commission, which observed that the text was informed by three aims: helping governments identify relevant types of legislation and enforcement mechanisms, encouraging companies to implement the normative substance, and laying 'the groundwork for the binding international standard setting process'.[51] The final text of the Draft Norms basically built on the idea that the effective implementation of human rights obligations in relation to business operations assumes the integration into companies' own codes of conduct and rules of operation, complemented by internal accountability mechanisms.[52] This was to be supplemented by periodic monitoring and verification by the UN and other international as well as national mechanisms to handle human rights obligations of business.[53] At the national level, states were to establish and reinforce the necessary legal and administrative framework for ensuring implementation.

The text of the final version of the Draft Norms covered TNCs[54] as well as 'other business enterprises'.[55] With regard to 'other business enterprises', the Draft Norms would apply to businesses with any relationship with transnational enterprises, if the impact of its activities was not entirely local or the activities involved violations of the right to security.[56] Additional information and guidance was provided by a Commentary.[57] The Draft Norms recognised that states are primary duty bearers with regard to human rights, adding that TNCs have responsi-

[49] Report of the sessional working group, 2nd session (n 38), para. 28.
[50] Report of the sessional working group, 4th session (n 40), paras 28–29.
[51] Report of the sessional working group, 2nd session (n 38), para. 33.
[52] Draft Norms, para. 15, Commentary to para. 15; Weissbrodt and Kruger (n 36) at 915.
[53] Draft Norms, para. 16, Commentary to para. 16; Weissbrodt and Kruger, ibid. at 915–21.
[54] Draft Norms, para. 20.
[55] Ibid., section I, Definitions para. 21.
[56] Ibid., para. 21, referring to definitions in paras 3 and 4.
[57] Sub-Commission on the Promotion and Protection of Human Rights (2003) Commentary on the Norms on the Responsibilities of Transnational Corporations

bilities to respect human rights 'within their respective spheres of activity and influence'.[58] The notion of 'sphere of influence' was not defined, although the Commentary sought to provide some clarification. Overall, the text addressed a set of 'General Obligations' and a series of specific human rights issues: rights to equal opportunity and non-discriminatory treatment, right to security of persons, rights of workers, and respect for national sovereignty with regard to human rights. In addition to mainstream human rights issues, the text of the Draft Norms included certain consumer and environmental issues, phrased as obligations ('Obligations with regard to consumer protection' and 'Obligations with regard to environmental protection').

The preamble of the Draft Norms referenced the UDHR as a common standard of achievement for all peoples and all nations to be striven for by governments, other organs of society and individuals. It built on this to assert that 'transnational corporations and other business enterprises, as organs of society, are also responsible for promoting and securing the human rights set forth in the Universal Declaration of Human Rights'.[59]

In the preambular part as well as in the definition of human rights in the final paragraph in the operative (substantive) part of the document, the Draft Norms referred extensively to international human rights law. They also referred to the ILO Tripartite Declaration of Principles concerning Multinational Enterprises and Social Policy and the OECD Guidelines for Multinational Enterprises. Human rights were defined broadly: according to the main text of the Draft Norms, human rights were understood to:

> include civil, cultural, economic, political and social rights, as set forth in the International Bill of Human Rights and other human rights treaties, as well as the right to development and rights recognised by international humanitarian law, international refugee law, international labour law, and other relevant instruments adopted within the UN system.[60]

Among many other instruments, the preamble set out such instruments as the Rio Declaration, the Plan of Implementation from the World Summit on Sustainable Development (Johannesburg 2002) and the UN Millennium Declaration. The references in the Draft Norms to sources in treaties and customary international law were explained by the draftsman

---

and Other Business Enterprises with Regard to Human Rights, UN Doc. E/CN.4/Sub.2/2003/38/Rev. 2.

[58] Ibid., para. 1.
[59] Draft Norms, preamble.
[60] Ibid., art. 23.

as providing a legal authority, 'as a restatement of international legal principles applicable to companies'.[61] As those instruments address themselves to states, there was, in principle, nothing new in the Draft Norms' assertion that 'States have the primary responsibility to promote, secure the fulfilment of, respect, ensure respect of and protect human rights recognized in international as well as national law', nor in the continuation that states' responsibilities include 'ensuring that transnational corporations and other business enterprises respect human rights'.[62]

The major novelty contained in the Draft Norms was their explicit recognition in (what might become) an instrument of international law that transnational corporations and other business enterprises, as 'organs of society', are responsible for promoting and securing the human rights set forth in the UDHR.[63] In that context, the Draft Norms stated in their main text that:

> [w]ithin their respective spheres of activity and influence, transnational corporations and other business enterprises have the obligation to promote, secure the fulfilment of, respect, ensure respect of and protect human rights recognized in international as well as national law, including the rights and interests of indigenous peoples and other vulnerable groups.[64]

The Norms suggested that TNCs and other enterprises, as particular types of non-state actors, have human rights responsibilities or even obligations that are independent of those of the host or home state of the enterprise. Notably the wording applied with regard to states was 'responsibility', whereas the term used with regard to business enterprises was 'obligations'. According to the Draft Norms, within their 'spheres of influence' TNCs and other business enterprises have 'obligations to promote, secure the fulfilment of, respect, ensure respect of and protect human rights'. These tasks are normally defined as obligations (binding duties) of states under international human rights law, whereas responsibility often refers to softer political or moral duties.

The Commentary introduced the notion of due diligence in the context of business actions and human rights by noting that business enterprises 'shall have the responsibility to use due diligence in ensuring that their activities do not contribute directly or indirectly to human abuses, and that they do not directly or indirectly benefit from abuses of which they

---

[61] Weissbrodt and Kruger (n 36) at 913 with references at fn. 72.
[62] Draft Norms, para. 1.
[63] Ibid., preamble.
[64] Ibid., para. 1.

were aware or ought to have been aware'.[65] As will be seen in Chapter 5, the notion of corporate due diligence for human rights was one of the few elements of the Draft Norms to survive throughout the mandate of the SRSG, which followed the Human Rights Commission's rejection of the Draft Norms. Due diligence is included as part of the corporate responsibility to respect in the UN Framework that resulted from the SRSG's 2005–08 mandate,[66] and forms a major part of the elaboration of the corporate responsibility to respect in the UNGPs.

The Draft Norms' assertion that business entities have obligations for human rights was one of the major points of contention. At stake was whether and to what extent non-state actors may bear human rights obligations at all, and if so, how far those obligations extend. Related to this, the understanding of the notion of an enterprise's 'sphere of influence' was also a major point of contention. The term still figures in the Global Compact, but this particular notion did not survive the SRSG process with regard to clarification of business responsibilities for human rights, as will be elaborated in Chapter 5. Another significant point of contention concerned implementation provisions, and particularly the possibilities and potential difficulties to enforce the Draft Norms as international standards, given the absence of a relevant international enforcement machinery. Indeed, enforcement by national authorities would be highly contingent on each states' willingness and institutional capacity to ensure effective enforcement. A third notion that has been contentious in the discourse on business responsibilities for human rights, 'complicity', does not actually feature in the Norms. 'Complicity' is noted in the second Principle[67] of the UN Global Compact. The notion entered the debate on the Draft Norms through a consultation on business and human rights undertaken in late 2004 by the Office of the High Commissioner for Human Rights (OHCHR) in cooperation with the Global Compact Office. 'Complicity' formed part of the mandate of the SRSG, along with 'sphere of influence'[68] as elaborated in Chapter 5.

---

[65] Sub-Commission on the Promotion and Protection of Human Rights (n 57), Commentary (b) to para. 1.

[66] See further Chapter 4 and UN Framework, paras 56–64.

[67] Principle 2 of the Global Compact says, 'Businesses should make sure they are not complicit in human rights abuses' (United Nations Global Compact, 'The ten principles of the UN Global Compact: Principle two: Human Rights', available at https://www.unglobalcompact.org/what-is-gc/mission/principles/principle-2 (last accessed 5 January 2017)).

[68] Commission on Human Rights (2005) Human Rights and transnational corporations and other business enterprises, UN Doc. E/CN.4/2005/L.87, 15 April 2005, para. 1.

124 *Changing sustainability norms through communication processes*

In preparing the text, the working group consulted with some civil society organisations. In accordance with the general process for international human right law-making, human rights NGOs were from the outset considered an integral part of civil society to be consulted.[69] Consultations only in the later stages of the drafting process came to involve some business associations, such as the International Business Leaders Forum and the World Business Council for Sustainable Development.[70] That was so despite the fact that it had already been observed at the working group's second session that the input of companies, unions, NGOs and other interested parties should be sought in regard to the appropriate legal nature of the text that the working group was working on.[71] Some business organisations did not perceive the process to be sufficiently inclusive,[72] and some large business organisations opted out of the consultations, explaining that they simply objected to the overall approach of the Draft Norms with regard to businesses having responsibilities for human rights.[73]

After the Sub-Commission on the Promotion and Protection of Human Rights approved and released the final version of the Draft Norms in August 2003,[74] the text was referred to the Human Rights Commission for formal adoption.

The Commission discussed the Draft Norms at its annual session in 2004, but was unable to reach agreement and decided to take up the issue again at its next session, which was to take place in 2005. In its resolution issued at the 2004 meeting the Commission stated that the Norms 'as a draft proposal' had 'no legal standing'.[75] When it re-convened in 2005, the Commission did not deal further with the Draft Norms. Instead, it adopted the resolution that led to the process resulting in the UN Framework and UNGPs.

At the 2004 session of the Commission on Human Rights, the Norms

---

[69] Report of the sessional working group, 1st session (n 37), para. 32.

[70] For a more detailed account of the drafting process and stakeholders included, see Buhmann, K. (2018) *Power, Procedure, Participation and Legitimacy in Global Sustainability Norms: A Theory of Collaboratory Regulation*, Routledge, Ch. 3 (3.2.1).

[71] Report of the sessional working group, 2nd session (n 38), para. 29.

[72] Backer (n 10) at 321–7; Hearne (n 48).

[73] Hearne, ibid.

[74] In the form of a resolution: Sub-Commission on the Promotion and Protection of Human Rights (2003) Norms on the Responsibilities of Transnational Corporations and Other Business Enterprises with regard to Human Rights, UN Doc. E/CN.4/Sub.2/2003/12/Rev.2.

[75] Commission on Human Rights (2004) *Decision 2004/116*, UN Doc. E/CN.4/2004/L.73/Rev.1, 16 April 2004.

were received with hesitation by a number of member states, particularly some with strong corporate lobbies against regulation of human rights responsibilities of business.[76] Extensive lobbying had taken place by groups in favour of as well as groups opposed to the Norms. A group of business organisations, comprising i.a. the International Chamber of Commerce (ICC), the International Organisation of Employers (IOE), the United States Council of International Business, and the Confederation of British Industry had lobbied against the Norms.[77] Seeking to avoid a rejection of the text and therefore of the effort to develop guidance or eventually requirements for businesses with regard to human rights, a group of NGOs had urged the Commission to avoid a rushed decision, observing that 'the UN Norms deserve a chance to be more carefully studied (. . .) before any action is taken'.[78]

Despite the Commission's decision, the Draft Norms continued to linger for some time within the UN Human Rights system as well as externally. The Draft Norms were included in a multi-stakeholder consultation and report undertaken by the OHCHR at the request of the Commission in 2004 and 2005, respectively, on initiatives and standards on business and human rights. At its 2006 (and final) session, the Sub-Commission on the Promotion and Prevention of Human Rights recommended that the Human Rights Council (which had then replaced the Commission on Human Rights) adopt the Norms. It also requested that the Council establish a body to monitor compliance with the Norms.[79] None of the recommendations was adopted by the Human Rights Council. The Draft Norms feature indirectly as part of the background for the establishment of the mandate of the SRSG in 2005. Parts of the Draft Norms' substantive provisions were critically assessed by the SRSG in his first ('interim') report (February 2006) (see below Chapter 5). The Draft Norms were applied in pilot schemes ('road-tested') by a group of companies organised

---

[76] D. Kinley and R. Chambers (2006) 'The UN Human Rights Norms for corporations: The private implications of public international law', 6(3) *Human Rights Law Review* pp. 447–97.

[77] A. Warhurst and K. Cooper in association with Amnesty International (2004) *The 'UN Human Rights Norms for Business'*, Maplecroft: United Kingdom, 26 July 2004, at 15 with references.

[78] Ibid.

[79] International Service for Human Rights (2006) Sub-Commission on the Promotion and Protection of Human Rights, 58th session (Geneva, 7–25 August 2006) Item 4: Economic, Social and Cultural Rights, Geneva 2006; B. Thiele and M. Gomez (2006) 'Highlights of the fifty-eighth session of the United Nations Sub-Commission on the Promotion and Protection of Human Rights', 24(4) *Netherlands Quarterly of Human Rights* pp. 703–14, at 711 with references.

in the Business Leaders Initiative for Human Rights (BLIHR) for several years.[80]

Yet the Draft Norms were not specifically mentioned in the mandate of the SRSG, which was drafted by the Human Rights Commission at its session in 2005.[81] This was criticised by NGOs and some other stakeholders including some states.[82] The omission to explicitly mention the Draft Norms in the SRSG mandate resolution has been explained to mean that the Draft Norms might feed into the process, but that the process generally was to consider business responsibilities for human rights in a wider normative and regulatory perspective.[83]

As noted, the primary draftsman of the Draft Norms, Professor David Weissbrodt, had indicated that the Draft Norms were intended to evolve into a binding instrument.[84] In other contexts, however, he has described the intention in more open terms, indicating that 'the Norms are not legally binding, but are similar to many other UN declarations, principles, guidelines and standards that interpret existing law and summarize international practice without reaching the status of a treaty'.[85] This suggests

---

[80] The 'road-testing' of the Draft Norms which took place 2003–06 included various activities, such as the development of human rights management systems and implementation of specific human rights initiatives as part of participating companies' regular activities. The 'road-testing' was intended as an effort to see what aspects of the Norms were operational for business and which ones could be revised to become more operational. Issues identified as needing clarification included environmental and consumer protection and implementation mechanisms. See Business Leaders Initiative for Human Rights (2006) Report 3: Towards a 'Common Framework' on Business and Human Rights: Identifying Components, London, June 2006; see also Hearne (n 48); T. Webb (2004) Analysis: Human rights Norms at the UN, *Ethical Corporation*, 24 October 2004.

[81] Commission on Human Rights (n 68).

[82] See for example the comment by the representative of Mauritania at the occasion of the Human Rights Commission's vote on the resolution calling for the appointment of a Special Representative on business and human rights, United Nations (2005) Press Release: Commission requests Secretary-General to appoint Special Representative on Transnational Corporations. Commission on Human Rights, 20 April 2005, available at http://www.unhchr.ch/huricane/huricane.nsf/view01/F92E35AD92F360D3C1256FEA002BF653?opendocument (last accessed 19 January 2013; website has been removed).

[83] Information provided in 2006 to author by Danish Government representative who took part in the negotiation of the resolution.

[84] D. Weissbrodt and M. Kruger (2005) 'Human rights responsibilities of businesses as non-state actors'. In P. Alston (ed.) *Non-State Actors and Human Rights*, New York: Oxford University Press, pp. 315–50, at 339; Weissbrodt and Kruger (n 36) at 913.

[85] Weissbrodt (n 43) at 136.

a law-in-process approach, that might or might not proceed towards a legally binding instrument. Perhaps as a result of that confusion, perhaps due to limited knowledge on the complex process of international law-making, perhaps due to political reasons, and perhaps a combination of all of the above, in part of the business community the Draft Norms were described as already close to being a treaty.[86]

Although the title given to the instrument, 'Norms', was novel and contributed to confusion about the legal character and status of the instrument, the Draft Norms as such are best regarded as law-in-process input from a specialised body within the UN Human Rights system for possibly more formalised soft or hard regulation. Regardless of the novel title, the Draft Norms resemble much other early international law in terms of a drafting process, which begins with a law-in-the-making text that may gradually become couched and adopted in a traditional form of international soft law and even hardened into international treaty law through a process of revisions, refinements and sometimes more radical amendments. Moreover, in restating existing international law, the Draft Norms were not that unusual. For example, that approach resembled that which had shortly before been adopted to provide guidance on protection of Internally Displaced Persons through an instrument of international law.[87]

4.3.2 System-specific Communication

Negotiation summaries in session reports and other available statements relating to the debates that led to the Draft Norms generally applied legal or political system logics. The statements were addressed from transmitters with the same logic as direct and intended recipients, that is, other experts in the Working Group, involved civil society in consultative status (human rights NGOs), and members of the Sub-Commission to which the Working Group reported. Arguing in the legal and political logic was successful in activating the rationality of the recipients and paving the way for the acceptance of Working Group's and Sub-Commission's acceptance of the Draft Norms. By contrast, arguments in legal and political logic did not resonate with business associations. This combined with the perception of large business associations of being excluded from the process,

---

[86] T. Webb (2005) Comment: Lobby groups and NGOs should rethink their approach to the UN Norms, *Ethical Corporation*, 23 April 2004.

[87] M. Mutua (2007) 'Standard setting in human rights: critique and prognosis', 29(3) *Human Rights Quarterly* pp. 547–630.

resulting in opposition by a small number of business associations, which were, however, large and influential with their host governments.

In the time between the submission of the Draft Norms to the Commission and the Commission's formal debate in early 2004, business associations that opposed the initiative issued statements arguing against the idea and text of the Draft Norms. In November 2003, a joint statement submitted by ICC and the IOE to the Sub-Commission that drafted the Norms argued that the Draft Norms 'are counterproductive to the UN's ongoing efforts to encourage companies to support and observe human rights norms by participating in the Global Compact'.[88] Drawing on conventional international law doctrine, the three-page statement built on legal system rationality – that is, a rationality that was different from the economic rationality of the organisations that submitted the statement. In this manner the statement argued that the Draft Norms would run against the interests of national and international society in terms of implementation of human rights, and that it would shift responsibility and accountability from states to companies. It stated that the Draft Norms were 'circumventing national political and legal frameworks and establishing international legal obligations for multinational companies that do not exist at the national level and do not apply to domestic companies'.[89] The statement also employed a combination of political and economic rationality to refer to public policy interests that companies share or to which they contribute. Thus, it referred to companies' interest in 'improvement of social conditions, which are an important factor for stable development', and in conclusion noted that 'the draft "norms" would greatly discourage the very investment that is the best hope for economic development and improved human rights'.[90] Indicating that company self-regulation as well as existing intergovernmental tools (including the OECD Guidelines and the UN Global Compact) 'are designed to supplement' national law to protect human rights,[91] the submission also endorsed co- or self-regulation complementary to conventional command-control public law, suggesting in legal rationality terms that companies contribute to the implementation of states' international human rights obligation because they self-regulate

---

[88] International Chamber of Commerce and International Organisation of Employers (2003) 'Joint views of ICC and the IOE on the draft "Norms on the Responsibilities of Transnational Corporations and Other Business Enterprises with regard to Human Rights",' submitted to the United Nations Commission on Human Rights, 24 November 2003.
[89] Ibid.
[90] Ibid.
[91] Ibid.

based on international soft law. The total argument built was that business responsibilities for human rights should be left to companies themselves, and that institutionalisation of human rights responsibilities would be detrimental to legal and public policy interests of national governments as well as of the UN.

The ICC-IOE statement also employed legal system rationality to critique the Draft Norms for mixing voluntary action and mandatory requirements. Both are referred to as 'obligations', thus underscoring that the Draft Norms were perceived – or at least portrayed in the statement – to establish hard law for companies. At the same time, the statement sought to counter the idea that the Norms, if adopted, could be legally binding since 'many of the instruments they are drawn from are not themselves legally-binding'.[92] In this, the submission noted the Draft Norms' reference to a diversity of soft law instruments, such as the ILO Tripartite Declaration, OECD's Guidelines for Multinational Enterprises and the Global Compact. The statement also drew on legal system logic to argue that the Draft Norms might conflict with companies' obligations under national law in host states, for example to pay taxes. Presenting an arguably extreme example, the implicit argument was that paying taxes in host states where human rights violations take place might make a company complicit in the state's violations. One paragraph introduced economic system rationality, which in combination with legal system considerations created the argument that the Draft Norms would both force companies to break contracts and counteract legal certainty for contract partners. Even if the argument was far-reaching in comparison with the text of the Draft Norms, arguments like this deployed the political and legal rationality of regulators to refute the Draft Norms with national authorities and international organisations. Since regulators and policy-makers normally do not support tax avoidance and do encourage legal certainty in their own states as well as host states, the arguments would resonate directly with policy-makers and regulators. If those recipients were to challenge the views presented in the submission, they would risk challenging their own views on tax payment and on legal certainty in developing countries and emerging economies, both of which had been major focal points in politics of the UN, the World Bank, and many Global North-based states in the 1990s.

Applying the model introduced in Chapter 3, Figure 4.1 below illustrates some of these dynamics.

Partly due to corporate lobbying, partly due to opposition with some

---

[92] Ibid.

130 *Changing sustainability norms through communication processes*

Transmitter
Human Rights experts

Context
Human rights experts in UN human rights setting
Audience-specific: A: human rights experts; civil society
Towards end: B: companies

Message
"Businesses have obligations for their impact on human rights"

Code (audience-specific)
A) a) Legal system interests (business respect, promotion and securing of human rights within their 'sphere of influence')
b) Political system interests (business contributions to human rights policy goals; also consumer and environmental objectives)

B) Legal and political system interests (same as under A a) and A b))

Contact
(Establishment of 'irritation' based on understanding within sub-system of interests at stake)

Recipient
A) States, civil society
B) Companies

Reaction
Internalisation of externalities mixed
⇨ A) Mixed acceptance
⇨ B) Resistance

A: Perturbation internalisation: support for and acceptance of Draft Norms
Productive contact because connected with core functions

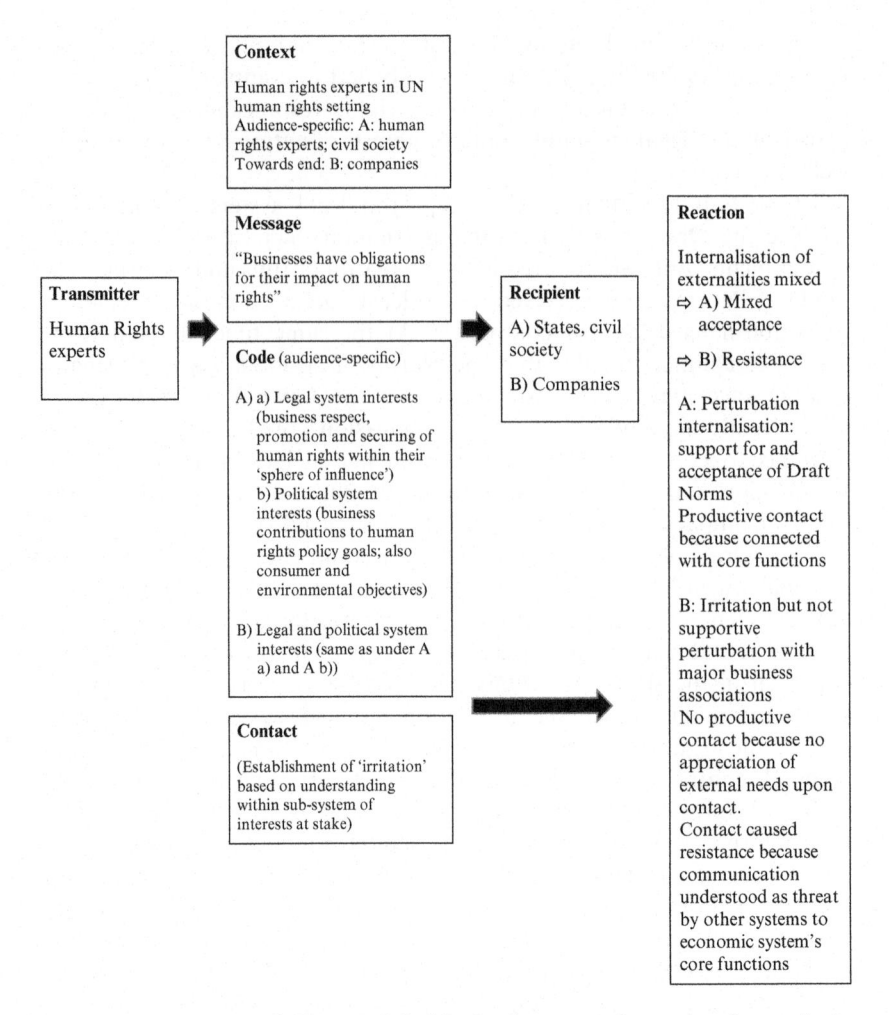

B: Irritation but not supportive perturbation with major business associations
No productive contact because no appreciation of external needs upon contact.
Contact caused resistance because communication understood as threat by other systems to economic system's core functions

Figure 4.1   UN Draft Norms: Model of relations and reaction for analysis of system-specific interest-based arguments

governments, the Draft Norms failed being approved by the Commission on Human Rights. The opposition was most likely caused by a plurality of factors, including the Draft Norms' use and elaboration of particular terms, the extent of and process for inclusion of business, and uncertainty concerning the intended regulatory implications for businesses (and for states). Within that context, arguments made by some large business organisations as well as governments opposed to the Draft Norms claimed that the idea of the UN developing norms for business conduct with regard to human rights went counter to the basic assumption of international law that states are bearers of international duties, and therefore also for human rights. The opposition suggests that the text of the Draft Norms and arguments that had been made in the process of promoting them had not successfully explained the case for business responsibilities for human rights. It had neither convinced governments of the benefits that might result from their effective implementation of their own obligations for human rights, nor convinced certain (perhaps few but influential) business associations of the benefits that they and their members might gain from an increased internalisation of societal expectations for business to take responsibility for their impact on human rights.

4.4 THE UNITED NATIONS GLOBAL COMPACT

4.4.1 The Originality of the Global Compact

The UN Global Compact became the first UN initiative to develop normative guidance for businesses with regard to their impact on society to be formally launched into operation. Whereas the Draft Code of Conduct and Draft Norms projects had made it to a full text, the texts were never adopted by the relevant regulatory bodies charged with the competence to agree on new international law instruments. By contrast, the Global Compact project did not aim at developing new normative international instruments of a legal character. Rather, the Global Compact was structured as a set of brief principles, which all rely on existing international law instruments that had been formally adopted and therefore had official status. Moreover, the Compact was set up in a manner that did not require the Compact's principles to be formally adopted by a UN body with the competence to agree on new legal instruments. (However, as elaborated below the Global Compact did obtain regular approval by the UN's highest political organ, the General Assembly, through a series of declarations on globalisation.)

The process to set up the UN Global Compact was launched almost at the same time as the drafting of the Draft Norms took off. In terms of delivering a result that was approved and adopted, the Global Compact process was more successful, even taking the differences between the Norms and Global Compact projects into account. The process resulted in agreement on nine Principles in three issue areas: human rights (Principles 1–2), labour rights (Principles 3–6), and environment (Principles 7–9). Announced in 2000, the original nine Principles within three issue areas build on international soft law in the respective issue areas: The UDHR, ILO's Declaration on Fundamental Principles and Rights at Work, and the Rio Declaration on Environment and Development.[93] A fourth issue area and Principle 10 on anti-corruption were added in 2004 with a normative reference to the UN Convention against Corruption,[94] which had been adopted in 2003.

The Global Compact differs from the Draft Norms by explicitly being only guiding, and by not laying claim to being regulatory or becoming any sort of legal text. However, in practical terms the differences were not crucial. That is so at least in view of the fact that the Draft Norms, if they had been adopted, would have been a law-in-the-making instrument, and in the line of international law-making most likely not have evolved into a conventional soft law instrument for some time, let alone into a legally binding convention. Moreover, there were considerable normative overlaps between the Draft Norms and the Global Compact. This is clear from the normative sources of the Compact and the detailed guidance provided by the Compact's website, which also elaborates on the international instruments that inform the principles and provide information on the more detailed human rights conventions that elaborate the UDHR standards, or the international labour conventions that embody the rights referred to by the ILO's 1998 Declaration. The normativity of the Global Compact may easily be underestimated because the text of each of the Principles is brief. However, with the Compact being mainly an internet-based instrument, the normative richness becomes obvious to those who explore the guidance provided by the ever deeper and ever more information-heavy links. The Compact's website has been subject to several revisions since it was first launched, but the ten Principles remain a core of the initiative in regard to guidance for companies for their actions with a particular regard to not doing harm.[95]

Whereas the Draft Norms were effectively dismissed by the Commission on Human Rights in 2004, the Global Compact was accepted in 2000 by a resolution adopted by the UN General Assembly, with support for the initiative renewed at regular (annual or bi-annual) intervals. Since then,

---

[93] United Nations General Assembly (1992) Rio Declaration on Environment and Development (United Nations Conference on Environment and Development: Annex 1: Declaration on Environment and Development), UN Doc. A/CONF.151/26 (Vol. I), 12 August 1992.

[94] United Nations General Assembly (2003) United Nations Convention against Corruption, UN Doc. A/58/422, 31 October 2003.

[95] See https://www.unglobalcompact.org/what-is-gc/mission/principles (revision January 2017, last accessed 13 January 2017).

the UN General Assembly has regularly supported the Global Compact through a series of resolutions on Public-Private-Partnerships.

The normative overlaps makes it relevant to consider what may explain the vastly different outcomes of the Global Compact project as compared to the Draft Norms project. Three obvious differences may account for part of the explanation: first, the Global Compact was an initiative launched by the UN Secretary-General, whereas the Draft Norms project was initiated by an expert working group under a Sub-Commission under the Human Rights Commission, which itself reported to ECOSOC and did not enjoy the standing in the UN hierarchy that the Human Rights Council does. Second, the Global Compact was explicitly not designed to become a legal instrument. In fact, the Secretary-General and his staff, who for practical purposes acted as the architects of the initiative, went to great lengths to highlight that the instrument was not 'regulatory', despite every intention, as noted, being to provide normative directives for businesses on their activities. There has never been any doubt that the Global Compact has no ambitions to become a legally binding instrument. (This, of course, is different from the situation when observance of one or more of the Global Compact Principles is made a legally binding requirement on a company through a contract between two or more economic entities, such as a buyer and a supplier.) Third, the Global Compact was developed through a multi-stakeholder process that involved business representatives. Whereas the Draft Norms process focused on civil society consultation, especially during the early parts of the process, the Global Compact process prioritised the inclusion of business representatives. Taking place during 1999 and early 2000 and therefore roughly at the same time as the early sessions leading to the Draft Norms, the process towards the Global Compact invited companies committed to CSR and CEOs with a similar commitment to take part in the efforts to debate the normative foundations and organisation of the initiative.[96] Almost representing an inversion of the Draft Norms process and almost leading to a similar failure, the Global Compact process only invited civil society organisations representing human rights, labour and environmental expertise to join the process some time after it had already begun, and the invitation only went out to selected organisations.[97] The inclusion of civil society succeeded in

---

[96] Ibid.

[97] Three NGOs were selected in the area of human rights: Human Rights Watch, Lawyers Committee for Human Rights and Amnesty International. Four environmental NGOs joined the Compact: the World Wildlife Fund for Nature, the International Union for Conservation of Nature, the World Resources Institute and the International Institute for Environment and Development. Save

134 *Changing sustainability norms through communication processes*

averting an almost fully-fledged legitimacy crisis, and the Compact initiative was successful in gaining support with public and private stakeholders, although resistance remained with parts of the UN system[98] and some academics[99] even after it was launched in mid-2000.

Two additional and partly interrelated points may be as important for the Compact's success as compared to the fate of the Draft Norms, in particular regarding the role that lobbying by business associations opposed to the initiative appears to have played. The first of these concerns is the setting and context in which the idea of the Global Compact took off. The second concerns the arguments with which the benefits of the Compact were explained to businesses, starting with the speech by the Secretary-General that also effectively kicked off the process to develop the Global Compact, although it had not been expected or even intended to lead to such an initiative.

4.4.2 The Discursive Evolution of the Global Compact and its Normative Guidance

Without an original ambition to become what it soon did, the Global Compact project took off during the World Economic Forum in 1999, a meeting for large economic actors. A speech[100] delivered by Kofi Annan, who was then the Secretary-General of the UN, presented the idea of business cooperation with the UN as an alternative to political or legal measures which might restrict the liberty of business. At the same time, the objective was tied to the goals of the UN as established in the UN Charter (that is, to maintain international peace; develop friendly relations among

---

the Children, the Ring Network and Transparency International were selected for their particular competencies in key areas. The ILO generally represented labour concerns. G. Kell and D. Levin (2002) 'The evolution of the Global Compact Network: an historic experiment in learning and action', paper presented at The Academy of Management Annual Conference 'Building Effective Networks', Denver, August 11–14, 2002, http://www.unglobalcompact.org/docs/news_events/9.5/denver.pdf (last accessed 22 January 2017), at 10.

[98] P. L. Fall and M. M. Zahran (2010) 'United Nations corporate partnerships: The role and functioning of the Global Compact', United Nations: Joint Inspection Unit, UN doc. JIU/REP/2010/9.

[99] Nolan (n 9).

[100] K. Annan (1999) Address of Secretary-General Kofi Annan to the World Economic Forum in Davos, Switzerland, 31 January, UN Press release SG/SM/6881, 1 February 1999 (Secretary-General proposes Global Compact on human rights, labour, environment, in address to World Economic Forum in Davos), http://www.un.org/News/Press/docs/1999/19990201.sgsm6881.html (accessed 17 December 2016), also reprinted in McIntosh, Waddock and Kell (n 14) pp. 28–31.

nations; achieve international cooperation in solving international problems of an economic, social, cultural, or humanitarian character, and in promoting and encouraging respect for human rights and for fundamental freedoms for all without distinction; and for the UN to be a centre of harmonisation for these ends).[101] The role of social expectations on business and the pressure that social groups exert on political decision-makers and legislators came across as key reasons in explaining the background and idea of the initiative to the audience. The Secretary-General observed that the past years had shown 'that the goals of the United Nations and those of business can, indeed, be mutually supportive' and proceeded to 'challenge' the business leaders present 'to join me in taking our relationship to a still higher level. I propose that you, the business leaders gathered in Davos, and we, the United Nations, initiate a global compact of shared values and principles, which will give a human face to the global market'.[102]

The speech played on the economic interests at stake for companies and their rationality of opportunities for profit and reducing loss. It articulated those interests in the light of the pressure that concerned stakeholders and networks may exert on governments and intergovernmental organisations to introduce restrictions on the international trade regime in order to balance trade and human rights, labour rights and environmental practices. Referring to the legislative power of governments and the UN (through governments) to introduce measures towards engaging companies in contributing to public policy objectives, the speech built an argument for economic actors to self-regulate (become 'allies in' UN efforts to 'improve labour conditions, human rights and environmental quality')[103] rather than to become regulated. This part of the argument combined economic system interests related to trade and investments with references to political system rationality, articulating the UN goals as policy objectives and concerns of 'various interest groups', and noting a potential use of law that might restrict international business ('to load the trade regime and investment agreements with restrictions').[104] That led up to an assertion combining legal and policy objectives of the UN goals to deliver the key point on the benefits to companies resulting from their self-regulating activity with regard to themselves and their business relations, stating that companies can 'uphold human rights and decent labour and environmental standards directly'.[105]

---

[101] United Nations Charter, art. 1.
[102] Annan (n 100).
[103] Ibid.
[104] Ibid.
[105] Ibid.

While the speech was initially only intended to turn business managers and CEOs to pay more attention to their social impact,[106] its effects by far exceeded that objective. A number of the audience members approached the Secretary-General to inquire how they might join the 'compact' that he had referred to in the speech. This was the impetus for the Secretary-General and his close staff to set in motion a process to develop what soon became known formally as the UN Global Compact.[107] The original three issue areas and their core normative sources also took point of departure in the speech, thereby tapping into the support that it had received. The Secretary-General called on the audience to 'embrace, support and enact a set of core values in the areas of human rights, labour standards, and environmental practices' and added:

> Why those three? In the first place, because they are the areas where you, as businessmen and women, can make a real difference. Secondly, they are the areas in which universal values have already been defined by international agreements including the Universal Declaration, the International Labour Organisation's Declaration on Fundamental Principles and Rights at Work, and the Rio Declaration of the United Nation's Conference on Environment and Development in 1992. Finally, I chose these three areas because they are ones where I fear that, if we do not act, there may be a threat to the global market, and especially to the multilateral trade regime.[108]

Overall, the speech built an argument that respect for international law on human rights, labour rights and environmental sustainability would benefit businesses directly, based on the very fact that the principles are based in universal standards and that 'if we do not act', the long-term sustainability of the global market and the multilateral trade regime may be at risk.[109] Moreover, it argued that businesses can contribute to promoting the goals of the UN according to its Charter. The combined argument, therefore, was that businesses may act socially as well as economically (safeguarding their economic interests) responsibly by upholding human rights, labour rights and environmental standards. This line of argument, which underscored the economic benefits of business paying respect to international standards and societal needs, differs markedly from that which was promoted as part of the process towards the Draft Norms, which focused on the adverse impacts that businesses caused and referred

---

[106] Personal communication on 8 November 2007 with John Ruggie, who in his capacity as Assistant Secretary-General took part in writing the speech.
[107] Ibid.; Kell and Levin (n 97).
[108] Annan (n 100).
[109] Ibid.

to obligations. The Secretary-General's Davos speech referred to business rationalities and spoke of businesses as partners in a joint endeavour, underscoring that this might reduce the risk of limitations on business and promote or open up business opportunities. The Draft Norms referred to potentially legally binding obligations, which could be understood to limit business opportunities. UN staff involved in establishing and promoting the Global Compact continued along the former line of argument, speaking to businesses by activating their rationalities.[110] However, they also invoked public policy rationalities when addressing governments. That occurred in resolutions addressing the UN General Assembly, which is composed of the UN's Member States. Initially not making direct reference to the Global Compact, these bi-annual resolutions were proposed in order to secure formal UN support for the initiative.[111]

The Compact's principles and general structure were developed in detail through a consultative multi-stakeholder process, which involved the UN Secretary-General and representatives for his office, as well as the ILO, the United Nations Environment Programme (UNEP), the OHCHR, the Secretary-General of the ICC (which readers are reminded throughout this book refers to the International Chamber of Commerce, and not the International Criminal Court) and representatives from a number of companies, especially TNCs. By March 1999, the ILO, UNEP and OHCHR had decided to develop a website on the (then) nine principles, which were evolving. In July 1999, the Secretary-General and heads of ILO, UNEP and OHCHR met with the ICC's president and Secretary-General and around 15 CEOs. Contacts were also established with the IOE, representing employers.[112] Discussions at this time focused on trade, which according to two of the Global Compact's architects, Georg Kell and

---

[110] See further, K. Buhmann (2014) *Normative Discourses and Public-Private Regulatory Strategies for Construction of CSR Normativity: Towards a Method for Above-National Public-Private Regulation of Business Social Responsibilities.* Copenhagen: Multivers, esp. Ch. 4 (4.1.1).

[111] See especially UN General Assembly, Towards global partnerships: Resolution adopted by the General Assembly [on the report of the Second Committee (A/60/495 and Corr.1)], UN Doc. A/RES/60/215/, 29 March 2006 (passed 22 December 2005); UN General Assembly, Towards global partnerships: Resolution adopted by the General Assembly, UN Doc. A/RES/58/129, 19 December 2003; UN General Assembly, Towards global partnerships: Resolution adopted by the General Assembly, UN Doc. A/RES/56/76, passed 11 December 2001; UN General Assembly, Towards global partnerships: Resolution adopted by the General Assembly, UN Doc. A/RES/55/215, passed 21 December 2000; and Buhmann, ibid., Ch. 4. (4.1.2.1).

[112] Kell and Levin (n 97).

David Levin, was perceived by business 'as a tool to secure and perpetuate economic liberalization'.[113] By November 1999, it was decided to shift collaboration with business, from business organisations to individual CEOs with an explicit CSR commitment.[114] Initial networking between various types of stakeholders did not prove easy, partly due to divergence in priorities between business and civil society and civil society's apprehension that the UN was about to compromise its integrity by collaborating with business.[115] According to Georg Kell, a first meeting with business representatives, held in London and comprising around 30 corporations from various countries, 'discussed methods of operationalizing the Global Compact but became mired in unproductive cross talk, partially due to the incongruence of civil service and business parlance'.[116] However, despite an admitted 'failure to define structures and operational concepts, the meeting ended with a strong commitment to continue collaboration' and 'a powerful message from these business representatives that the cooperation of labour and NGOs was needed to make the initiative credible'.[117]

Representatives for the international labour movement (the International Confederation of Free Trade Unions (ICFTU) and the International Federation of Chemical, Energy, Mine and General Workers' Union (ICEM)) only became involved in the development of the Global Compact somewhat later in the process. When that happened, they expressed support for the Global Compact as a modality for promoting ILO core labour rights. Much of the labour movement and some employers' associations had originally been hesitant towards the idea of the Global Compact.[118] The international labour movement (comprising both unions and employers organisations) and the ILO as such have long grappled with CSR as a notion and how to handle it.[119] Eventually, however, the process was made sufficiently inclusive and the strategic argumentation convincing for the initiative to gain support among stakeholders from the labour movement and civil society as well as business.

Speeches and other statements made in the context of the development

---

[113] Ibid.
[114] Ibid.
[115] Global Compact Critics Blog, at: http://www.globalcompactcritics.net/ (last accessed 31 January 2013; website has been closed).
[116] Kell and Levin (n 97).
[117] Ibid.
[118] Ibid., at 8.
[119] M. Hopkins, (2006) 'Commentary: What is Corporate Social Responsibility all about? 6 *Journal of Public Affairs* August–November, pp. 298–306 at 301; see also International Labour Office (2003) 'Corporate social responsibility: Myth or reality?', Geneva: ILO labour education series 2003/1.

of the Global Compact or explaining the Compact to various audiences show that the Global Compact was developed through a discursive strategy that emphasised economic concerns and benefits to companies, while the institutional legal dimensions of the set-up were downplayed. Downplaying institutional legal dimensions meant that those dimensions which would cause the Global Compact to be considered to possess qualities or features of legal institutions, such as formally binding codes of conduct, enforcement mechanisms or complaints handling, were described in ways that generally denied that the Global Compact holds such dimensions. The political system issues of the Global Compact idea and set-up were referred to but did not play a major role. From the outset, it was made clear that the Global Compact normatively related to UN objectives on human rights, labour standards and environment, and that the normative sources for the Global Compact and its principles were international law instruments on those issues.

4.4.3 System-specific Communication

With the formal launch of the Global Compact in mid-2000 and the acceptance given to the initiative by the UN General Assembly, the Global Compact project was successful in developing normative guidance for businesses with regard to their social impact. Building on a close connection to UN goals, the Compact was set up to have a particular focus on human rights, labour standards (in particular core labour rights, which are also human rights), the environment and from 2004 anti-corruption. The process was successful in obtaining broad stakeholder agreement on the Global Compact Principles, allowing the initiative to be officially launched only 18 months after Kofi Annan's speech in Davos. From the outset and as demonstrated by the Davos 1999 speech, Kofi Annan and other Global Compact architects who worked closely with him argued the relevance of human rights and other UN goals to businesses by articulating the economic benefits to companies of actively working with the UN on these issues, and of adopting the principles. Such statements activated the economic rationality by referring to potential economic losses, such as those that might directly or indirectly result from a larger body of binding rules pertaining to business conduct, or economic sanctions by market actors.

The majority of statements on the Global Compact related to its creation, objectives and method of work employed arguments that incorporated system-specific interests of the recipient or recipients. Thus, statements addressing audiences that comprise companies made reference to economic system interests (such as international trade, freedom of enterprise, reputation, risks and risk management, or simply profits), and those that address civil society organisations concerned with the impact of business on environmental and social sustainable development made reference to related public policy objectives. Those that addressed the UN General Assembly or other audiences of politicians and international lawmakers made reference to the UN objectives in terms of public policy and/or legal objectives of the UN and of states.

UN staff involved in setting up the UN Global Compact applied system-specific language with emphasis on the particular interests of a specific audience in order to cause change within or by the systems to which the specific communications were addressed. Statements intended to make the private sector or its organisations support or join the Global Compact were made in economic system logic. Those that aimed at generating General Assembly support for cooperation with the private sector or express such support through the adoption of resolutions were phrased in political and legal system language with particular emphasis on the UN goals. Those that aimed at convincing civil society of the Compact's potential to address and promote public policy interests were phrased in language that activated their political system logic with an emphasis on specific sustainability issues or potentially adverse or positive business impact.

The website and its links elaborated the Global Compact Principles by providing details and references to international law standards established in conventions on human and labour rights. The statements presented the Global Compact to companies as a method to pre-empt hard regulation through self-regulation, while at the same time contributing to UN Goals based on a set of principles linked to international declarations. To civil society and states, the statements presented the initiative as a modality to involve the private sector in the solution of public policy and legal objectives based on international law on human rights, labour rights, environmental sustainability and (since 2004) anti-corruption. UN staff who formed part of the Global Compact architects addressed the international labour movement or employers in statements that made reference to social development for workers or business in wording that aligned both with the legal objectives of international labour law, policy objectives of social and business development in a wider sense, and power issues related to the role of the international labour movement. Although statements made by UN staff did not neglect the particular interests of the UN within the Global Compact issue areas, the majority of statements gave more attention to the system-specific interests of recipients than those of the transmitter.

Drawing on the model outlined in Chapter 3, Figure 4.2 depicts examples of the deployment of system-specific arguments:

Two steps forward, one back 141

Transmitter	Context			Reaction
	Setting-up and explaining the UN Global Compact Audience-specific: Civil society, states, companies, International labour			

Context

Setting-up and explaining the UN Global Compact
Audience-specific: Civil society, states, companies, International labour

Message

A) "Global Compact assists in implementation of UN goals"

B) "Global Compact participation assists in pre-empting hard law"

Code (audience-specific)

A) a) Political system interests (public-policy objectives on social and economic development, environmental sustainability)

b) Legal system interests (respect and fulfilment of human and labour rights; non-corrupt practices, respect environmental law)

B) Economic system interests (trade options; reduce risks that affect profits)

Contact

(Establishment of 'irritation' based on understanding within sub-system of interests at stake)

Transmitter

Global Compact architects (UN staff working with UN Secretary-General/UN Global Compact Office)

Recipient

A) States, civil society, intl. labour movement

B) Companies

Reaction

Internalisation of externalities

⇨ A) Accept

⇨ B) Accept; self-regulation

(A + B) Perturbation/ internalisation: UN Global Compact as a means towards protections of system-specific interests

A: a) Public policy interests

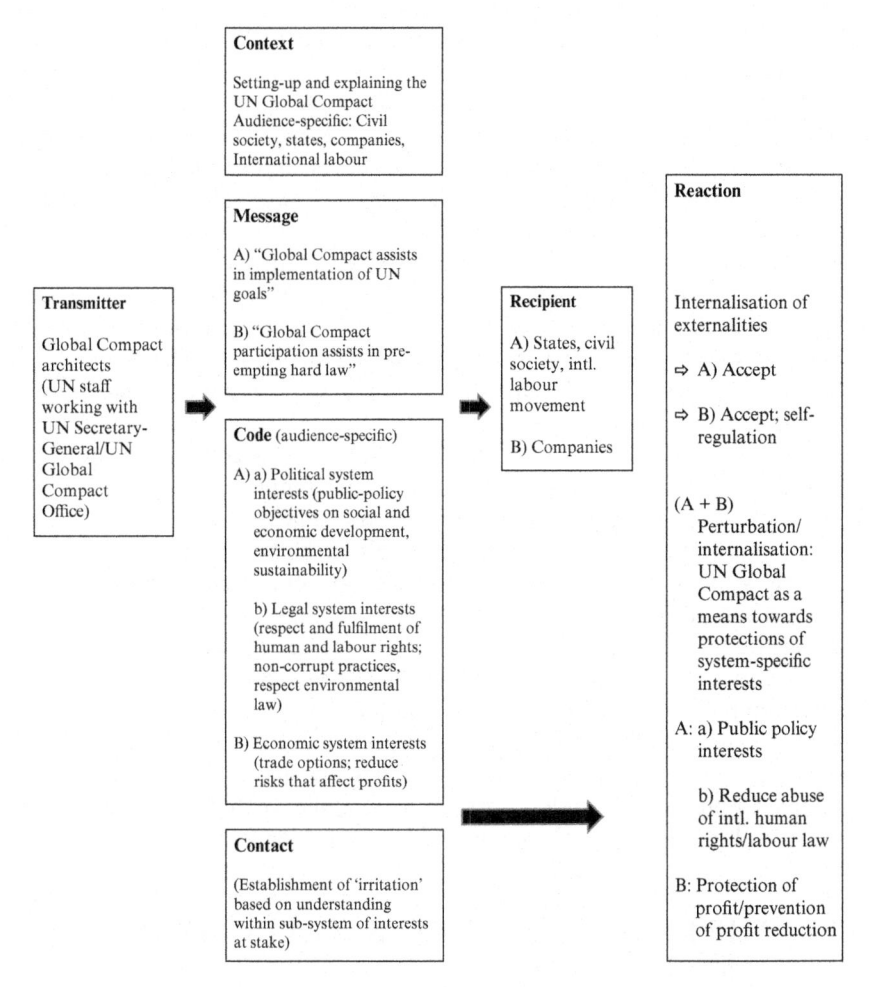

b) Reduce abuse of intl. human rights/labour law

B: Protection of profit/prevention of profit reduction

Figure 4.2   UN Global Compact: Model of relations and reaction for analysis of system-specific interest-based arguments

Arguments relating to the system-specific interests of the recipient drew on system-specific logic represented in terminology, language, observations or considerations as linguistic means to establish irritation and cause perturbation within the recipient sub-system(s). For states, civil society and the labour movement, perturbation led to adaptation to accept the idea of the Global Compact as a regulatory method under the UN to promote human rights, labour rights, environmental sustainability and anti-corruption. For businesses, it led to acceptance of the normative foundations on which the Compact builds, and to let these normative foundations feed into self-regulation.

By including business organisations and CEOs in the process of developing the Global Compact initiative and its Principles, businesses were given an active say, reducing the risk that they would baulk at the Global Compact as an initiative that sought to impose duties on them or counter it as an effort to shift public obligations on to business. Moreover, this enabled business representatives to be exposed to the concerns, needs and expectations of other stakeholders, including UN bodies charged with human rights and the environment, the ILO and labour organisations, and civil society organisations. In line with the theory of social autopoiesis and in combination with statements deploying economic system logic, businesses were therefore exposed to irritation, which generated internal perturbation that eventually supported a process of accepting new norms for business conduct, expressed by the Global Compact Principles.

Civil society participation was limited to a small number of organisations, but those that participated brought a high degree of expertise on the issue areas to the process and offering practical insights on the implication of business impact on the ground. This fed into the website's detailed guidance, which spells out how businesses can act to implement the Compact's principles, and explains how their economic activities may affect human rights, labour, the environment, or how they should act to avoid being involved in practice of corruption. As the website's detailed guidance is mainly addressed to companies that have committed to the Global Compact's principles, it speaks to an audience that already accepts the overall normative guidance offered by the principles.

4.5 THE EUROPEAN MULTI-STAKEHOLDER FORUM ON CSR

Because of the success that the UN as a global organisation had in developing the Global Compact and obtaining broad stakeholder support for the normative guidance provided by the ten Principles, it could have been expected to be simple for the EU, a Global North-based regional organisation with a strong policy and legal commitment to human and labour rights in national, international and even transnational relations, to develop and achieve stakeholder approval of a somewhat similar initiative and even to exceed the Global Compact in ambitions. Between 1999 and 2004 the EU's three political institutions – the European Parliament, Council, and the Commission – sought to develop what they referred to as a Code of Conduct or a European framework on CSR. However, the final output, which was published in a report resulting from a multi-stakeholder process (the European MSF on CSR) comprising a number of European business associations and civil society, was quite a long way from the original ambitious objectives expressed by, in particular, the European Parliament and the Commission. To place the two empirical EU cases into the overall context, the main European policy measures on CSR that framed those two cases are introduced below in section 4.5.1 before the MSF is discussed in section 4.5.2 and the CSR Alliance in section 4.6.

4.5.1 EU Policy Initiatives Towards Normative Guidance on CSR 1999–2002

With a strong human rights focus, EU activities towards setting norms for CSR began in 1999 when the European Parliament adopted two policy resolutions, one targeting the international trade system and international labour standards,[120] the other proposing a 'Code of Conduct' for European TNCs.[121] The text of the resolutions paid considerable attention to international human rights law as a normative source for CSR. The Parliament also argued that a legal basis should be created for the development of EU law on company conduct, and offered proposals for alternative regulatory modalities in the absence of a legal basis in the EU treaties for introducing coercive law requiring companies to engage in CSR. It should be noted that the European Parliament may launch such initiatives as invitations to the Commission and Council to develop detailed policies, but it does not have the powers to develop and adopt them on its own.

The Parliament highlighted international human rights law as its intended normative source for business conduct with regard to social impact. The resolutions provided examples of specific rights and explicit reference to both hard and soft law instruments from the UN and the ILO, including but not limited to ILO core conventions, the ICESCR, the ICCPR, the ILO Tripartite Declaration of Principles concerning Multinational Enterprises and Social Policy and the OECD Guidelines for Multinational Enterprises. Human rights and international labour law issues were strongly present in the substance of the suggested Code

---

[120] European Parliament (1999) Resolution on the Communication from the Commission to the Council on the trading system and internationally recognised labour standards (COM(96)0402 – C4048896), A4-0423/98, adopted on 13 January 1999, OJ 1999 C104/63 14 April 1999.

[121] European Parliament (1999) Resolution on EU standards for European enterprises operating in developing countries: towards a European Code of Conduct, OJ C 104/180, EP Resolution A4-0508/98, adopted on 15 January 1999.

of Conduct. Whereas the environment was noted only in general terms, extensive reference was made to international human rights and labour standards, indicating that those international law elements were given high priority by the drafters. Several specific rights covered by international labour law and international human rights law (occupational health and safety, freedom from forced, bonded and child labour, several types of women's and indigenous peoples rights, all of which are covered by both of these types of international law) were mentioned specifically in addition to a general reference to 'basic human rights'.[122]

In its 'Resolution on the trading system and internationally recognised labour standards', the European Parliament also called on the Commission to take action by proposing that a Code of Conduct be drawn up based on ILO fundamental principles and other 'minimum applicable international standards'.[123]

The European Commission followed up by issuing two policy papers: a Green Paper on 'Promoting a European Framework for Corporate Social Responsibility' issued in 2001,[124] and a Commission Communication on 'Corporate Social Responsibility: A business contribution to sustainable development'[125] issued in 2002. The Green Paper argued that corporations should take social responsibility on a voluntary basis. It stressed that human rights form an important dimension of CSR, particularly in relation to international operations and global supply chains, and made reference to soft law instruments such as the ILO Tripartite Declaration and the OECD Guidelines.[126] The Communication stated, inter alia, that corporations should exercise social responsibility in relation to the third world. It explicitly encouraged companies to take ILO labour standards and OECD's Guidelines as minimum standards in their codes of conduct.[127]

In 2006, a new Commission Communication linked CSR especially to the so-called Lisbon Goals (elaborated below), but retained reference to some human and labour rights aspects related to non-EU rela-

---

[122] European Parliament Committee on Development and Cooperation (1998) Report on EU standards for European Enterprises operating in developing countries: towards a European Code of Conduct, A4-0508/98, 17 December 1998, at 17.
[123] European Parliament (n 121), para. 19.
[124] Commission of the European Communities (2001) Promoting a European Framework for Corporate Social Responsibility COM(2001)366.
[125] Commission of the European Communities (2002) Corporate Social Responsibility: A business contribution to sustainable development COM(2002)347.
[126] Commission of the European Communities (n 124) s. 2.2.3.
[127] Commission of the European Communities (n 125), s. 5.1.

tions.[128] However, the 2006 Communication had abandoned the idea of a European 'Framework' or specific set of normative guidance for CSR. The 2005 launch of the SRSG process, which was supported by EU States, may have been a partial reason for that decision. However and as importantly, as elaborated in the following, the results of the MSF process that was launched based on the 2001 Green Paper and the 2002 Communication were not encouraging for the EU Commission to take another go at developing a specific and ambitious European normative 'Framework' on CSR.

Several of the EU's so-called Lisbon Goals on employability, inclusiveness, lifelong learning and responsible competitiveness were referred to by the Commission in its 2001 Green Paper, and the 2001 and 2006 Communications on CSR. These 'goals' are related to human rights, although that point is rarely made explicit. The Lisbon goals (not to be confused with the 2009 'Lisbon Treaty' (Treaty on the Functioning of the European Union, TFEU)) are contained in the so-called Lisbon Strategy, an EU policy which was adopted in March 2000 by EU heads of state and government.[129] The Lisbon goals were formulated as welfare society policy objectives with particular reference to the political economy interests of employment, inclusive and cohesive societies and international competitiveness. Some of the Lisbon goals, however – especially those on lifelong learning, equal opportunities and social inclusion – correspond to legal claims or rights to non-discrimination in the labour market and beyond. These claims and rights are provided by constitutions or statutory law in some EU Member States. They are also legal obligations of Member States under, at least, the ICESCR and the European Social Charter[130] (a Council of Europe treaty that is the social and economic rights sister instrument of the civil and political rights oriented European Convention on Human Rights (ECHR)). In EU terminology, the Lisbon Goal of 'responsible competitiveness' refers to a policy aim according to which European companies are to be competitive in the global market without violating international core labour rights or working with suppliers who violate these rights.

---

[128] Commission of the European Communities (2006) Communication from the Commission to the European Parliament, the Council and the European Economic and Social Committee: Implementing the Partnership for Growth and Jobs.

[129] See Council of the European Union (2000) Presidency conclusions, Lisbon European Council, 23 and 24 March 2000.

[130] Council of Europe (1961) European Social Charter, Strasbourg, ETS No. 35; Council of Europe (1996) European Social Charter (Revised), Strasbourg, ETS No. 163.

As a means to achieving those public policy objectives, in March 2000 the European Council made 'a special appeal to companies' corporate sense of responsibility regarding best practices on lifelong learning, work organisation, equal opportunities, social inclusion and sustainable development'.[131] This, too, underscores the implicit human rights elements of the Lisbon Strategy. When the Strategy was revised in 2005 it was decided to place renewed focus on growth, innovation and employment (with considerable focus on employment and jobs), and to encourage the strengthening of social cohesion and the mobilisation of national and community resources in the Strategy's economic, social and environmental dimensions. The European Council stressed that to achieve the goals, the EU would strive to make the regulatory environment more business friendly, adding, however, that 'business must in turn develop its sense of social responsibility'.[132] Thus, CSR was widely drawn upon by EU institutions to promote the Lisbon goals and general EU human and labour rights objectives in various contexts at around the same time as the Draft Norms and the Global Compact were developed and rejected or launched, respectively.

In the absence of a legal basis for the EU to legislate on a CSR Code of Conduct and similar initiatives as proposed by the Parliament, efforts to turn policy into institutionalised practice would have to be based on other measures within the EU's competences. The 2001 Green Paper was the first actual EU policy document on CSR, setting out to a large audience of stakeholders what might become EU policy. It listed elements to be considered in a CSR policy, in particular related to societal need and potential benefits of CSR from public and private (business) perspectives, the appropriate form of regulation and the normative role to be played by international human rights and labour law. As a policy document from the Commission, the Green Paper was addressed to EU policy-makers, particularly the European Parliament, the Council, Member States, organisations such as social dialogue partners and others with access to EU policy and law-making in the substantive fields covered by the document. The audience also included a number of stakeholders without direct access to EU policy and law-making, such as companies in Member States. Such actors were invited to provide responses through a consultation process.

Overall, the Green Paper demonstrated that to the EU, CSR was

---

[131] Council of the European Union (n 129).
[132] See European Union: Council of the European Union (2009) Presidency Conclusions, Brussels European Council, 18–19 June 2009, EU Doc. 7619/1/05 REV 1, 19 June 2009.

considered a modality towards the implementation of public policy aims (generally related to welfare state policy objectives of an economic or social nature) as well as the implementation outside the EU of international law instruments or standards to which the EU is committed. The title of the Green Paper invoked the ambition of a European 'framework' for CSR, and the text of the Green Paper made it clear that that framework was envisaged to embody strong references to international human rights and labour law as well as some aspects of international environmental law.[133]

In line with arguments that promoted the Global Compact idea, the EU Green Paper drew on a combination of references to the economic interests of companies and to social and environmental policy objectives to build a case for companies to contribute to public policy objectives. CSR was defined as voluntary,[134] but the subtle message was that authorities may actively act to promote CSR, because CSR is not just about companies' economy but also about the political economy and the realisation of social and environmental public policy objectives.[135] Having outlined the policy objectives, the Green Paper proceeded to elaborate the business case by referring to CSR as an investment to reduce risks to the company.[136]

The Green Paper established a connection between EU policy on sustainable development and intergovernmental initiatives and international law instruments related to CSR and core labour rights. It stated that EU measures on CSR must 'reflect and be integrated' in the context of the Global Compact, key ILO instruments and the OECD Guidelines.[137] The argument developed a normative international law connection in that it specifically set out that 'observance of core ILO labour standards (...) is central to' CSR, and that the OECD Guidelines 'benefit from the commitment of adhering governments to promote' business observance.[138] Through this, an international law dimension was integrated into the proposed EU understanding of CSR. On the backdrop of the previously made argument on economic interests of companies that CSR was held to present (that is, the 'business case'), the argument articulated a connection between business values and interests that would resonate with business managers, and EU political economic interests that would be meaningful to states and their authorities.

---

[133] Commission of the European Communities (n 124) para. 8.
[134] Ibid.
[135] Ibid., para. 11.
[136] Ibid., para. 12.
[137] Ibid., para. 17.
[138] Ibid.

The final part of the Green Paper[139] dealt with the consultation process to bring forth the intended European framework for CSR. That process would eventually become the European MSF on CSR. The Commission proposed a participatory process involving public authorities as well as business and other non-state actors to partake in developing the framework.

Throughout, the Green Paper made more use of political or legal rationality arguments than economic system references to the 'business case' or other considerations alleging economic benefits of CSR for companies. As well as expressing common practice of political authorities like the Commission, this would in practice resonate with the target audiences of the Green Paper, which included Member States, EU institutions and CSR-concerned NGOs. However, not addressing companies by interests specific to their sub-system may have had an effect on business views on the MSF process and their engagement with the idea of a normative framework on CSR for European businesses. As will be seen below in section 4.5.2, the business sector obtained significant influence on the MSF output's limited substantive references to international human rights law.

4.5.2 The MSF: Procedure, Process and Output

4.5.2.1 The 2002 Communication's provision of procedural and normative details for the MSF

In addition to European policy objectives and CSR, the 2002 Communication set the organisational and management structure for the MSF and set forth detailed normative guidance for the work of the MSF towards the intended European framework on CSR. This included recommendations for the MSF to look to international human rights and labour law as normative sources for the substantive guidance to be provided to European companies. The OECD Guidelines and ILO fundamental conventions were highlighted as key 'agreed instruments' of relevance for CSR.[140]

In terms of organisation, the Communication announced that the MSF was to be chaired by the EU Commission. Participants would comprise around 40 European representative organisations of employers, employees, consumers and civil society as well as professional associations and business networks. Other EU institutions would be invited with observer status. A steering group with representatives from the Commission and

---

[139] Ibid., paras 89–94.
[140] Commission of the European Communities (n 125) at 5.

leading participating organisations would be in charge of daily management.[141] The Forum's working method was to be based on two plenary ('High Level') meetings each year at the political level, and theme-based roundtables.

The objectives set out for the MSF were both ambitious and specific. They were phrased in clearly regulatory terms, in most cases of a legal system character (such as 'guiding principles', 'codes of conducts, to be based on internationally agreed principles, in particular the OECD Guidelines', 'development of commonly agreed guidelines', 'definition of commonly agreed guidelines . . . supporting the ILO core conventions')[142] rather than a (purely) political character. The Commission 'invited' the MSF to:

> address and to agree by mid-2004 if possible on guiding principles on the following issues:
> - the relationship between CSR and competitiveness (business case);
> - the contribution of CSR to sustainable development, in particular in developing countries, and to gender mainstreaming;
> - SME-specific aspects (tools, coaching/mentoring practices by large enterprises, supply chain aspects);
> - effectiveness and credibility of codes of conducts, to be based on internationally agreed principles, in particular the OECD guidelines for multinational enterprises;
> - development of commonly agreed guidelines and criteria for CSR measurement, reporting and assurance;
> - definition of commonly agreed guidelines for labelling schemes, supporting the ILO core conventions and environmental standards; (. . .).[143]

Notably, the reference to ILO instruments was to conventions and not to declarations (such as the ILO 1998 Declaration on Fundamental Principles and Rights to Work) or other soft law instruments. As ILO's conventions are hard law (binding) and detailed, this suggests that the product that the Commission intended to result from the MSF was to be based on those detailed instruments as normative sources. Most if not all issues presented as CSR aspects under the EU employment and social affairs policy ('quality employment', 'lifelong learning', 'information', 'consultation and participation of workers', 'equal opportunities', 'integration of people with disabilities')[144] have clear parallels in

---

[141] Ibid., at 17–18.
[142] Ibid., at 18.
[143] Ibid.
[144] Ibid., at 19.

international human and labour rights law, in particular international labour law under the ILO and the Council of Europe's European Social Charter, as well as the UN Declaration on the Rights of Disabled Persons.[145]

Along with general references to bribery and environmental pollution, the OECD Guidelines and specific core labour rights ('child or forced labour')[146] were also emphasised in relation to public funding of business activities. The Communication also welcomed labelling schemes to promote transparency and verifiable criteria. While observing that participation should be voluntary, the Commission emphasised also that labelling schemes should draw on ILO core labour conventions to set minimum standards.[147]

In sum, CSR was described as a modality towards the implementation of public policy objectives related to employment, environment, human rights and labour rights, including the implementation of labour and human rights outside the EU's territory. With CSR defined in the Communication as voluntary, CSR-promotion by EU authorities was argued to be justified with reference to alleged benefits for companies as well as societies. Referring to ILO fundamental conventions and the OECD Guidelines, the Communication provided specific normative guidance for the (intended) normative substance of the output of the MSF.

4.5.2.2 The MSF process and output

The European MSF on CSR was finally launched on 16 October 2002. Chaired by the EU Commission, the MSF had a membership of 18 organisations representing trade unions and workers' cooperatives, industrial and employers and commerce organisations, and NGOs engaged in human rights, consumers' interests, fair trade and sustainable development. Observer status was held by 11 institutions or organisations, including the European Parliament, the EU Council, the Global Compact, OECD, ILO and UNEP.[148] The activities of the Forum were supported from within the existing financial, human and administrative resources of

---

[145] The UN Convention on the Rights of Persons with Disabilities was only adopted in December 2006, that is, four years after the publication of the Communication.
[146] Commission of the European Communities (n 125) at 22–3.
[147] Ibid., at 16.
[148] European Multistakeholder Forum on CSR, Composition, http://circa.europa.eu/irc/empl/csr_eu_multi_stakeholder_forum/info/data/en/CSR%20Forum%20composition.htm (last accessed 12 March 2013; website has been removed).

the European Commission.[149] High level meetings and topical roundtables were prepared by a Coordination Committee composed of representatives from the Commission and from participating organisations. The Coordination Committee was comprised of up to two representatives from each of the following organisations that were invited to nominate representatives: the European Trade Union Confederation (ETUC), the Union of Industrial and Employers' Confederations of Europe, the European Business Network for Corporate Social Responsibility (CSR Europe),[150] the environmental NGO group Green G8, and the Platform of European Social NGOs which represented and coordinated views of human rights and other social aspect oriented civil society organisations.

On the website, the MSF was described as 'the centrepiece of the Commission strategy for promoting CSR and sustainable development, as set out in the CSR Communication of July 2002'.[151] The Commission's introduction to the MSF referred to the Lisbon Strategy and the EU Strategy for Sustainable Development, labour rights and to promotion of governance in the context of globalisation. On the MSF's website page on the objectives, composition and operational aspects, the Commission introduced the MSF as an initiative with a regulatory aim, referring to both policy implementation and promotion of international 'core labour standards', that is, standards contained in ILO core labour conventions, and 'social and environmental governance'.[152] The objectives of the MSF were presented as follows:

---

[149] European Multistakeholder Forum on CSR, *Objective, composition and operational aspects,* http://circa.europa.eu/irc/empl/csr_eu_multi_stakeholder_for um/info/data/en/CSR%20Forum%20Rules.htm (last accessed 12 March 2013; website has been removed).

[150] According to information at the website of CSR Europe in 2008 and 2013, the organisation described itself as a non-profit organisation established in 1996 by former Commission President Jacques Delors with the objective of helping companies achieve their economic goals while placing CSR in the mainstream of business practice. See CSR Europe website (http://www.csreurope.org/, as of 15 February 2013) and Euractiv (2004) Corporate Responsibility: Interview news: The new Member States will bring fresh ideas and new views to the CSR debate, *Euractiv,* 4 May 2004. On the evolution of the organisation and its political priorities against those of other organisations involved in the European CSR project, see also D. Kinderman (2013) 'Corporate social responsibility in the EU, 1993–2013: Institutional ambiguity, economic crises, business legitimacy and bureaucratic politics', 51(4) *JCMS: Journal of Common Market Studies* pp. 701–20.

[151] European Multistakeholder Forum on CSR, Home, http://circa.europa.eu/ irc/empl/csr_eu_multi_stakeholder_forum/info/data/en/csr%20ems%20forum.htm (last accessed 12 March 2013; website has been removed).

[152] European Multistakeholder Forum on CSR (n 149).

> With the overall aim to foster corporate social responsibility, the [MSF] shall promote innovation, transparency and convergence of CSR practices and instruments through:
>
> - Improving knowledge about the relationship between CSR and sustainable development (including its impact on competitiveness, social cohesion and environmental protection) by facilitating the exchange of experience and good practices and bringing together existing CSR instruments and initiatives, with a special emphasis on SME specific aspects;
> - exploring the appropriateness of establishing common guiding principles for CSR practices and instruments, taking into account existing EU initiatives and legislation and internationally agreed instruments such as OECD Guidelines for multinational enterprises, Council of Europe Social Charter, ILO core labour conventions and the International Bill of Human Rights.[153]

In terms of system-specific rationality, the points made would be more likely to activate the internal logic of policy-makers and regulators of whom there were few at the MSF as well as NGOs concerned with human and labour rights, rather than that of businesses associations of which there were many at the MSF.

Representing industry and employers, UNICE (a business association, now BusinessEurope) in a statement delivered at the High Level meeting in October 2002 articulated CSR as 'voluntary and business-driven'.[154] UNICE argued that CSR should not entail simply shifting government duties to the private sector, and emphasised that governments themselves have a role with regard to implementation of the policy objectives and legal instruments.[155] Associations for smaller businesses, commerce and handicrafts supported these views.[156]

The Social Platform, a group of 38 European NGOs and networks in the social sector, expressed hesitation towards the voluntary approach.

---

[153] Ibid.

[154] European Multistakeholder Forum on CSR (2002) High Level meetings, 16 October 2002, Agenda, Statements, Philippe de Buck – Secretary General, UNICE, http://circa.europa.eu/irc/empl/csr_eu_multi_stakeholder_forum/info/data/en/CSR%20Forum%2020021016%20statements%20UNICE.htm (last accessed 12 March 2013; website has been removed).

[155] Ibid.

[156] European Multistakeholder Forum on CSR, High Level meetings, 16 October 2002, Agenda, Statements, Alain Wolf – Adviser to the Presidency, CEEP; EU Multistakeholder Forum on CSR, High Level meetings, 16 October 2002, Agenda, Statements, Xavier R. Durieu – Secretary General, Eurocommerce, http://circa.europa.eu/irc/empl/csr_eu_multi_stakeholder_forum/info/data/en/CSR%20Forum%2020021016%20statements%20CEEP.htm (last accessed 12 March 2013; website has been removed).

They held that CSR should not replace regulation, but be complementary to 'regulatory instruments',[157] in context suggesting that this was to be understood as conventional top-down or command-control law. They argued that the normative baseline must be provided by international standards, thereby implicitly arguing that international labour law and other CSR-relevant international standards should form a normative source for (European) CSR normativity.[158]

Following the first Roundtable meetings, at the time of the High Level meeting in December 2002 and two months into the MSF process, discursive struggles were on a course leading away from the debate on international standards and the role these should have for CSR substance, and from "a framework of guiding principles". The agreed themes for the Roundtables[159] made no mention of international standards. Rather than discussing international law as a normative source for CSR, the debate was mainly on activities that could be funded by governments to build knowledge on CSR as opposed to being undertaken by business.

Based on a joint proposal from UNICE, ETUC, European Platform of Social NGOs, Green 8 and CSR Europe, the fourth High Level meeting in November 2003 adopted an outline for the MSF Final Report, comprising three parts. Part One was proposed to be a '[r]eaffirmation of International and European agreed principles, standards and conventions', Part Two an analysis of CSR-determining factors, and Part Three on future initiatives and recommendations.[160] The reasoning provided indicates that the pertinent international standards and instruments form part of the external environment of companies but do not go beyond this, and would be suggested to do no more in the report. In other words, the normative standards and instruments would not be presented as applying to companies

---

[157] European Multistakeholder Forum on CSR, High Level meetings, 16 October 2002, Agenda, Statements, Anne-Sophie Parent – Member Social Platform Management Committee http://circa.europa.eu/irc/empl/csr_eu_multi_stakeholder_forum/info/data/en/CSR%20Forum%20021016%20statements%20Social%20Platform.htm (last accessed 12 March 2013; website has been removed).

[158] Ibid.

[159] European Multistakeholder Forum on CSR (2002) High Level meetings, 19 December 2002, Minutes, http://circa.europa.eu/irc/empl/csr_eu_multi_stakeholder_forum/info/data/en/CSR%20Forum%20021219%20minutes.htm (last accessed 12 March 2013; website has been removed).

[160] European Multistakeholder Forum on CSR (2003) High Level meetings, 13 November 2003, Joint Proposal for a Final Report format from the Coordination Committee, http://circa.europa.eu/irc/empl/csr_eu_multi_stakeholder_forum/info/data/en/CSR%20Forum%20031113%20report%20structure.htm (last accessed 12 March 2013; website has been removed).

directly as specific although soft normative expectations, neither would a normative framework be proposed to flesh out those standards with regard to companies. Part One of the report would formally honour the MSF mandate. However, it would do little in providing substantive input to CSR normativity, let alone a strong human rights normativity. This came out in the introduction to the proposal, which emphasised that MSF participants had 'agreed on the need to "take into account"' existing EU law and specific international law instruments, but proceeded to note only that the report's Part One would 'reaffirm this statement by listing those principles and conventions' and 'setting them in the context of the forum's work'.[161] In other words, the pertinent instruments were not to be specifically integrated in the two other parts of the report, nor would guidance be developed on how companies could internalise the norms on conduct contained in the instruments. Despite these inconsistencies with the ambitions that had been expressed by the Commission, the proposal was adopted as the foundation for the Final Report, which as will be seen largely built upon the proposal.

The fifth and final High Level meeting took place on 29 June 2004. The main point on the agenda was the presentation of the Final Report, which constituted the MSF output. Following its presentation, MSF participants debated the report. UNICE, ETUC, CSR Europe, the Social Platform and the Green 8, CEEP, Eurocommerce, Amnesty International and the International Federation for Human Rights (FIDH) all made statements. The discussion and presentations at the meeting demonstrate that despite the adoption of the report, disagreement persisted. In particular, contention remained on the role of international human rights law and particular international law instruments as a source for the normative substance.

The text of the Final Report[162] itself is a testimony to the extent of disagreement and antagonism among MSF stakeholders on the role they were willing to award to international law instruments on human and labour rights as well as the environment as normative sources for CSR.

The introduction to the Final Report reiterated the origin, objectives, organisation and process of the MSF, but with a somewhat different weighting of elements than when they were originally presented by the Commission at the first High Level meeting in October 2002. In the Final Report, the objective is described briefly, indicating the aim of creating convergence of CSR practices and establishing common guiding principles

---

[161] Ibid.
[162] European Multistakeholder Forum on CSR (2004) Final Results and recommendations.

based on instruments of international law. As before, the set of instruments specifically mentioned to be taken into account for the MSF's 'exploring the appropriateness of establishing common guiding principles for CSR practices and instruments' included both international soft law and international hard law: 'existing EU initiatives and legislation and internationally agreed instruments such as OECD Guidelines for multinational enterprises, Council of Europe Social Charter, ILO core labour conventions and the International Bill of Human Rights'.[163] However, the report listed only a limited set of instruments to act as direct sources for CSR. Overall, human rights were dealt with almost exclusively only in Part One of the report. This influenced the remainder of the report because Part One did not deal with human rights as a source of CSR normativity, nor did it provide guidance on how companies may engage with human rights.

Instead of going into detail on the substantive impact that the instruments could or should have, the report's Part One, which is a brief part of the overall document, contained a comprehensive list of international instruments. In terms of key instruments, it provided little precision on the implications for companies, let alone specific guidance on conduct. The main instruments noted as 'important reference texts and instruments'[164] for CSR were the ILO Tripartite Declaration, the OECD Guidelines, and the UN Global Compact. While these are, indeed, important in that they deal directly with issues related to social responsibilities of business and as noted by the report were 'both developed with the involvement of business and directly addressed to them',[165] they are also non-binding instruments that at most serve as guidance for companies. Instruments offering more detailed guidance or which had a stronger international law character were simply taken note of with the comment that they 'contain values that can inspire companies when developing their CSR, which in turn can play a role in reinforcing and making tangible the values these texts represent'.[166] This applied to the UDHR, the ICESCR, the ICCPR, the ECHR, the EU Charter and the ESC, as well as the 1998 ILO Declaration on Fundamental Principles and Rights at Work. Thus, the actual international law instruments repeatedly emphasised by the European Parliament and the Commission prior to and at the launch of the MSF were relegated in the Final Report to playing a secondary role. By contrast, the three

---

[163] Ibid., at 2–3.
[164] Ibid., at 6.
[165] Ibid.
[166] Ibid.

instruments emphasised by the MSF – the ILO Tripartite Declaration, the OECD Guidelines and the UN Global Compact – had not been specifically mentioned by the Commission prior to the establishment of the MSF. Moreover, the international law instruments that inform the Global Compact Principles were not noted by the report in the same context as the Compact but as possible sources of inspiration. This suggests that the drafters of the report may not have been aware that the UDHR and ILO's 1998 Declaration are direct normative sources for the Global Compact, or that if they were, they wished to relegate the human and core labour rights norms provided by those international law instruments to a lesser role for European CSR.

The MSF Report did not explain what role the 'reference' international law treaties or declarations should take for companies, nor how companies should understand or relate to the OECD Guidelines, the ILO Tripartite Declaration or the Global Compact. The wording is too vague to set actual norms of conduct for companies. All three instruments existed prior to the establishment of the MSF. Overall, Part One of the MSF Final Report therefore appears to have no sign of change in terms of CSR normativity through the MSF in the creation of a shared understanding of CSR, and even less in terms of the formulation of an actual normative framework.

Moreover, in the report's Part Three, the international instruments listed in Part One were noted as 'reference texts'[167] without an explanation of what that meant. There was no indication of intent for that text to inform company action normatively. With regard to raising awareness, the recommendations addressed governments as the main actors. While it is natural that governments play a role in relation to instruments of international law, the recommendations in the Final Report considerably played down the role of companies and the significance of these instruments for companies in relation to CSR. That was particularly so if compared with the views expressed in the 1999–2002 documents from the European Parliament and the Commission. Also, the responsibility was effectively returned from companies to governments, particularly stressed by phrasing such as a recommendation by the Forum that 'when fulfilling their responsibilities in relation to the texts in Part One, national, European and international public authorities co-operate closely with stakeholders in order to better understand how to promote these values and principles (. . .).'[168] The absence of specificity of the values and types of actions or situations that may give rise to CSR-action to be considered by companies

---

[167] Ibid., at 12.
[168] Ibid.

is striking. The vagueness is underscored by the very general listing of the normative texts in Part One, couched in titles of documents without the mentioning of specific standards. Moreover, under the heading 'Raising awareness of core values and key principles embodied in the reference texts', the report deployed legal system rationality in a number of contexts where the message partly is for governments to attend to legal obligations and policy objectives themselves, rather than expecting (let alone requiring) companies to lift the burden.

The MSF was intended by the Commission as a forum for business to learn from civil society and others to strengthen their CSR engagement. However, the Final Report recommended that 'national European and international authorities [should] co-operate closely with stakeholders' to learn about and internalise companies' needs and business perspectives 'when fulfilling their responsibilities'[169] (that is, responsibilities of authorities, not of businesses) in relation to the texts in Part One in which the report referenced international law instruments. Along with other elements of the Final Report, this indicates that the interest of business, especially those opposed to the idea of CSR based normatively in international instruments including those on human rights, had obtained hegemony in the construction of CSR during the MSF. This had come about as a result of business organisations deploying a discursive strategy in which they applied the political and legal logics of public authorities and regulators to argue a case for policy concerns associated with CSR, and particularly its human rights and labour elements, as being tasks and obligations for the EU and its Member States, not for business. Because the EU Commission and civil society organisations also mainly employed political or legal system logics, they were not able to engage business support for a more ambitious result as they might have by more forcefully articulating the economic benefits that businesses may gain from CSR.

The EU Commission's internalisation of the arguments that had been deployed by business is evident in a statement at the final High Level meeting by the European Commissioner for Employment and Social Affairs. This statement was delivered by the head of the part of the EU Commission that had taken in lead in establishing the MSF and setting its ambitious goals. The Commissioner indicated that the EU Commission, on the one hand, found that the process had been beneficial in creating a product that had the potential of encouraging companies of all sizes to reflect on their impact on society and on society's expectations of them,

---

[169] Ibid.

and therefore have a more solid foundation for self-regulating. On the other hand, it also indicated that the Commission had given up reaching the original objective of a specific guiding framework incorporating international human and labour rights and environmental concerns to the extent suggested prior to and at the launch of the MSF. The statement presented the implementation and enforcement of human and labour rights as a matter for and responsibility of states, whether EU Member States or third states. Although in principle this is in accordance with international law doctrine, it is a fair distance away from the role that international law could have taken in relation to CSR, had the MSF agreed to establish a more detailed framework for CSR among European companies based on specific international instruments and standards.

Civil society organisations were not pleased with the result. They had consistently argued that CSR should be normatively based on international law instruments or specific standards, and that formal law should be developed in order to institutionalise socially responsible business conduct because business self-regulation was seen to be insufficient. At the final High Level meeting, NGOs once more addressed the role to be played by international human rights law and argued in favour of hard regulation on CSR, which in their view should be made by authorities. NGOs that had made several statements jointly during the MSF, at the final High Level meeting appeared and made their statements on an individual basis. Several of these statements are lengthy and suggest frustration at the outcome of the MSF and with its limited results in terms of anchoring CSR normativity in international human rights law. Through the statement from the Social Platform, a group of NGOs argued that an effective CSR framework should build on principles and standards contained in international law and be subject to mandatory reporting and other legal requirements. They pointed out that 'the Commission, Council and Parliament, which have not taken active part in the Forum, must now take the lead role in the development of an effective EU framework for CSR' because 'what CSR needs to become efficient is proactive and consistent public policies to create the right enabling environment and ultimately to ensure accountability by all companies'.[170] In doing so, they articulated a need that the Commission,

---

[170] European Multistakeholder Forum on CSR (2004) High Level meetings, 29 July 2004, Agenda, http://circa.europa.eu/irc/empl/csr_eu_multi_stakeholder_forum/info/data/en/CSR%20Forum%20040629%20speech%20Social%20Platform.htm (last accessed 12 March 2013; website has been removed).

Council and European Parliament move towards a firmer regulatory framework for CSR than that which MSF stakeholders were able to agree to in the Final Report.

NGO statements generally displayed severe disappointment with the limited substantive results of the MSF process. The minutes from the final High Level meeting relating the points made by MSF participants noted that civil society organisations 'deplored that the international dimension of the discussion had been underplayed'.[171] The wording suggests that the Commission, as the drafter of the minutes, was aware of the dissatisfaction of these organisations with the MSF output. The strong wording of the minutes also suggests that the Commission agreed with NGOs that the end-result was disappointing. That point is highlighted by the Commission's initiative to set up the CSR Alliance, discussed below, and the continued references to human rights law as a normative source at that occasion.

Despite the approach to CSR as voluntary, the intended output was ambitious in terms of normativity and particularly its emphasis on international labour law as well as the OECD Guidelines. Based on the European Parliament's call for a Code of Conduct, the Commission's framing of the output was an ambition approximating a European version of the Global Compact (perhaps even offering advanced guidance) that would provide businesses with detailed guidance for managing their societal impacts, particularly in regard to labour. This would have approximated the sort of hard law regulation that was not possible due to the limitations of EU jurisdiction and conferred powers. The end result, however, did not meet those ambitions. It did not provide normative guidance beyond what was already available, and contented itself with referencing very soft instruments as key normative sources without any strong message for firms to self-regulate in accordance with those instruments. The MSF's Final Report was vague in relation to business responsibilities for human rights as well as in specific normative guidance for CSR. Moreover, rather than developing detailed recommendations for business in regard to specific actions, it made recommendations for governments to make it simpler for managers to do business, and for EU Member States to act to live up to their own state duty to ensure that human rights are respected and implemented. Thus, in terms of contents, the MSF report did not deliver on the intended objective.

---

[171] European Multistakeholder Forum on CSR, Final High Level meeting, 29 June 2004, Minutes.

4.5.3 System-specific Communication

During the MSF process up to and including the Final Report, political system and legal system language and considerations were common. Arguments focused on the roles and responsibilities of authorities and companies and what governments could do to assist companies in carrying out their roles and responsibilities. Use of economic system language and related considerations was somewhat more limited. It was mainly but not exclusively deployed by economic actors, including underscoring their points on not shifting public roles on to companies.

The MSF process debates were marked by polarisation between the views of business and NGOs on CSR. Business sought to direct the construction of CSR towards retaining the voluntary approach, thus working along the CSR definition made by the Commission and at the same time deploying legal system logic. Even if the point was that CSR was *not* to be mandatory, the mere deployment of the logic resonated with the EU Commission and confirmed its own suggested understanding of CSR. Moreover, business arguments did not bring in international law. Combined with the reference to CSR being voluntary, this contributed to constructing an idea of CSR that was not associated with international law as a normative source for CSR. NGOs, on the other hand, argued that CSR was not to be an alternative to regulation in the sense of conventional law-based approaches. They, too, deployed legal system logic, invoking the mandatory/voluntary code and referring to international law as a normative source for CSR. Doing so they deployed arguments suited to activate the rationality of the Commission, but not that of business. Eventually, business statements were more effective in shaping the outcome, perhaps because they started from the perspective of the existing understanding of CSR (CSR as voluntary) which was also the idea promoted by the Commission. This connects to the deployment of stabilising and de-stabilising strategies, discussed in Chapter 6. NGOs argued that international standards should be a baseline without, however, making clear whether this was for governmental regulation or as a normative source for business self-regulation on CSR.

The Final Report's statement that CSR should not be 'used to shift public responsibilities to companies'[172] (made already in the report's Introduction) framed the MSF output both in regard to the form of regulation for CSR and the role to be played by international law as a source for CSR normativity. That argument sought to counter efforts by EU

---

[172] European Multistakeholder Forum on CSR (2004) Final Results and recommendations, at 3–4.

institutions to involve companies in implementing public policy objectives, including the impact that companies could have on human and labour rights implementation outside the EU's jurisdiction. By implication, the overall message was that CSR should not be subjected to formal legal regulation, nor should human rights or labour rights play a particular part. Such business deployment of legal and political logic had the effect of activating the Commission's rationality into accepting the claims that businesses made. In other words, this led the Commission to internalise the business demand that only public organisations have a responsibility for the delivery of public goods or implementation of human rights.

Assessed against the MSF Final Report, analysis of the argumentative structure indicates that employers' and business organisations' arguments, which referred to policy objectives of the Commission and the legal obligations of the Commission and Member States, affected the construction of CSR towards increased emphasis on the 'voluntary' element and hardly any on the 'compliance' ('mandatory') aspects. It also suggests that the strategy of private sector organisations to communicatively engage authorities' own legal obligations and responsibility to implement policies led to a decrease in expectations on companies, rather than increasing these and detailing substantive standards of conduct based in international human rights law. Limited efforts from the Commission and civil society to argue economic system considerations for companies did not offset the effects of business' arguments. As a result, the original MSF objective towards a guiding framework on CSR with considerable specific reference to detailed international law instruments and standards was watered down in the Final Report to a list of general and very soft set of very soft 'guiding instruments'. Instead of a detailed normative framework on CSR, the MSF presented authorities with clearly articulated expectations on what authorities could do through legislation to ease companies' tasks as profit-seeking economic actors and assist them in benefiting economically from engaging in CSR. The elaboration of CSR normativity that had been intended by the Commission resulted instead a more open-ended general understanding with limited normative elements and emphasis on the non-mandatory character.

Initially, the MSF in its mandate and debate expressed clear links between CSR, European and international law, and the aims of the Lisbon Strategy that expressed public policy objectives related to employment. In later meetings, the links to legal instruments, including international law as normative sources, were downplayed in favour of a debate on CSR as voluntary rather than mandatory. The connection between business action and implementation of public policy objectives was also played down. The MSF led to a construction of CSR according to which CSR is voluntary in the sense that it is neither based on public nor private law, and should

162 *Changing sustainability norms through communication processes*

be regulated through neither. Further, the CSR construction that evolved during the MSF also articulates CSR as distinct from international law normativity prescribed in specific standards of conduct contained in detailed hard and soft international human rights law instruments, and as informed directly only by a small number of soft instruments that indirectly refer to specific norms of conduct.

The use and impact of system-specific language usage is exemplified in Figure 4.3.

Context

Constructing CSR normativity through the EU MSF
Interaction: business organisations, 'social dialogue partners', NGOs, EU Commission

Transmitter

A) EU Commission
B) EU Commission
C) Business organisations
D) Civil Society

Message

A) "CSR creates value for society => a role for authorities in regulating CSR"
B) a) "CSR is voluntary, to be business driven"
   b) "CSR to build international law norms"
C) a) "Public policy objectives and legal obligations = EU and Member States' responsibility"
   b) "Authorities should ensure legal framework so that business may benefit from CSR"
D) "International law to inform CSR"

Code (audience-specific)

A) Political system code
B) a) Legal system code
   b) Legal system code
C) a) Political and legal systems code
   b) Legal system code
D) Legal system code

Contact

Establishment of 'irritation' based on understanding within sub-system of interests at stake.

Recipient

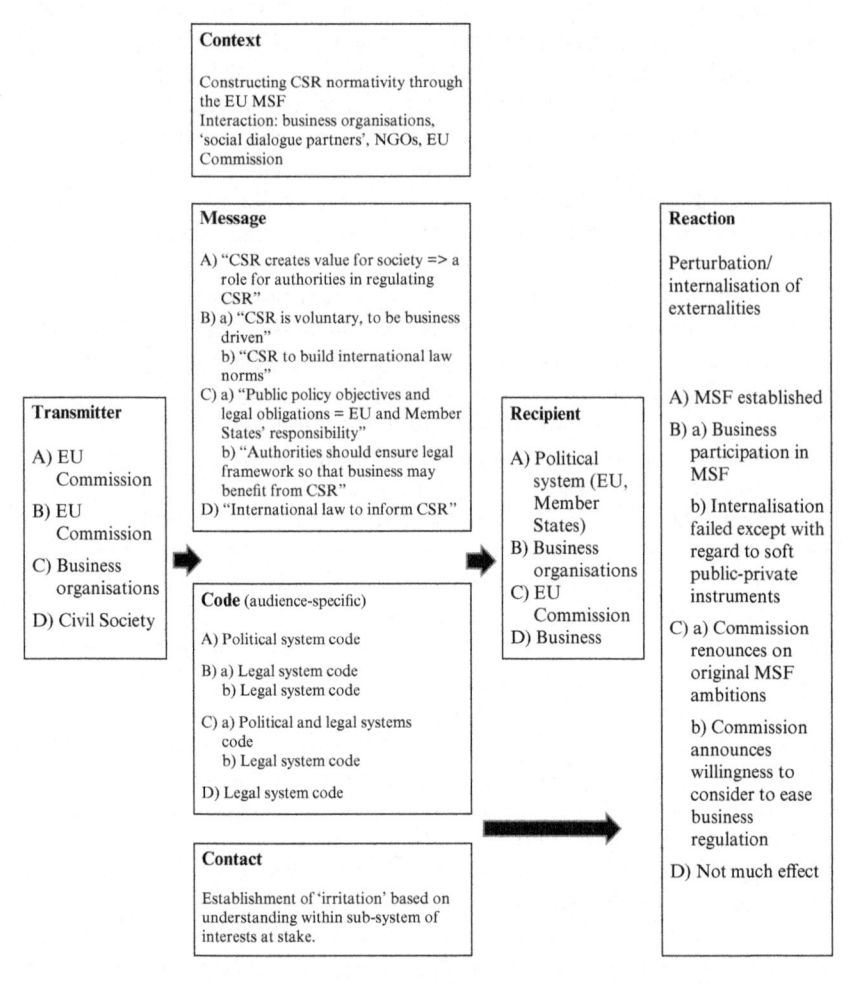

A) Political system (EU, Member States)
B) Business organisations
C) EU Commission
D) Business

Reaction

Perturbation/ internalisation of externalities

A) MSF established
B) a) Business participation in MSF
   b) Internalisation failed except with regard to soft public-private instruments
C) a) Commission renounces on original MSF ambitions
   b) Commission announces willingness to consider to ease business regulation
D) Not much effect

Figure 4.3 EU MSF: Model of relations and reaction for analysis of establishment of MSF and system-specific interest-based arguments in discursive construction of CSR normativity

Figure 4.3 confirms that system-specific language mimicking the code of the recipient was clearly effective in achieving results intended by the transmitters. In the case of the Global Compact, the intended result was a change in business attitudes to CSR and responsibilities for human rights. In the case of business associations in the MSF, the intended result was no change from the status quo in regard to responsibility for public policy implementation, so that public policy tasks, including those related to human rights, would remain with public authorities. The figure also confirms that statements arguing in the code of the transmitter were not effective to generate perturbation if that code differed from that of the recipient.

A combination of factors may explain the disconnect between the ambitious objective and the actual output of the MSF process. The procedural design favoured business associations, most of which enjoyed experience in the negotiations on labour law-making in the EU context. A majority of the civil society organisations lacked similar experience from the EU. In fact, the experience of some of those organisations from UN law-making, in particular organisations familiar with UN human rights law-making, may have contributed to their extensive deployment of political and legal system logics. By doing so, these civil society organisations may have added to the irritation that businesses were already causing to the Commission. As a result, they may also have contributed to the perturbation within the Commission that at the end of the MSF process made the Commissioner for Employment and Social Affairs talk about EU and Member State obligations for human rights, rather than about business responsibilities for their social impacts. Moreover, as a result of engaging in the CSR discourse in a way that from the outset articulated CSR as voluntary action, the Commission established a foundation for the MSF's discursive construction of CSR as precisely that – voluntary. The emphasis on CSR being voluntary was strengthened by the 2002 Communication on which the MSF was founded. However, unintended by the Commission and in contrast to the Global Compact, the discursive construction of CSR through the MSF led to an understanding according to which CSR is not only voluntary, but also normatively distinct from international legal instruments other than some of a very soft character.

Power struggles within the Commission may have further favoured the interests of business.[173] Between them, the participating business associations were adept at articulating their concern with a juridification of CSR

---

[173] See Buhmann, K. (2011) 'Integrating human rights in emerging regulation of Corporate Social Responsibility: The EU case', 7(2) *International Journal of Law in Context* pp. 139–79; Buhmann (n 70).

and enhanced business responsibility for labour rights and other human rights in a manner that shifted the assumption of responsibility or duty to act from businesses to governments (the EU and its Member States). In this, the evolution of the discursive construction of CSR that took place with the EU MSF offers an example of an argumentative strategy that was reversed if compared to that applied for the establishment of the Global Compact, in which the UN Secretary-General and his staff successfully convinced business of the benefits they would gain from self-regulating in accordance with enhanced social expectations and public policy needs. The EU Commission did not deploy similar arguments until after the MSF Final Report, when the Commission tried once more to set up an initiative to make businesses take their responsibility for human rights more seriously, as seen in the next section.

4.6 THE CSR ALLIANCE

Following the 2002–2004 MSF and its output, the Final Report, the EU Commission in 2006 launched a new initiative, aiming once more to place international human rights law as a strong normative source for EU-based businesses in regard to CSR. The new initiative, the CSR Alliance, was introduced with a new Commission Communication on CSR, which bore the pompous title, 'Implementing the Partnership for Growth and Jobs: Making Europe a Pole of Excellence on CSR'.[174] The 2006 Communication invited European companies to strengthen their commitment to CSR and 'behave responsibly wherever they operate, in accordance with European values and internationally agreed norms and standards',[175] which include labour and human rights.

The CSR Alliance was organised to comprise businesses and the EU Commission, and to deliver insights on 'best practice'. Work within the Alliance mainly consists in meetings of business only.

'Best practice' products of the Alliance are relatively limited, but do contain some references to human rights and relevant normative guidance.[176]

---

[174] Commission of the European Communities (2006) Communication from the Commission to the European Parliament, the Council and the European Economic and Social Committee: Implementing the Partnership for Growth and Jobs.
[175] Ibid., at 5.
[176] CSR Alliance (2008) Toolbox: Equipping companies and stakeholders for a competitive and responsible Europe, Brussels: CSR Europe.

The Communication produced by the Commission after the MSF and the MSF Final Report had a significantly different focus than the 2002 Communication and the 2001 Green Paper. There was no ambition to deliver a European Framework for CSR, and the issue focus was as much on internal EU needs as on policies related to external affairs.

The Communication that announced the Alliance referred to the same limited range of international law and CSR instruments that had been mentioned in the MSF Final Report. Although the references were limited to the instruments agreed to by the MSF, these steps indicate that the Commission persisted in an aim of getting companies to respect human rights and to draw on CSR for that purpose, but also that it was struggling with how to make companies internalise this expectation. The Communication also indicates that NGO arguments in the final stages of the MSF, including at the final High Level meeting, had had an effect on the Commission in terms of creating perturbation that led the Commission to insist on human rights law as a normative source for CSR and seek to promote that objective through the CSR Alliance.

4.6.1 System-specific Arguments

To obtain business support for setting up the Alliance, the Commission visibly changed its argumentative strategy from the one it has applied during the MSF. The Alliance was announced in an EU policy document (the 2006 Communication), which like the 2001 Green Paper and the 2002 Communication was couched mainly in political rationality language, as is normal for a document addressing policy makers. However, an Annex to the 2006 Communication deployed a much more economic system oriented logic, making use of arguments that were clearly intended to resonate with business.

The Commission employed legal and political system language in the main part of the Communication. It still articulated CSR as a voluntary modality for business but also a modality towards implementation of public policy objectives, including respect for human rights, core labour standards and environmental protection in developing countries. Economic system language was used more sparsely, mainly to indicate benefits that business may gain from CSR. In the Annex the Commission shifted to extensive usage of economic system language, both on its own and in combination with legal or political system language, articulating the Alliance as voluntary and CSR as well as the Alliance as combining business and public policy interests.

In the main text of the Communication, the Commission noted that CSR practices can contribute to a number of public policy objectives, including higher levels of labour market inclusion and recruitment from disadvantaged groups, job creation, investment in skills development and life-long learning, and greater respect for human rights and core labour standards, especially in developing countries.[177] These are all in accordance with the Lisbon Goals that were guiding for much EU policy at the time in the social area. However, the Annex, which describes the Alliance in detail, deployed a series of economic rationality oriented statements that would resonate directly with business. It described CSR as business-driven, explicitly recognised businesses' economic role in society, and referred to CSR as meaningful for business to achieve a better image in society and therefore better conditions for entrepreneurship, innovation and economic success.[178] It also described CSR as being basically imbued with human rights as a means through which companies may contribute to the rule of law and human rights. Thus, from the Commission's perspective CSR was still seen as a means to policy ends, especially human rights, and the Alliance was intended to stimulate company self-regulation on human rights and other CSR-related public policy objectives. But the argumentative strategy was radically changed into one that sought to activate economic rationality and therefore create irritation that would generate internal perturbation leading to acceptance of the demands explained by the Commission.

By contrast, addressing EU and Member State politicians and authorities, the main Communication text was kept mainly in political and legal system logic. It described the Alliance as a political umbrella for new or existing CSR initiatives by large companies, SMEs and their stakeholders. With a focus on intra-EU political human rights-related priorities at the time, which emphasised creating new employment opportunities in response to growing unemployment, it was characterised as 'a vehicle for mobilising companies in the interests of job creation, economic growth and sustainable development'.[179] Its activities would include fostering innovation and entrepreneurship to societal needs, mainstreaming CSR into EU policies, particularly with regard to employability and diversity, working conditions, and promotion of CSR globally in accordance with the three ILO, OECD and UN regulatory instruments noted as main reference texts by the MSF Final Report.

For the current analysis, in view of the outcome of the MSF process the main points are that the Alliance was set up, and therefore the arguments that were deployed by the Commission for that purpose. The establish-

---

[177] Commission of the European Communities (n 174) at 4.
[178] Ibid., Annex.
[179] Ibid., at 6.

ment of a new initiative comprising business with the aim of promoting guidance for CSR was a success, especially when compared with the resistance with which business had met the EU's Commission's ambitions for the MSF. The fact that the outputs of the Alliance relate to human rights issues, such as non-discrimination and diversity in the work place, also suggests that the Commission's argumentative approach had softened the previous opposition. It had successfully activated the economic rationality with companies to make them embrace non-discrimination and diversity as beneficial to business. Several companies were doing so already, but the MSF showed that they met the idea of public initiatives to promote and shape CSR with resistance. The Commission's argumentative strategy to set up the CSR Alliance changed that by invoking the economic logic.

Figure 4.4 depicts the system-specific logic usage deployed for getting the CSR Alliance established.

Context

Constructing CSR normativity through the CSR Alliance Interaction: EU and MS political system, business organisations

Transmitter

A) EU Commission

B) EU Commission

Message

A) "CSR modality to promote Lisbon Goals" (employment, inclusiveness, etc.)
B) "Globalisation of trade necessitates business self-limitations"
"CSR matters to big and small companies to improve performance"

Code (audience-specific)

A) Political system code

B) Economic system code

Contact

(Establishment of 'irritation' based on understanding within sub-system of interests at stake)

Recipient

A) Political system (EU, Member States)

B) Business organisations

Reaction

Perturbation/ internalisation of externalities

A) CSR Alliance launched as new CSR initiative from EU Commission

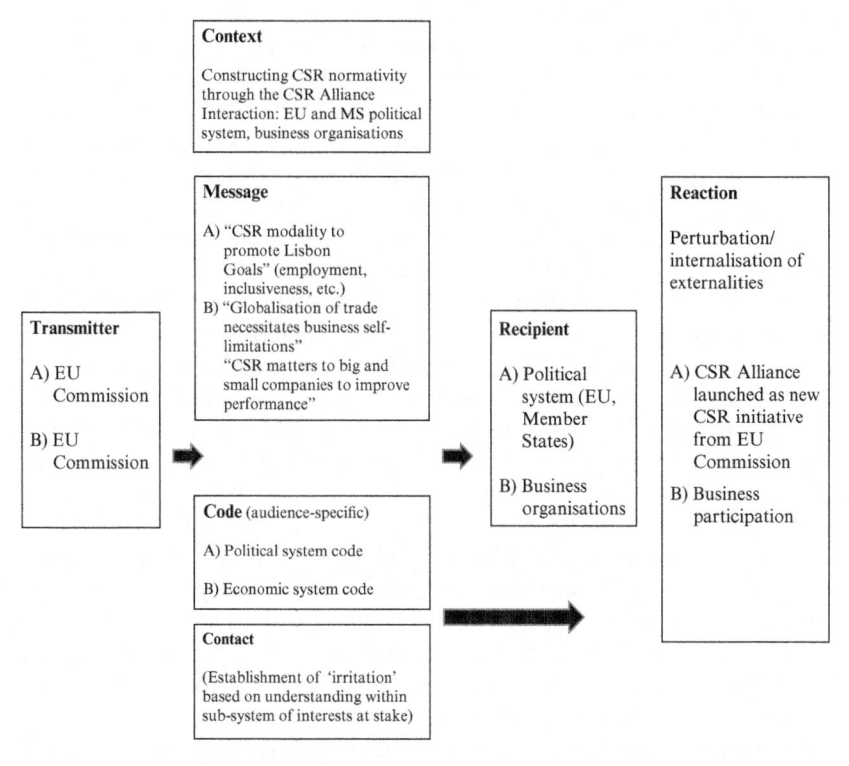

B) Business participation

Figure 4.4   CSR Alliance: Model of relations and reaction for analysis of system-specific interest-based arguments for establishment of CSR Alliance

The first specific output of the CSR Alliance, a 'CSR Toolbox', was publicised in December 2008. The 'toolbox' was developed by CSR Europe but introduced as a CSR Alliance output. Available information on the 'Toolbox' focus areas suggests that international human rights and labour law feature as sources of normative guidance, for example with regard to occupational health and safety, gender issues in employment, treatment of foreign workers and supply chain management.[180]

4.7 SUMMING UP

This chapter has shown that prior to the SRSG process, the evolution of normative guidance for business in relation to human rights, explicitly and within a broader CSR context, progressed unevenly. Two major trends can be observed: efforts tended to be more successful if they did not portend to aim at establishing binding rules for business. Furthermore, they encountered less resistance from business if they explained the significance of human rights to business in terms of economic system rationality. That applied regardless of whether the argument articulated the benefits that respecting human rights means for managing risks to the reputation and business opportunities of a company; or whether it presented business internalisation of external human rights demands and expectations as way to preserve the possibility for a company to decide for itself what CSR action to engage in without highly specific directives from authorities.

The Draft Norms originated as an expert contribution to potential new international law. Developed by an expert in collaboration with his expert colleagues in the Sub-Commission and through a process that involved civil society organisations in consultative status with the UN, originally mainly civil society organisations representing actual or potential victims of human rights abuse were invited to contribute views and opinions. This was in line with conventional UN law-making on international law. Organisations representing business were involved at a later stage. The process was successful in developing a normative output – the Draft Norms – but not in achieving the necessary support among members of the UN's Commission on Human Rights for the Draft Norms to be formally adopted by the Commission. Had they been adopted, they might have been formally provided with the status of an international soft law instrument, which might eventually have progressed into a process of further negotiations and revisions towards a binding instrument (a treaty),

---

[180] See CSR Europe (n 176).

that one day may have gained political support for adoption. However, in the line of international law-making, even if the text had been adopted by the Human Rights Commission the Draft Norms that carried an innovative title for an international law instrument and therefore did not make an explicit claim to being awarded formal soft law character nor hard law status might also have stayed a law-in-process text.

The initiative to establish the Global Compact was successful in terms of setting up a new type of intergovernmental mode for regulating companies. The Compact provides specific guidance for conduct for companies, with a firm normative anchoring in international law on human rights, labour standards, environmental responsibility and anti-corruption. The Global Compact initiative originally met with considerable hesitation among states (whose representatives make up the UN General Assembly), civil society, the international labour movement and parts of industry. The argumentative strategy helped convince stakeholders to support and work with the approach and its linkages to international law, including human rights law. It did so in appealing to recipients by arguing the benefits of the Global Compact precisely in terms of the interests of each specific audience.

The MSF originated as an initiative by the EU Commission in order for business, the labour movement and civil society to develop and agree to a guiding framework on CSR. The Commission intended the normative output to draw strongly on international law instruments, in particularly the OECD Guidelines and ILO core labour conventions as well as the International Bill of Human Rights. From the outset, the Commission articulated CSR as voluntary and going beyond what was required by formal law. During the negotiations business, industry and employers' organisations consistently argued that CSR should not be subjected to regulation through public law. These groups avoided making reference to specific normative standards, such as international law declarations or conventions. Civil society organisations, by contrast, consistently noted a need for hard regulation of business impact on society and for international law instruments to form a key normative source. Due to business organisations' mastering system-specific arguments that resonated with the legal logic of public organisations, the responsibility for human rights was directed back to states and the EU, rather than being shared with companies. This was not matched by deployment of system-specific logic by the EU Commission or civil society. The discursive construction of CSR through the MSF led to an understanding according to which CSR is not only voluntary, but also normatively distinct from international legal instruments other than those of a very soft character.

In regard to the establishment of the CSR Alliance, the difference between the main Communication and the Annex shows that the EU Commission had begun to deploy two different argumentative approaches, each one targeting the specific audience. By addressing businesses in their system-specific logic, the Commission was able to gain business support for the new initiative, the CSR Alliance. As it was to be comprised of businesses, this allowed the CSR Alliance to be set up. That, in itself, was a success when seen on the backdrop of the MSF and the manner in which business successfully made the Commission revert its ambitions for business to engage actively with human and labour rights as part of CSR. Imbued with normative guidance similar to that which the Commission had provided for the MSF, the CSR Alliance was set up to carry on the task that the Commission had originally had for the MSF. This underscores the significance of the Commission's deployment of economic rationality when addressing business in regard to the proposal of the CSR Alliance.

The discursive shift in language (particularly in the 2006 Communication Annex) towards greater usage of economic system logic parallels that which businesses used successfully in the MSF to argue by mimicking the code of recipients. In the MSF, business had argued that the political and legal objectives informing the Commission's take on CSR were really tasks to be taken care of by the EU and Member States. Reversed in the 2006 Communication in terms of the transmitter and recipient, and therefore the system-specific logic that was used, deployment of economic system logic functioned to frame the argument and the construction of CSR and the Alliance. That was done in such a way as to cause irritation that led to perturbation with business. It was therefore able to stimulate change within the economic system in a manner that led to business acceptance of a need to engage in developing some normative guidance on CSR, albeit still not a very far-reaching change.

The progress to establish normative guidance for businesses with regard to their impact on human rights was marked by at least one step back for each two steps forward. Getting TNCs and their social impacts on to the UN agenda through the establishment of a TNC Committee in the 1970s and the UN's Draft Code of Conduct was significant as the backdrop of the state-centrist international human rights regime, but when the Code of Conduct project was abandoned, that progress was not carried into fruition. Adopting soft guidance under the ILO and the OECD in the 1970s were important steps forward, as was the evolution of the Draft Norms in itself. However, the harsh dismissal of the Draft Norms by the UN Commission on Human Rights as a text that 'as a draft proposal' had no legal standing[181]

---

[181] Commission on Human Rights (2004) Decision 2004/116.

was a major step backwards. It displayed that the international human rights system was not at all ready to formally adopt broad and comprehensive norms for business on human rights, especially not in a form that might develop into formal international soft or hard law. Getting businesses to accept that they had a role to play in working for the UN's goals through the Global Compact initiative and obtaining agreement on the Global Compact Principles were important steps forward. But the outcome of the EU's MSF, which aimed at developing what would have been a European version of the Global Compact and perhaps gone beyond Compact in ambition showed that within a region that is host to a large number of the world's TNCs, business opposition to such an endeavour was considerable. On the backdrop of the advance obtained with the adoption of the UN Global Compact and agreement on the international law instruments that inform the Principles, the manner in which the MSF final report from 2004 referenced the Global Compact and its informing instruments, including the UDHR and ILO's 1998 Declaration, was a step backwards. It did not move the normative discourse forward. On the backdrop of the outcome of the MSF, the EU Commission's getting business support for setting up the CSR Alliance and for the Alliance to have a focus on human rights, among other issues, was a small step forward. A similarity in the argument deployed by the EU Commission in its 2006 Communication Annex and that which is described in the following chapter as used by the SRSG may have played a part, as discussed below. Moreover, the EU Commission's establishment of the CSR Alliance may also suggest that the agreement that had led UN Commission on Human Rights to propose the SRSG mandate in 2005, spilled over on the EU too. Yet the outputs of the Alliance have not been impressive in terms of normativity for business on human rights.

Overall, these four case studies show that participants in a multi-stakeholder regulatory process can significantly influence the normative output by communicating in the logic of those with whom action or non-action is desired with regard to the proposed or intended change towards sustainability. This can be used both to promote change through acceptance and integration of new norms (as in the case of the Global Compact, and perhaps the CSR Alliance with regard to business), or stifle action by 'freezing' responsibility with a particular functional societal group (as in the case of the Draft Norms with regard to the UN Commission on Human Rights, or the MSF with regard to the EU Commission). This confirms the pertinence for both theory and practitioners of having awareness of the system-specific interests and binary codes corresponding to audience rationalities in accordance with the theory of autopoiesis.

On this backdrop of a complex stage for intergovernmental initiative to construct and agree on normative guidance for businesses with regard to their impact on human rights, Chapter 5 proceeds to the main case study, the SRSG process. Resulting in the UN Framework and eventually the UNGPs, that process succeeded in obtaining stronger and more broad-based support for comprehensive guidance than had been the case for any of the previous inter-governmentally initiated projects with regard to normative guidance for business and human rights.

5. From incremental steps to emerging regime

Chapter 5 is concerned with how the SRSG process led to the construction of business responsibilities for human rights that is found in the UN Framework and UNGPs. Taking point of departure in the SRSG process 2005–08 that delivered the breakthrough noted in Chapter 1, the chapter analyses the argumentative strategies of stakeholders within business and civil society that were made to the SRSG, as well as responses and explanations by the SRSG in speeches and reports. Statements are analysed by looking at the use of arguments that referred to the logic of the recipient, looking at how the capacity of statements to invoke the rationality of the recipients can be observed through changes in stances in later texts. The chapter also discusses whether and how this contrasts with statements that referred to the logic of the transmitter. Finally, the SRSG's argumentative construction of the concept human right due diligence is considered on the backdrop of his de-construction of the 'sphere of influence' and upholding the 'complicity' concept. The chapter proceeds chronologically: section 5.1 considers the period from the Draft Norms to the resolution establishing the SRSG mandate; and sections 5.2, 5.3 and 5.4 each of the following years of first mandate term. Section 5.5 considers the clarification of 'complicity' and 'sphere of influence' that rejected the 'sphere of influence' and introduced human rights due diligence. Section 5.6 considers the second mandate term, which led to the UNGPs and their adoption by the Human Rights Council. Section 5.7 is the concluding analysis of how the outputs of the SRSGs mandate terms were argued into acceptance.

Forming part of the empirical part of the study, this chapter changes focus to a process that emerged at the backdrop of the UN Commission for Human Rights' dismissal of the Draft Norms. Like the Draft Norms and the other case studies referred to in Chapter 4, the SRSG process was set within a broader CSR context. This influenced some of the arguments throughout the process and particularly during the first term (2005–08), until the SRSG process clearly branched off into the emergent discourse of BHR. This occurred with the UN Framework's defining BHR as entailing duties for states and responsibilities for businesses in a pattern of interaction and with an explicit normative foundation in the International Bill of Rights and ILO fundamental conventions. That led to the further elaboration into the UNGPs, as well as the influence that the emergent BHR regime has been having on the CSR discourse, particularly in intergovernmental and hybrid CSR guidance and policy instruments.

Based on recommendations in a resolution by the Commission on Human Rights, the 2005–08 mandate of the SRSG was defined by the UN Secretary-General to comprise identification and clarification of 'standards of corporate responsibility and accountability' for companies with regard to human rights; elaboration on the role of states in 'effectively regulating and adjudicating the role of' business with regard to human rights; and research and clarification of the implications for companies of 'concepts such as "complicity" and "sphere of influence"'.[1] In addition, the mandate holder was asked to develop materials and methodologies for undertaking human rights impact assessments of the activities of companies and to compile a compendium of best practices of states and companies.[2] The human rights impact assessment and best practice elements of the mandate and SRSG work are mainly operational and will not be addressed in this study. This also applies to stakeholder submissions specifically on those issues.

The analysis builds on statements made in reports and other written texts by the SRSG and stakeholders, who either participated directly in meetings under the SRSG process or contributed through written submissions. The documents are comprised of two main types, of which only the first is suited for the analysis of functional system-specific arguments. This type consists of letters to the SRSG from NGOs, business organisations, companies, academics and other stakeholders, containing views and proposals intended to feed into the SRSG mandate and work, and replies from the SRSG as well as responses in his annual reports and background reports. Most of these texts inform the general analysis without being quoted or summarised. A limited selection of quotes are given to illustrate examples of argumentative strategies or illustrate a point made for the analysis. Summaries of key texts have been rendered in a general way. The other type of documents consists of background documents for meetings and meeting reports prepared by or for the SRSG and his team. Within this type, the former contains suggestions

---

[1] Commission on Human Rights (2005) Human rights and transnational corporations and other business enterprises, para. 1, sub-paras (a), (b) and (c).
[2] Ibid., para.1, sub-paras (d) and (e).

and ideas proposed by the SRSG or invited specialists prior to thematic or other consultations. The other type contains summaries of debates and conclusions. Both are generally of a relatively broad nature in terms of the social system-specific functional interests represented although they tend to reflect the concern of the SRSG in relation to issues and policy-cum-regulatory needs connected to the mandate issues. Some are summaries that respect the 'non-attribution rule' or 'Chatham House rule' under which many consultations and other meetings were held. This means that statements made at the meetings were rendered in the minutes or reports without identification of institutional affiliation or names of the individuals who made a statement. For this reason, these documents do not lend themselves to the same type of discourse analysis as texts that have a clearly identified submitter set within a functional sub-system. The summaries nevertheless are important for an analysis of the SRSG process as they indicate the line of direction of the debates, as well as conclusions and gradual development of priorities and other choices made by the SRSG during his mandate. The main points therefore serve the analysis in terms of documenting the impact made by previous statements of the SRSG or contributions by other actors, including through statements that derive from a named organisation or person (the first type of documents mentioned above).

The SRSG process was marked by a large number of stakeholders and a broad composition of its multi-stakeholder consultations, as well as outwardly communicated efforts at conducting such consultations in an intergovernmental context.

A chronological approach allows for understanding the discourse evolution as it evolved during the SRSG process, and to appreciate the interdiscursivity when statements draw on or otherwise relate to statements made earlier in the process. Accordingly, the analysis is divided into periods corresponding to steps leading up to and including the first, second and third reports of the SRSG first mandate, as well as the period of the second mandate. The first mandate term concluded with the Human Rights Council's resolution to 'welcome' the UN Framework proposed with the 2008 report. The Council asked the SRSG to elaborate the guidance offered by the Framework into operational details through the second SRSG term (2008–11) that resulted in the UNGPs. Accordingly, the major discursive struggles on what was to be understood by business responsibilities for human rights took place in the period after the UN Commission on Human Rights dismissed the Draft Norms, up to the Human Rights Council's decision to 'welcome' the UN Framework. This period is the main one addressed in here through statements from stakeholders and the SRSG. The second mandate term was a period of fine-tuning, based on the agreement reached with the UN Framework.[3]

5.1 FROM THE DRAFT NORMS TO THE RESOLUTION ESTABLISHING THE SRSG MANDATE

Prior to and between the Commission on Human Rights' 2004 debate on the Draft Norms and the establishment of the SRSG mandate in 2005, several business organisations, human rights NGOs, academics and some others issued statements on the Norms and the future course on human rights responsibilities of business. As seen in Chapter 4, statements from business organisations and news media interviews with representatives from such organisations indicate that at least part of the private sector harboured reservations towards the Draft Norms and towards the general idea of recognising business responsibilities for human rights. That tendency continued after the Norms were first debated by the Commission for Human Rights in 2004. Statements and other reports on civil society views, especially from Amnesty International and other human rights NGOs, advocated in favour of formulating human rights duties for companies. Taken together, these stances represent the position from which the SRSG process developed its arguments and evolving argumentative strategy. It is also on this basis that changes can be observed on discursive strategies of business and civil society organisations during the SRSG mandate in terms of construction of business responsibilities for human rights and recognition of the role of human rights law as a relevant source of norms for business conduct and their economic impact on society.

5.1.1 General Argumentative Structure and Strategy

In an interview published in *Ethical Corporation*, a news magazine on CSR, soon after the UN Human Rights Commission's 2004 debate on the Draft Norms the vice president of US Council of International Business Adam Greene[4] argued along lines that resemble those made in the joint statement on the Draft Norms by the ICC and the IOE in November 2003,

---

[3] Compare De Schutter, O. (2013) Foreword. In S. Deva and D. Bilchitz (eds). *Human Rights Obligations of Business: Beyond the Corporate Responsibility to Respect?* Cambridge University Press, pp. xv–xxii.

[4] B. Hearne (2004) 'Analysis: Proposed UN Norms on human rights shelved in favor of more study', *Ethical Corporation*, 3 May 2004.

which was discussed in Chapter 4 (section 4.3). Greene made extensive use of legal system considerations in criticising the Draft Norms and the general idea of human rights responsibilities in terms of the role and power of business and of states, arguing that the Draft Norms and the idea of business responsibilities were problematic from a democratic and thus political perspective as well as from a legal perspective. The argumentative strategy accorded with reservations on limitations on the freedom of enterprise and the distinctions between roles and limitations of business and states that had been raised in the legal academic US debate on CSR. Greene referred to the limited legal authority of businesses and legal guarantees for companies in national law. The Draft Norms were described as 'a radical re-write of international law'[5] that would shift obligations from states to corporations. This suggests that the point of departure was taken in conventional general international law without regard to the horizontality doctrine of international human rights law and its recognition of states' duties to respect individuals against abuse caused by other individuals or organisations. Along related lines, he observed that the 'primary problem lies in the lack of implementation of legal guarantees at the national level',[6] suggesting that any issue with business impact on human rights is caused by public governance failures. Drawing on civil rights as examples of human rights ('censorship, restrictions on freedom of religion or of the press'), in the interview he presented the idea of business responsibilities for human rights as an absurdity, observing that 'the idea that you can solve these things by ignoring government's role and looking only at companies is absurd'.[7] Making reference only to civil rights of a type that are closely associated with violations by non-democratic governments does make the connection to business look somewhat absurd, especially when discussed from the perspective of business being expected to solve the problem. Reference to child labour, occupational health and safety or other social or economic rights that are more often associated with business impact would have brought forward a different message, showing how the connection between business and human rights is not an absurdity. Moreover, stating that the approach taken by the Draft Norms was to disregard governments and look 'only at companies'[8] was a simplification, as the text of the Draft Norms recognised that states have 'primary responsibility' for human rights. It underscores the statement's

---

[5] Ibid.
[6] Ibid.
[7] Ibid.
[8] Ibid.

objective of depicting the Draft Norms as out of touch with the fundamentals of human rights law and international law.

In another interview to the same magazine, the US Council for International Business argued that paying taxes to human rights abusive regimes might be considered a violation of the company's human rights responsibilities.[9] The statement implicitly referred to another CSR concern that surfaced in 2003–04, discussing whether companies' evasion of paying taxes in states where profits were made might be considered socially irresponsible, even though it might be strictly speaking in accordance with applicable tax law. By bringing the tax and compliance argument into the human rights and complicity context, the statement connected two different currents of the CSR discourse and tied them together through legal system based language on tax-paying companies complying with national law ('the simple act of paying taxes – as required by national laws').[10] In doing so, the statement built an argument that the claim that companies have human rights duties may give rise to situations that clash with companies' legal obligations to comply with host state law to pay taxes.

NGOs sought to draw attention to the need to integrate human rights in a globalisation process that they perceived to be dominated by economic concerns and trade rights. Amnesty International argued that business statements presenting the Draft Norms as an effort to shift government responsibilities on to companies disregarded the focus of the Draft Norms on companies' 'sphere of influence'.[11] In *Ethical Corporation*, Amnesty International explained that the Draft Norms only expected companies to do what was within their sphere of influence, and not to take on the role of governments.[12] Following the Human Rights Commission's 2004 dismissal of the Draft Norms, Amnesty voiced concerns held by many civil society organisations that were eager to preserve the Draft Norms as the foundation of such work. In a statement published in January 2005, Amnesty dramatically challenged the Commission's intentions and integrity, asking whether the Commission lived up to being 'the UN's chief guardian of Human Rights'.[13] Amnesty argued that the adverse social

---

[9] B. Hearne (2004) 'Proposed UN Norms on human rights: Is business opposition justified?', *Ethical Corporation*, 22 March 2004.
[10] Ibid.
[11] Ibid.
[12] Ibid.
[13] Amnesty International (2005) 2005 UN Commission on Human Rights: The UN's chief guardian of human rights?, AI Index: IOR 41/001/2005, 1 January 2005.

effects of the economic power and impact of businesses must be countered through human rights standards and accountability of an enforceable character. In an opening that would aim to resonate with business managers, the initial part of the statement drew on economic system rationality to set out factors ('capital, labour, technology and other resources'),[14] which form the foundation of business expansion beyond national territories. The statement proceeded to integrate legal system rationality to explain that such economic processes have resulted in increasing numbers of companies operating beyond 'the regulatory capacities of any one national system'.[15] Drawing briefly on political-economic interests on the positive impact of business on society in terms of provision of employment and other 'benefits for countless millions of persons',[16] the statement reverted to explaining the adverse impact of business on human rights through legal system logic in combination with economic system references to business practices. Amnesty argued that some companies abuse human rights through their employment practices or the effect of their production processes on workers, communities and the environment; and that others are implicated in abuses through their association with repressive governments or political authorities and the activities of their security forces.[17] In combining different rationalities and also referring to some of the societal good that businesses do, the statement addressed both businesses and regulators with the aim of stimulating their appreciation of the need to prevent the adverse societal effects of transnational business. Formally addressing the Human Rights Commission, the statement would be suited to reaching a broader audience that would include business.

Having established the reasons and problems of business impact on human rights with a potentially mixed broad audience, Amnesty's January 2005 statement switched to legal system observations to argue a need to proceed from voluntary instruments to a course that would be more likely to lead to corporate human rights accountability, that is, hard law-based monitoring, enforcement and sanctions. Referring to three main intergovernmental CSR initiatives – the OECD Guidelines, the Global Compact and the ILO Tripartite Declaration – Amnesty observed that 'voluntary initiatives have not been sufficient'[18] to prevent human rights abuse or ensure accountability.

This Amnesty statement followed the style of many others from civil

---

[14] Ibid.
[15] Ibid.
[16] Ibid.
[17] Ibid.
[18] Ibid.

society at this stage in mainly applying legal system logic, but it differed by applying economic system considerations in combination with legal system logic. For example, it referred to foreign investment, alleging that investors and some host governments shared complementary economic interests to such an extent that it kept host governments from undertaking adequate monitoring of firms' conduct. However, by focusing on government practices as the general point of departure, the still limited usage of economic system logic differed from arguments introduced by the SRSG and some NGOs at a later stage, which referred explicitly to business interests in managing risks.

Amnesty deployed additional reference to economic system interests in order to strengthen the argument on the need and benefits of international standards. Amnesty argued that 'global standards on human rights responsibilities' for business would not only be of benefit to victims of human rights, but also to companies through feeding into national law and 'help establish compatible legislation across national borders to guide company operations'.[19] Making implicit reference to the idea of a 'level playing field' for companies in regard to their social responsibilities and societal impact, the statement characterised global standards (such as the Draft Norms) as beneficial to companies.

The diversity and antagonism of views, even within sectors, are underscored by a series of governmental statements relating to the Commission's 2005 resolution that recommended to the Secretary-General to establish the SRSG mandate. These are indicative of the diversity of states' interests and their impact on the construction of business social responsibilities, particularly with regard to human rights. Some governments opposed the idea of the Draft Norms and other forms of UN regulation of business responsibilities for human rights. In comments on the Draft Norms made in late 2004 to the Human Rights Commission, the Government of Australia opposed a mandatory approach.[20] Referring only to corporate social responsibilities (or CSR), the statement avoided direct mention of human rights. The argument invoked an alleged 'principle' that CSR guidelines 'should be voluntary', and asserted that the Draft Norms 'represent a major shift away from voluntary adherence' and that 'the need for such a shift' had not been demonstrated.[21] Comments from the representa-

---

[19] Ibid.
[20] Australian Government statement on the draft UN Norms, late 2004, quoted in D. Kinley *et al.* (2007) 'The politics of corporate social responsibility', at 40; see also J. Nolan (2005) 'The United Nation's compact with business', endnote 27.
[21] Australian Government statement, ibid.

tives of the US and South Africa, two of three states that voted against the resolution, underscore the lingering struggle among Commission members and the states they represented on the appropriateness and need of public – let alone international – regulation of business responsibilities for human rights.

A detailed statement made by the US representative to explain why that government voted against the proposed resolution[22] presented the business obligation to 'obey the law' as basically meaning '[honouring] the human rights of all individuals with whom they have contact'.[23] However, if that might sound ambitious with regard to the expectations on business, the statement noted that business involvement in adverse effects on human rights boils down to states' obligations, arguing that 'human rights obligations apply to states, not non-state actors, and it is incumbent upon states when they deem necessary to adopt national laws that address the obligations of private actors'. The statement did not, however, refer to the horizontality doctrine that later became part of the reasoning for the UN Framework's State Duty to Protect. Rather, it referred to states' own discretion to adopt national legislation that addresses 'the obligations of private actors'.[24] The US Government's statement proceeded to emphasise the contributions that business makes to society, referring to public policy interests (employment, income for individuals, essential goods and services, education, training and healthcare) and presenting business contributions in terms of political-economic objectives closely related to social and economic human rights. After setting forth the benefits of business to society and human rights, the statement observed that the proposed Commission resolution treated business 'as potential problems rather than the overwhelming positive forces for economic development and human rights that they are'.[25] Combined with reference to intergovernmental recognition of the 'value of the private sector to development',[26] the statement portrayed business as beneficial for public policy objectives, bringing forth the message that regulation of business conduct with regard to human rights was irrelevant, unnecessary and ultimately damaging to

---

[22] United States (2005) Explanation of no-vote, Commission on Human Rights, Item 17: Transnational Corporations, April 20, 2005 (on file with author); see also (but with a somewhat imprecise summary of the first part of the statement) United Nations (2005) Press Release: Commission requests Secretary-General to appoint Special Representative on Transnational Corporations.
[23] United States, ibid.
[24] Ibid.
[25] Ibid.
[26] Ibid.

key UN policy interests. The point was underscored when the statement argued that 'the anti-business agenda pursued by many in [the UN] over the years has held back the economic and social advancement of developing countries'.[27] Thus, the government of the US suggested that voting against a resolution aiming to promote the course of UN guidance on human rights for businesses, would in fact benefit the socio-economic development of developing countries. Implicitly it would therefore also benefit the possibilities of developing countries to provide for access to public goods or services that are associated with corresponding social or economic human rights. In arguing that establishing duties for companies in relation to human rights would be detrimental to policy objectives of international development, the government of the US deployed arguments quite similar to those of the large business associations opposed to the Draft Norms.

In a complete contrast to the approach of the US, the South African representative sought in vain to have the resolution amended to include a specific reference to the Draft Norms, and in the end voted against the resolution because it made no reference to the Norms.[28]

The Commission's resolution that proposed the establishment of the SRSG mandate was sponsored by 38 states[29] representing most continents (although a majority from Europe). The resolution was adopted by the Commission by a roll-call vote of 49 in favour to three against, with one abstention.[30] Already the preamble of the mandate resolution indicates that the Commission in 2005 made an effort to include and address

---

[27] Ibid.

[28] United Nations (2005) Press Release (n 22); see also Amnesty International (2005) 2005 UN Commission on Human Rights: Amnesty International welcomes new UN mechanism on Business and Human Rights, Public statement, IOR 41/044/2005 (Public) 21 April 2005. Detailed explanation of the South African statements and explanation of the no-vote has not been available to this author.

[29] Argentina, Austria, Belgium, Canada, Chile, Croatia, Cyprus, Czech Republic, Denmark, Estonia, Ethiopia, Finland, France, Germany, Greece, Guatemala, Hungary, India, Ireland, Italy, Latvia, Lithuania, Luxembourg, Malta, Mexico, Netherlands, Nigeria, Norway, Poland, Portugal, Romania, Russian Federation, Slovakia, Slovenia, Spain, Sweden, Switzerland and United Kingdom of Great Britain and Northern Ireland.

[30] The result of the vote was as follows: *In favour*: Argentina, Armenia, Bhutan, Brazil, Canada, China, Congo, Costa Rica, Cuba, Dominican Republic, Ecuador, Egypt, Eritrea, Ethiopia, Finland, France, Gabon, Germany, Guatemala, Guinea, Honduras, Hungary, India, Indonesia, Ireland, Italy, Japan, Kenya, Malaysia, Mauritania, Mexico, Nepal, Netherlands, Nigeria, Pakistan, Paraguay, Peru, Qatar, Republic of Korea, Romania, Russian Federation, Saudi Arabia, Sri Lanka, Sudan, Swaziland, Togo, Ukraine, United Kingdom and Zimbabwe.

concerns that had led to the mixed reception of the Draft Norms. The preamble 'recognizes' that TNCs can 'contribute to the enjoyment of human rights'.[31] It employs economic system oriented language in setting out the means and forms of such contributions, for example through investment and employment. Legal system interests and considerations on the promotion of human rights are listed only after the recognition of business contributions. 'Responsible operation' of TNCs was stated prior to but in the same sentence as 'effective national legislation',[32] thus signalling to the audience that the role of nation states remains significant as well. Referring to 'channelling the benefits of business towards'[33] the promotion of respect for human rights, the impact of business on human rights was worded in an affirmative way rather than with emphasis on adverse impact. Opening the resolution on a positive note rather than a business-critical note sent an including message and a note of recognition to those in the audience who represented business interests or, as the government statements above show, were concerned with such interests. The resolution mentioned economic system consideration prior to listing of legal and specific human rights considerations.[34] That too suggests an intention on the part of the sponsoring states to signal acknowledgement of business concerns (including with those states that had opposed the Draft Norms on economic system grounds), and to establish a business relevant context for future work on business responsibilities for human rights.

Specific instructions for the mandate holder (the SRSG) to adopt a broad stakeholder consultation approach also suggest that the drafters of the Human Rights Commission's resolution wanted to ensure that business be included in the process towards the output of the mandate. Through this element of the resolution, the Commission indicated to the wide group of stakeholders with an interest in the subject that the proposed process was to be different from the one which had led to the Draft Norms. The resolution requested the mandate holder 'to consult on an ongoing basis with all stakeholders'[35] and listed not only states and intergovernmental organisations but also 'transnational corporations and other business enterprises, and civil society, including employers' organi-

---

Against (3): Australia, South Africa and United States. *Abstention* (1): Burkina Faso, see United Nations (2005) Press Release (n 22).
[31] Commission on Human Rights (2005) Human rights and transnational corporations and other business enterprises, preamble.
[32] Ibid.
[33] Ibid.
[34] Ibid.
[35] Ibid, para. 3.

zations, workers' organizations, indigenous and other affected communities and non-governmental organizations'[36] among organisations to be consulted. In listing companies prior to NGOs when enumerating the types of non-state actors to be consulted, the resolution sent a message on the importance that was attached to the inclusion of business in the process. In doing so, the Commission explicitly introduced a different approach than that which had been applied for the process towards the Draft Norms. Importantly, the resolution's instructions for the multi-stakeholder process to be inclusive of business also showed that the character of the approach that led to the UN Framework and UNGPs was not simply an idea of the SRSG, something that might have been a somewhat accidental or haphazard experiment. The explicit inclusion of business in the process was a decision by the UN's then key political human rights body.

The resolution contained another instruction, which also sent a message to companies, civil society and other concerned organisations that the Commission was aware that certain sectors may be particularly prone to cause adverse impact on human rights. This was an instruction to the SRSG and the UN's administrative human rights body, the OHCHR, to jointly convene annual meetings with executives from specific sectors 'to consider (. . .) the specific human rights issues faced by those sectors, to raise awareness and share best practice'.[37]

From the institutional perspective these steps may be perceived as the UN giving in to business interests. However, viewed from systems-thinking they signal a recognition of the rationality of economic actors and an effort to advance their appreciation of human rights.

5.1.2 Analysis

Conflicting stances at play around and following the presentation of the Draft Norms set a complex basis for the SRSG process. Arguments invoking legal system considerations dominated, especially in statements from organisations and states opposed to the idea of an institutionalisation of human rights responsibilities for business. However, legal system logic was also employed in statements arguing in favour of institutionalising human rights responsibilities for business. The conflict was very much articulated as an 'either/or' between, on the one hand, voluntary action and, on the other, hard law and enforceable account-

---

[36] Ibid.
[37] Ibid., para.5.

ability. Statements speaking into political and legal system rationalities were employed by some large business organisations to argue against an institutionalisation of business responsibilities for human rights as conflicting with public policy objectives. In terms of systems-specific logic, there was only limited usage of economic system logic, and an extensive usage of legal and political system observations to support claims and arguments.

The usage of system-specific language during this period indicates that actors may strategically employ the language of the sub-system whom they want to influence. That is particularly clear in this case in terms of political and economic system language. To a certain extent – as in the case of the ICC and the US Council for International Business – use of legal system language would also resonate with the rationality of the recipients (such as the UN Human Rights Commission) whom transmitters sought to influence. In general, however, the extensive use of legal system language was probably largely due to argumentative custom with international organisations in the field of human rights law. Departing from that habit, the Commission on Human Rights applied all three system-specific rationalities in the preamble to the SRSG mandate.

Statements made in the time between the Human Rights Commission's discussion of the draft UN Norms in 2003 and its resolution establishing the SRSG mandate demonstrate that the debate was marked by contention and antagonism between governments, and between civil society and business organisations. The international labour movement sided with business organisations rather than with civil society in relation to UN development of standards for business responsibility for human rights. International business organisations and the labour movement argued against the UN developing standards of conduct on human rights for business. These organisations employed conventional international law doctrine on international obligations being state obligations to support their arguments.

Business organisations and ICFTU employed legal and political system language to address international law-makers and policy-makers. By referring to international law doctrine and policy objectives on democracy, these organisations addressed recipients in the system specific language of their audiences, presenting arguments apt to cause perturbation within their systems. The US government's deployment of political system language, especially on business contributions to international development, also had the potential to cause a degree of perturbation among states and civil society through inserting irritants relating to their policy objectives on international development and social and economic rights.

5.2 FIRST MANDATE YEAR: FROM ESTABLISHMENT OF MANDATE TO 2006 ('INTERIM') REPORT

Setting out the direction of the mandate's work was a major activity during the first year of the SRSG's 2005–08 term. That activity culminated with the presentation of the SRSG's first report in 2006. Often referred to as the SRSG's 'interim' report, the 2006 report basically closed further discussion on the Draft Norms under the mandate. As noted, the Commission on Human Rights had already closed its own discussion of the Draft Norms in 2004, and did not refer to the Draft Norms in the mandate for the SRSG. Even so, there had been some expectation among stakeholders that the SRSG would revert to the Draft Norms, perhaps even resuscitate them. As the future fate of the Draft Norms in relation to the SRSG's work was unknown to many stakeholders, several statements made during the first year continued to refer to that document, and therefore carried on efforts to construct the substance and regulatory form of business responsibilities for human rights from the divergent perspectives of involved actors.

5.2.1 General Argumentative Structure and Strategy

5.2.1.1 Stakeholder statements

A statement from Amnesty International issued immediately upon the Commission's adoption of the mandate resolution demonstrates the role that the Draft Norms were still believed, or argued by many stakeholders, to hold. This was apparent for example in the statement that '[t]he UN Norms are the most comprehensive statement of standards relevant to companies in relation to human rights'.[38] References to 'provisions' and 'standards', holding companies 'accountable' and identification of 'mechanism to ensure these standards are adhered to'[39] exemplifies extensive legal system orientated language, both mirroring tradition and style in human rights NGOs' interaction with the UN human rights system, and habitual style of communication with a legal environment. Amnesty International argued that the SRSG process should lead to specific standards and accountability or enforcement mechanisms. Employing legal system language and being quite specific in its expectations, Amnesty argued that the SRSG should identify 'further standards',[40] indicating

---

[38] Amnesty International (n 28).
[39] Ibid.
[40] Ibid.

that the standards should go beyond or add to those identified in the Draft Norms. The standards should be of a type to enable companies 'to be held accountable', and the SRSG should develop 'mechanisms to ensure' adherence to the standards.[41]

In a statement issued in June 2005, the International Commission of Jurists (ICJ), an NGO, argued in favour of applying 'due diligence' in the human rights and business context.[42] The ICJ applied the term in relation to states' duties. With an audience of public as well as private and company lawyers, ICJ supported the idea of making it clear to companies that they should not disregard their impact on human rights. 'Due diligence' processes are common in corporate law activities of law firms in relation to mergers and acquisitions to identify legal liability and financial risks to the company. For this reason, it is a notion familiar to corporate management as the conduct of due diligence assessments is a normal procedure by carefully managed companies in relation to the conduct of others. 'Due diligence' had not been employed in the text proper of the Draft Norms, but was noted twice in the Norms' Commentary, in both cases referring to companies.[43] Due diligence has been applied also in human rights case law and literature in relation to states' duty to protect against third party human rights abuse.[44] ICJ's statement emphasised the human rights obligations of states and noted that through the Draft Norms 'the duty of states to exercise 'due diligence' in relation to companies' was 'spelt out in human rights language'.[45] As will be seen, 'due diligence' was picked up by the SRSG and his team as well as some stakeholders who provided statements and comments to the SRSG process. In relation to due diligence, the SRSG, however, shifted focus from states to companies. The notion gained a prominent role as part of the *corporate responsibility to respect* human rights, which was formally introduced with the 'protect, respect and remedy' framework of the SRSG's 2008 report.

A brief September 2005 letter from Amnesty International to the then newly appointed SRSG differs from several other statements that were

---

[41] Ibid.
[42] International Commission of Jurists (2005) Corporate Accountability, International human rights law and the United Nations, Geneva, 9 June 2005.
[43] Draft Norms, paras A(b) and C(d).
[44] The Inter-American Court of Human Rights and the Maastricht Guidelines on Violations of Economic, Social and Cultural Rights, among others, have applied the notion of state due diligence in the human rights context, referring to the state's lack of care to prevent human rights violations by non-state actors. See J. A. Zerk (2006) *Multinationals and Corporate Social Responsibility,* at 84, 86.
[45] International Commission of Jurists (n 42).

made as part of the SRSG process by NGOs and other non-business stakeholders, especially at the early stage of the process, through its relatively extensive deployment of references to economic system logics. Like one of Amnesty's statements before the adoption of the SRSG's mandate resolution, the September 2005 statement referred to a tension between states' economic interests and their obligations to protect human rights. It argued its point on the need for normative international standards on business and human rights by relating economic interests and activities of companies to public policy and legal duties of states and the UN, such as by articulating companies ('if effectively regulated') as potential providers of 'an enabling environment for the enjoyment of human rights'.[46] Several points mentioned in the letter, such as a reference to states being unwilling or unable to protect human rights, were later addressed by the SRSG in several of his annual reports, including the 2008 report that proposed the UN Framework. Although brief and worded in a suggestive rather than definite style, the letter and argumentative strategy made an imprint on the output of the SRSG process in terms of attention paid to the practical effects on human rights of governance gaps at the national level as a result of conflicts between, on the one hand, a state's economic interests including to attract business activities and investment and, on the other, its human rights obligations. Amnesty's letter applied a combination of political and legal system logic with some elements of economic system considerations. Amnesty argued a case for 'a UN set of universally recognized normative standards applicable to business'.[47] Less effective on the SRSG output than the reference to governance gaps, Amnesty suggested to the SRSG that the Draft Norms serve 'as a base for identifying human rights responsibility'.[48] The OECD Guidelines and ILO Tripartite Declaration, both of which are international soft law instruments that make reference to human rights, were identified as 'useful source materials'.[49]

Connecting to legal system and public policy goals, Amnesty argued that business activities can provide 'an enabling environment for the enjoyment of human rights' but that this requires that business is effectively regulated.[50] Economic system references linked the specific activities of business and their potential negative impact on public policy and legal objectives. For example, Amnesty observed that 'the activities of companies can have

---

[46] Amnesty International (2005) Letter to Professor John Ruggie, 16 September 2005, AI ref UN 260-2005.
[47] Ibid.
[48] Ibid.
[49] Ibid.
[50] Ibid.

serious negative impact on the protection of human rights'.[51] The statement encouraged the SRSG to have regard to communities caught between ineffective public governance and economic interests, in particular where a host state is unwilling or unable to protect human rights.[52]

Held soon after the SRSG's appointment, a consultation on human rights and the extractive industry in November 2005 also provided views and information that fed into the SRSG's work. The consultation was held as a follow-up to the mandate resolution, which contained a point on an annual meeting with senior executives from companies and experts from a particular sector to be held by the OHCHR in cooperation with the SRSG. The Human Rights Commission had asked that the meetings deal with specific human rights issues encountered by those sectors to raise awareness and share best practices. Discussing existing initiatives and standards relevant to the extractive sector, the consultation sought to clarify human rights responsibilities of business in the sector, and examined ways to strengthen protection of human rights in the extractive sector. A report prepared by the Office of the High Commissioner[53] indicates that business participants emphasised compliance with national law as the foundation for their practices, arguing that governments should make sure they enforce national law according to their own international obligations and do so rather than count on business to honour non-implemented international standards within national jurisdictions. According to the consultation report, 'NGO participants identified a need for a universal human rights standard in the area of business and human rights, [whereas] employer groups and business participants emphasized the need for enforcement of appropriate national legislation accompanied by practical action on the ground in support of human rights.'[54] Indicating a level of disagreement in relation to the meeting's recommendations, the report notes that '[i]t is important to emphasize that the recommendations were not agreed by the meeting' and provides a list of recommendations 'indicative of the range of views expressed in the final session'.[55] Recommendations were diverse and included to develop standards of

---

[51] Ibid.
[52] Ibid.
[53] United Nations High Commissioner for Human Rights/Commission on Human Rights (2005) Report of the United Nations High Commissioner for Human Rights on the sectoral consultation entitled 'Human Rights and the extractive industry', 10–11 November 2005, UN Doc. E/CN.4/2006/92, 19 December 2005.
[54] Ibid., para. 33.
[55] Ibid., para. 37.

conduct that might but need not be binding; and clarification of accountability mechanisms for business impact on human rights.[56]

A statement made by the chairman of Anglo-American plc (a large mining company) and a joint NGO submission from members of the ESCR-Net Corporate Accountability Working Group[57] give an indication of the divergence of views held in regard to business responsibilities for human rights. The statement delivered by the Chairman of Anglo-American plc first noted that some companies are willing to take on responsibility for their impact on society.[58] Following that point, however, it proceeded to highlight government obligations for human rights. The way these obligations were presented was reminiscent of some of the arguments made by some large business organisations and governments prior to the establishment of the SRSG mandate. The statement's opening section was on 'The responsibilities of governments' and was worded primarily with reference to international law, arguing the doctrinal view of international law that international obligations are borne by states. It referred to 'governments [as bearers of] the prime responsibility' for human rights, empowered to 'establish the laws which ensure that human rights are protected and promoted in their countries'.[59] By arguing that governments enjoy, individually or collectively, through the UN 'the right to apply forms of coercion when individuals or groups fail to respect the human rights of others' and that 'the rest of us do so out of morality, social or commercial pressure',[60] the statement articulated business responsibilities as fundamentally differing from those of states from the legal system doctrinal perspective. It deployed legal system logic to this effect. Doing so in a context in which states and intergovernmental organisations were participants is indicative of an explicit argumentative strategy designed to invoke the legal system rationality of governments. The argument aimed to activate states' and intergovernmental organisations' logic to the effect that they would shift their regulatory focus on human rights from business responsibilities to authorities' obligations. This resembled some of the

---

[56] Ibid., paras 38–41.
[57] ESCR-Net Corporate Accountability Working Group (2005) Joint NGO submission: Consultation on human rights and the extractive industry, final version 9 December 2005, available at http://www.escr-net.org/usr_doc/ESCR-Net_on_HR_and_Extractive_Industry.pdf (last accessed 4 February 2013; website removed).
[58] M. Moody-Stuart (2005) Mark Moody-Stuart on Business and Human Rights, 17 November 2005, available at http://www.unglobalcompact.org/NewsAndEvents/news_archives/2005_11_17.html (last accessed 4 February 2016).
[59] Ibid.
[60] Ibid.

From incremental steps to emerging regime 191

arguments that had been made in the context of the EU's MSF as well as by companies and governments opposed to the idea of the Draft Norms. Based on the success of that type of argumentative structure in those contexts, it might have been expected to be equally successful for averting further steps in the UN context. However, the Anglo-American plc argument and similar statements were part of a larger picture, and as the SRSG mandate evolved during the first term, system-specific argumentative strategies came to be increasingly deployed by other stakeholders too.

While the statement made by the NGO-coalition ESCR-net at the consultation on the extractives sector also used legal system logic, they viewed business responsibilities for human rights differently from Anglo-American plc. In a statement presented at the extractives consultation, ESCR-net introduced its contribution by employing legal system language to argue that a change in international law was required to deal with human rights and business through international standards that must 'ultimately be enforceable'.[61] Referring to business-related human rights abuse as 'violations', the statement equated abuse caused by companies with the legal character of abuse caused by governments.

Another example of a civil society statement, in a February 2006 submission to the SRSG submitted just before the release of the SRSG's first report, Interfaith (an investor group favouring socially responsible investment) deployed legal system logic combined with some reference to economic system interest of business to argue that 'a minimum set of standards'[62] would be good for business. Making reference to the idea of a 'level playing field', the organisation observed that several companies had 'acknowledged that they want to know the "rules of the road"', arguing that a minimum set of standards would reduce uncertainty and therefore be beneficial to business. This reasoning can be detected in the later 2007 and 2008 reports by the SRSG. While the SRSG was exposed to many sources, the application in his reports of wording and proposals made by stakeholders suggests he paid attention to arguments that could be useful for achieving understanding across functional sub-systems of the benefits of normative guidance on business responsibilities for human rights.

5.2.1.2 SRSG statements

In a speech delivered in October 2005, a few months after the inception of the mandate, the SRSG set out his understanding of the institutional

---

[61] ESCR-net Corporate Accountability Working Group (n 57).
[62] Interfaith Center for Corporate Responsibility (2006) Letter to John Ruggie, 6 February 2006.

framework for the issues to be addressed under the mandate. The SRSG first deployed a combination of legal and economic system logics, focusing on firms' interests. Later, the argument mainly deployed legal system related observations on accountability as a counterweight to the economic and legal rights of companies under international trade law. He next introduced political system considerations in adding that companies' leverage might serve towards public policy objectives. He observed that 'some companies have made themselves and even their entire sectors targets by doing bad things on a big scale, as a result of mistakes, short-sightedness or malfeasance',[63] and that such actions caused societal demands for greater corporate accountability.[64]

Much like the approach and analyses of the SRSG in his other capacities as an academic[65] and advisor to the UN Global Compact, the main argument was that international law had developed to provide increased protection of the rights of TNCs, and that companies had also emerged as participants in some areas of 'international standards setting'.[66] Having thus established that companies had both benefited from international law and had taken to making rules themselves, the SRSG proceeded to argue that the imbalance between corporate rights and duties fuelled calls for businesses to consider their impact on human rights, and by many actors for increased corporate accountability.[67] The SRSG proceeded to counter one of the arguments against business responsibilities for human rights, which held that establishing such responsibilities would allow states not to honour their international obligations. He drew on legal system logic ('if governments everywhere did what they are supposed to')[68] to remind states as well as other stakeholders that slack state delivery of their obligations contributes to the societal 'urgency' of the need for institutionalising business responsibilities for human rights.

In a speech at a seminar in London in December 2005, the SRSG laid out what was to become a main thread of the mandate's work and reporting with a focus on 'weak governance zones'[69] as areas that particularly

---

[63] SRSG (2005) 'Opening remarks', Wilton Park conference on Business and Human Rights, 10–12 October 2005.
[64] Ibid.
[65] E.g., J. G. Ruggie (2004) 'Reconstituting the global public domain – issues, actors and practices', 10(4) *European Journal of International Relations* pp. 499–531.
[66] SRSG (n 63).
[67] Ibid.
[68] Ibid.
[69] SRSG (2005) 'Remarks', Business and Human Rights seminar, Old Billingsgate, London, 8 December 2005.

call for businesses to take responsibility for their impact on human rights. Making reference to implications for companies, which derived from the US Alien Torts Claims Act and emerging extraterritorial legislation pertaining to business actions, the statement addressed the economic risks that companies may encounter if they disregard human rights ('As companies are discovering at their peril') and connected this to legal system observations ('operations in weak governance zones do not occur in "law free zones"').[70] Presenting a turn of 'prevailing ideas, ideologies and institutional practices' to 'catch up with new economic and social forces' as being of benefit to both business and human rights in a general sense,[71] the speech combined divergent interests of functional sub-systems into a statement that implicitly referred to economic, political and legal system logics at once ('the alternatives would be bad for business and human rights alike').[72] The speech built on this to call on 'the business and human rights communities'[73] to work on shared interests rather than differences. This is significant because it clarified that the SRSG was not on the side of either, but set on assisting towards the development of a shared foundation.

At the same time, the SRSG explained that a hard law approach was not his priority. Making reference to the mixed results and range of international criminal law, he argued that the idea of imposing direct obligations on companies under international law contradicted an aim of achieving 'practical results',[74] similar to what he would later refer to as his 'principled pragmatism' for achieving results on the ground for victims of corporate human rights abuse.

The focus on weak governance zones was followed up by an announcement at the end of December 2005 that the SRSG had asked IOE to undertake a project on effective ways for companies to deal with dilemma situations encountered in 'weak governance zones'. IOE was to liaise with its members and other business organisations, including ICC and the Business and Industry Advisory Committee (BIAC) to the OECD.[75] Recall that IOE and ICC had been strongly opposed to the Draft Norms. Engaging them in work on human rights dilemmas in weak governance zones might look like letting the fox into the henhouse. Instead, as will be

---

[70] Ibid.
[71] Ibid.
[72] Ibid.
[73] Ibid.
[74] Ibid.
[75] SRSG (2005) Announcement by John Ruggie, Special Representative of the UN Secretary-General on business and human rights, regarding initiative by International Organization of Employers, 21 December 2005.

elaborated below (section 5.3.1.1), the move resulted in a change in stances within those organisations, leading to enhanced support among them and their members for the SRSG process and its foundations. Thus, the change applied not only to the work and recommendations of the SRSG, but also to the idea of businesses having responsibilities for human rights as well as normative base in international human rights law.

5.2.2 The 2006 ('Interim') Report

The SRSG's interim report[76] was published only seven months into the mandate, in February 2006.[77] The report was addressed to the UN Commission on Human Rights and was published by the Commission (just as the later SRSG reports were published by the Human Rights Council). While written mainly in political and legal system language, the report also contains some economic system references, mainly comprising observations on the profit-oriented system made up of private corporations. The report set out the approach as a pragmatic one based on basic principles of international human rights law.

The report observed that in the current globalised world, it is relevant to consider engaging companies in relation to human rights in terms of legal as well as economic and political considerations. Making reference to the state-based international order and the role of the UN, the opening paragraphs suggested that a shift in the international order to include companies not only as holders of rights, but also of bearers of duties is a necessary consequence of the fact that companies have come to play significant 'public' roles,[78] that is, for example take on tasks that are traditionally governmental obligations and exercise power that resembles that of governments. The report explained that such a shift was necessary because:

> The United Nations was created to provide a State-based international order. In 1945, States were the sole international decision-makers of any significance;

---

[76] Commission on Human Rights (2006) Interim report of the Special Representative of the Secretary-General on the issue of human rights and transnational corporations and other business enterprises, UN Doc. E/CN.4/2006/97, 22 February 2006.
[77] The report contains an introduction and two main parts. Part I, 'Framing the Issues', contains three sections: A: Globalization (paras 9–19), B: Abuses and correlates (paras 20–30), and C: Existing responses (paras 31–53). Part II, 'Strategic Directions', contains two sections: A: The Norms (paras 56–69) and B: Principled pragmatism (paras 70–81).
[78] Commission on Human Rights (2006) Interim report (n 76).

they were the subjects of their joint decisions and were responsible for enforcing those decisions. (. . .) [W]hat once was external trade between national economies increasingly has become internalized within firms as global supply chain management, functioning in real time and directly shaping the daily lives of people around the world.[79]

Having thus established through legal and economic system logics that the UN and states have acted to promote and protect the economic interests of companies, the report added political system logic in describing how company actions have led to 'increased demands for greater corporate responsibility and accountability'.[80] It proceeded to refer to public policy aims of the UN, such as the Millennium Development Goals (MDG), the provision of medicines in poor countries, mitigating climate change and generally curbing human rights abuses.[81] Connecting to economic system logic, it built in an argument that 'good practices' may be turned into a 'competitive advantage'[82] for companies that actively seek to avoid human rights problems.[83] It elaborated by referring to the UDHR and combining economic system considerations with those of the legal and political systems by noting that 'securing respect for human rights' should be 'a central aim of governance at all levels', both private and public.[84]

Through use of economic system references, the report argued that the logic and features of the economic system may cause human rights to be violated, unless the basics of the economic system's objective of making profits and its institutional manifestations are subjected to control. Again, the argument combined the interests of public policy, (human rights) law and business and their respective social systems by identifying 'the core challenge of business and human rights'[85] in terms that relate to all three functions. To operationalise the methods for addressing shared challenges, the report made reference to governance as a steering issue that resonates with all three social sub-systems. Building on that, it qualified the specific shared challenge as 'devising instruments of corporate and public governance to contain and reduce' tendencies of companies to abuse human rights.[86]

Presenting results of a survey of instances of business violations of

---

[79] Ibid., paras 9–11.
[80] Ibid.
[81] Ibid.
[82] Ibid.
[83] Ibid.
[84] Ibid.
[85] Ibid.
[86] Ibid.

human rights, the SRSG proceeded to explain that these tend to take place in 'weak governance' zones,[87] including states with low levels of rule of law. Proposed response options were described not as legal reactions, but as 'policy responses'.[88] Legal terminology such as *de lege ferenda* or 'legal policy' was not used, perhaps deliberately avoided. At the most, the statement contained reference to 'policy preferences about what the law should become'.[89] As will be seen, an insistence by the SRSG on his work being policy oriented rather than legal standard setting – as the Draft Norms had been perceived by some to be – was carried through throughout the first mandate to the 2008 report, which proposed the UN Framework that was referred to by that report as a 'policy framework'. This insistence was upheld despite the various references to (non-)'doctrinal' debate, 'evidence-based findings', and to 'providing conceptual clarification',[90] all of which suggest that legal system considerations might emerge.

As to the Draft Norms, the SRSG concluded that the Norms contained 'useful elements',[91] but that they were lacking in terms of precision and conceptual clarity. This led him to discard the Draft Norms altogether for the purposes of the work under the mandate in order to clear the table of what he described as misconceptions, and of doctrinal debates on the Norms, their aims, substance and intended or possible future regulatory form.

Despite the declared pragmatic approach, much of the 2006 report's second part was a marked transition from the policy-oriented observations in the first part of the report to specific international law reasoning. In the latter, the report also drew on legal theory and method to establish the current legal status of human rights obligations of states and companies. It made the point that current 'instruments that do have international legal force (...) impose obligations on States' and that 'all existing instruments specifically aimed at holding corporations to international human rights standards' are voluntary. It did, however, recognise that companies may be held liable 'for committing, or for complicity in, the most heinous human rights violations amounting to international crimes'. Legal system language was also employed in the report's conclusion that international law had not yet been 'transformed to the point where it can be said that the broad array of international human rights attach direct obligations to corporations'.

---

[87] Ibid.
[88] Ibid., e.g., paras 28 and 29.
[89] Ibid., para. 65.
[90] Ibid., para. 7.
[91] Ibid., para. 57.

Having established what effectively came to serve as a legal doctrinal foundation for the mandate's work on business responsibilities for human rights, the report proceeded to combine legal and public policy considerations into a statement that recognised that there 'are legitimate arguments in support of the proposition' of direct obligations for corporations in some situations. The argument took its point of departure in international law doctrine in stating that such arguments are particularly relevant when governments lack the will or capacity to enforce their obligations. It proceeded to incorporate some political implications in adding that as a result, 'the classical international human rights regime, therefore, cannot possibly be expected to function as intended'. It further combined international law doctrine and legal politics, with an implicit element of public policy interests in the statement that 'there are no inherent conceptual barriers to States deciding to hold corporations directly responsible' but that propositions made are not 'about established law; they are normative commitments and policy preferences about what the law should become'. Thus, although it did not use the terminology, the report did establish its point of departure in mainly traditional international law doctrine (*lex lata,* or existing applicable law) with limited recognition of international law obligations on companies, and consequently constructed possible changes as issues of politics of law (*lex ferenda,* or the law as it should ideally be).

The interim report proceeded to set out the future course of the mandate's work in line with what the report referred to as 'principled pragmatism'.[92] Several paragraphs indicated that responsibilities of business with regard to human rights are not just matters of law in the strict sense or of politics, but also of social norms and moral considerations. Alluding to how a company may self-regulate in response to expectations of its environment, the report described 'individual company policies and voluntary initiatives' as 'a reflection of how social expectations influence' their conduct.[93] No direct reference was made to reflexive law. The report, however, employed a line of thinking indicative of related observations or ideas on how business organisations may react to externalities. The report presented social expectations of business as complementary 'where the capacity or willingness to enforce legal standards is lacking or absent'.[94] The topic of social expectations remained significant in the subsequent SRSG reports.

---

[92] Ibid., para. 81.
[93] Ibid., para. 74.
[94] Ibid., para. 75.

The essence of the 'principled pragmatism' in terms of method and expected outcome was set out in wording that combined legal system language and political system considerations. The approach was described by applying UN Charter-like language, referring to 'strengthening the promotion and protection of human rights' and public policy aims of creating change that affects 'the daily lives of people'.[95]

The 'principled pragmatism' was elaborated by the SRSG in a letter issued shortly after the report as considering 'whatever measures work best in creating change where it matters most'.[96] That approach may also account for the relative absence of legal terminology in relation to the legal policy aspects of the SRSG's work. By avoiding reference to the mandate and its outcome in terms of legal policy or *de lege ferenda,* the SRSG worked around legal system worded objections and implied impracticable consequences like those that the Draft Norms encountered.

5.2.3 Analysis

During the first year of the mandate prior to the presentation of the SRSG's first report, civil society stakeholder statements favouring the development of standards of conduct for business referred to international human rights law and to the Draft Norms as a basis for further work. Recall in this context that the Draft Norms referenced a large number of hard and soft instruments on human rights as well as on some other types of rights. Some statements also referred to specific soft law instruments that addressed labour rights or human rights. Doctrinal legal system language and arguments dominated in stakeholder statements during the first year of the mandate prior to the SRSG's presentation of his first report. While business persisted in referring to doctrinal international law on international obligations being state obligations, NGOs made connections between national and international law and different aspects of (national) law that protects individuals. As exemplified by the Secretary-General of ICJ and one statement from Amnesty International, economic system logic on the benefits that companies might derive from an institutionalisation of human rights responsibilities for business was making its way into arguments. Political system language was deployed only sparsely by civil society, in particular by Amnesty International to argue that standards on human rights conduct for business would benefit public policy objectives.

---

[95] Ibid., para. 81.
[96] SRSG (2006) Letter to Olivier de Schutter and Antoine Bernard, FIDH. 20 March 2006.

From incremental steps to emerging regime 199

The deployment of legal system logic and reference to doctrinal international law, which was made by business, parallels that which was noted above in relation to business statements prior to the adoption of the SRSG mandate. This suggests that the approach persisted among many companies with regard to an actual institutionalisation of human rights responsibilities for companies.

SRSG statements at this time drew on all three involved system-specific logics, that is, the economic, the legal and the political. Charged with the process set up under the mandate resolution, the SRSG in that capacity was not himself part of a functional system, but rather acted as a medium for the Commission on Human Rights and later the Human Rights Council. This meant that his interest was not a particular version of business responsibilities for human rights, but to deliver on his task under the mandate, and therefore to forge agreement among the involved functional sub-systems on as advanced a normative instrument on business responsibilities for human rights as he considered to be feasible. In consequence, he employed legal system logic both to draw attention to the discrepancy between companies' rights under international trade law and their limited duties as to their impact on societies, and to states' obligations to implement and enforce their international obligations in national law. Thus, although the SRSG employed international legal system doctrinal arguments, contrary to business statements did so with a clear message that human rights are not only a matter for states. He employed economic and political system logic to strengthen the argument that business enterprises have responsibilities for human rights by drawing up implications to companies and states alike of neglecting human rights.

In terms of the form of regulation, civil society organisations argued in favour of a hard institutionalisation of human rights standards for business and did so through legal system logic reference to violations, accountability, mechanisms to ensure adherence, and legal certainty. Business argued against such standards, recommending instead voluntary codes and schemes functioning through dialogue, learning and exchanges. The SRSG did not favour hard law measures in terms of direct obligations on companies, explaining with reference to both political and legal system logic that such measures would not deliver the practical results nor the certainty called for by other actors within a reasonable time for victims affected by corporate human rights abuse. On the other hand, he did not explicitly reject either approach, or some combination.

Only a small number of stakeholder submissions were made to the SRSG during the first year of the mandate prior to his presentation of the interim report. Statements made in the phase between the Commission of Human Rights' 2004 session and the establishment of the mandate were intended to influence the work of the then-still-to-be-appointed SRSG. Comparison between stakeholder statements, the interim report, and the SRSG's own speeches suggests that statements in legal, political and economic system logics all had an impact on the SRSG's 2006 report. The analysis also suggests more specific findings. First, two types of arguments were particularly effective in terms of influencing the SRSG's findings transmitted in the interim report. The first type comprised legal logic arguments, argued on the basis of conventional international law doctrine of states' obligations for human rights. This type of '*lex lata*' argument was mainly made by business organisations and business representatives. As we shall see, from the 2007 report and onwards, the SRSG expanded the doctrinal international law argument by applying the specific horizontality human rights doctrine to support the implications of the state duty to protect. However, in the 2006 report the influence of the conventional doctrinal international law argument was still stronger than the newer and specialised horizontality doctrine that later came to dominate. Second, in terms of the weight with which the Draft Norms might have carried over into the SRSG mandate, critique of the Draft Norms couched in legal logic arguments focusing on weaknesses from a legal perspective of precision and conceptual clarity won the case for the future of the Draft Norms. This was to the detriment of softer arguments on the Draft Norms' value as a basis for an inventory of human rights standards for business. The former type of argument was mainly made by business organisations, the latter by NGOs. This finding is interesting both in terms of observations on what types of stakeholders were successful in arguing their case, and in terms of the type of arguments that turned out to be influential in the context. For the Draft Norms, the hard legal argument based on conventional legal and international law doctrine won out, not only in influencing the pre-mandate debate in the Human Rights Commission, but also in the arguments made by the SRSG in his dismissal of the UN Norms to clear the slate for work on the objectives set by the mandate resolution.

The analysis also indicates that although the SRSG refused to approach his mandate from a doctrinal perspective, the classical legal doctrinal argument was in fact quite influential for the interim report. Stakeholders who mastered the international law doctrine were successful in influencing the direction of the future debate on human rights and business. This is not by itself surprising in a highly legal context as that of international law-making, including processes of 'law-in-the-making'. From a more general point of view, however, the fact that the doctrinal argument was more successful somewhat stands the SRSG's allegedly 'non-doctrinal' approach on its head. The antagonistic debate on the Norms prior to the SRSG mandate led the SRSG to take issue with the Draft Norms and discard them based on deficiencies argued on the basis of legal doctrine and applicability, rather than simply revise the text. As already indicated and to be elaborated in the following, legal doctrine continued to influence the SRSG's arguments, but with increased integration of newer international law doctrine, in particular on states' duty to protect. Doctrinal arguments in the interim report suggest that the SRSG strategically sought to address the Human Rights Council in the legal system logic that the Council's rationality would appreciate, generally employing legal system doctrine to anchor his work and its suggestions within the general international law background framing the mandate, while labelling his strategy non-doctrinal in order to be able to work pragmatically across system-specific interests.

Legal doctrine formed a significant part of the wording and argumentative strategy in the interim report, especially towards the conclusion. Political and economic system logics were employed by way of introduction to frame the issue and establish the urgency of addressing the adverse impact of business on public policy concerns. The interim report's usage of economic system language was mainly made with reference to adverse impact on society.

These points serve to indicate what type of argument was successful in the context, that is, what argument was the most influential. In the case of the interim report, the stakeholder that happened to master that successful argument was business. The result may also partly be an effect of the fact that a sector-specific consultation was held with the extractive industries prior to the publication of the interim report. That gave industry an opportunity to contribute targeted views on the mandate, background, and its possible outcome.

The attention paid by NGOs to the lessons and needs of victims of corporate human rights violations also had some influence. Stakeholders' urging of the SRSG to consider local communities became stronger with the on-going development of the mandate's work. In relation to the interim report, however, the argument to consider victims, which became voiced in legal as well as economic and political terms, was among the most influential imprint of NGOs' statements.

Economic system arguments on the risks to business that may result from their disregard of human rights carried some influence. Such arguments, made by NGOs and SRI organisations, were limited at this phase, yet they appear to have made an impact on the interim reports seen through its references to the risk for litigation and its statement that weak governance zones are not 'law free zones'. This suggests that a combination of economic system concerns of business and the combined economic- and-legal risk aspects (the economic losses in a wide sense that may result from litigation) was successful. As the analysis below will show, SRSG arguments on company interests in respecting human rights in terms of risk management became more prevalent during the second and third year of the mandate.

5.3 SECOND MANDATE YEAR: FROM 'INTERIM' REPORT TO 2007 REPORT

During the second mandate year, the SRSG held workshops with legal experts to discuss extraterritorial legislation as a tool to improve the accountability of transnational corporations for human rights violations and corporate responsibility for human rights under international law.[97] He held regional consultations to gain perspectives on the overall issues covered by the mandate and to learn about broader stakeholder concerns.[98] In Asia (Bangkok) the consultation was on human rights issues in supply chains; in Africa (Johannesburg) on human rights issues for businesses operating in conflict zones, and in Latin America (Bogota) on the social license to operate, in particular with regard to local communities and indigenous peoples. Workshop participants included NGOs and trade unions, business, governments, international organisations and academics, mainly from the region where each workshop took place. Background and discussion papers were prepared by academics and other expert stakeholders for some of the consultations and workshops.[99] Workshop and background paper themes reflect the diversity of issues covered under the mandate. The key substance of the meetings was rendered by summary

---

[97] For details, see E. Wilmhurst (2006) Human rights and transnational corporations: Legislation and government regulation, Chatham House, 15 June; SRSG (2006) 'Summary report: Seminar of legal experts: extraterritorial legislation as a tool to improve the accountability of transnational corporations for human rights violations', Brussels, November 3–4; SRSG (2006) 'Summary report: Workshop on attributing corporate responsibility for human rights under international law', NYU School of Law, Friday, November 17.

[98] SRSG (2006) 'Summary report: Asian regional consultation: Held by the Special Representative of the Secretary-General on human rights and transnational corporations and other business enterprises', Bangkok, June 26–27 at 1.

[99] E.g., R. Casey (2006) *Meaningful Change: Raising the Bar in the Supply Chain Workplace Standards*, Friedrich Ebert Stiftung and Harvard University John F. Kennedy School of Government; O. De Schutter (2006) *Extraterritorial Jurisdiction as a Tool for Improving the Human Rights Accountability of Transnational Corporations*, Belgium: Louvain, December 2006; 'Revenue sharing and fiscal management: Discussion paper' (2006) draft for discussion 28 July 2006.

reports from each of the meetings. Consultations were also held on human rights impact assessment and on human rights and the financial sector. Feeding into the SRSG reports in a general sense, three major analytical products were developed by the SRSG and his team: a mapping of state obligations for corporate acts under the UN human rights treaty system; a report on state responsibilities to regulate and adjudicate corporate activities, focusing on the core human rights treaties; and a report on business recognition of human rights, looking at global patterns and regional and sectoral variations.[100]

For the purposes of the current study the main point is that a general 'do-no-harm' perspective (for companies to respect human rights) was proposed at the workshop on attribution of corporate responsibility for human rights under international law and made its way to the UN Framework.

A number of submissions were made to the SRSG, both in the context of workshops and outside of these. Some submissions contained detailed analytical descriptions of jurisprudence and treaty law in relation to elements of the SRSG's mandate, offering stakeholder insights and expertise of the author groups.[101]

5.3.1 General Argumentative Structure and Strategy

In response to the publication of the interim report, a number of NGOs and others submitted comments to the SRSG or published comments elsewhere. SRSG replies are not specifically analysed in here as they were mostly of a general character, clarifying issues but without contributing in a material sense to be observed in later steps of the mandate work.

5.3.1.1 Stakeholder statements

One particularly comprehensive NGO statement represented points that others made in less detailed fashion. In a position paper dated 15 March 2006 the Federation Internationale des Ligues des Droits des l'Homme

---

[100] M. Wright and A. Lehr, (2006) *Business Recognition of Human Right: Global Patterns, Regional and Sectoral Variations*, a study conducted under the direction of John G. Ruggie, Harvard University, UN Secretary-General's Special Representative for Business and Human Rights, 12 December 2006.

[101] See for example the report Forest Peoples Programme and Tebtebba Foundation (2006) 'Indigenous Peoples' rights, extractive industries and transnational and other enterprises: A submission to the Special Representative of the Secretary-General on human rights and transnational corporations and other business enterprises', 29 December.

(FIDH) argued in favour of retaining the Draft Norms.[102] The position paper mainly employed legal systems logic in its argument on the need for human rights standards for business. The position paper took issue with some of the SRSG's findings in order to present a case for 'the adoption of universal standards applicable to all companies'. To make that point, the position paper employed legal system language derived from the UN Charter, making reference to the 'promotion and protection of human rights'. It also suggested that 'universal standards' should be binding and enforceable, as evident for example through reference to such legal system wording as 'modes of direct accountability'.[103]

The paper set out what it considered to be weaknesses in the interim report, highlighting a failure to recognise precedents in international criminal law to impose human rights obligations on individuals.[104] Also, it introduced the terminology of the state duty to protect against human rights abuse by non-state actors, bringing a key point into the discursive construction of business responsibilities for human rights that was to be highly influential. Without prejudice to the significance of contributions made by other actors, the FIDH paper demonstrates the impact of the on-going multi-stakeholder consultative process throughout the mandate. It shows the effects on both illuminating and influencing the output of the multi-stakeholder process, especially when stakeholders deployed an argumentative strategy that assisted the SRSG in clarifying, appreciating or arguing a point in his communication with other stakeholder groups and deploying the relevant logic. For the SRSG's construction of the state duty to protect as set forth in Pillar One of the UN Framework and UNGPs, the legal logic was relevant. The state duty to protect aspect of international human rights law had been mostly absent both in the SRSG debate until then, and during the debate on the Draft Norms, except for some academic treatises.[105]

The FIDH report also took issue with the interim report's decon-

---

[102] FIDH (2006) 'Position paper: Comments to the interim report of the Special Representative of the Secretary-General on the issue of Human Rights and Transnational Corporations and other business enterprises, February 22, 2006', 15 March, http://www.fidh.org/IMG/pdf/business442a.pdf (last accessed 4 February 2013; website has been removed).

[103] Ibid., at 3, 7.

[104] In a response dated 20 March 2006 the SRSG pointed out that he had in fact addressed the development of international criminal law and evolving obligations of individuals in the interim report (paras 62–64), see SRSG (n 96).

[105] N. Jägers (2002) *Corporate Human Rights Obligations: In Search of Accountability.* Antwerp: Intersentia; A. Clapham (2006) *Human Rights Obligations of Non-State Actors,* New York: Oxford University Press.

struction of the 'sphere of influence' concept and its observations on 'complicity'. Those observations will be reverted to below in the section 5.5, but it is worth noting here that FIDH's legal logic oriented critique was reflected in clarifications in the UN Framework and a complementary detailed report on 'sphere of influence' and 'complicity'.

The FIDH statement also drew on legal theory to critique some of the findings of the interim report, including some of those that had been voiced by business and government actors with regard to the Draft Norms. It employed legal system logic to refute the SRSG's 'implicit argument, that international human rights law imposes obligations only on states'.[106] The FIDH position paper addressed several of the SRSG's references to the protection of companies' interests under international trade law, thus meeting (and seeking to counter) the SRSG on his own argument by challenging its basic premise, at least as that was perceived by FIDH. The statement observed that 'the recognition of an international legal personality to transnational corporations should not be seen as a prerequisite to the imposition of obligations on such entities, just like it has not been considered a prerequisite for the recognition of rights to these actors, for instance, under free trade agreements'.[107] This legal logic argument served the SRSG in pushing his points on corporate responsibilities for human rights. Points on corporate legal personality, particularly in the context of national law implementation of international criminal law, were subsequently addressed by the SRSG in his 2007 and 2008 reports.

A statement submitted in May 2006 by a large group of NGOs argued in favour of achieving corporate accountability for human rights through the adoption of global standards, which should build on international human rights and humanitarian law and other 'internationally recognized principles'.[108] Much of the statement was characteristic of the style and form of argument of NGO statements to the SRSG on the interim report, with the exception of the above FIDH statement that contributed to bringing the state duty to protect aspect of international human rights law into the debate. Like most other NGO statements, it was also kept mainly in legal system logic based in international law. Business responsibilities were referred to as derived from states' obligations under international law. However, this statement also set out the connection between states and businesses with regard to human rights in a way that was later found in the

---

[106] FIDH (n 102) at 7.
[107] Ibid., at 7–8.
[108] Human Rights Watch and others (2006) 'Joint NGO letter in Response to Interim Report 1', 18 May, http://www.fidh.org/IMG/pdf/Joint_NGO_Response_to_Interim_Report.pdf (last accessed 4 February 2013; website has been removed).

UN Framework. Along with explanations from human rights experts, the arguments proved useful for the SRSG's quest to elaborate a connection between the roles of states and businesses in terms that would resonate with both. The NGO statement referred specifically to 'responsibilities' of business and to the 'obligation [of states] to protect', translating into states' 'duty to ensure that businesses act' in accordance with each state's international obligations.[109] This line of thinking later appeared in Pillar One and Two of the UN Framework. The statement said, inter alia:

> While states are the primary duty-holders under international law, including human rights and humanitarian law, it should not be forgotten that businesses also have responsibilities under these legal regimes. Indeed, as part of their obligation to protect human rights under their jurisdiction, states are under a duty to ensure that businesses act accordingly.[110]

The NGO statement also argued for accountability for companies and 'the adoption of universal standards on business and human rights'[111] as the means towards that end. That part of the argument was less concrete and more programmatic than the argument in the same statement on the state duty to protect and business responsibility to respect. As further discussed below, it appears that the programmatic parts of this and other statements were less influential, probably because they were vaguer and less suited for immediate adaptation into the SRSG's texts.

A submission made by the civil society organisation International Alert at the regional consultation in Johannesburg[112] emphasised the experience of companies that acted on human rights grounds during the apartheid times in South Africa. Referring to specific cases, the statement referred to moral as well as economic logic informed motivation that may drive some managers or other individuals to take responsibility for their company's human rights impact, considering for example 'the pressure of the market' or 'a desire to protect the company's reputation'.[113] It argued that ethical, economic systems or even institutionalised soft law or voluntary measures such as sector-specific principles or the Global Compact are not sufficient and called for 'guidance on the ground level so that they can develop their procedures'.[114] The statement thus described a need for specific norms that

---

[109] Ibid.
[110] Ibid.
[111] Ibid.
[112] International Alert (2006) 'Speech by Salil Tripathi', Johannesburg, 27–28 March.
[113] Ibid.
[114] Ibid.

companies may rely on in their day-to-day operations. Similar reasoning is found in the 2007 report and the UN Framework.

Among a relatively limited number of business statements following the SRSG's interim report, the International Council on Mining and Metals (ICMM) submitted statements in March 2006 and October 2006. Referring to voluntary transnational schemes that had been developed to address severe human rights risks related to natural resource extraction particularly common in 'weak states' (schemes like the Kimberley Process and the Voluntary Principles on Security and Human Rights), the March 2006 statement developed its points from the perspective of public policy interests. Thus, ICMM developed an argumentative strategy resembling that which had been employed by some companies in the MSF process, but also combined references to public policy objectives with economic logic.

ICMM argued that greater recognition should be made by the SRSG of the benefits that mining may provide to 'the poorest countries of this world',[115] partly as a result of foreign investment. The statement deployed references to the economic system rationality of companies, including 'incentives', 'performance', 'economic benefits' and 'protect[ion] of investments' combined with references to public-policy interests of host and local governments and communities. It made reference to public policy concerns as well as interests in presenting the mining industry as both having a 'social and environmental impact' and creating 'constraints and opportunities for enhancing human rights performance'.[116] The statement articulated the industry's interest in, and alleged will to engage in, voluntary regulation as based on the 'unusually strong incentive' that firms in the mining industry have 'to develop positive relations with local communities'.[117] Tying business organisations' economic rationality (including long-term protection of investments) to overall societal interests, the statement deployed reference to public policy interests ('mitigating environmental impact', 'creating local economic benefits', and 'sensitivity to the concerns of local governments')[118] to elaborate on the ways in which industry may contribute to social concerns without a need for formalised regulation.

---

[115] International Council on Mining and Metals (2006) 'Submission to UN Secretary General's Special Representative on Human Rights and Business: Clarity and consensus on legitimate human rights responsibilities for companies could accelerate progress', March 2006.
[116] Ibid.
[117] Ibid.
[118] Ibid.

Drawing on a combination of political and economic system considerations, the statement developed an argument that investing in, and by implication the activities of, the mining sector are beneficial to host countries from the public policy objective perspective of promoting economic growth and development.

ICMM's March 2006 statement closed with a strong call for governments to take action to honour their national and international obligations. Reminding its audience that 'basic welfare provision, after all, is a core task for the state'[119] and that debates over companies' responsibilities would not arise if 'governments ensured rights were upheld',[120] it drew on legal system language to reinforce the mining industry's argument against mandatory regulation on business responsibilities. This argument resembles the one made by the Anglo-American plc chairman under the extractives sector consultation in 2005, and like that one also resembles arguments made by business organisations during the EU's MSF and to refute the Draft Norms. But as observed above, those strategic arguments did not have the influence in SRSG process that they had had previously. As was already becoming apparent, the SRSG was developing a strategy of arguing in a manner to invoke perturbation with business. This was an inversion of what especially the extractives sector and large business associations had been aiming to do vis-à-vis authorities through an argumentative strategy invoking the rationality of states. As will be discussed further below and in Chapter 6, as the SRSG came increasingly refer to the state duty to protect and to play on business rationality through stabilising and de-stabilising arguments, his arguments on business responsibilities gained in strength.

ICMM's second submission set out a number of recommendations for the SRSG from the mining industry. Under the title 'How the UN SRSG can help spread good practice and tackle critical issues',[121] the submission contained a general commitment on the part of the ICMM members to advance industry good practice on human rights.[122] Essentially, however, the statement built an argument that more attention should be paid to governments' obligations for human rights, and that voluntary initiatives are preferable to international standards for the purpose of regulation of companies. Through a combination of legal and economic system logics

---

[119] Ibid.
[120] Ibid.
[121] ICMM (2006) 'Second submission to UN Secretary General's Special Representative on Human Rights and Business: Mining and Human Rights: How the UN SRSG can help spread good practice and tackle critical issues', October 2006.
[122] Ibid., at 1, 13.

with a few references to political system interests, the argument referred to the obligations of governments and to legislation and the challenges that various types of companies face with regard to human rights (presented in economic system terminology as 'performance'). The conclusion drew on legal system logic to both underscore 'the fundamental role of governments' and argue increased focus of 'existing, human-rights related, multi-stakeholder initiatives' and 'implementation by governments of existing international commitments'.[123]

Similar to some of the arguments made by business associations during the European MSF that came to be incorporated into the MSF Final Report, the ICMM statement effectively sought to roll the issue of business impact on human rights back to the discussion on states' obligations under international law, deploying legal system language to argue that point. The point was stressed further in a subsequent paragraph, which drew on legal system language to argue 'broader implementation of targeted voluntary initiatives' as 'the most effective response' and argued that governments should be encouraged to implement 'their existing legal commitments'.[124] However, some points that were argued with reference to economic system logic fed into the SRSG reports along with other statements to the same effect. This was the case with the ICMM's suggestion for a clarification of the responsibilities of business and those of states. Thus, eventually and drawing once more on economic system considerations but this time combined with policy objectives of socio-economic development, the ICMM moved towards a call for increased guidance for business organisations. Adding legal system observations, the organisation argued that the solution may be provided by 'more clearly defining states' and companies' respective responsibilities'.[125] Points similar to those lines of the argument are found in the UN Framework, and were also made in the SRSG's 2007 report's distinction between the roles of states and business. This, too, supports the observation that operational suggestions setting out ways for the SRSG to phrase and explain business responsibilities as both related to compliance with applicable law passed by states and also being independent from states' duties, were useful for influencing the SRSG's work.

In December 2006, the study[126] on the role of business in weak governance zones which IOE, ICC and BIAC had undertaken at the invitation

---

[123] Ibid., at 1.
[124] Ibid., at 3.
[125] Ibid., at 6.
[126] IOE, ICC, BIAC (2006) 'Business and human rights: The role of business in weak governance zones: Business proposals for effective ways of addressing dilemma situations in weak governance zones', Geneva, December 2006.

210 *Changing sustainability norms through communication processes*

made by the SRSG during the first mandate year was published. Recall that the SRSG had invited IOE, ICC and BIAC to identify effective ways for companies to deal with dilemma situations encountered in weak governance zones. Recall further that both ICC and IOE had taken a very strong stance against the Draft Norms and the general idea of business responsibilities for human rights. Yet, contrary to those former positions the December 2006 study referred to international law as a 'fall-back'-position for companies operating in zones of weak governance where national law is not in place or enforced. The 2006 study is an indication of the internal reflection and self-regulation that may result among business (or other) actors when invited into interaction with public institutions with potentially regulatory powers.[127] The IOE/ICC/BIAC study set out the role to be played by international human rights law as a normative source for company conduct through specific reference to 'the principles of relevant international instruments where national law is absent'.[128] More specifically, it stated, 'All companies (. . .) are expected to obey the law, even if it is not enforced, and to respect the principles of relevant international instruments where national law is absent.'

One of the study's recommendations referred to the practice of due diligence, employing the legal term in an economic context of companies in conflict zones and elsewhere. As noted, during the SRSG process references to due diligence had previously been employed by ICJ and some other stakeholders with regard to states' obligations. The recommendation in the IOE/ICC/BIAC-study spurred a shift in the SRSG process, for references to the due diligence concept to be moved from the state sphere into the strict business sphere. Suggesting that due diligence belongs to the set of ordinary considerations that a carefully managed company will undertake to avoid risks of a law-related character to its economic nature, the study of the three large organisations urged 'clients and business partners'[129] to '[p]erform due diligence, which should include a human rights assessment and impact project to determine the national human rights situation.'[130]

This is also an example of intertextuality drawing on the Draft Norms and its Commentary, which had applied the due diligence term to companies rather than states. As will be noted below, similar usage of the due diligence term was found in the SRSG's 2008 report that proposed

---

[127] See further, K. Buhmann (2018) *Power, Procedure, Participation and Legitimacy in Global Sustainability Norms*.
[128] IOE, ICC, BIAC (n 126) para. 15.
[129] Ibid., para. 19.
[130] Ibid.

the UN Framework, suggesting that the IOE/ICC/BIAC study may have had an influence on the arguments employed by the SRSG to present his recommendations. That is noteworthy taking into account the role that this risk-based due diligence approach has come to have. It was not just a major point of the UNGPs' elaboration of the points set forth in the UN Framework. The approach has spread beyond human rights, particularly in the application in the 2011 revision of OECD's Guidelines and its uptake by the EU and application in the EU's Non-Financial Reporting Directive.[131] What is interesting here is not that business organisations' argument had an influence on the output of the SRSG process, but that the argument resulted from an invitation from the SRSG to those business organisations to engage actively with the issue at stake, whose relevance and appropriateness they had previously rejected. This confirms that what looked like letting the fox into the henhouse in fact changed the fox so that it would be more inclined to protect the chickens or hens. This is an important contribution to insights on the value of reflexive law type regulation that encourages those with whom change is sought to contribute to developing the solution (rather than opposing it or engaging in protest and lobbying like the response to the Draft Norms, which were understood by the IOE and its partners as a result of a non-participatory process).

A statement from Asian civil society organisations presented at the regional consultation in Bangkok in June 2006 made reference to different types of human rights violations by companies in the region, especially by the extractive industries. Drawing largely on legal system considerations, focusing on 'accountability' and expressing strong support for '"codification" of the global standards'[132] for TNCs with regard to human rights, the statement advocated a formalisation of standards and measures that would reach companies acting in states in which the government violates human rights.

Differing somewhat from NGO submissions at the occasion of the SRSG's consultations in Johannesburg and Bangkok, a civil society declaration submitted for the Bogotá consultation built its arguments on legal system considerations and the situation of TNCs, combined with specific references to the economic system and framed within political system observations. Like some of the SRSG's statements, the submission

---

[131] K. Buhmann (2016) 'Juridifying corporate social responsibility through public law'.

[132] Asian civil society statement to U.N. Special Representative on transnational business and human rights at the Asia Regional Consultation, Bangkok, Thailand, 27 June 2006.

referred to the strengthening of 'interests and rights'[133] of companies. Through a combination of economic logic references (tying the argument to observations on company conduct and economic interest based actions) and legal system logic, the statement made several concrete recommendations to the SRSG, including for the development of a normative human rights framework compulsory for companies and of a framework which would ensure adequate and effective access to judicial remedy in cases where companies threaten or negatively impact human rights. The latter point was one of those addressed in detail at the workshop, which also discussed alternatives to court based conflict resolution, including through creative solutions that integrate legal and non-legal mechanisms for the purpose of negotiation.[134] With some variations such points eventually came to be addressed by the SRSG's 2008 report in relation to judicial and non-judicial remedies.

An October 2006 submission from the Interfaith SRI group drew on economic system logic to argue in favour of mandatory reporting and for the development of baseline human rights criteria to be employed by stock exchanges. The basic argument was that mandatory reporting will deliver transparency and reinforce companies' willingness to observe human rights through the creation of a 'level playing field'. Like a previous submission from the same group,[135] this one stood out through its specific economic system logic, which was deployed to argue the case for standards and other regulatory measures. Similar considerations are found in the SRSG's reports, which encouraged companies to report on their human rights impacts, and states to require or encourage such reporting. This, too, suggests that the line and style of argument had an impact on the output of the SRSG process and intertextuality between arguments. The submission stated:

> [W]e recognize the limitations of a voluntary reporting model. There is a clear need for some form of mandatory reporting in this area in order to establish a level playing field where all companies report basic, baseline data on their human rights performance. Currently, few companies are willing to produce truly transparent reports unless they believe they have 'a good story to tell.' This disparity of disclosure creates significant market inefficiencies that mask

---

[133] Declaration of the Social, Non-Governmental and Union Organizations and Indigenous and Affected Communities. Bogotá, 18–19 January 2007.
[134] SRSG (2007) Summary report: Latin America consultation: Held by the Special Representative of the Secretary-General on human rights and transnational corporations and other business enterprises, Bogotá, January 18–19.
[135] Interfaith Center for Corporate Responsibility (n 62).

the true nature of corporate behavior, and enhance already substantial obstacles to meaningful progress.[136]

Also making use of economic system logic, the submission highlighted the significance of human rights for reputation, work-stoppage and litigation risks to businesses. It further built its argument on economic system logic through direct reference to the 'business case' and by referring to company acknowledgment that specific standards of conduct would be of benefit to business. The statement explicitly incorporated litigation risks and other 'risks to shareholders associated with corporate violations of human rights'[137] in the understanding of the business case.

5.3.1.2 SRSG statements

In a statement made in Germany in June 2006 at a meeting organised by the Fair Labor Association and the German Network of Business Ethics,[138] the SRSG outlined some key directions of his future work, in particular of the role of states in relation to business and human rights. Taking a point of departure in company practices and reasons for non-compliance, the SRSG built on this combined application of economic and legal system logics to argue that more emphasis should be given to the part that governments play. Echoing points made by ICMM as well as his own views on governance gaps on several occasions, the SRSG built an argument that human rights problems in the business sector are basically due to government failure. With this statement the SRSG made it clear that the policy objectives of the UN indeed required attention to be paid to state obligations. He met companies on their arguments on states not fulfilling their own obligations, but as we shall see below did not use this to release companies of human rights responsibilities. Instead, he adopted the state duty argument to elaborate the State *Duty to Protect*, explaining implications for business in terms of compliance with law, which forms one part of Pillar Two as developed in the UN Framework. He also drew on this to elaborate the complementary part of Pillar Two on the need for companies to self-regulate to cover 'gaps' between international human rights law and the law that applies in their operating context.

---

[136] Interfaith Center on Corporate Responsibility (2006) Letter to John Ruggie, 10 October.
[137] Ibid.
[138] SRSG (2006) 'Remarks', delivered at forum on Corporate Social Responsibility, co-sponsored by the Fair Labor Association and the German Network of Business Ethics, Bamberg, Germany, 14 June.

In the statement the SRSG further combined economic and legal system considerations into a recommendation to the audience to strengthen their emphasis on social responsibility as a requirement in government procurement policies. Introducing aspects on the ways in which governments and legislators may draw on the mechanisms of the economic system to induce socially responsible practices in business organisations, the SRSG opened a new track in his argumentative strategy. Attention paid to the economic system and its mechanisms as drivers for social responsibility and business self-regulation from the public as well as the private perspective was to complement other parts of the SRSG's argumentative strategy as the mandate term proceeded.

In a speech in November 2006 to a meeting of the Canadian extractive industry operating in developing countries,[139] the SRSG outlined some preliminary findings based on the legal expert workshops he had staged on the emergence of an international legal environment of corporate liability for human rights. Those findings and the implications for corporations were to feed into the SRSG's 2007 report in more detail. At seven printed pages, the speech is relatively long compared with many other of the SRSG's published speeches. It was perhaps the length, perhaps the audience, perhaps the stage of the mandate work, or perhaps a combination of the three, which allowed the SRSG to address a number of issues with significant implications and messages to members of the extractives sector. As the argument developed, it related to argumentative strategies of the extractive industries themselves in previous stages of the mandate's work, but presented them so as to encourage the industry to consider their impact on society rather than relying on legal doctrinal ideas of human rights being state obligations. In this speech, which addressed corporations operating in countries where corporate human rights abuse may be particularly prone to arise, the SRSG stressed the legal aspects, implicitly also suggesting their implications in economic system logic in terms of litigation risks and costs, reputation risks, and other risks potentially affecting the profits of a company. Whereas industry had repeatedly deployed legal system language to articulate human rights as state obligations, the SRSG articulated liability and complicity for business-related human rights abuse as increasingly part of companies' reality, with implications for their economic performance.

The statement exemplifies an emerging emphasis by the SRSG on legal

---

[139] SRSG (2006) 'Remarks at public session', National Roundtable on Corporate Social Responsibility and the Canadian Extractive Industry in Developing Countries, Montreal, 14 November at 3.

aspects of business impact on human rights and associated economic risks to companies. The expert legal workshops held by the SRSG during the second mandate year contributed to the new emphasis on liability and complicity, but related ideas appeared in some stakeholder submissions. The SRSG reacted to businesses' practice of mainly addressing the mandate issues in legal system logics by responding in the same type of logic, but by addressing legal issues with economic implications for business. By way of first addressing government responsibilities, the statements developed the potential implications for company liability if governments decide to enact extraterritorial legislation. The economic consequences of extraterritorial legislation are particularly significant for companies which, like many extractive industry TNCs, are incorporated in states with well-functioning legal systems but carry out much of their work in 'weak governance' states. The statement finally highlighted the economic risks to companies as well as state agencies involved in export funding that may effectively contribute to exploiting governance gaps resulting from national and international institutional weaknesses.[140]

During the final part of the second year and prior to the publication of the 2007 report, the SRSG gave strengthened emphasis to state obligations to regulate and adjudicate, with a particular focus on export credit agencies and international financial institutions. A multi-stakeholder sectoral consultation was undertaken in cooperation with the OHCHR in Geneva on 16 February 2007. The consultation covered a range of topics, spanning from government obligations to voluntary financial sector initiatives, and from the role of public funding institutions such as export credit agencies to responsibilities of private financial institutions.[141] The report indicated considerable disagreement on many issues, but it also suggests a certain degree of agreement that financial institutions have responsibility in relation to human rights. The report confirms that a shift in the SRSG's attention and argumentative strategy was taking place, with strengthened emphasis on the interrelationship between the state duty (to protect) and economic risks to companies arising out of their adverse human rights impacts. In this context, the SRSG highlighted the role of public funding agencies providing financial means for companies that may be involved in human rights violations. Moreover, attention was paid to the risks posed

---

[140] Ibid., at 6.
[141] UN High Commissioner for Human Rights/Commission on Human Rights (2007) 'Report of the United Nations High Commissioner for Human Rights on the sectoral consultation entitled "Human Rights and the Financial Sector",' 16 February 2007, UN Doc. A/HRC/4/99, 6 March 2007.

to economic system actors by human rights violations in which they are involved directly (as producers, buyers, etc.) or indirectly (as funders).

That shift was apparent also in a speech delivered at a meeting in February 2007 in London.[142] Here the SRSG made some points, somewhat similar to those made to the Canadian extractive industry in November 2006, in which he stressed the risks that legal liability for human rights abuse may cause to companies. At the London meeting, which was organised by Amnesty International, the UK United Nations Association and the law firm Clifford Chance, the SRSG elaborated the line of argument from his previous stance of emphasising obligations for human rights as obligations for nation states, noting that '[n]othing prevents states from imposing international responsibilities directly on companies'.[143] By putting into such plain words the formal capacity of states to regulate companies' human rights responsibilities under international law the statement brought additional clout to other arguments presented by the SRSG to make clear that human rights do – or should – matter to companies and their managers. This speech added a new legal system informed argument to the argument made in Canada in November 2006 on liability risks, and to the economic system, political system and moral arguments made previously. Alluding to the powers of states to regulate companies through international law, the speech also played on the incentives for companies to self-regulate rather than to be subjected to formal regulation. As noted in Chapter 2 (section 2.1.2), organisational research suggests that companies sometimes prefer to self-regulate in order to pre-empt formal governmental regulation. The SRSG noted again that current international law practice and theory, however, did not 'support the claim that companies have direct human rights obligations under international law'[144] and that gaps remain in terms of governance and protection of victims. On that basis, he made a point that was to reappear in later statements and the UN Framework, referring to 'the court of public opinion'[145] as complementary to courts of law. Alluding in this way to the power of media and the market – consumers, investors and others – to hold companies accountable in reputational and economic terms, the SRSG's speech connected economic and legal systems observations to bring forth another argument on the significance that human rights observance may hold for companies based on economic system interests. The statement

---

[142] SRSG (2007) 'Prepared remarks at Clifford Chance', London, 19 February.
[143] Ibid.
[144] Ibid.
[145] Ibid.

underscored that non-judicial stakeholders hold companies economically to account for observance of international human rights law, although they are not legally bound by such standards.

The argument also characterised soft law as an important standard-setting mechanism, which is not just 'well-known'[146] but worthy of further consideration. The speech referred to conventional international soft law, such as ILO declarations and OECD guidelines, as well as hybrid public-private regulation on CSR, such as the Kimberley Process and the Voluntary Principles on Business and Human Rights. Addressing an audience that generally is concerned with hard (human rights) law, this type of argument allowed the SRSG to set the stage for future recommendations on soft law measures. The speech elaborated on the regulatory potential of soft law. It suggested that the merits of soft law are at least partially due to a multi-stakeholder character that tends to characterise its development as well as implementation. The latter argument would resonate with civil society organisations among the audience. It would also resonate with law firms by implicitly suggesting a case for business opportunities in advising companies on how to stay on the right side of soft law standards and mechanisms. Employing legal system logic, the speech noted that multi-stakeholder or public-private 'hybrid initiatives have direct effect'[147] suggesting an immediate normative effect on business organisations, as opposed to the (compliance) effect that comes about through state law passed to implement that state's international obligations.

Turning finally to states, the SRSG referred at this time explicitly to the state duty to protect, a term which was to become increasingly prominent towards the 2008 report (the UN Framework). Addressing an audience gathered at a large London law firm, the SRSG's references to 'uncertainty' giving cause for concern in relation to states' duty to protect and 'its implications with regard to preventing and punishing abuses by business enterprises'[148] would resonate with many among the audience. Audience members looking for business opportunities in advising business clients would also be apt to pay attention to the economic prospects flowing from the combined legal and economic system language reference to states' extraterritorial jurisdiction to companies that states 'support with taxpayer funds or by other means',[149] e.g., through export credits and similar state funded schemes.

---

[146] Ibid., at 4.
[147] Ibid., at 5.
[148] Ibid., at 6.
[149] Ibid.

5.3.2 The 2007 Report

Published in February 2007, the SRSG's second report, 'Business and Human Rights: Mapping international standards of responsibility and accountability for corporate acts'[150] relates to various elements of the mandate's sub-paragraphs (a), (b), (c) and (e), i.e., standards of corporate responsibility and accountability with regard to human rights, the role of states in effectively regulating and adjudicating the role of transnational corporations and other business enterprises with regard to human rights, including through international cooperation; the notion of corporate 'complicity'; and some practices of states and transnational corporations and other business enterprises in relation to human rights. The report was accompanied by four detailed addenda (sub-reports) on those issues and a companion report on human rights impact assessment (sub-paragraph (d) of the mandate). The focus of the main report was on the state duty to protect, corporate responsibility and accountability for international crimes, corporate responsibility for other human rights violations under international law, soft law mechanisms and self-regulation.

The SRSG referred to his 2007 report as a 'mapping' or inventory of a number of issues related to the mandate. In fact, it is a detailed presentation and discussion of a range of issues at the core of the international law debate relating to business responsibilities for human rights with a particular regard to the issues covered by the report, indicated in the preceding paragraph. The list of contents itself gives an indication of the shift in focus that distinguishes this report from the 2006 interim report. Except for a few paragraphs in the introduction and the conclusion, the 2007 report discussed most issues using legal system logic and terminology rather than related political or economic system logic and terms. Following on the style and observations that were made in the second part of the 2006 report, which also adopted a primarily legal approach to the issues under consideration within the mandate, the 2007 report confronted many of the international law and other law-related topics of contention that were propounded by various stakeholders in debates on the Draft Norms and/or had been present in other debates on business social responsibilities. Based on international law doctrine, scholarship and studies by the SRSG's team, the report took issue with arguments proposed by both sides of the

---

[150] Human Rights Council (2007) 'Business and Human Rights: Mapping international standards of responsibility and accountability for corporate acts', report of the Special Representative of the Secretary-General on the issue of human rights and transnational corporations and other business enterprises, UN Doc. A/HRC/4/35, 9 February.

previous debate. In addressing both the state duty to protect directly (as the first chapter of the report) and corporate responsibility in terms of a legal scholarship informed analysis of responsibility and accountability for international crimes, the report countered the continued relevance of both the business side's arguments on (sole) state obligations, and the civil society side's arguments that dealing with the business and human rights problem can only be solved through the setting of global binding standards. The report offered an understanding of business and human rights that was based on the idea that states do have obligations relevant to business conduct, and that new standards and types of regulatory instruments are emerging, which impact on legal and social expectations of companies. Establishing this created new common ground for both (or all) sides to consider also the benefits and weaknesses of intergovernmental soft law and of corporate self-regulation. Having established that both warrant merit but also suffer from weaknesses, the report was able to move on to its conclusion. Only here did the 2007 report revert in a higher degree to the sort of political science and economic system logic and arguments that was prevalent in the 2006 report. Those parts perhaps also spoke particularly to readers outside the legal community – in particular politicians and government lawyers, being the makers of possible future hard or soft (inter)governmental law on the matter, as well as the business sector. The conclusion was still mainly argued from a legal system perspective.

The report's substantive chapters incorporated observations on 'social expectations', demonstrating attention being paid to social norms and expectations. Social norms and expectations also were to become an issue to be addressed in the UN Framework that was presented the following year. The SRSG's references to social expectations not only indicate the role that such expectations played in relation to clarifying normativity during the SRSG process as such, but also suggest openness towards the capacity of such expectations to permeate the norm-creating process of business social responsibilities in a wider sense.

The report opened with a paragraph framed to place the issue of human rights responsibilities of businesses in a clearly economic context, while also demystifying the capacity of the economic system to handle the challenges by itself. The report made reference to economic system considerations on efficiency and sustainability of 'markets', noting that certain legal system institutions protect rights and interests of companies. The opening reference to economic system interests and the legal system as a protector of those interests 'in the marketplace' was directly woven into a pattern of international law and political developments that have shaped the economic conditions of business as well as the social and legal conditions impinging on their abilities to cause 'individual and social harms' and impose 'costs on people and communities – including human rights abuses'.[151] After establishing the need to bring balance to the extent of corporate economic rights and social impact caused by businesses to society, the report explained that such a task is not achieved overnight. It even acclaimed the Commission of Human Rights with recognising this. This created a connection to the findings and recommendations brought forth in the report, pre-empting critique or opposition by those who might see the SRSG's report as straying somewhat from the typical focus of UN Human Rights Special Procedures.

The argumentative structure created an approach that would resonate with the Commission and governments to draw on the logic of the economic system in order to involve the business sector in being 'part of the solution' rather than only as the cause of the problem. Finally, the introductory part of the report spelled out that governments 'need to be joined by other social actors and to utilize other social institutions, including market mechanisms' to achieve their goals.[152] The framing of the interdependence between governments and non-state actors prepared the ground for recommendations for governments and the Human Rights Council and the private sector as well as civil society to work together to address problems of business-related human rights abuse.

The concluding paragraphs picked up on the initial statements in a way that wove the 'misalignment' between, on the one hand, economic forces and actors, and on the other hand, governments' roles and capacities into the legal framework established in the five substantive chapters. As part of its concluding arguments, the report referred to governments as functioning according to the mechanisms of the economic system. Doing so would indicate to the report's audience that the SRSG recognised that states' competition for 'access to markets and investments' bears part of the blame for ineffective prevention of business-related human rights abuse.[153]

Having referred to the negative impact on victims of human rights violations by business, the report built an argument which suggested that all societal actors have an interest in recognising the connection between human rights and globalisation. The report proceeded in legal as well as economic system logic to argue the benefits that business may gain from greater legal clarity on the standards and expectations to which business are held to account. Bringing 'the courts of public opinion'[154] into the

---

[151] Ibid., paras 1–2.
[152] Ibid., para. 4.
[153] Ibid., para. 82.
[154] Ibid., para. 84.

argument, it added a twist on accountability in acknowledging – and making plain – that companies may face political or economic system reactions (market-based sanctions) even if legal institutions are not in place. It created an argument that – without a clear legal framework and with courts lacking jurisdiction and/or clear standards on the basis of which to assess TNCs' or other business organisations' conduct – non-judicial stakeholders function as 'courts', and corporations may find themselves in a situation of legal and societal uncertainty. Connecting to the 'governance gap' noted previously by the SRSG, the argument was built that absence of clear legal standards reflecting social expectations creates legal and economic uncertainty for companies and leads to 'predictability gaps'.[155] By employing political, legal and economic system logics, the SRSG included a range of interest groups in the conclusions, recognising interests and broadening the reach beyond the Human Rights Council. The report stated:

> This report has identified areas of fluidity in the business and human rights constellation, which in some respects may be seen as hopeful signs. By far the most consequential legal development is the gradual extension of liability to companies for international crimes, under domestic jurisdiction but reflecting international standards. But this trend is largely an unanticipated by-product of states' strengthening the legal regime for individuals, and its actual operation will reflect variations in national practice, not an ideal solution for anyone. No comparably consistent hard law developments were found in any other areas of human rights, which leaves large protection gaps for victims as well as predictability gaps for companies – who may still get tried in 'courts of public opinion'.[156]

With the report and its presentation to the Human Rights Council, the SRSG took the opportunity to ask the Council to extend his mandate for another year. It was made clear that the 2007 report did not contain final recommendations.[157] Having asked the Human Rights Council to extend the mandate by one year until 2008, the SRSG in the final paragraph of the 2007 report indicated that his recommendations the following year would be both of a political and legal nature, touching on 'legal and policy measures that states and other social actors could take' and entailing options to create and deliver effective remedies for victims.[158] Thus, the SRSG prepared the ground for bringing forth recommendations

---

[155] Ibid.
[156] Ibid.
[157] Ibid., para. 9.
[158] Ibid., para. 88.

that would address not only the Human Rights Council or states, nor only companies or victims, but all of those. Referring to policy and legal measures, he also prepared the ground for acceptance that the measures he would propose might differ from the types of measures conventionally expected from Human Rights Special Procedures, and that they would not comprise simply a new draft international instrument in place of the Draft Norms.

The report's substantive chapters covered a variety of subjects from a descriptive and analytical perspective based in international law doctrine (jurisprudence, treaty and customary law, and doctrinal case law) and general legal doctrine. In a chapter on the state duty to protect, the report states that 'international law firmly establishes that states have a duty to protect against non-state human rights abuses within their jurisdictions, and that this duty extends to protection against abuses by business entities'.[159] This was substantiated by detailed reference to UN treaty provisions and treaty body General Comments, concluding that '[c]urrent guidance from the Committees suggests that the treaties do not require states to exercise extraterritorial jurisdiction over business abuse. But nor are they prohibited from doing so'.[160] It suggested that '[i]ndeed, the increasing focus on protection against corporate abuse by the UN treaty bodies and regional mechanisms indicates growing concern that states either do not fully understand or are not always able or willing to fulfil this duty'.[161]

In a chapter on corporate responsibility and accountability for international crimes, the report described and provided an analysis of individuals as subjects of direct responsibility under international criminal law. The report argued that long-standing doctrinal arguments over whether corporations could be subjects of international law, 'which impeded conceptual thinking about and the attribution of direct legal responsibility to corporations, are yielding to new realities'. Corporations are increasingly recognised as rights-holders as well as duty-bearing participants at the international level. The rights' aspect was exemplified by international investment law, and the duty aspect by international environmental law.[162] Referring to the drafting process of the International Criminal Court Statute and the practice as well as criminal law legislation of some states, the report argued that criminal liability for companies in a capacity as

---

[159] Ibid., para. 10.
[160] Ibid., para. 15.
[161] Ibid., para. 16.
[162] Ibid., para. 20.

individuals bearing legal personality is found both at international and national levels. It argued that corporate complicity is recognised both at international and national level, and that domestic level extraterritorial provisions could be extended to corporations. Referring to specific forms of regulation that may promote business self-regulation to internalise societal expectations, it demonstrated that states may use incentive-based and smart-mix regulation law to shape corporate culture.

Based on a survey of Fortune Global 500 companies (large TNCs), the report found that companies refer to the full range of human rights, but also that companies do not necessarily recognise the rights on which they have the greatest impact. On voluntary corporate codes on human rights it observed that companies may be using 'elastic' or flexible interpretations of international instruments. The description and assessment of voluntarism and its effects also drew on economic system logic and practices, such as corporate reporting and materiality standards. It noted that similar to public-private soft-law initiatives, the credibility of voluntary accountability mechanisms is enhanced by processes involving participation, transparency, and review.[163]

The report's findings referred extensively to workshops held during the first 18 months of the mandate. The influence of the legal experts' workshops is particularly noticeable. The impact of business and civil society contributions was less strong, but detectable in some parts of the report. Obviously, arguments on states' obligations were met through pulling the issue of the state duty to protect right at the beginning of the report. The state duty to protect, to be implemented through various means, constitutes much of the foundational point for the findings, arguments and recommendations in the report. This includes criminalisation of corporate conduct or other ways of holding companies to account through national law and international law. It also formed the foundations for observations and recommendations on alternative means available to states for creating a corporate culture respectful of human rights, such as through incentives and reporting requirements that may complement regulation and adjudication, forming part of what the UNGPs refer to as smart-mix regulation.[164]

In general, the 2007 report was received with acceptance and appreciation by many stakeholders. As will be seen from the sections below on stakeholders' comments, it did not receive as critical and questioning responses as the 2006 report. The message to states and other stakeholders

---

[163] Ibid., para. 80.
[164] UNGP No. 3 and Commentary.

was that '[i]n sum, the state duty to protect against non-state abuses is part of the international human rights regime's very foundation. The duty requires states to play a key role in regulating and adjudicating abuse by business enterprises or risk breaching their international obligations'.[165]

5.3.3 Analysis

During the second year of the mandate, the usage of legal system language persisted but underwent a shift towards the obligations of states to actively protect against human rights violations at the horizontal level rather than simply to observe their international obligations at the vertical level. This also entailed articulation of implied obligations for companies in terms of compliance with national law. Even with this somewhat common point of reference in international law doctrine, views continued to question the appropriateness of institutionalising human rights responsibilities for companies, and both business organisations and some other stakeholders continued to refer to governments as primary duty holders for human rights as well as for public policy objectives. The SRSG shifted usage of economic system language to increasingly referring to specific interests of specific companies, thus bringing the argument closer to decisions made by daily management of a company than the abstract references to international trade benefits that had marked the first mandate year. Political system language was invoked by business organisations, for example ICMM to argue that business activities benefit the public policy activities that the UN and governments sought to address through the SRSG process. It was also deployed by the SRSG as a modality to encourage other organisations to address the needs and activities of governments in order to bring their leverage into play on business.

In their comments to the 2006 interim report and suggestions to the SRSG for his further work, civil society continued to call for regulation of companies through an international law mechanism. Business organisations argued in favour of voluntary mechanisms, including through reflexive law type co-regulation.

Not surprisingly in the context of the SRSG process, international human rights continued to hold a prominent place as a source of norms for company conduct. Civil society organisations called for specific guidance for companies. But business organisations, too, acknowledged international human rights law as a normative source for responsible business conduct.

---

[165] Human Rights Council (n 150) para. 18.

Arguments on the state duty to protect (such as FIDH comments, and perhaps related arguments made by other actors but rendered only in non-attribution form, as well as expert legal opinions not directly covered in this study) influenced the 2007 report by updating the process in relation to this particular human rights law aspect of international law theory. In other words, when addressing core institutional legal issues of duties and rights, an argument drawing on institutional legal logic to refute outdated positions was effective. On the backdrop of the generally accepted doctrinal approach of states' obligations under international human rights law and arguments made by business organisations addressing the UN and governments in the code of the legal system, this allowed the SRSG to apply a particular argumentative strategy. That strategy bought into previously made arguments by business organisations on states' international obligations and company compliance with national law by developing implications based on doctrinal international law. Only the SRSG applied the specialised doctrine of international law, i.e. the horizontality doctrine. When linked to economic observations on free trade and its benefits to business, etc., the combined strength of the argument would resonate with business by causing perturbation with their core rationality.

While the SRSG's argumentative strategy became more concretely focused on the state duty to protect and specific decisions and activities of business enterprises as well as impact of social expectations, NGOs continued to argue in more general and abstract terms, with broad references to international human rights law and public policy implications of business activities. In some cases, however, NGOs argued through specific recommendations. Feeding into the 2007 report as well as, in particular, the 2008 report, whether they were made by civil society or companies, the influence on the SRSG's work of such specific recommendations was clearly stronger than abstract arguments.

Perhaps most interestingly, also feeding into the form of regulation of CSR from the regulatory strategy perspective, the SRSG's invitation to IOE, ICC and BIAC to develop guidance for business activities in conflict zones resulted in an acknowledgement of international law as a fall-back position when national law is not in place or not enforced. This eased the SRSG's referencing international human rights law as a normative source for business conduct, and also catered for a fundamental agreement among all key stakeholder types – business organisations, civil society, or (inter-)governmental organisations – for the remainder of the SRSG on the basis of which to develop specific guidance for companies as well as states.

The 2007 report was drafted mainly in technical legal language. In this, it differed from the 2006 interim report, which made more use of political and economic system language. Given that it was addressed to the Human Rights Council, the usage of legal system language was a logical engagement with the formal audience. From this perspective, it is also not surprising that the five substantive chapters were not only drafted in this type of language, but also address the complexities and possible legal avenues from the perspective of international law and legal theory. The use of legal system language and observations does, however, indicate a considerable degree of juridification of a topic that the SRSG had previously described as highly political. The aim may have been dual: partly to de-politicise the debate by fixing it in legal doctrine and solid legal analysis; and partly to provide a point of departure for operational recommendations based in findings and facts of a (solid) legal nature that would not be questioned the way political suggestions and arguments are. Readers without a background in law would likely find some difficulty in appreciating the analysis and discussion in the five substantive chapters. Those readers might be expected to read the introduction and, perhaps, the conclusion. They could be expected to appreciate the social and economic system considerations made in the introductory and concluding chapters, and on that basis the findings of the report.

5.4 THIRD MANDATE YEAR: FROM 2007 REPORT TO UN FRAMEWORK

During the third year of the 2005–08 mandate, the SRSG organised several multi-stakeholder consultations to provide insight on a diversity of topics: Business and human rights in conflict zones: The role of home states (Berlin, 5 November 2007); multi-stakeholder initiatives[166] (The Hague, 6–7 November 2007); business and human rights: the role of states (Copenhagen, 8–9 November 2007); corporations and human rights: accountability mechanisms for resolving complaints and disputes (Massachusetts, USA, 11–12 April and 19–20 November 2007); and the

---

[166] Multi-stakeholder initiatives are understood by the SRSG generally to refer to initiatives whose stakeholders combine at least the private sector and civil society (see P. Brown (2007) 'Principles that make for effective governance of multi-stakeholder initiatives: updated, final version', UN SRSG/CCC Expert workshop on improving human rights performance of business through multi-stakeholder initiatives 6–7 November 2007, December 2007; and implicitly the SRSG's 2007 report (Human Rights Council (n 150)). This narrow definition of multi-stakeholder initiatives focusing mainly on private for-profit and non-profit actors differs from the one generally applied in this study which considers public-private CSR initiatives to be multi-stakeholder initiatives.

corporate responsibility to respect human rights (Geneva 4–5 December 2007).

In addition to the overall issues addressed at the multi-stakeholder consultations, the SRSG made use of the consultations to introduce and test reception of elements that were to be presented in the report. Following a practice that the SRSG had adopted at some meetings held during the second year of the mandate, the consultations offered opportunities to softly break ideas that might go into the final report and to obtain reactions and responses from stakeholders across the range in terms of functional social sub-systems as well as regions.

Brief summary reports published after the consultations[167] are kept in non-attributional style, meaning that views cannot be attributed to particular actors or particular social system interests. In June 2007, the SRSG met with UN human rights treaty bodies, with the dual aim of learning about treaty bodies' practice and experience under the treaties[168] and identifying areas where further clarification could be helpful to increase states parties' as well as other stakeholders' understanding of the state duty to protect against human rights abuse caused by business organisations.[169] The meetings fed into the 2008 report in a general sense and are not addressed separately in here.

5.4.1 General Argumentative Structure and Strategy

5.4.1.1 Stakeholder statements
In March 2007 the Clean Clothes Campaign, an NGO engaged in responsible supply chain management, made recommendations and suggestions

---

[167] Background papers and reports are available through the Business and Human Rights resource centre's SRSG portal Multi-stakeholder consultations – 2007 Consultations, meetings and workshops at: http://www.business-humanrights.org/SpecialRepPortal/Home/Consultationsmeetingsworkshops/Multi-stakeholderconsultations/2007 (last accessed 27 December 2016); an addendum to the SRSG's 2008 report provides a combined summary of the multi-stakeholder consultations (Human Rights Council (2008) 'Summary of five multi-stakeholder consultations', UN Doc. A/HRC/8/5/Add.1, 23 April 2008).

[168] SRSG (2007) 'Meeting between the SRSG on Human Rights and Business and Treaty Bodies, 19/06/07', Background paper: Mapping States parties' responsibilities to regulate and adjudicate corporate activities under the United Nations' core human rights treaties: Main trends and issues for further consideration; SRSG (2007) 'Meeting with UN Special Procedures', Geneva, June 19.

[169] OHCHR (2007) 'Human rights impact of corporate activity: Request for information from Special Procedures', Geneva 1 May; OHCHR (2007) 'SRSG to meet with treaty bodies', Geneva, 5 June.

especially in relation to labour conditions in supply chains.[170] Contrary to many other NGOs, this organisation supported the idea of a non-binding instrument, pending the long-term objective of a binding arrangement. The statement employed legal system logic to argue that national law is not sufficient as 'that state-centric model of governance'[171] on which it builds is 'increasingly incapable of addressing supply chain issues, which move beyond national borders'.[172] Based on this, it argued that voluntary initiatives may complement national law and may contribute to 'the development of a global regulatory framework'.[173] Worded in operational terms, the Clean Clothes Campaign suggested that particular attention be paid to grievance and complaints mechanisms and that the 'possibility of appointing an ombudsperson at UN level (. . .) be explored'.[174] As will be seen, both the issue of grievance and complaints mechanisms and that of an international ombudsman were addressed by the SRSG in his 2008 report. Although grievance and complaints mechanisms had been argued by other stakeholders too, the terms used and the particular reference to an ombudsman suggest that the specificity of the Clean Clothes Campaign submission may have been particularly influential. That is underscored by fact that another suggestion for a similar institution (a global ombudsman) was made by another NGO just prior to the release of the 2008 report, that is, at a time when the UN Framework would already have been drafted.

Indeed, the ombudsman proposal was also made in a case study in a February 2008 submission by CIDSE, a group of development NGOs.[175] This was one among other recommendations to the SRSG with a view to reducing the risk of human rights violations and improving access to justice, including measures for greater and global accountability for all companies. A number of short- and medium-term measures were also proposed in language that relied on economic system rationality combined with references to international soft law and other guidance for businesses. CIDSE recommended that governments restrain access to public finance (such as export credit, investment guarantees) for companies that did not

---

[170] Clean Clothes Campaign (2007) Letter to John Ruggie, Amsterdam, 23 March 2007, available at http://www.business-humanrights.org/Documents/Clean-Clothes-Campaign-letter-Ruggie-23-Mar-2007.pdf.
[171] Ibid.
[172] Ibid.
[173] Ibid.
[174] Ibid.
[175] CIDSE – Développement et la Solidarité (2008) CIDSE submission to the Special Representative of the United Nations Secretary-General on Business and Human Rights: Recommendations to reduce the risk of human rights violations and improve access to justice, February 2008.

meet the 'highest internationally accepted standards including the OECD Guidelines for Multinational Enterprises [or the] the ILO core labour standards'.[176]

Overall, CIDSE observed that while states have primary responsibility under international law, this does not mean that other actors 'are, or should be, free from any direct responsibility for human rights'. It argued that in order to live up to its role of limiting and governing the exercise of power, international human rights law must continue to develop to account for the growing power of actors other than states to affect the human rights enjoyment of individuals and communities.[177] Although much of the submission reiterated points made by the SRSG, the overall message of the statement was a critique against the current approach taken and the work being done so far in regard to victims.

Several comments from civil society stressed the situation of victims of corporate human rights abuse as a particular lacuna in the work of the SRSG until then, including in the 2007 report. This critique of the SRSG's work for not paying attention to victims struck ground during the third mandate year. The results were noticeable both in the work of the SRSG (and his team) feeding into the 2008 report, and in the 2008 report itself. As one of the responses, the SRSG initially outlined activities to gain and include information on abuse of human rights alleged to be caused by business.[178]

A submission from the NGO ESCR-net in September 2007 indicates that the NGO community felt strongly about the interests of victims.[179] In a letter from October 2007, a group comprising of around 150 NGOs, SRI organisations and individuals voiced concern with the general direction of the work of the SRSG in terms of looking at non-binding guidance and with what they felt was too limited attention paid to victims. It contained some programmatic wishes for a world with less human rights violations, but the statement also made some proposals of a relatively more concrete character than many other NGO submissions during the mandate. Mainly applying legal system logic, but interspersing references to political rationality in line with some of the SRSG's own statements addressing

---

[176] Ibid.
[177] Joint NGO letter on work of the mandate, 10 October 2007 (available at the Business and Human Rights Resource Centre SRSG portal in version dated 25 October 2007).
[178] SRSG (2007) Letter to Niko Lusiani, 29 August 2007 (see further below on 'Form of regulation').
[179] International Network for Economic, Social and Cultural Rights (2007) Letter to John Ruggie, 5 September (see further below on 'Form of regulation').

governments, the submission offered recommendations 'that might be included in [the SRSG's] final report to the Human Rights Council'. The submission noted:

> As you have rightly recognized, the expansion of global markets has not been matched with sufficient protection for the people and communities that are the victims of such human rights abuses. In many cases, abuses involving businesses arise in a vacuum of effective human rights protection, in which governments fail to take appropriate steps to prevent abuses and perpetrators are not held to account, and in which obstacles to justice compound the original abuses by depriving victims of their right to an effective remedy and reparation.[180]

The letter generated a response from one of the 'grand old men' of business and human rights, Sir Geoffrey Chandler, who was the founder of the Amnesty International UK Business Group and its chair 1991–2005. Reacting partly to some of the programmatic elements of the letter, the response is interesting for the way in which it deployed a combination of legal and political system logic by referring to normative guidance for companies and the concerns of labour law, and economic system rationality in encouraging civil society to support guidance that would be practically applicable to market actors. The statement spoke of 'universal human rights principles, applicable to all companies, which will enable stakeholders and the market to bring influence to bear on non-financial performance and so change it for the better'.[181] Calling for support for practical guidance rather than studies on impacts, it observed that 'if we want a change in corporate behaviour we need to talk in language intelligible to the practitioner, not in the abstract language of lawyers'.[182]

5.4.1.2 SRSG statements

The SRSG responded to calls for a legally binding instrument by referring to international law experience indicating that such processes can be protracted. In several statements he argued that an ordinary instrument of international law would likely take far too long in being drafted, with no certainty that it would ever be adopted. Drawing on legal system logic designed to resonate with the human rights objectives of the Human Rights Council and human rights NGOs, the argument built was that a

---

[180] Joint NGO letter (n 177).
[181] G. Chandler (2007) Open letter to the signatories of the 10 October letter to the Special Representative of the UN Secretary General for business and Human Rights, 15 October.
[182] Ibid.

softer approach would be more effective for addressing the situation and needs of victims, here and now. The SRSG stated:

> We can all agree that statements of principles, soft law declarations, and international treaty instruments will play a role in the future evolution of the human rights regime, as they have done in the past. But we also need to acknowledge that progress on that front is slow at best. The recently adopted Declaration on the Rights of Indigenous Peoples marks a major milestone. But it has been twenty-two years in the making, it is not a binding legal instrument, and even if it were to be developed into a treaty, ratification remains a voluntary act on the part of individual states. In the meantime, some initiatives of far more recent origin that critics dismiss for being purely 'voluntary' are already being enacted through domestic laws, regulations, and policies.[183]

Prior to the presentation of the 2008 report, most of the SRSG's speeches delivered outside the multi-stakeholder consultations addressed sub-issues under the mandate of particular relevance or interest to the audiences. In line with the approach that had been introduced prior to the 2007 report, the statements introduced elements that were later expanded in the report, and some statements tested responses to those elements. The SRSG also took issue with some of the topics that had been controversial in the debates surrounding the Draft Norms. Indicating a continuation of the focus on the state duty to protect against business violations of human rights, which had become clear during the second year and the 2007 report, some speeches were delivered to institutions or gatherings under intergovernmental bodies with particular business interests, such as international financial institutions.

At one of those meetings, in a speech to an international business forum organised by the World Bank in October 2007 the SRSG addressed bilateral investment treaties and host government agreements.[184] The speech developed an argument that legal instruments (such as bilateral investment treaties), which provide for insulation of companies from legislative or regulatory changes in their host states, may be detrimental to human rights. Establishing a connection to the overall international development objectives of the World Bank and its particular focus on economic development, the SRSG articulated the problem as one that needs to be addressed for the sake of sustainability of international trade and globalisation in general. The argument was built through a combination of legal

---

[183] SRSG (2007) Letter to Ms Julieta Rosi, 15 October.
[184] SRSG (2007) 'Remarks at plenary session on "Business and the rules of the game: From rule-takers to rule-makers?"', 12th International Business Forum, World Bank, Washington D.C., 8–10 October.

and economic system logic, with legal system logic particularly referring to protection of business interests provided by international or national law and weak control by parent companies under corporate law. The speech deployed economic system logic to refer to sourcing issues and investment interests, and placed them in the legal context.

The statement introduced the three-pronged approach that was to become the main topic of the 2008 report, and which we now know as the three Pillars of the State Duty to Protect, the Corporate Responsibility to Respect, and Access to Remedy. This allowed the SRSG to test the reception of the three-pillared framework before it was formally launched. The SRSG talked about the situation of victims of corporate human rights violations, thereby including the topic he had been urged to consider since the Human Rights Council debate of the 2007 report and in NGO submissions. The manner in which the topic of victims was introduced at the same time served to reduce expectations that the SRSG would announce a proposal for a conventional international law instrument, even a soft law instrument. The speech was rounded off with a statement on the pragmatic way in which the SRSG sought to address the governance gaps he had repeatedly referred to during the mandate term. Emphasising 'workable guiding principles',[185] this too served to prepare stakeholders not to expect a hard law proposal from the SRSG, but rather a set of normative guidelines of benefit to the public policy interests at stake as well as being practicable to business organisations.

The statement's reference to closing law-free zones and to do so through the identification of 'workable guiding principles',[186] was significant in view of the fact that the framework, which was soon after introduced in full with the 2008 report, was referred to by the SRSG as a 'policy framework'. By both referring to closing 'law-free zones' and 'guiding principles', the statement indicates that there is more of a legislative-regulatory aim to the three-pillared framework than is indicated by the 'policy' wording. The reference to 'guiding principles' does not place itself squarely in the considerations or language of one particular social sub-system. Most, if not all, social sub-systems have principles, and most actors approve of principles for some purpose. A reference to 'principles', therefore, had the potential to resonate with a broad audience comprising several social sub-systems with otherwise non-aligned interests, while at the same time suggesting a strong normative substance. Even so, as will be seen from the discussion below, there was a considerable overlap or con-

---

[185] Ibid.
[186] Ibid.

nection between the 'principles' suggested with the UN Framework's three pillars and international human rights standards.

Referring both to closing law-free zones and guiding principles served as a way to balance between expectations and apprehension, perhaps particularly among business, that the SRSG's work would lead to public regulation of business behaviour. At the same time, it also suggests that despite a wariness of reverting to a situation like the 'stalemate' surrounding the Draft Norms, the SRSG recognised a need for regulation, even if in a soft-law form. Moreover, it suggests that he approached this need in terms that differed from the ordinary legal language as well as the conventional process of international law-making, in favour of a broad multi-stakeholder process outside the rooms at the New York or Geneva UN headquarters where international law is traditionally debated.

In a speech in early 2008 at a meeting for the Working Group on arbitration and conciliation under the UN Commission on International Trade Law (UNCITRAL), the SRSG addressed some of the same topics as those from the World Bank meeting. Although slightly briefer, the statement had a stronger use of economic system considerations and interests.[187] As in several other statements, the SRSG referred to imbalances between the legal protection of business interests and the challenges it places on business to reduce adverse impact on society.

5.4.2 The 2008 Report: Protect, Respect and Remedy: A Framework for Business and Human Rights

5.4.2.1 Overview

Published in April 2008 and entitled 'Protect, Respect and Remedy: A Framework for Business and Human Rights', [188] the third and final report from SRSG's first term proposed the three-pillared normative guidance that has since become known as 'The UN Framework'.

The 2008 report introduced a normative framework 'rest[ing] on differentiated but complementary responsibilities' for businesses and states, and

---

[187] SRSG (2008) Statement of the UN Secretary-General's Special Representative on Business and Human Rights, Professor John Ruggie, to the UNCITRAL Working Group II (Arbitration and Conciliation), 48th session, New York, USA, 4–8 February.

[188] Human Rights Council (2008) 'Protect, respect and remedy: A framework for business and human rights,' Report of the Special Representative of the Secretary-General on the issue of human rights and transnational corporations and other business enterprises, John Ruggie, UN Doc. A/HRC/8/5 7 April 2008 ('UN Framework').

elaborated on the implications. Structured around a series of recommendations for both states and businesses, the framework established three complementary and mutually supportive principles (now typically referred to as 'Pillars': (1) the State Duty to Protect against human rights abuses by third parties, including business; (2) the Corporate Responsibility to Respect Human Rights; and (3) the joint task for states and businesses to respond to a need for more effective Access to Remedy for victims.

Responding to one of the issues for clarification prescribed by the declaration that established the mandate task, a special companion report addendum[189] elaborated on the main report's clarification of the concepts of 'sphere of influence' and 'complicity'. Another addendum contained a summary of the five multi-stakeholder consultations held in 2007,[190] and a third was a survey on the scope and patterns of alleged corporate-related human rights abuse.[191]

Similar to the 2007 report and in both cases reflecting the fact that the Human Rights Council and governments were the formal audience, many of the substantive chapters of the 2008 report were mainly worded in legal system language with strong references to legal doctrine and institutions.

The 2008 report also made specific recommendations to UN human rights bodies and other intergovernmental bodies for them to promote business responsibilities for human rights in doctrine, clarification and practice, including through supportive public agency actions. UN human rights treaty bodies were encouraged to make recommendations to states concerning the duty to protect. The report also recommended a revision of the human rights provisions of the OECD Guidelines because it found that many of the voluntary codes of conduct that existed at the time were more ambitious than the then most recent (2000) version of the Guidelines.

The state duty to protect (Pillar One) was described as an integral part of the proposed UN Framework. Building on already existing requirements of international law on states, it requires that states 'take all necessary steps to protect against human rights abuses by non-State actors, including by business, affecting persons within their territory or jurisdiction. The duty includes to prevent, investigate, and punish the abuse, and to provide access to redress'.[192] The corporate responsibility to respect human rights

---

[189] Human Rights Council (2008) 'Clarifying the concepts of "Sphere of Influence" and "Complicity"', UN Doc. A/HRC/8/16, 15 May.

[190] Human Rights Council (n 167).

[191] Human Rights Council (2008) 'Corporations and human rights: a survey of the scope and patterns of alleged corporate-related human rights abuse', UN Doc. A/HRC/8/5/Add.2, 23 May 2008.

[192] UN Framework, para. 18.

(Pillar Two) was defined as avoiding infringements on the rights of others and addressing adverse impacts that may occur, or in essence that businesses should do no harm. This entails acting with 'due diligence', i.e., having in place 'a process whereby companies not only ensure compliance with national laws but also manage the risk of human rights harm with a view to avoiding it',[193] while the specific scope of human rights-related due diligence depends on the context in which a company is operating, its activities, and the relationships associated with those activities.[194] Access to remedy (Pillar Three) is both a part of and complementary to the state duty to protect as well as the corporate responsibility to respect. The SRSG noted that victims' access to formal judicial systems is often the most difficult where the need is greatest, and that non-judicial mechanisms are 'seriously underdeveloped' from the company level up through national and international spheres. Without adequate remedy, the duty to protect could be rendered weak or even meaningless. As part of the corporate responsibility to respect, grievance mechanisms help identify, mitigate, and possibly resolve grievances before they escalate and greater harm is done. Based on specific research undertaken under the mandate, the 2008 report also noted that in order to conform to general human rights principles for remedy institutions, non-judicial mechanisms – whether state-based or independent – be legitimate, accessible, predictable, rights-compatible, equitable and transparent.

In highlighting the state duty to protect and in stating it as the first of the three parts of the three-pillared framework, the UN Framework adopted a classical international law view of duty bearers for international human rights. Through this, the three-pillared framework took a point of departure in doctrinal international law (on states being duty bearers), as well as in human rights law (on the duty to ensure the protection of human rights in horizontal relationships between individuals and/or corporations). Adopting the doctrinal view of horizontal human rights obligations, it asserted that it is the obligation of states to protect individuals and communities against human rights violations by (other) non-state actors.[195] The Framework emphasises that the duty to protect is not limited to core legislative, judicial and core executive bodies. It does so through concrete references to state agencies that are some distance from core state bodies, such as implementing or executive agencies with very specific mandates of a business-related character (such as export credit agencies), i.e., agencies

---

[193] UN Framework, para. 25.
[194] Ibid.
[195] J. H. Knox (2008) 'Horizontal human rights law'.

that differ from those normally associated with human rights (legislatures, courts, top executive authorities such as ministries or local government). Three points that emerge from the UN Framework's clarifications under the state duty to protect are particularly significant. The first is that the Framework eliminated doubts about the ranking between state duties and corporate responsibility: the state duty to protect is absolute. The second point is that the report, at least in principle, eliminated doubt about what human rights may be subject to corporate responsibility for human rights: the report states the full spectrum of internationally recognised human and core labour rights as relevant in this respect. Third, the report implicitly recognised that for the Framework to be applicable in a legal context, it must be precise and not employ terms which are too vague.

The SRSG had indicated that most governments take a relatively narrow approach to issues arising out of business impact on human rights agenda, and that human rights concerns are poorly integrated into other 'policy domains' that directly shape business practices. What the SRSG addressed as 'policy', perhaps due to his pragmatic approach, functioned as a soft way of telling states that they do not take the state duty to protect sufficiently serious across the range of their substantive tasks and agencies, and that they need to expand it with regard to national state bodies. Doing so may require taking national measures, which some would refer to or consider to be 'policy'. However, state agencies like export credit agencies are by default state bodies, just like courts or ministries, and therefore as such they should understand and observe the state duty to protect. If they do not, it flows from the state's international obligations that legislatures or higher executive bodies should issue directives or conduct training to ensure that (lower) executive bodies understand and observe their duty to protect.

According to the UN Framework, 'policy' actions that states can take to fulfil their duty to protect also include 'an urgent policy priority' 'to foster a corporate culture respectful of human rights at home and abroad'.[196] Suggesting possible influence from civil society statements recommending state action to promote business respect for human rights, the 2008 report proposed that states encourage a corporate culture respectful of human rights by requiring sustainability reporting and other measures which support and strengthen market pressures on companies to respect human rights.[197] This is noteworthy as it relates to the interface between coercive law and incentives based on public regulatory modalities condu-

---

[196] UN Framework, para. 27.
[197] Ibid., para. 30.

cive to inducing corporate self-regulation on CSR and related issues, in particular through reflexive regulatory modalities. This carried into the UNGPs through their encouragement of states to apply a smart mix of regulatory modalities.

By limiting his wording to 'policy' rather than to wording suggestive of the legal system, such as politics of law or *lex ferenda*, the SRSG maintained the overall idea that his work was not intended to have a legal impact or result in legal requirements on companies. In reality, its numerous references to 'policy actions' in the context of the state duty to protect and to companies' obligations to comply with national law under the corporate responsibility to respect were meant to have an impact on law in home as well as host states. The UN Framework is clearly normative, suggestive of soft law despite references to 'policy' in its title and substance.

Alluding to the preamble of the UDHR in its explanation of the corporate responsibility to respect (Pillar Two), the UN Framework acknowledges that companies may be considered 'organs of society', but also observes that they are 'specialized economic organs', thus recognising that their tasks and functions in society differ from those of states. As such, 'their responsibilities cannot and should not simply mirror the duties of States'.[198] According to the SRSG, the corporate responsibility not to infringe on the rights of others goes beyond complying with national laws. On this issue the UN Framework leaves the terrain of legal doctrine and established legal institutions, venturing into the field of 'social expectations' and 'courts of public opinion'.[199] Striking this note, the Framework referred to a point that has been demonstrated to be of considerable significance for business in relation to the general CSR field: risk and general reputation management. Alluding to the role that social norms have as 'sources' for the development of legal norms, the SRSG created an argument on social expectations as normative sources, which is designed to go to the heart of companies and provide understanding: social expectations and 'courts of public opinion' may not be established legal institutions. Often, as in the area of business and human rights, social expectations are neither in accordance with a conventional doctrinal approach, nor would the 'judgments' of the courts of public opinion in terms of consumer or investor decisions necessarily stand in a court of law. But both are facts of social and economic life. In terms of economic consequences both may be as important to a company, if not more, as a fine issued by a court of law.

The UN Framework constructed corporate responsibility to encompass

---

[198] Ibid., para. 53.
[199] Ibid., para. 54.

respect for the full list of internationally recognised human rights and international core labour rights. It explained that a specific list of human rights for business responsibilities would be counterproductive, as there would be a risk that some right, which might turn out to be violated by a company, would not be included.[200]

In the UN Framework the SRSG proposed a due diligence process for companies to become aware of, prevent, and address adverse human rights impacts. 'For the substantive content of the due diligence process, companies should look, at a minimum, to the international bill of human rights and the core conventions of the ILO, because the principles they embody comprise the benchmarks against which other social actors judge the human rights impacts of companies.'[201] According to the UN Framework, core elements of human rights due diligence comprise a human rights policy, undertaking human rights impact assessments, integrating human rights throughout a company, and tracking and reporting performance. The UN Framework's due diligence was elaborated in the companion report on 'complicity' and 'sphere of influence', which also explained the reasoning by extensive reference to economic system rationality (see further below section 5.5).

Under Pillar Three, the creation of a 'global ombudsman' was mentioned as a possibility for increased access to remedy, which may be subject to 'careful consideration'. Its inclusion indicates that similar to arguments that spurred increased focus on victims during the third year of the mandate, this particular proposal had been made in a way that was effective in becoming integrated into the SRSG's output. With specific but non-attribution reference to proposals by 'some actors', the Framework noted the idea of a global ombudsman empowered to receive and handle complaints. The Framework listed some points to be considered for such an institution to be effective.[202] It was also observed that company-based remedy mechanisms should operate through dialogue and mediation rather than the company itself acting as adjudicator.

5.4.2.2 Report substance and arguments

At the very opening of the UN Framework, the second paragraph of the report was couched in a combination of economic, political and legal system language. This tied the three sub-systems of key stakeholders and their interests together and prepared the ground for the report's subse-

---

[200] Ibid., paras 59–63.
[201] Ibid., para. 58.
[202] Ibid., paras 82–103.

quent analysis, findings and recommendations. Referring to the positive impact that business may have on human rights and to the wider societal potential of business, the paragraph moved towards arguing a need for an institutionalised regulatory framework for business to deliver on that potential, for the benefit of society and for business itself.[203] It observed, among others, that 'markets work optimally only if they are embedded within rules, customs and institutions. Markets themselves require these to survive and thrive, while society needs them to manage the adverse effects of market dynamics and produce the public goods that markets undersupply'.[204]

Setting out its approach and at the same time anticipating some potential or already voiced objections to the decision not to propose binding standards, the report drew particularly on legal and economic system logics.

In setting out the state duty to protect, the 2008 UN Framework report initially explained how globalisation and the expansion of international trade law have benefited corporations through granting and protection of rights, but it progressed to draw extensively on international law doctrine. State duties, founded in international law, had also formed a key argument in the business-driven sub-discourse against specific business responsibilities for human rights at the time of the debate on the Draft Norms and at times during the SRSG mandate. However, the UN Framework drew on the doctrine to send a message to states that many currently understand the principle too narrowly. It indicated that states often 'get the balance' wrong in favour of trade and other economic considerations, and that this may in fact be detrimental to companies. It observed:

> Governments should not assume they are helping business by failing to provide adequate guidance for, or regulation of, the human rights impact of corporate activities. On the contrary, the less governments do, the more they increase reputational and other risks to business.[205]

The Framework proposed possible modes of implementation of the state duty to protect, such as to strengthen corporate culture favourable to human rights; to ensure policy alignment between human rights and economic considerations, including trade; to ensure better guidance and support at the international level; and to work towards innovative

---

[203] Ibid., para. 2.
[204] Ibid.
[205] Ibid., para. 22.

solutions to business operations in conflict zones. These were articulated as 'not intended to insist on specific legislative or policy actions'.[206] That approach in fact left options open, including the legislative one at the national as well as international level. For the national level, this was underscored by an indirect reference to legislation-based incentives.[207] For the international level, it was emphasised by reference to the OECD Guidelines, which were described as 'currently the most widely applicable set of government-endorsed standards focused on corporate responsibility and human rights' but also as a set of standards in need of an update and revision.[208]

The corporate responsibility to respect was explained and presented through a combination of primarily legal system and economic system considerations. The legal considerations were drawn on to strengthen the economic argument, highlighting the risks that are posed to business by not respecting human rights. The way in which the corporate responsibility to respect was articulated as independent from states' duties lent it a degree of legal character. The report did not argue that the corporate responsibility is a conventional legal responsibility. Nor did it say it is not legal, or is entirely voluntary. The responsibility to respect is constructed as dual, comprising the – undoubtedly legally binding – obligation to comply with national law, and the responsibility to observe social expectations of business.[209] It was constructed as a responsibility that may occasionally be met by sanctions by courts, suggesting it is a responsibility based in conventional law. In addition, it was backed with reference to non-legal mechanisms and social expectations, which in previous paragraphs in the 2008 report had been noted as possible pre-cursors for law.[210]

---

[206] Ibid., para. 28.
[207] Ibid., para. 32.
[208] Ibid., para. 46.
[209] Ibid., para. 54.
[210] After submission of the report, the SRSG elaborated on the background for the choice of the term 'responsibility'. At a meeting in January 2010, the SRSG emphasised with regard to the corporate responsibility to respect that the term 'responsibility' was chosen deliberately because the corporate responsibility to respect is not currently a legal duty under international law. He also explained that the use of the phrase 'do not harm' was not intended to mean a passive responsibility or disclose the relevance of affirmative acts required to meet the responsibility. See Mandate of the Special Representative of the Secretary-General on the Issue of Human Rights and Transnational Corporations and other Business Enterprises (2010) 'Closing governance gaps: Application of the UN "Protect, Respect, Remedy" Framework', Expert Multi-stakeholder consultation, 20 January 2010 in Berlin; hosted by the German Federal Ministry for Economic Cooperation and

The report explained:

> In addition to compliance with national laws, the baseline responsibility of companies is to respect human rights. Failure to meet this responsibility can subject companies to the courts of public opinion – comprising employees, communities, consumers, civil society, as well as investors – and occasionally to charges in actual courts. Whereas governments define the scope of legal compliance, the broader scope of the responsibility to respect is defined by social expectations – as part of what is sometimes called a company's social licence to operate.[211]

Moving on to elaborate the due diligence required to 'discharge the responsibility to respect', the Framework presented this as a version of a process that many companies are already familiar with, often as a process required by law. As elaborated below, this argument bought into the practice of due diligence already common with many companies and TNCs, although the focus of human rights due diligence differs fundamentally from the conventional legal liability or financial risk due diligence. While conventional due diligence is about protecting the company from risk from its environment, the human rights due diligence is about protecting society from risk caused by the company. The UN Framework described due diligence in the human rights context as a process which may substantively build on the standards contained in the International Bill of Rights (UDHR, the ICESCR, the ICCPR) and the ILO core conventions. The reasoning was based on the observance that other social actors simply hold businesses to account, in non-legal ways, for compliance with those instruments.[212]

The main 2008 report dealt with the concepts of 'sphere of influence' and 'complicity' in two sub-chapters.[213] This part of the SRSG's construction of business social responsibilities will be reverted to below (section 5.5). The main report stated that the SRSG found the concept of the corporate 'sphere of influence' to be misleading and to lack precision for application in a legal context. Thus, once more, the context of the report was implied to belong to the legal system and rationality, although the report does not say so outright. By implication then, the three-pillared framework has a legal character. The concept of complicity was discussed in terms of its legal meaning and also with regard to application in

---

Development (BMZ), organised by InWEnt – Capacity Building International, Germany, last page of document.
[211] UN Framework, para. 54.
[212] Ibid., para. 57.
[213] Ibid., paras 65–81.

non-legal context, as 'an important benchmark for social actors'.[214] The report found the concept to be workable in a legal context and upheld it for the three-pillared framework.

The third Pillar on access to remedy was argued mainly using legal system logic, in contrast to the parts of the UN Framework related to Pillar One and Two, which deployed legal as well as political and economic logic and observations. In fact, this marks a consistent approach throughout the Framework: addressing the concerns and core issues under each of the pillars mainly in the logic or logics that responded to the rationalities of key stakeholders in regard to the particular pillar. In the case of Pillar One, which addresses itself to states, legal and political functions are key, therefore rendering legal and political rationalities apt. In the case of Pillar Two, which in the Framework was presented to a broad group of stakeholders but for take-up would need to be accepted by businesses, economic system rationality was thus central. This explains usage of terms like the social licence to operate, social expectations and the implied reputational and other economic effects of the 'courts of public opinion'. Such terms are not normally found in international human rights instruments, but were required for business managers reading the UN Framework to relate to and appreciate what Pillar Two meant to them. Pillar Three, which is of core significance to victims of business-related human rights abuse, was also an effort to respond to the concerns of human rights NGOs. Given that the NGOs had mainly been arguing in legal rationality, the response to them was appropriately made in that same code. At the same time, this resonated with governments with particular regard to the judicial part of their legal functions. For company-based remedies too, the legal system approach was deployed in regard to the institutional features and requirements.

The 2008 report was presented to and discussed by the Human Rights Council in June 2008. Following the presentation, the Human Rights Council on 18 June 2008 by a resolution[215] that was adopted unanimously[216] 'welcome[d]' the three-pillared framework presented with the 2008 report. The Council's decision marked the first time a UN human rights body with a political composition (as opposed to the expert composition of treaty bodies and the former Sub-Commission) was in full agree-

---

[214] Ibid., para. 75.
[215] Human Rights Council (2008) 'Mandate of the Special Representative of the Secretary-General on the issue of human rights and transnational corporations and other business enterprises', Human Rights Council Resolution, 8/7June 2008.
[216] The resolution was adopted without a vote, i.e., unanimously by state members of the Human Rights Council.

ment in taking an affirmative approach to a proposal to promote business responsibilities for human rights. This development also marked a significantly different approach within the Human Rights Council, compared to the reception and debate of the UN Norms at the Commission of Human Rights in 2004. While obviously several factors were at play, the analysis of deployment of system-specific arguments demonstrates that arguing in a manner that resonates directly with those with whom change is desired played a significant part in this.

The argumentative strategy that had been applied by the SRSG specifically targeted the audience for whom a particular pillar or required action was addressed. This is even more obvious in the companion report that provided detailed information and reasoning on the SRSG's 'clarification' of the 'sphere of influence' and 'compliance'. Here too, despite the SRSG's outward insistence on not being doctrinal, legal doctrine was employed extensively by the SRSG to construct the understanding of those concepts and to develop his recommendations in the 2008 report. The following section shows how this happened.

5.5 CLARIFICATION OF 'COMPLICITY' AND 'SPHERE OF INFLUENCE': REJECTING 'SPHERE OF INFLUENCE' AND INTRODUCING HUMAN RIGHTS DUE DILIGENCE

Recall that as explained in Chapter 3, the legal system's rationality turns around the binary code legal/illegal and related distinctions. A range of types of phenomena described in language that presumes a legal/illegal or related distinction therefore indicates use of legal system language. Such phenomena include 'crime', 'liability', 'enforcement', and 'abuse'. Also 'rights', 'complicity', 'infringe' or 'infringement', and 'respect' all indicate legal system language. The usage of legal system language and its combination with other system-specific language is particularly noteworthy in the SRSG's work to clarify 'complicity' and 'sphere of influence'. In the UN Framework and UNGPs, the SRSG employed a strategy of creating perturbation by indicating how legal system phenomena may emerge from economic system actions, either through uncertainty based on the imprecision of the 'sphere of influence' concept, or as risks based on 'complicity'. This section will demonstrate how legal and economic system language was deployed by the SRSG to create perturbation among the Human Rights Council and business organisations – formal and informal recipients, respectively – in order to cause acceptance and internalisation. Figure 5.1 (displayed in the subsequent analytical section 5.7.1) offers a graphical depiction with examples.

The issues of 'sphere of influence' and 'complicity' carried over to the SRSG mandate from preceding debates on human rights and business, in particular the debate on the Draft Norms. The Draft Norms made a single, but centrally placed reference to 'sphere of influence'. The Commentary to the Norms did not contain references to 'sphere of influence', but the term was used by the Global Compact.

The 2005–08 mandate asked the SRSG to 'research and clarify the implications for transnational corporations and other business enterprises of concepts such as "complicity" and "sphere of influence"'.[217] A concept that is not established in legal discourse, 'sphere of influence' has been causing problems for academics within law. By contrast, 'complicity' is already an established term within criminal law, and as such has been easier for lawyers to relate to 'complicity' in the context of business and human rights.[218] The business community was hesitant towards the application of the concept of complicity in a context related to international human rights law, outside national law jurisdiction. There was some acceptance of the 'sphere of influence' as a concept to assist companies in relating to the extent of their impact on society. There was, however, no agreement or full understanding of the application or applicability of the concept, nor of its implications. By contrast, company lawyers and others with a background in law expressed difficulties with relating to the 'sphere of influence' concept, which was perceived to be vague and imprecise.[219]

The SRSG approached the clarification of the concepts of 'complicity' and 'sphere of influence' through a process that involved expert meetings, submissions from individuals and multi-stakeholder consultations. Both concepts were also referred to during meetings and in submissions other than those which specifically aimed at their clarification. Points made in stakeholder consultations carried over into the UN Framework and its detailed companion report, while points made at the expert meetings can be seen in the Framework in regard to application in a legal context.

During the multi-stakeholder workshops and other meetings, the issues of 'sphere of influence' and 'complicity' surfaced at several occasions. The fact that the Global Compact applied the 'sphere of influence' concept had previously led business representatives to endorse it and explain its useful-

---

[217] Commission on Human Rights (2005) Human rights and transnational corporations and other business enterprises, para. 1(c).

[218] See, for example, the discussion and example in O. De Schutter (2006) 'The challenge of imposing human rights norms on corporate actors'. In O. De Schutter (ed.) *Transnational Corporations and Human Rights*, Oxford: Hart, pp. 1–40.

[219] K. Buhmann (2014) *Normative Discourses and Public-Private Regulatory Strategies for Construction of CSR Normativity*, Ch. 4 (4.2.6).

ness from the business perspective.[220] The 'complicity' concept was mainly referenced by legal experts (partly to clarify it) and NGOs concerned with corporate accountability.[221]

'Complicity' was addressed only briefly in the SRSG's 2006 ('interim') report and only with little detail as to the substance of the concept. The report highlighted sectors and actions likely to encounter complicity situations, and the legal sources on which the SRSG drew to clarify the concept. It noted that the extractive industries account for most allegations of the worst abuses of human rights, 'up to and including complicity in crimes against humanity. These are typically related to acts committed by public and private security forces protecting company assets and property; large-scale corruption; violations of labour rights; and a broad array of abuses in relation to local communities, especially indigenous people'.[222] Citing legal practice from national law (especially the US) and customary international law, it argued that 'emerging practice and expert opinion increasingly suggest that corporations may be held liable for committing, or for complicity in, the most heinous human rights violations amounting to international crimes, including genocide, slavery, human trafficking, forced labour, torture and some crimes against humanity'.[223] The report also observed that the Global Compact introduced the concepts of 'complicity' and 'spheres of influence' into the CSR debate, where they had 'taken on a life of their own'.[224]

On 'sphere of influence', the 2006 report was more eloquent in terms of independent effort to clarify the notion. The report both suggests that consensus on the concept had been emerging among business, and that the concept was too elusive to form a basis for establishing legal obligations. The former was noted in the general part of the report, the latter in the part of the report in which the SRSG discussed (and criticised) the Draft Norms. While the diagnosis of the 'sphere of influence' as elusive and unsuited as a basis for establishing binding obligations was made in the discussion of the Draft Norms, the implications apply to the general

---

[220] See in particular, Moody-Stuart (n 58).
[221] See, for example, the discussion and example in O. De Schutter (2006) 'The challenge of imposing human rights norms on corporate actors'; Clapham (n 105) at 563–4; ESCR-Net Corporate Accountability Working Group (n 57); summary of Amnesty International's submission in United Nations High Commissioner for Human Rights/Commission on Human Rights (2005) 'Report of the United Nations High Commissioner for Human Rights on the sectoral consultation entitled "Human Rights and the extractive industry"'.
[222] Commission on Human Rights (2006) Interim report, para.25.
[223] Ibid., paras 61–62.
[224] Ibid., para. 40.

usage of the concept and to its application in a legal context. The SRSG's argument deployed initially built on economic system related logic. It referred to core conditions or actors surrounding a company's operations and therefore its possibilities to exist and make profits, from employees to host country. Only after making that point did it proceed to elaborate the problems facing the application of the concept. This was based on legal system language and observations. Thus, the SRSG subjugated the application of the concept from a combined economic and legal perspective, to the legal application. The deployment of both the economic and legal rationalities is in line with the two different system-specific points of departure for this discussion. Eventually, however, the difficulties that the application encountered from the legal perspective were made to win out, indicating that legal rationalities trumped the economic rationalities in the reasoning leading to the UN Framework and in significant parts of the substance of the Framework's text. However, as will be discussed below, this did not mean that the SRSG rejected business perspectives. Rather, he deployed a combination of rationalities in his reasoning, with the objective of achieving support for his recommendations and to ensure appreciation with stakeholders of the points made.

In its March 2006 Position Paper, FIDH commented both on 'sphere of influence' and 'complicity'. Although mostly framed as a counter-critique of the SRSG's critique of the Draft Norms, the statement also brought attention to the conceptual challenges in applying the concepts. FIDH argued with a point of departure in states' obligations for human rights, drawing on a combination of legal and economic system concerns in order to substantiate the need for clearer definition of the boundaries between companies' and states' responsibility in relation to complicity and sphere of influence. The underlying argument suggested that clarity will provide increased legal certainty for companies, in combination with the interest of companies in avoiding the economic effects of legal liability. On 'sphere of influence', FIDH took its point of departure in the Global Compact, but developed this in the direction of procedural obligations. Presenting its argument with an overall basis in legal system considerations and adding some public policy oriented *lex ferenda* observations, FIDH suggested that 'the more powerful a company – that is, the closer the company comes to possessing the influence traditionally held by states – the more reasonable it would seem to impose compliance with internationally recognized human rights'.[225] FIDH delivered an equally detailed and legal system-logic based comment on 'complicity'. It referred to companies'

---

[225] FIDH (n 102) at 9–10.

own increasing acceptance of responsibility for complicity in terms that are almost completely phrased through legal system logics, although they refer to activities within the economic system.[226] Amnesty International argued along similar lines that the organisation deployed at the sectoral consultation on the extractive industries in November 2005, but qualified this by relating it narrowly to states' obligations. That statement, too, was developed almost completely in legal system logic.[227]

In their December 2006 report on ways of addressing dilemma situations in weak governance zones, which was developed in response to the SRSG's invitation to the organisations to develop human rights guidance for business in conflict zones, IOE, ICC and BIAC placed 'sphere of influence' in the context of economic activities of companies. The report's statement also drew on legal system logic to refute the applicability of the 'sphere of influence' concept as a 'basis for imposing legally binding obligations on companies'.[228]

In his 2007 report to the Human Rights Council, the SRSG had employed several legal system observations on 'complicity'. For example, the SRSG noted that 'corporate complicity' may be placed in the larger context of 'criminal or civil wrongs' from the perspective of 'most national legal systems' and international tribunals' 'standard for individual criminal aiding and abetting liability'.[229] On 'sphere of influence', it also employed legal system observations. It noted the absence of a 'legal pedigree' and its relation to the 'state duty to protect'.[230]

The concepts of 'sphere of influence' and 'complicity' were addressed in greater detail in the dedicated companion report to the main 2008 report. The main 2008 report that introduced the UN Framework drew up the main issues and conclusions, applying arguments that are strongly built on legal system considerations. The underlying reasoning was elaborated in the companion report. Both reports underscore the extent to which the SRSG's work is informed by legal doctrine. The insistence on discarding the 'sphere of influence' concept because it does not fit with legal considerations further underscores that the SRSG worked towards an aim of developing a framework for business responsibilities for human rights that would be operational from a legal perspective, even if the framework itself did not lay claim to a legal title or even to having a soft law character. As a result of the absence of enforcement mechanisms at the international level,

---

[226] Ibid.
[227] Amnesty International (2006) Letter to John Ruggie, 27 April.
[228] IOE, ICC, BIAC (n 126) para. 17.
[229] Human Rights Council (n 150) para. 31.
[230] Ibid., para. 87.

considerations on the clarity required for legal obligations to be enforced by national courts played a part.

The main report opened the discussion on 'sphere of influence' in the section that introduced and explained the corporate responsibility to respect. Initially, the report briefly discussed the concept in the context of the Draft Norm's distinction between (states') primary and (companies') secondary obligations for human rights. It argued that that emphasis was wrong, in 'defining a limited list of rights linked to imprecise and expansive responsibilities, rather than defining the specific responsibilities of companies with regard to all rights'.[231] The report eventually rejected the 'sphere of influence' because it found that it 'conflates two very different meanings of influence', one being the ability to cause harm, the other influence ('leverage') over other actors causing harm.[232]

In effect, supported by the companion report, the main report deconstructed the concept of 'sphere of influence' – at least in terms of feasibility of application to the corporate responsibility to respect – in favour of the concept of 'human rights due diligence', a new concept that was introduced by the UN Framework and as indicated has since become very influential in both BHR and CSR. Leaving the details of the argument to the companion report, the main report added economic system logic to its legal system considerations in order to recommend due diligence in place of the rejected concept of 'sphere of influence'.[233]

On 'complicity', the argument developed differently, even though founded on essentially the same basis, i.e., on legal system logic. Again drawing on the due diligence notion, the main report added economic system considerations to legal system logic to build its argument in favour of upholding the concept of 'complicity' in regard to business and human rights. It observed that avoiding complicity is part of the corporate responsibility to respect, and can be achieved through due diligence processes.[234] It emphasised that companies may incur economic costs if met with claims of complicity in human rights abuse. It observed that claims of complicity can impose reputational costs and even lead to divestment without legal liability being established.[235] In line with the point on the 'courts of public opinion', the SRSG observed that even when a company's deriving a benefit from a human rights abuse is not likely on its own to bring legal liability, benefiting from abuses may carry negative implications for com-

---

[231] UN Framework report, para. 51.
[232] Ibid., para. 68.
[233] Ibid., para. 72.
[234] Ibid., paras 73–81.
[235] Ibid., para. 75.

panies in the public perception.[236] To underscore that point, the SRSG referred to international human rights law, noting that in 'international criminal law, complicity does not require knowledge of the specific abuse or a desire for it to have occurred, as long as there was knowledge of the contribution'.[237]

The companion report elaborated and underscored those points partly based on arguments already brought forth or tested during the mandate. The summary provides the essence of the report. It builds on the SRSG's assessment of the feasibility of applying the two concepts, including in particular the legal system informed reasoning on (lack of) precision of 'sphere of influence' and case law and international criminal law informed clarification of 'complicity'. In both cases, the SRSG's findings relate to the legal system informed concept of corporate due diligence. The report established due diligence process as a feasible operational approach for companies to respect human rights. It related human rights due diligence to complicity through the means of economic system based considerations on adverse human rights impact as a risk emerging from companies' business relationships. The companion report also observed that because the concept of 'sphere of influence' was 'too broad and ambiguous a concept to define the scope of due diligence required to fulfil the responsibility to respect' the UN Framework had set out the human rights due diligence approach as a more viable alternative. It also observed that avoiding complicity is 'an essential ingredient in the due diligence carried out to respect rights because it describes a subset of the indirect ways in which companies can have an adverse effect on rights through their relationships'.[238]

To justify the due diligence concept, a legal system informed argument was combined with economic system considerations on risks. The report noted the corporate interest in managing economic effects that may result from compliance allegations and litigation risks. The discursive strategy applying system-specific rationality, which was employed by the SRSG to argue due diligence as an element of business responsibilities for human rights, is further evident in the SRSG's rejection of the concept of 'sphere of influence' in favour of 'due diligence'. His explanation and guidance on how companies may avoid complicity served the same purpose. For the concept of 'sphere of influence', which had been mainly developed and applied by businesses or in a business-oriented context, such as the Global Compact, the SRSG applied legal system observations to indicate that the

---

[236] Ibid., para. 77.
[237] Ibid., para. 80.
[238] Human Rights Council (n 189) Summary.

concept should be discarded. For the concept of 'complicity', which is well known in the legal system, he added economic system considerations to legal system logic in order to connect due diligence and complicity avoidance as risk management.

The evolution of due diligence as part of the corporate responsibility to respect was a case of interdiscursivity in which previous statements influenced later ones. During the SRSG process, the application of due diligence shifted focus from states to companies. Some statements reached back to previous ones to shape the construction of the substantive contents of the term in the specific context for which due diligence was finally recommended. Recall that the ICJ had referred to due diligence,[239] but had done so with reference to states' obligations. Recall further that the guidance for companies working in conflict zones, which ICC, IOE and BIAC had developed during 2006,[240] urged companies to perform due diligence. The SRSG's main 2008 report and the accompanying report specifically on 'complicity' and 'sphere of influence' adopted the due diligence term exclusively with regard to companies. Even when he recommended that export credit agencies require clients to perform due diligence, the actual due diligence exercise is required by the private sector actor.

The SRSG's deconstruction of the 'sphere of influence' in favour of human rights due diligence was based on an argumentative line of reasoning that rejected the former in favour of the new human rights oriented risk-management cousin of the well-known due diligence approach that many companies are familiar with as an economic risk mitigation tool related to business activities. This argumentative strategy was designed to resonate with the business audience, which would have to accept the shift from the 'sphere of influence', already an established term under the Global Compact, to due diligence in the human rights context. The line of argument also rejected the 'sphere of influence' as legally incoherent or simply not belonging to the universe of the legal system. The latter argumentative strategy was designed to speak to and resonate with the Human Rights Council, which would also have to accept the introduction of due diligence in the specific context of business and human rights. In both cases, the argumentative structure prepared the ground for the shift of terms by invoking the stabilising effect from the perspective of each of the audiences – the economic one of business, and the legal one of the Human Rights Council – of rejecting the 'sphere of influence' concept.

---

[239] International Commission of Jurists (2005) 'Corporate accountability, international human rights law and the United Nations'.
[240] IOE, ICC, BIAC (n 126) esp. para. 19.

We shall revert in Chapter 6 to the SRSG's playing on the stabilising and de-stabilising effects on system-specific interests to advance his arguments.

The companion report connected complicity to the due diligence concept, suggesting a combination of economic and legal system interests of companies in avoiding complicity. It expanded the focus to a company's 'relationships associated with those activities'.[241] The final paragraphs, therefore, incorporated aspects of what had been discussed under the concept of 'sphere of influence', and did so with clear reference to complicity and due diligence. Moreover, the final paragraphs deployed legal system rationality only in the first and final part, but used economic system logic throughout. The latter referred to the benefits that due diligence may present to companies in order to reduce complicity risks, and the process aspects of integrating human rights concerns throughout a company's activities and relationships to others.

In conclusion, the SRSG's clarification of the concept of 'complicity' leaned heavily on a combination of legal system logic interspersed with economic system logic. The point of departure was taken in the legal 'pedigree' of 'complicity', just as the non-legal 'pedigree' of 'sphere of influence' was used as a point of departure for de-constructing that concept in favour of one with a clearly legal pedigree, i.e., due diligence. In the case of 'complicity' too, the legal system-based arguments are interspersed with economic system considerations. The argumentative strategy often deployed a combination of system-specific language that underscored the economic interest of companies in obtaining clarity of a legal character of what is expected of them and what they can expect in terms of legal liability and sanctions as well as economic decisions by other economic actors. Again, this shows that the SRSG relied strongly on legal arguments and legal doctrine, despite the claim to be non-doctrinal. But in so doing, he combined legal doctrine with political or economic logic to build arguments that would resonate with the particular audience that he was addressing at the time. This tailored argumentative strategy enabled the outputs of his two terms, the UN Framework and the UNGPs, to obtain broad acceptance. The extent and depth of this was groundbreaking for a UN effort at normative guidance for TNCs to be adopted by an international law-making body. Similar support had not emerged for the Drafts Norms, nor the UN's TNC Code of Conduct project. The support for the UN Framework led to the second SRSG mandate, in which the UN Human Rights Council asked the SRSG to operationalise the UN Framework into what became the UNGPs.

---

[241] Human Rights Council (n 189) para. 72.

5.6 FROM THE UN FRAMEWORK TO THE UNGPS

With the same resolution that 'welcomed' the UN Framework in 2008, the Human Rights Council established a second three-year mandate term for the SRSG.[242] The second term, too, was charged on John Ruggie, who was tasked with 'operationalising' the UN Framework 'with a view to providing more effective protection to individuals and communities against human rights by, or involving [companies] and to contribute to the consolidation of existing relevant norms and standards and any future initiatives, such as a relevant, comprehensive international framework'. The resolution asked the SRSG to continue applying the multi-stakeholder approach he had adopted for the first mandate term.

The resolution did not specify what form the 'operationalisation' of the three-pillared framework could or should take. This left open the possibility that the operationalisation might entail a degree of international regulation, for example a soft law form. The reference to providing 'concrete and practical recommendations' and 'concrete guidance' did not exclude a law-like form of guidance, but also did not presume that the end result will be a conventional legal instrument, such as a treaty.

The resolution's request to the SRSG to 'continue' the multi-stakeholder consultations approach not only endorsed the approach taken during the first term but also institutionalised it. It was no longer to be seen as a somewhat unusual approach adopted by a particular UN Special Procedures mandate-holder in response to instructions in the mandate resolution from 2005, but an established, recognised and welcomed practice to promote understanding, mutual learning and consensus among actors from diverse social sub-systems, to promote and protect all human rights in areas where they may be impacted by business action. This embodies a *de facto* endorsement by a high-level UN body of a reflexive regulatory approach to the continuous development of the international human rights regime, extending from state duties to 'differentiated but complementary' corporate responsibilities, and from judicial to non-judicial and company-level remedies. The potential that this may have for sustainability governance in other areas underscores the significance of understanding the discursive dynamics at play for such a process to deliver normative results.

During the second mandate term, the SRSG continued the practice

---

[242] Human Rights Council (2008) 'Mandate of the Special Representative of the Secretary-General on the issue of human rights and transnational corporations and other business enterprises'.

established during the first mandate of holding various types of consultations.[243] Moreover, pilot projects were carried out with companies to apply the UN Framework and gain input for the elaboration, particularly with regard to Pillar Three.[244]

A few months after the extension of the mandate, the SRSG made a statement to the UN General Assembly.[245] The main part of the statement was more or less a restatement of previous overviews of the UN Framework. The final paragraph, however, stood apart. It stressed that 'success will depend on the continued cooperation of all stakeholders' to achieve 'tangible results where they matter most in the daily lives of people and communities whose rights are adversely impacted by the economic forces that have been threatening our planet'. Beyond the obvious call for cooperation by stakeholders, this also reads as a message to states, business and civil society alike that the 'operationalisation', including what it might entail in terms of regulation, co- and self-regulation, will not succeed for the benefit of all interests unless they actually do cooperate. Addressing this statement to the General Assembly, the SRSG both informed the General Assembly of the significance of a multi-stakeholder regulatory approach to promoting the protection and respect of human rights in a business-related context, and obtained its tacit endorsement.

A news release from ICC following a presentation by the SRSG of his report at ICC International Headquarters in Paris in April 2008 stated that 'Professor Ruggie's presentation was received very positively by the ICC commission and was followed by a rich and constructive exchange of views with commission members.'[246] In view of the fact that the 2008 report in fact proposed more extensive business responsibilities for human rights than did the Draft Norms, and that it suggested that states

---

[243] Mandate of the Special Representative of the Secretary-General on the Issue of Human Rights and Transnational Corporations and other Business Enterprises (2010) 'Mandate consultation outline', October 2010; J. G. Ruggie (2013) *Just Business*.

[244] C. Rees (2011) *Piloting Principles for Effective Company-Stakeholder Grievance Mechanisms: A Report of Lessons Learned*, CSR Initiatives, Harvard Kennedy School, Cambridge, MA; Ruggie, ibid.

[245] SRSG (2008) 'Statement by Prof. John Ruggie, Special Representative of the Secretary-General on human rights and transnational corporations and other business enterprises', 63rd session of the General Assembly, Third Committee, Agenda Item 64(b): 'Promotion and protection of human rights: Human rights questions, including alternative approaches for improving the effective enjoyment of human rights and fundamental freedoms', New York, 27 October 2008.

[246] International Chamber of Commerce (2008) UN Special Representative Ruggie addresses business audience, ICC News, Paris, 27 April 2008.

strengthen regulation, adjudication and the creation of human rights compliant corporate cultures by introducing reporting requirements, criminal law measures and incentives, etc., ICC's reception indicates a considerable shift in attitude over the four-year period since the Draft Norms were debated by the Commission on Human Rights in 2004. This suggests that the extensive and inclusive consultation process may have contributed to this, along with the SRSG's invitation to ICC, IOE and BIAC to develop guidelines for companies in weak governance conflict zones. In combination, consultations and the guideline formulation process appear to have resulted in an enhanced understanding of human rights with the ICC (and perhaps other organisations); learning about the foundations and normative substance of other social actors' expectations of business in relation to human rights; and finally in internal reflection leading to a degree of self-regulation and/or willingness to self-regulate.

The 'operationalisation' took point of departure in the detailed linking of the well-established state duty to protect and business responsibilities established with the UN Framework. Because fundamental agreement had been reached,[247] the SRSG's discursive task shifted focus to a detailed elaboration of what states and businesses must do to live up to the three pillars of the state duty to protect, corporate responsibility to respect, and for both to provide access to remedy. The 2009[248] and 2010[249] reports and other statements applied the approach that the SRSG had adopted in the final part of the first mandate, of testing guidance steps. The system-specific language use became less legal doctrinal, especially for Pillar Two, in which arguments invoking economic system rationality were used to explain the benefits that business may gain from respecting human rights, for example through managing risks through a human rights due diligence process. For Pillar One and the state-based remedy parts of Pillar Three, the SRSG continued to apply a legal systems logic through explanations

---

[247] See also, O. De Schutter (2013) 'Foreword'. In S. Deva and D. Bilchitz (eds). *Human Rights Obligations of Business: Beyond the Corporate Responsibility to Respect?* Cambridge University Press, pp. xv–xxii.

[248] Human Rights Council (2009) 'Business and human rights: Towards operationalizing the "protect, respect and remedy" framework', Report of the Special Representative of the Secretary-General on the issue of human rights and transnational corporations and other business enterprise. UN Doc. A/HRC/11/13, 22 April 2009.

[249] Human Rights Council (2010) Business and human rights: Further steps toward the operationalization of the "protect, respect and remedy" framework', Report of the Special Representative of the Secretary-General on the issue of human rights and transnational corporations and other business enterprises, John Ruggie. UN Doc. A/HRC/14/27, 9 April 2010.

that were designed to activate the rationality of governments in regard to their human rights obligations. Political system logic was also applied, particularly to clarify to states that business-caused adverse impact on human rights reduces their opportunities to deliver on human rights-related public policies and task. To avoid this happening, home and host states should legislate and engage in other efforts to close governance gaps and prevent businesses from causing such impact.[250]

As the UN Framework became a reality and was being operationalised through the process leading to the UNGPs, many stakeholder meetings and reports took to discussing the implications of the UN Framework among themselves. This meant that they focused more on implementation and less on influencing the construction of the output than had been the case during the first SRSG term. Reports from civil society to contribute insights to the elaboration were predominantly on access to remedy. Consistent with the legal logic focus in Pillar Three, they made extensive use of legal terms and observations.[251] Also using legal logics, other civil society statements argued that the UNGPs were unsuitable for addressing corporate human rights abuse.[252] Such arguments made around the time of the Human Rights Council's meeting to decide whether to adopt the UNGPs indicate that at that time, some civil society organisations were troubled with the prospects of a soft law instrument. This and some academic critique issued during and after the second SRSG term suggest that although the SRSG process was successful in generating acceptance for the output of the two terms to ensure their adoption by the Human Rights Council and, as importantly, ensure that lobbying did not obstruct

---

[250] E.g., Mandate of the Special Representative of the Secretary-General on the Issue of Human Rights and Transnational Corporations and other Business Enterprises (2009) 'Responsible contracting', 25 and 26 June 2009 Paris, France: Summary Report; Mandate of the Special Representative of the Secretary-General on the Issue of Human Rights and Transnational Corporations and other Business Enterprises (2010) 'Closing governance gaps.'

[251] E.g., The Corporate Responsibility Coalition (2010) 'Protecting rights, repairing harm: How state-based non-judicial mechanisms can help fill gaps in existing frameworks for the protection of human rights of people affected by corporate activities,' November 2010.

[252] E.g., Human Rights Watch (2011) UN Human Rights Council: Weak Stance on Human Rights, News release 16 June 2011; Alianza Social Continental *et al.* (2011) Statement to Delegations on the Human Rights Council 2011, 17th session, Agenda Item 3: 'Civil Society Organisations respond to Ruggie's Guiding Principles regarding human rights and transnational corporations and other business enterprises'; FIAN International (2011) CSOs and social movements front Human Rights Council today: Ruggie's Guiding Principles unsuitable for addressing corporate human rights abuses, 31 May 2011.

the adoption, the process had not been fully successful in convincing civil society and some other stakeholders of the soft law approach taken.

The report that was eventually issued in 2011 at the end of the second SRSG term and adopted by the Human Rights Council in June 2011, contains the UNGPs. Among the 31 principles, all with commentaries, ten relate to Pillar One, the State Duty to Protect; 14 relate to Pillar Two, the Corporate Responsibility to Respect; and seven to Pillar Three, Access to Remedy. Among the Pillar Two principles, several elaborate on actions that businesses should take to spell out their human rights commitments into policies and human rights (risk-based) due diligence.

The next section discusses in more detail the argumentative approach for the due diligence process introduced by the UN Framework and elaborated by the UNGPs for companies to identify, prevent, mitigate and account for how they manage their adverse impacts.

5.7 ARGUING THE OUTPUTS OF THE SRSG TERMS INTO ACCEPTANCE

5.7.1 Communicating in System-Specific Logics

The UN Framework was both the foundation for the UNGPs and the culmination of the first mandate. As such, the UN Framework and the argumentative strategy that led to the 2008 report responded not only to stakeholder points made during the third year of the SRSG's first mandate, but also to some points or argumentative trends that occurred during the first two years (2005–07), and prepared the ground for the continued discursive construction of BHR through the elaboration during the final three years (2008–11).

A shift occurred in argumentative strategies and structures among several groups of actors during the mandate terms. From the inception of the mandate, the SRSG both argued with reference to state duties (noting that states have 'primary responsibility for human rights' and referring to governance gaps), and to economic or related risks to companies that may result from their engaging in actions that cause human rights abuse. The SRSG's arguments using legal system logic and reference to state duties and other legal aspects of legal system rationality became predominant towards the final part of the mandate. In doing so, the arguments shifted from the conventional international law 'state duty' doctrine to the more nuanced human rights law version of the 'state duty to protect', which entails obligations for states to engage in efforts to protect against human rights abuse caused by businesses. Even so, the SRSG's arguments continued to also refer to economic system rationality, especially in statements addressing audiences comprising business representatives or actors involved with the private sector (such as the World Bank's International Business Forum,[253] referred to in section 5.4.1.2). Making the connection to the economic risks to business and therefore the economic system's logic, the SRSG also argued in legal logic to persuade businesses, and particularly corporate lawyers, of the benefits of human rights due diligence.

Business arguments remained structured around legal system language with an emphasis on state obligations for human rights. However, in the second part of the first mandate term – particularly after the publication of the IOE/ICC/BIAC study[254] in late 2006/early 2007 – it shifted towards increased recognition of international law as a relevant normative source for company action. This suggests that a combination of factors were at play: in line with the communicative element in reflexive law and autopoiesis, reaching out to the organisations that had been the most opposed to normative guidance on human rights for business challenged those organisations to come up with normative guidance that in fact relied on international human rights law. Simultaneously, the SRSG's deployment of a combination of economic and legal logics facilitated business appreciation of the benefits of understanding and working with human rights as being in the longer-term interest of business. In this, the SRSG also played on system-specific interests through a stabilising and de-stabilising argumentative strategy, as elaborated in Chapter 6. Indicating a practice-oriented approach consistent with assumption on which legal autopoiesis builds, some statements observed that a change in corporate behaviour requires talking in language that resonates directly with the business practitioner rather than the language of legal practitioners (in particular, the statement by Sir Geoffrey Chandler in October 2007,[255] noted in section 5.4.1.1).

Throughout the SRSG process, civil society organisations applied an argumentative strategy employing legal system rationality, arguing for harder regulation and more legal accountability. However, as a medium for the Human Rights Council rather than a representation of a social sub-system, the SRSG was not particularly receptive to legal system arguments per se. Rather, he was receptive to arguments that contributed to his knowledge on the specificities of the international human rights law regime, in particular the state duty *to protect*. He was also receptive to

---

[253] SRSG (2007) 'Remarks at plenary session on "Business and the rules of the game"'.
[254] IOE, ICC, BIAC (n 126).
[255] Chandler (n 181).

arguments that assisted him in moving the process towards agreement on a normative output, or which indicated human rights gaps in the work (such as the situation of victims of human rights abuse). The SRSG's receptiveness to arguments on the need for victims to have access to remedy may be understood partly in that light, as the Third Pillar was important for civil society support. Among civil society proposals, especially those that were concretely worded were successful in being taken up in SRSG reports (for example, the proposal on a global ombudsman, which was made by Clean Clothes Campaign and CIDSE, and the proposals for governments to require transparency to strengthen market pressures).

The SRSG himself employed legal system language to address civil society statements calling for a legal framework for business and human rights, explaining that the often-protracted process of formal international (hard) law-making was the reason why he sought to develop a different regulatory modality. Some civil society statements (e.g., during the 2005–08 term on the role of export credit agencies and related institutions on business-related human rights abuse) indicate that civil society adopted or even internalised SRSG arguments and employed these in subsequent statements. The SRSG employed political system logic as a general framing of his mandate and the way that human rights, companies and public policy concerns relate. This allowed him to create an understanding with national governments with a focus on public policy objectives, therefore also creating support among national civil servants or political appointees in the Human Rights Council.

In sum, the SRSG process confirms the observation in Chapter 4: that communication in the system-specific logic of the recipient is a significant channel for influencing the perceptions of the recipient by stimulating its understanding and appreciation of the needs or demands of its environment. It may appear obvious that to make someone else appreciate one's own point, one should communicate in a manner that resonates with the audience. However, how to communicate like that? The answer is, in fact, not obvious if not informed by a theory. The theory of autopoiesis offers an entry point in suggesting that the key is in activating the recipient's inherent functional rationality, and that this can be done through linguistically using the logic of the recipient. Figure 5.1 offers examples of system-specific communication by the SRSG, business and civil society and its results.

For the purposes of the current chapter's analysis, two main findings emerge. First, the SRSG's arguments on economic system effects of business-related human rights abuse facilitated business acceptance and internalisation of international human rights law as normative source for business conduct. This combined with, or was supported by, the reflexive

From incremental steps to emerging regime 259

Context

SRSG mandate

Message

A) "Failure to respect human rights affects a company's social licence to operate"
B) "Human rights are state obligations"
A) "Companies must be held to account for their impact on human rights"
B) "States must live up to their international obligations"

Transmitter

A) SRSG
B) Companies
C) Civil society
D) SRSG

Recipient

A) Companies
B) SRSG (civil society, UN, states)
C) SRSG
D) States

Code (audience-specific)

A) Economic system interests

B) Legal system interests (duties, *lex lata*)

C) Public policy-cum-legal system (*lex ferenda*)

D) Legal system interests (duties, *lex lata*)

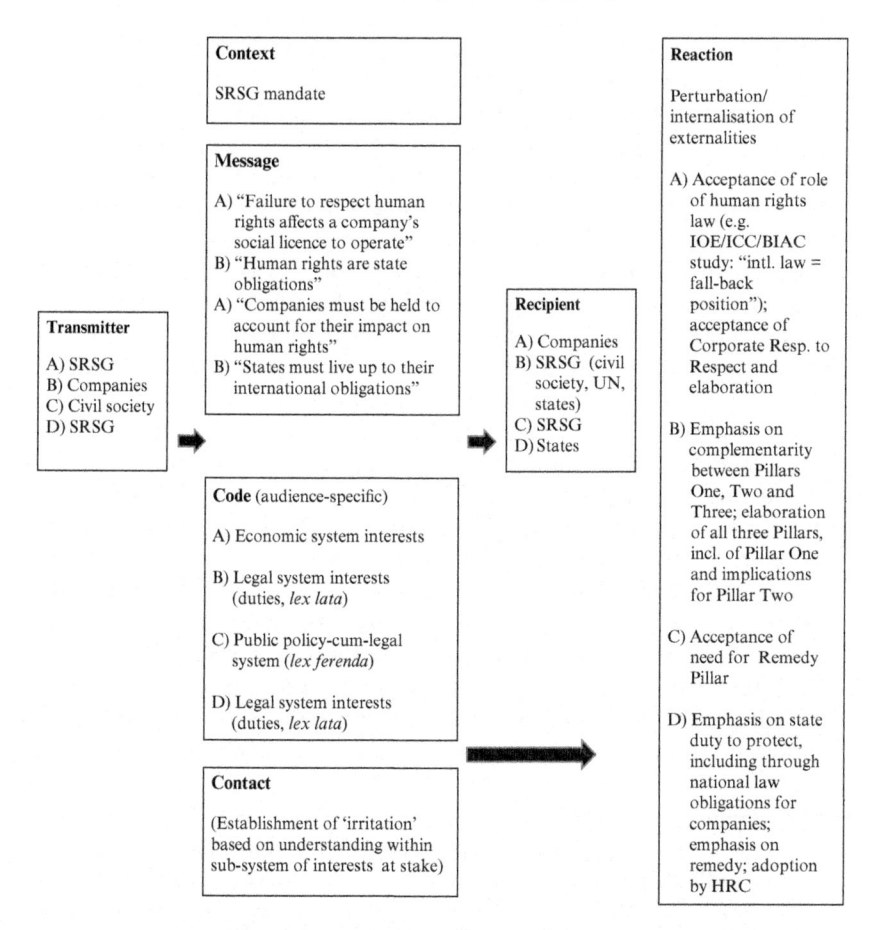

Contact

(Establishment of 'irritation' based on understanding within sub-system of interests at stake)

Reaction

Perturbation/ internalisation of externalities

A) Acceptance of role of human rights law (e.g. IOE/ICC/BIAC study: "intl. law = fall-back position"); acceptance of Corporate Resp. to Respect and elaboration

B) Emphasis on complementarity between Pillars One, Two and Three; elaboration of all three Pillars, incl. of Pillar One and implications for Pillar Two

C) Acceptance of need for Remedy Pillar

D) Emphasis on state duty to protect, including through national law obligations for companies; emphasis on remedy; adoption by HRC

Note: This figure is designed with a point of departure in points (a) and (b) of the 2005–2008 mandate: identification and clarification of 'standards of corporate responsibility and accountability' for companies with regard to human rights; elaboration on the role of states in 'effectively regulating and adjudicating the role of' business with regard to human rights.

Figure 5.1 SRSG process: Model of relations and reaction for analysis of system-specific interest-based communication for discursive construction of business responsibilities for human rights

law approach of inviting business representatives to help define guidance. Second, the SRSG's approach shifted from limited usage of legal system language towards extensive usage of legal system language, combined with an emphasis on the economic implications of legal system observations and considerations. The latter is particularly clear in relation to arguments on economic risks that human rights abuse may cause to companies. Still, the SRSG avoided direct references to changing the law (*lex ferenda*), presenting many of his proposals for new or amended law simply as 'policy proposals'. The SRSG was also successful in having the Human Rights Council (and states represented at the Council) accept the decision not to aim at a binding international law instrument, but rather to work through softer measures that could guide companies to internalise respect for human rights standards into their practices without a protracted process of formulating a declaration or convention. That line was supported or at least accepted also by both civil society and business. In both cases, the SRSG's approach was to address audiences in their own system-specific logics in ways that also highlighted the implications for their system-specific concerns that might result from other interests and rationalities, that is, those that guide the actions of other functional sub-systems.

Following the adoption of the UN Framework and the UNGPs, academic observers have been divided as to their efficacy and authoritative character. Some academics within international human rights law and other fields had felt that the UN Framework was a missed opportunity to propose a set of binding legal standards of human rights obligations for companies.[256] Others have argued that the UN Framework outlined a path forward and would gain status as an authoritative document.[257] Following the adoption of the UNGPs as well, there has been academic critique of both process and output,[258] but also recognition of the contri-

---

[256] E.g., C. M. O'Brien (2011) 'The UN Special Representative on Business and Human Rights: Re-embedding or dis-embedding transnational markets?' In C. Joerges, and J. Falke (eds) *Karl Polanyi, Globalisation and the Potential of Law in Transnational Markets*, Oxford: Hart, pp. 323–57; S. Deva (2011) '"Protect, respect and remedy": a critique of the SRSG's framework for business and human rights'. In K. Buhmann, L. Roseberry, and M. Morsing (eds) *Corporate Social and Human Rights Responsibilities: Global Legal and Management Perspectives*, Houndmills, Basingstoke, Hampshire New York: Palgrave Macmillan, pp. 108–28; A. J. D. Regil (2008) 'Business and human rights: Upholding the market's social Darwinism'. In *Human Rights and Sustainable Human Development*, The Jus Semper Global Alliance, October 2008; T. J. Melish and E. Meidinger (2012) 'Protect, Respect, Remedy and Participate: "New Governance" lessons for the Ruggie Framework'. In M. Radu (ed.) *The UN Guiding Principles on Business and Human Rights: Foundations and Implementation*, Martinus Nijhoff Publishers, pp. 303–36.

[257] C. Ochoa (2008) 'The 2008 Ruggie Report: A framework for business and human rights', 12(12) *ASIL Insight* 18 June 2008.

[258] E.g., C. Parker and J. Howe (2012) 'Ruggie's diplomatic project and its missing regulatory infrastructure'. In R. Mares (ed.) *The UN Guiding Principles on Business and Human Rights: Foundations and Implementation*, The Hague:

butions that the SRSG process and its outputs offer to the onward course for business and human rights[259] and even for adding to the CSR discourse.[260] Like other academic analysis of normative frameworks, case law and jurisprudence, the critique of the outputs of the SRSG process is part of an on-going effort to contribute suggestions for improvements for the future. The details of the academic debate exceed the focus of this book.

5.7.2 Settling the Understanding of Business Responsibilities for Human Rights and Its Core Elements

The SRSG process succeeded in constructing the idea of business responsibilities for human rights as based on all human rights, with a point of departure in international human rights law, in particular the International Bill of Rights and the eight ILO fundamental conventions (on the four core international labour rights). The normative understanding established in the UN Framework and elaborated in the UNGPs combines both (under Pillar One) the legal obligations of states to protect; and (under Pillar Two) the legal compliance duty of companies to respect as well as the social expectation on business to respect human rights even beyond the legal obligation to comply with national law. To this it added (under Pillar Three) the responsibility to provide judicial and non-judicial remedies, including for companies to provide grievance mechanisms. Through the

---

Martinus Nijhoff Publishers, pp. 273–301; F. Wettstein (2013) 'Making noise about silent complicity: The Moral Inconsistency of the "Protect, Respect and Remedy" Framework'. In Deva and Bilchitz (n 3) pp. 243–68; D. Bilchitz (2013) 'A chasm between "is" and "ought"? A critique of the normative foundations of the SRSG's Framework and the Guiding Principles'. In Deva and Bilchitz, ibid. pp. 107–37; S. Deva (2013) 'Treating human rights lightly: a critique of the consensus rhetoric and the language employed by the Guiding Principles'. In ibid. pp. 78–104; J. Bonnitcha and R. McCorquedale (forthcoming) 'Is the concept of "due diligence" in the Guiding Principles coherent?', *European Journal of International Law*, available at SSRN http://papers.ssrn.com/sol3/papers.cfm?abstract_id=2208588.

[259] E.g., A. Sanders (2015) 'The impact of the "Ruggie Framework" and the "United Nations Guiding Principles on Business and Human Rights" on transnational human rights litigation'. In J. Martin and K. E. Bravo (eds) *The Business and Human Rights Landscape: Moving Forward, Looking Back.* Cambridge: Cambridge University Press, pp. 288–315; F. Wettstein (2015) 'Normativity, ethics, and the UN Guiding Principles on Business and Human Rights: a critical assessment', 14(2) *Journal of Human Rights* pp. 162–82.

[260] F. Wettstein, (2015) 'Business and Human Rights: implementation challenges.' In D. Baumann-Pauly and J. Nolan (eds) *Business and Human Rights: from Principles to Practice,* Routledge, pp. 77–89; Buhmann (2016) 'Public regulators and CSR'.

agreement that was reached in the Human Rights Council, the floating signifier of business responsibilities for human rights was 'fixed' or settled, at least for a time. (The process towards a UN treaty on business and human rights, which is on-going at the time of writing, presents a new effort at hegemony over the concept and its implications for states and businesses. The treaty process was initiated in 2014[261] by a group of states with the support of civil society and some academics who felt that the UN Framework and UNGPs were not sufficiently strong.)

The settling of the discourse on business responsibilities for human rights that resulted from the SRSG process has led to a conception that is both narrower and much wider than the CSR concept. BHR is narrower than CSR in that it encompasses only human rights. It is wider in the sense that it encompasses not only actions 'beyond what is required by applicable law' (a voluntary element), but also actions required of companies by law in their home states or countries of operation (a mandatory element). It is also wider in that it covers both states and companies, and elaborates the understanding of the state duty to protect to encompass state organs that are indirectly involved in business activities through funding of private sector activities.

The clarification during the first SRSG term of both of the concepts 'sphere of influence' and 'complicity' differs from the general construction of the corporate responsibility to respect. As will be elaborated in Chapter 6, it offers an interesting example of how a legal concept can be argued into acceptance with another sub-system by articulating it as an essentially stabilising element to avert de-stabilisation. The SRSG's deconstruction of 'sphere of influence', the proposal to adopt due diligence instead, and the acceptance of 'complicity' all lean heavily on legal system logic to build the argument. Further, the argument for due diligence incorporated economic system considerations on economic loss or risks that companies may encounter by not having policies or due diligence processes in place. The results differ, as do the points of departure, but the purpose is the same: To build an argument on the desirability from a legal or an economic system perspective of the certainty that due diligence, a legal system-based concept, can provide for businesses in relation to meeting social expectations of their responsibility for human rights. The system-specific argumentative approach may be depicted as follows (Figure 5.2).

---

[261] Human Rights Council (2014) 'Elaboration of an international legally binding instrument on transnational corporations and other business enterprises with respect to human rights.'

From incremental steps to emerging regime 263

Context

SRSG mandate point (c): 'complicity' and 'sphere of influence'

Message

A) "'Sphere of influence' has no legal pedigree lacks clarity for application in legal context; due diligence is established legal concept"

B) a) "Complicity in human rights abuse causes liability and reputational risks to a company"
b) "human rights due diligence enables companies to identify and manage risks"

Transmitter

A) SRSG

B) SRSG

Recipient

A) Human Rights Council

B) a) Formally: Human Rights Council
b) Informally: companies

Reaction

Perturbation/ internalisation of externalities

A) Accept rejection of 'sphere of influence' in favour of due diligence

B) a) Accept notion of company complicity in human rights abuse

b) (Intended) company performance of due diligence to identify and avoid causing risks to human rights

Code (audience-specific)

A) Legal system interests (clarity = precondition for application)

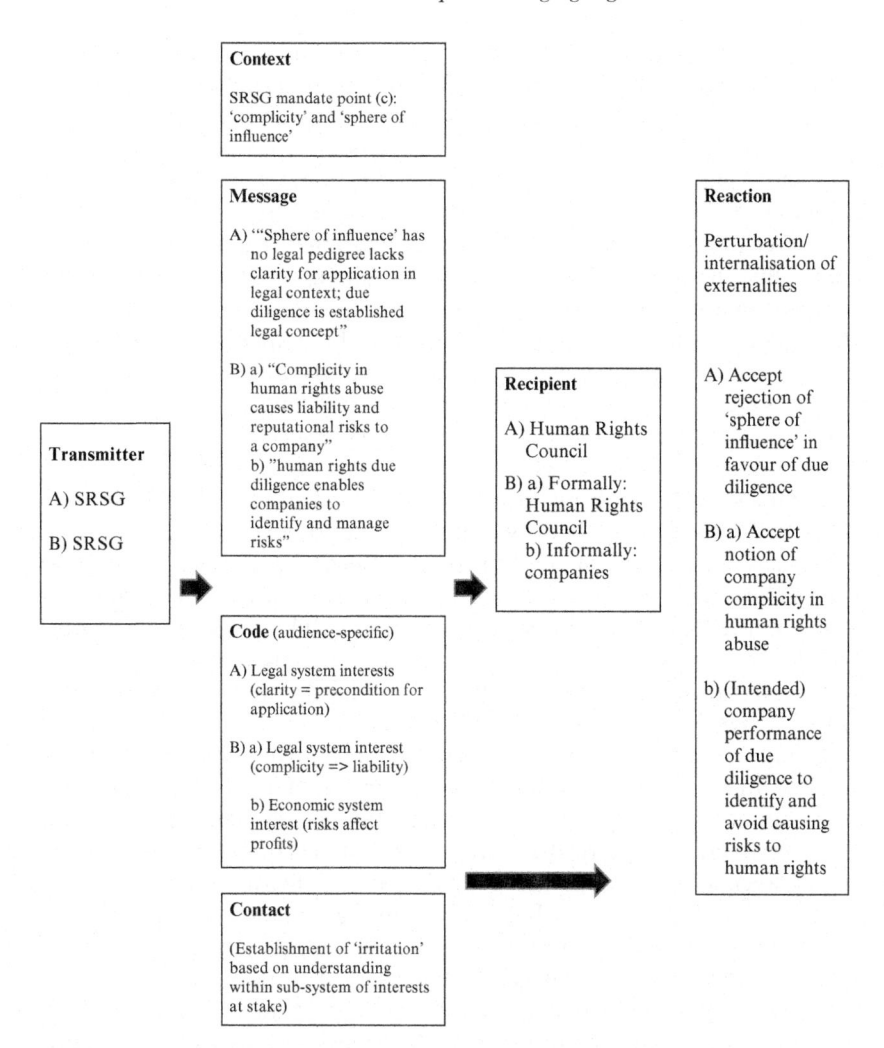

B) a) Legal system interest (complicity => liability)
b) Economic system interest (risks affect profits)

Contact

(Establishment of 'irritation' based on understanding within sub-system of interests at stake)

Note: Clarification of the implications for transnational corporations and other business enterprises of concepts such as 'complicity' and 'sphere of influence'.

Figure 5.2   SRSG process – 2005–2008 term – mandate point (c): Model of relations and reactions for analysis of system-specific interest-based communication in discursive construction of business responsibilities for human rights: 'complicity', 'sphere of influence' and human rights due diligence

Economic system logic was deployed to build the argument for companies to accept the existence and growth of social expectations on them to take responsibility for their impact on human rights. An allegedly non-doctrinal point of departure served to build what was essentially an argument that was based in law and legal doctrine. A legal system-based foundation was present throughout: in references to legal or non-legal 'pedigree', in reference to national or international criminal case law and to liability, in reference to (legal) certainty, and in reference to established legal terminology as tools for companies to apply in order to assess their actions with regard to their human rights impact. This weight on system-specific legal logic deployment differed from the remainder of the SRSG's statements, including in the main 2008 report. As noted above, the dedicated companion report to the 2008 report offered its concluding arguments upon a backdrop of economic system logic addressing companies by emphasising risks and legal system logic addressing the Human Rights Council by way of framing the context for the conclusion. The (de-)construction of the 'sphere of influence' and 'complicity' offer particularly clear examples of the significance of not only mastering system-specific logics, but also playing on this to build a case for normative change with the audience in order to preserve its system-specific interests.

The clarification of the concepts of 'complicity' and 'sphere of influence' shares with the remainder of the SRSG's work a leaning towards defining or hinging concepts or actions substantively and procedurally on law. In the UN Framework, the extensive use of legal system logic and the common interspersion of this with economic system logic served a purpose of creating perturbation not only with the Human Rights Council to appreciate and accept the SRSG's recommendations on 'sphere of influence' and 'complicity', but also within the business community as an informal, but significant recipient of the 2008 report's messages and the guidance it provides. Legal system logic served to transmit messages to the Human Rights Council in order for it to understand and, if required, act. Resonating with the rationality of business organisations, economic system logic in that context served as a sort of coating for the (perhaps bitter) pill of increased human rights normativity for business action. That coating may have been perceived by the SRSG as necessary to make companies understand the implications of the law-based findings that were made on 'complicity' and 'sphere of influence' and the applicability of human rights due diligence. Supported by the SRSG's playing on de-stabilising and stabilising arguments, it helped stimulate perturbation in the economic system for companies to internalise social expectations.

After its publication the SRSG's 2008 report came to be commonly referred to as the 'Protect, Respect and Remedy Framework'. During the second mandate term of the SRSG (2008–11) the report came to be referred to widely as the 'UN Framework', with the reference to the UN in that short-hand title suggesting an official endorsement which the framework did not actually enjoy. The Human Rights Council's 'welcoming' was an unusual step, applying an unusual term, and not a formal adoption. Even before the publication of the UNGPs the UN Framework came to be widely applied and to influence a number of official documents. It directly influenced the 2011 revision of OECD's Guidelines for Multinational Enterprises[262] as well as the EU's 2011 Communication on CSR[263] and transparency requirements for corporate reporting that were announced in the Communication. Thus, it not only broke ground within the UN system by obtaining agreement for guidance on business and human rights. It expanded that to other intergovernmental organisations. Perhaps the single most obvious example of this is the broad uptake and application of the risk-based due diligence approach that was developed by the UN Framework and elaborated by the UNGPs. In being applied to general CSR issues, for example by OECD's Guidelines and the EU's Non-Financial Reporting Directive, the BHR regime is coming to shape CSR.[264]

Chapter 6 follows up on the analysis in Chapters 4 and 5 through a comparative analysis and synthesis of argumentative strategies and their effects on the views of stakeholders representing other functional subsystems or logics than that of the transmitter of a statement.

---

[262] OECD (2011) Guidelines for Multinational Enterprises, 2011 revision, Paris: OECD Publishing, available at http://www.oecd.org/daf/internationalinvestment/guidelinesformultinationalenterprises/48004323.pdf.

[263] European Commission (2011) 'A renewed EU Strategy 2011-14 for Corporate Social Responsibility'.

[264] See further, K. Buhmann (2016) 'Juridifying Corporate Social Responsibility through Public Law, assessing coherence and inconsistencies against UN guidance on Business and Human Rights', 11(3) *International and Comparative Corporate Law Journal* pp. 194–228.

PART III

Arguing for change

6. Argumentative strategies

Chapter 6 compares and synthesises the insights of the five case studies with regard to argumentative strategies and their influence on the output of each of the regulatory processes as well as the outcome in terms of formal acceptance of the output. It opens by observing that the significance of communicating in the system-specific logic of the audience does not mean that all must work according to the logic of the market. Rather, deploying the economic system's logic is the key to making companies internalise the needs and expectations of society, and therefore stimulate their consideration of social needs, inclusive of respect for human rights. The chapter identifies three trends in argumentative strategies and considers the use, impact and complementarity of these: system specific interest-based arguments (section 6.2); stabilising and de-stabilising arguments (section 6.3) and specificity of proposals for change (section 6.4). Section 6.5 concludes the chapter by considering the role of the case studies towards the discursive construction of business responsibilities for human rights and the emergence of the BHR regime.

6.1 INTRODUCTION

6.1.1 Background and Objective

Chapters 4 and 5 showed that participants in the processes to develop normative guidance on business responsibilities for human rights experienced varying degrees of success in influencing and determining the outputs to accord with their concerns, and to preserve or even promote their interests. The analysis demonstrated that arguments invoking the system-specific logic of recipients tended to be more influential than those which invoked the logic of the transmitters. This, however, is not the full picture: it also became obvious in Chapters 4 and 5 that there were more nuances at play, as both the use of stabilising and de-stabilising arguments and the specificity of a proposal also played a part.

The finding that communicating in the system-specific logic of the audience can be significant does not mean that all functional sub-systems or the discourses on CSR or BHR must succumb to the logic of the market in order to influence businesses to take responsibility for their impact on society or work for sustainability. By contrast, deploying economic system logic is the key to making companies internalise the needs and expectations held by other stakeholders, and therefore advance business appreciation and consideration of social, environmental and other sustainability needs and interests of others. Understanding and being able to apply the logic of the market is therefore an avenue to induce change and acceptance with market actors of the priorities of political, legal and other functional sub-systems with regard to sustainability. This chapter develops that point through an analysis that compares and synthesises the findings in Chapters 4 and 5 with regard to identifying what argumentative strategies and combinations are the most effective in stimulating the intended acceptance and change of norms. The chapter does this by considering systems-specific interest-based communication, stabilising and de-stabilising argumentative strategies, and finally the specificity or generality of an argument.

The deployment of system-specific interests as part of an argumentative strategy was explained and exemplified in Chapters 4 and 5. These chapters showed considerable variation between practices of arguing a point through a statement that sought to induce change with a stakeholder from another functional sub-system by activating the core rationality of the audience. Some participants used that strategy more than others. In general, that argumentative strategy was mainly used by business associations, some of the Global Compact architects, and the SRSG, especially towards the end of the first mandate term. The EU Commission, too, did so when it addressed businesses in the Annex to the 2006 Communication, with aim of setting up the CSR Alliance.

To appreciate how the combination of stabilising and de-stabilising arguments can enhance the effect of the general approach of system-specific arguments, understanding what issues may be stabilised or de-stabilised is a first step. That is the topic of section 6.2 below, which discusses the interests and power issues at stake for key stakeholders in regard to different degrees of change that may result from a multi-stakeholder process to develop norms for business with regard to their social impact. The section also considers how the outputs of the case study processes measure up to their original ambitions and what this means for the change obtained through each process, and how the discursive outputs were shaped through system-specific interest-based communication. Next, section 6.3 considers the use of stabilising and non-stabilising arguments to reinforce a system-specific interests-based argument, providing examples from the case studies. Section 6.4 considers the significance of an argument being specific and easily operational, or more general, if principled. Section 6.5 concludes by considering the contributions of the discursive processes with regard to the emergence of the BHR regime.

This chapter builds on and re-combines elements from previous chapters. Recall that Laclau and Mouffe's discourse theory considers discourse as a way to obtain power (and for the purposes of the current study, promote or preserve system-specific interests) through constructing the meaning of 'floating signifiers', that is, concepts that have not yet found a finally determined meaning, such as 'CSR' or 'business responsibilities for human rights'. Recall also that Fairclough's textual analysis approach to discourse applies textual analysis as a way to understand how discourse constructs social phenomena, such as normative conceptions of what is constituted by CSR or business responsibilities for human rights. Chapters 4 and 5 focused on the usage of system-specific language in textual statements for constructing business social responsibilities with a particular focus on human rights. With this backdrop, Chapter 6 considers the effects and complementarity of the argumentative strategies through obtaining support for particular versions of understandings of what business responsibilities for their social impacts are, ultimately leading to the emergence of a regime on BHR.

As explained at the beginning of Chapter 4, Chapters 4 and 5 relayed the processes of the case studies with regard to the discursive construction of CSR, the general progression (and frequently also, regression) of the construction process of social responsibilities of business to be informed by international human rights law, and the deployment of system-specific logic of either the recipients or transmitters in a general sense. The focus of the current chapter is on what argumentative factors led to the specific outputs of the case studies (or in the case of the CSR Alliance, the launch and preliminary outputs). Consistent with the general outline, the main emphasis is on the SRSG process leading to the UN Framework and UNGPs, with the other case studies adding perspective to how and why the SRSG process differed and resulted in turning around previous business resistance, obtaining support for the idea of formal guidance on business and human rights issued by an intergovernmental organisation.

6.2 POWER, DISCOURSE AND COMMUNICATION IN SYSTEM-SPECIFIC LOGICS

6.2.1 Power Concerns with the Construction of Norms on Business Responsibilities for their Social Impacts

As observed in Chapter 1, power is a key issue for the purposes of discourse as a process, as well as the output of processes to discursively construct particular ideas or concepts. That is particularly the case for ideas or concepts whose meaning is open for debate, leading to struggle for hegemony in defining the meaning ('floating signifiers'). For the current purposes, power plays a role with stakeholders in a discourse as a subject to be promoted or preserved through the output of the process of construction of CSR normativity – that is, the result of the discursive process that evolved within each of the case studies. As a corollary, it also plays a role in the process, because participants in a multi-stakeholder process in anticipation of the outcome seek to discursively influence the construction of normativity on business social responsibilities, so that the output will accord with their system-specific interests.

As noted in Chapter 3, depending on their point of departure and aims, discourse participants may employ stabilising or de-stabilising strategies when arguing that business responsibilities for human rights should be voluntary or become mandatory. As part of this, they may employ a *lex lata* or a *lex ferenda* line of argument towards affecting recipients' stances on whether or not the law should change to establish obligations on companies in relation to their impact on society. Based on the interests that they want to preserve or promote, discourse participants may seek to stabilise or de-stabilise the role to be played by international human rights law as a normative source for business social responsibilities. Conservative stabilising strategies could argue that human rights are obligations for states and therefore should not be transferred onto companies as obligations or even expectations. De-stabilising strategies could argue that business social responsibilities should be normatively informed by or even established in international (human rights) law.

Consistent with the habermasian element in reflexive law theory[1] (see Chapter 1, section 1.3.2.2.2), the ability to influence the output of a multi-stakeholder regulatory process and obtain hegemony through the construction of the normative output may be based on the reasoned strength of the argument. The discursive usage of system-specific logics to cause perturbation within the (sub-)system(s) of recipients provides argumentative strength based on what is understood as reason by the audience, because the argument activates its rationality. Recall in this context also that Habermas does not insist on normative products being made as a result of full deliberation. He recognises that compromise may be necessary, and that this can be achieved through negotiation.

---

[1] G. Teubner (1983) 'Substantive and reflective elements in modern law'; see also K. Buhmann (2018) *Power, Procedure, Participation and Legitimacy in Global Sustainability Norms,* Routledge.

The autopoietic element in reflexive law theory allows for understanding how strategic usage of system-specific logics may be deployed in multi-stakeholder regulatory processes with the aim of stimulating recipients' appreciation of the transmitter's views and needs. As demonstrated by the analysis in Chapter 4 of the process that led to the Draft Norms and particularly their dismissal with the UN Human Rights Commission, the insights of systems-thinking that underpin social autopoiesis are not limited to strictly reflexive regulatory processes. They also help understand how specific system-specific interests can come to prevail in other regulatory processes that involve interests of more than one social sub-system.

At the time of the outset of this study between 1998 and 2005, the potential implications for governments, civil society and companies of a future normative construction of social responsibilities of business varied greatly. This marked all the five case studies and affected the discursive engagement with system-specific interests and concerns with change in other sub-systems. In terms of prospective outputs and longer-term outcomes, all was possible at the outset of each of the processes, because floating signifiers were still very fluid and open to struggles for fixing their meaning. At the time when the five processes were launched, three major types of possible change were likely, each with different stakeholders as winners or losers. The three types were: a hard institutionalisation (business obligations on their impact on society established through binding law), a soft institutionalisation (business responsibilities clarified in soft law), and status quo (no change). For each participant in each process, the prospect of 'winning' or 'losing' was not just a question of the fixation of the concepts. As important were the implications for power positions for each stakeholder group with their own constituencies and for their longer-term power vis-à-vis other functional sub-systems. The normativity that would be the output of the process to define CSR and, eventually, business responsibilities for human rights had the potential to cause major shifts in such power relations.

A *hard institutionalisation* would entail legally binding requirements in international law on businesses to act socially responsibly in specific ways, in particular in not causing human rights abuse and/or in contributing actively to the realisation of human rights. A legally binding requirement that firms do not act in ways that cause human rights abuse would restrict actions permitted by firms and would have implications for their resources made or spent, such as payment for production or services in low-wage countries with labour protection below the requirements of international labour standards and/or inefficient monitoring and enforcement of applicable labour law. A requirement that firms act in specific ways to contribute to human rights implementation could also be significant for resource priorities for many business organisations. As a result, such requirements could have potential economic effects on many actors in the private sector, be they TNCs, suppliers or even buyers. On the other hand, businesses that already respect human rights in their own practices and as an integrated element in their business relations, such as with suppliers, might benefit from a legal institutionalisation. This would result in a 'level playing field', which would in effect place those already playing according to the rules applying in that field at an advantage. They would already have their practices and economies tuned in to those (or related) rules, and could benefit economically from opportunities that might arise when other firms restructure their practices to comply with the new rules, or even withdraw from certain markets or activities due to reduced profitability.

The implications in terms of impact on system-specific interests go beyond the economic sub-system: some governments might also find that binding requirements on business with regard to human rights, particularly in the fulfilment of human rights, would ease resource requirements on themselves. For many NGOs, an institutionalisation would underscore their power and ability to act on the political stage. It would demonstrate their ability to obtain influence in shaping new norms in accordance with the perceptions of their constituencies. As a result, they may gain more members and become more powerful among their peers, and having proven their influence they can also expect to increase their power in negotiations with public regulators and negotiators, whether at national or international level.

A *soft institutionalisation* towards specific guidance for businesses in the form of non-binding international law on their social responsibilities would still have significant economic implications for a large number of businesses globally, whether TNCs, suppliers or even buyers. Some might perceive it as a way to invest in society and ensure that they meet society's expectations beyond binding law. To others, it might constrain economically conditioned practices that have benefited from governance gaps. Because market reactions or economic 'sanctions' (such as consumer boycotts or investors' decisions to divest) are not tied to legally binding rules, the profit implications might be as severe or almost as severe for such companies as in the case of a hard institutionalisation. In other cases, non-binding guidance on business conduct might put less strain on firms' economic resources and, as such, may be less likely to have as extensive direct economic effects as in the case of legally binding requirements.

Despite not being legally enforceable, a soft institutionalisation may nevertheless spill over on governments' interests through increased respect and realisation of human rights in states. For NGOs engaged in CSR or human rights, the political power-gain resulting from a soft form of institutionalisation rather than binding requirements many have been calling for, would possibly be considerably less than in the case of a hard institutionalisation. Organisations that have fought for a hard institutionalisation may even fear, risk or experience a loss of power with constituencies and public negotiators as the organisations are seen to be unable to achieve their commitments. For the international labour movement and national trade unions, a soft institutionalisation could appear less of an encroachment on their power as the international or national organisations charged with labour rights, than would a hard international law institutionalisation outside the auspices of the ILO.

Status quo might affect perceptions of international law as a regulatory system and its ability to adapt to changed structures following the emergence of economic non-state actors as agents in transnational activities as well as at the international stage. In particular, this relates to international law's ability to ensure a balance between societal interests and concerns, such as trade, human rights and social or environmental conditions. Business organisations that do not welcome limitations on the freedom of enterprise would emerge as the winners in terms of obtaining hegemony over the discourse and its output and in terms of economic power to benefit from unrestricted trade. Those that benefit from global, regional or local governance gaps would preserve their economic benefits resulting from unchanged practices, for example in production or sourcing from supplier countries. In the longer term, profit gains would not be certain as parts of the market do value social responsibility, and therefore self-regulation in the absence of binding rules, yet in the short term they might gain economically. Business organisations that accept certain limitations, so far on a voluntary basis, could stand as losers in the inter-business struggle for profits and inter-systemic power. Governments, international organisations like the UN, and NGOs that have sought to promote an institutionalisation of corporate responsibilities would be the losers in the political struggle for power to define business conduct. They would be perceived as unable to bring their concerns and ideas to bear in terms of changed values and practices relating to the market. Ultimately, international law and politics could stand as the main losers. Society would lose faith in international law, politics and related institutions, including the UN, because they had shown themselves to be weak and ineffective in the face of increasing economic and political power of business.

With the benefit of hindsight, it is possible to observe that the Human Rights Council's endorsement and adoption in 2008 and 2011 of the UN Framework and UNGPs brought the situation towards a combination of a soft institutionalisation with some hard institutionalisation elements. Pillar Two's social responsibility to observe social expectations is a soft institutionalisation. Pillar One's elaboration of the implication of the state duty to protect in regard to state obligations for their own economic activities and provision of detailed guidance for firms can be considered a hard institutionalisation. Although strictly speaking this was only an elaboration of already existing obligations for states under binding international law, debates under the first SRSG term showed that the knowledge of the implications of those obligations for state bodies was not well understood or even known.[2] Moreover, the implications of this under the compliance-part of the Pillar Two entails hard law implications for businesses, as governments might introduce additional obligations on companies. The process towards a treaty on human rights, on-going at the time of writing, may result in a harder institutionalisation, if it is successful in obtaining agreement on legally binding directives for businesses with regard to human rights. If the treaty process is not successful, it is possible that the failure of that political process will result simply in a retention of status quo as compared to when the treaty process was launched in 2014. However, there is also a risk that a failure will open up past disagreements and result in a regression from that which was obtained with the UN Framework and UNGPs, possibly to such an extent as to re-leash the situation that caused the dismissal of the Draft Norms.[3]

The system-specific interests sketched in relation to prospects for an institutionalisation of social and human rights responsibilities of business played into the multi-stakeholder regulatory processes of the Draft Norms, the Global Compact, the EU MSF, the CSR Alliance and the SRSG process. Participants' concerns with what was at stake influenced how they engaged in the effort to discursively construct a particular version of social responsibility for business, and specifically the form of institutionalisation that might result. The analysis in Chapters 4 and 5 demonstrates that the power concerns related to the output were observable in the manner in which actors discursively engaged in the multi-stakeholder processes. It shows that the manners in which the system-specific concerns affected were transformed into their statements varied greatly. Some organisations, in particular business associations, were adept at communicating in a manner

---

[2] Human Rights Council (2008) Summary of five multi-stakeholder consultations.

[3] Compare J. G. Ruggie (2016) Hierarchy or ecosystem?; L. C. Backer (2014) 'The Guiding Principles of Business and Human Rights at a crossroads: the state, the enterprise, and the spectre of a treaty to bind them all', *Coalition for Peace and Ethics,* Working Paper, Vol. 7, No. 1 (July 2014); see also J. R.-M. Wetzel (2015) *Human Right in Transnational Business: Translating Human Rights Obligations into Compliance Procedures,* Luzern Springer, pp. 198–200.

that aimed to resonate with the core interest of certain recipients, particularly governments. In that way they were able to create irritation, which in turn caused perturbation and affected views and political stances with public regulators so that the output was close to status quo. That was particularly the case with the process that lead to the Human Rights Commission's dismissal of the Draft Norms, and the MSF. Several public authorities and some NGOs, on the other hand, mainly communicated through logics corresponding to their own interests, and therefore were not very successful in generating irritation with business or the perturbation necessary for change in business practices. Deploying the logic of the economic system, the SRSG was able to turn business opposition into support for norms on human rights for businesses, even accepting approaches based on law.

The following sections will consider the dynamics at play to assess the argumentative strategies that were decisive in generating the agreement, which enabled the BHR regime to take off.

6.2.2 Assessing Outputs against Objectives: A Variety of Discursive Outcomes towards the BHR Regime

Chapter 4 showed that the process towards the *Draft Norms* was effective in developing a normative output based on the conventional UN approach to human rights law-making, involving experts and civil society primarily representing victims. However, the dismissal of the Draft Norms by the UN Human Rights Commission and the arguments that were raised against the Draft Norms by some governments (e.g., as explained in Chapter 4, the US and Australia) as well as some large business associations also indicated that when an intergovernmental organisation ventures beyond its conventional state-centrist focus in terms of those intended to be subjected to new norms of conduct, the limited inclusion of those stakeholders can lead to strong opposition, both directly and indirectly through lobbying of states. International lawyers know that new hard international law is rarely made quickly. However, it is not to be expected that businesses or even some NGOs were aware that simply naming a text 'Norms' and referring to it as such in an international law context was something completely different than those 'Norms' at any time attaining any binding or formally guiding effect. The prevalence of statements made by both businesses and some states, which alleged that the Draft Norms were twisting international human rights law in seeking to establish human rights norms for business, indicates that in addition to opposition against the mere idea of establishing obligations for business with regard to human rights, there was also confusion as to how or whether such a step was actually in line with international law.

Assessed against the self-defined objectives for the Draft Norms, the process of developing and debating them was not successful in generating support with the Commission on Human Rights. Political support among a significant number of the Commission's members would have been necessary for the Draft Norms to become accepted by the Commission, even as a 'law-in-the-making' text to be discussed and refined over subsequent meetings.

Chapter 4 also showed how the *UN Global Compact* evolved on the basis of a multi-stakeholder process organised and led by the office of the UN Secretary-General. The Global Compact was developed through a selectively composed multi-stakeholder group. Business organisations and specific CEOs and NGOs were invited to form part of the group. The overall objective was defined as involving business in the implementation of the UN Goals. The Global Compact was successful in constructing a normative framework commonly understood to be related to CSR, and to provide international law with a significant role as a normative source for the Global Compact principles. Recall in this context that principles 1 and 2 directly relate to human rights, based on the UDHR. Referring to the ILO's 1998 Declaration, principles 3, 4, 5 and 6 relate to (core) labour rights, which are also human rights. The environmental principles 7–9 and the anti-corruption principle 10 also incorporate international law elements. In sum, the process leading to the Global Compact constructed business social responsibilities as being founded on international declarations and conventions, with human rights law a defining normative source for six out of the original nine principles. It was effective in delivering on the stated objective of developing a 'compact' offering normative guidance for firms to support and help implement UN goals. From the outset, the Global Compact website has been leading readers to internet sites, which provide information on and reproduce the pertinent international law declarations and conventions for each of the principles. The ten Global Compact principles, however, do not themselves specify the pertinent declarations' or conventions' provisions as standards of conduct, nor do they require specific actions of participants. Furthermore, the principles are not legally binding on participants, and participation is based on voluntary commitment.

As also seen in Chapter 4, following the 2001 EU Green Paper on CSR entitled 'Promoting a European Framework on CSR' and the 2002 Communication, *the EU MSF* was established in 2002 by the EU Commission. Defining an objective that was described as 'ambitious' by the EU Commissioner for Social Affairs, who had taken a lead role in setting up the MSF, the EU Commission specifically suggested that the MSF explore the appropriateness of establishing common guiding principles for CSR practices and instruments. The Commission also specifically suggested that the MSF consider founding such principles on internationally agreed principles, in particular the OECD Guidelines and ILO fundamental conventions.

Although the MSF was chaired by the Commission, the Commission mainly had a managing role. The MSF's active members comprised business and industry organisations, labour organisations, and NGOs concerned with environmental, human rights, consumers' and development issues. As participants in EU 'social dialogue', an institutionalised process of industry, employers' and workers' organisations' participation in EU law-making on labour issues, business/industry and labour participants in the MSF enjoyed experience in the politics and practices of EU labour law preparation.

The MSF did not result in a specific normative framework, let alone specific principles, and therefore did not deliver on the objective intended by the EU Commission. The Final Report made only general reference to international human rights law as part of a framework for CSR in Europe. It did refer to international law instruments as 'reference instruments', but specifically only noted the ILO Tripartite Declaration, the OECD Guidelines, and the UN Global Compact as directly relevant to companies. The general omission of direct reference to detailed and conventional international human rights law instruments (hard and soft) indicates lack of agreement among MSF participants with respect to relating an EU CSR framework to detailed human rights standards.[4]

The MSF recommendations articulated CSR as voluntary in the sense of not being subject to requirements based in law. Rather than assuming enhanced responsibility for the social impact caused by business, the Final Report in effect passed responsibility for social or global concerns on human rights in general back to governments. Mirroring arguments made by business associations during MSF meetings, that was done with the message that governments should act by themselves to have public policy goals implemented and human rights respected, rather than asking companies to act directly. From this perspective too, the MSF did not deliver on its ambitious goal of developing a European normative framework for CSR, which had been originally hoped to entail common guiding principles for CSR practices and instruments founded on internationally agreed principles, in particular the OECD Guidelines and ILO fundamental conventions.

---

[4] Compare also J. Fairbrass (2011) 'Exploring Corporate Social Responsibility Policy in the European Union: A discursive institutionalist analysis', 49(5) *JCMS: Journal of Common Market Studies*. pp. 949–70.

In 2006 the EU Commission launched the *CSR Alliance* in partial response (or reaction) to the limited success of the MSF in delivering a European framework for CSR. An objective of the Alliance was to reinvigorate the EU's promotion of CSR with a strong human rights element by helping stimulate company self-regulation. The EU CSR Alliance was set up as a voluntary business network for the exchange of best practice on CSR and other activities to promote corporate self-regulation on CSR. The normative role of international human rights law was emphasised by the Commission at the launch of the CSR Alliance. Some tools developed by the CSR Alliance relate to human rights, particularly those which are also labour rights, yet they do not make direct reference to international human rights law. From that perspective, the CSR Alliance has not delivered very strongly on its objective. For the current purposes, however, the mere fact that it was possible for the Commission to get business support for the Alliance was significant at the backdrop of the debates during the MSF and its output. That support, however, came or at least was made to come about, at the price of excluding civil society participation. This led to a significant loss of legitimacy of the Alliance. It also reduced stakeholder pressure or 'irritation' on participating businesses. This may explain the somewhat limited activity of the Alliance as well as its limited outputs.

Chapter 5 presented how a shift in terms of development and agreement on quite extensive normative guidance on business responsibilities for their social impact with particular regard to human rights occurred between 2005 and 2011 through a process established by the UN. After the Draft Norms failed to generate general support at the UN Human Rights Commission, Professor John Ruggie was appointed SRSG. During the first term 2005–08 the SRSG was charged with identifying and clarifying standards of corporate responsibility and accountability with regard to human rights and elaborating on the role of states in regulating and adjudicating the role of business with regard to human rights, as well as clarifying the implications for companies of the concepts of 'complicity' and 'sphere of influence'. Moreover, he was asked to develop methods and materials for human rights impact assessment and compile best practices. During the second term 2008–11 the SRSG was charged with 'operationalising' the output of the first term. The *SRSG 2005–08* mandate term led to the formulation of the 'Protect, Respect and Remedy Framework' (now also referred to as the 'UN Framework'), which was 'unanimously welcomed' by the UN Human Rights Council in 2008. The second term lead to the UNGPs, which were adopted by the Human Rights Council in 2011. Both were developed through a multi-stakeholder process that included a wide range of NGOs, labour, business organisations and representatives of individual companies, representatives of governments and intergovernmental organisations, and academics. Both relate to the full spectrum of human rights based on the SRSG's finding that companies are capable of violating all human rights. International human rights law plays a strong normative role for the framework: both the UN Framework and UNGPs refer to the International Bill of Rights and ILO's fundamental conventions as minimum standards to which businesses should have regard. Moreover, international law doctrine on state obligations and in particular international human rights law doctrine on the state duty to protect against violations caused by third parties, such as companies, play a strong role for Pillar One and spills over into Pillar Two. The spill-over is due to the UN Framework's emphasis on the corporate responsibility to respect comprising the responsibility of complying with national law, in addition to the responsibility to observance of social expectations.

Both terms of the SRSG process were effective in delivering on their stated objectives, and the first term arguably even beyond that. To appreciate this it is useful to consider that in the human rights field, harm done is all too often not fully remediable. This does not mean that remedy and accountability are not important. But access to a remedy process, or the administration of a sanction targeting the company, the provision of a pecuniary compensation, an apology or other measures of reparation are not able to replace an arm or even a life or a provider lost in an occupational health and safety accident; a childhood lost to child labour; or agricultural land, home villages or religious sites demolished in favour of infrastructure projects. In emphasising ways to prevent businesses from doing harm, the SRSG did not overlook the mandate's elements on business accountability or states' regulation and adjudication. However, the SRSG pulled some of the focus on actions of businesses and states forward from the conventional *ex-post facto* focus of international and much other law: his concern was not first and foremost with sanctions when harm has occurred, but with setting out recommendations that would help prevent harm from arising. That *ex-ante* approach is a key element in the recommendations of Pillar Two for corporate human rights policies and the human rights due diligence process, and in Pillar One for all types of state bodies to ensure that they observe their state duty to protect, for policy coherence, and for states to develop guidance for firms and require or recommend due diligence and transparency on corporate human rights impacts. Pillar Three clarifies and identifies remedy steps to target situations when harm has occurred, or is perceived to have occurred, despite the preventative actions set out in Pillars One and Two. As a result of the wording of the 2008–11 mandate, the combination of an *ex-ante* and *ex-post* approach also informs the UNGPs and delivered on the objectives set out through operationalising the UN Framework. The process was successful in obtaining support that led to the UNGPs becoming unanimously adopted by the Human Rights Council.

The UN Framework is not legally binding, nor even explicitly characterised as guiding. During the 2005–08 term, the SRSG explicitly made clear that his aim was not to develop binding international rules, because these traditionally take years or even decades to reach sufficient agreement among states. Rather, he wanted to develop a framework which could quickly become operative for those it addresses, with positive effects for those who are, or may otherwise become, victims of human rights abuse caused by companies. The UN Framework set out recommended actions for governments as well as companies. Despite its official label as a 'conceptual and policy framework' it is in fact clearly normative. The normative aspect is enhanced in the UNGPs, which in terms of the title ('Principles') and style in effect set out soft law directives for firms and governments, and in case of the latter reinforce the UN Framework's recommendation on how authorities can observe and implement their binding obligations that already exist under international human rights law.

The 'policy' and soft law character, respectively, of the UN Framework and UNGPs are also consistent with the mandate's objectives, as no specific form was set out for the outputs. Looking back more than ten years after the first mandate was created, an output described as a 'policy' framework may appear unambitious. However, in view of the result of the Draft Norms process, at the time that was actually a rather courageous move, especially considering the extensive substantive normative guidance that is in fact offered by the UN Framework. From this perspective, the Framework could even be regarded as outperforming what was called for, as it did not just clarify and identify standards for business and the role for states, but also provided both types of actors with extensive normative guidance on how they could act to honour and implement those standards. In doing so it also brokered a normative basis that has enabled the emergent BHR regime to take on solidity and evolve in a manner that sets it apart from the general international human rights regime through its explicit emphasis on businesses having social responsibilities that go beyond compliance with national law. Even if based on a soft institutionalisation rather than so far a hard version, this was a decisive change from the previous efforts to develop normative guidance for businesses with regard to their social impact.

6.2.3 Shaping Discursive Outputs Through System-Specific Interests in Communication

From the previous section it transpires that none of the initiatives led to a fully-fledged hard institutionalisation. The Draft Norms process aimed at a soft institutionalisation initially, which might have turned into a hard institutionalisation, but the end result was *status quo*. The Global Compact led to a *soft institutionalisation*, with the 'voluntary' character of CSR not being addressed, but significant normative guidance developed with a strong basis in international law, including human rights law. The SRSG process led to *a combination of a hard and soft institutionalisation*: it emphasised the legal obligations of states and the implications for legal regulation and obligations of firms to comply with ensuing national law, and stressed that in voluntarily honouring social expectations business should consider international human rights law. It also made explicit that this should be the case where applicable national law falls short of the pertinent state's international obligations.

Resulting in a situation close to *status quo*, the MSF output emphasised the 'voluntary' character of CSR, and rejected formalised regulation as well as a strong normative foundation in international human rights law or the advancing of such normative guidance. A second effort by the EU Commission to develop an institutionalisation of CSR normativity, the CSR Alliance has moved towards *a slightly enhanced institutionalisation* by heeding the normative guidance provided by the Commission without doing so explicitly through direct reference to international human rights law.

Differentiated interests of stakeholders made themselves felt most strongly in the MSF process and in its output. The interests of certain economic actors prevailed to the detriment of the ambitious original objective of the Commission and the interests of civil society actors. Thus, industry and employers were able to obtain hegemony over the construction of CSR normativity and assert their influence on the output. By comprising only business organisations, the CSR Alliance carried over the power of business on further EU CSR work, and although the CSR Alliance 'Toolbox' does relate to human rights relevant issues, the role of international human rights law is vague and indirect.

By contrast, the Global Compact was both ground-breaking and quite effective in terms of constructing CSR normativity based on international law. Business was included throughout the process, but through careful selection of stakeholders supportive of CSR and the UN objectives. Economic system interests of leaving CSR to be 'voluntary' prevailed, but public policy interests related to the objectives of international human rights law came to be influential on the output. Public policy objectives and civil society interests were allowed to play a strong part in the output, explicated and institutionalised through basing the ten principles in international law instruments. Rather than business obtaining hegemony through strategic arguments, business interests in preserving CSR as 'voluntary' were accommodated because the UN made an effort not to question that idea in the discursive construction of the Global Compact.

Constituting an even stronger contrast to the EU MSF and its output and to the Draft Norms, the SRSG process was the most effective in regard to constructing a normative idea of business social responsibilities informed by international human rights law and as not only 'voluntary' action. Economic system interests were represented throughout the SRSG process, along with the concerns of civil society and public institutions. Originally strongly opposed to an institutionalisation of CSR and the definition of business responsibilities for human rights, economic system participants were swayed to recognising socially responsible action based on international human rights law as being in the general interest of companies. Public policy interests in business activity respectful of human rights obtained hegemony over the construction of a normative concept of business responsibilities for human rights in terms of both legal duties and social expectations. The approach and construction were approved even by those members of the Human Rights Council and business associations hosted in those states that had previously been opposed to the normative idea as well as the process.

The SRSG employed several strategies whose effects may be explained from the perspective of legal autopoiesis. In particular, he combined the argumentative strength of system-specific language with activities to induce reflection within social sub-systems, as exemplified by the 2006 IOE/ICC/BIAC study's reference to international human rights law as the normative fall-back position for businesses operating in conflict situations: here a virtual turn-around took place in the approach of the involved business associations, so that they adopted legal logic references or concepts to preserve their economic rationality interests. The SRSG's decision to engage organisations that had been opposed to the Draft Norms and had indicated that they had felt excluded from the Norms process, in subsequently developing guidance for companies on human rights dilemmas exposed them to the needs and expectations of stakeholders in their economic, political and legal environment. This caused a change in stances within those organisations and led to support at a general level for the work and recommendations of the SRSG.

The five processes did not function in isolation. Each built to some extent on steps taken and challenges met by one or more previous ones. This inter-discursive character is observable for example in the MSF Final Report's reference to the Global Compact, as well as in the considerations of the Global Compact that fed into the formulation of the SRSG mandate. It is also observable in the SRSG's deploying arguments resembling those of Kofi Annan in the speech that led to the Global Compact.

UN and EU initiatives in particular also built on experiences of the preceding initiative or initiatives within that organisation.

Participants involved in the process related to the Draft Norms, the establishment of the UN Global Compact and its principles, the SRSG process, the MSF and the initiation of the CSR Alliance had different interests and concerns at stake as regards the prospective outputs' significance for the future conduct of business, as well as the power during the process to influence stakeholders representing particular sub-systems. The variety of interests and objectives was already evident in arguments made during each of those processes, as described in Chapters 4 and 5 from the perspective of system-specific rationalities articulated or invoked. The following analysis shows how some were particularly adept at playing on the system-specific interests of others in order to shape the normative output that the former desired.

6.3 PLAYING ON SYSTEM-SPECIFIC INTERESTS: STABILISING AND DE-STABILISING ARGUMENTATIVE STRATEGIES

6.3.1 Stabilising and De-stabilising Arguments Strategies: General Observations on Deployment and Effects

It has been discussed and shown above that the deployment of system-specific language addressing (or 'mimicking') the interests of recipients enables transmitters to cause perturbation to stimulate recipients' acceptance of the views of the transmitters. As suggested in the theory sections in Chapters 1 and 3, stabilising or de-stabilising strategies can enhance the effect of such an argument. As the following analysis shows, the ability of participants to play on system-specific interests by mastering stabilising or de-stabilising strategies may be quite significant for their influence in a multi-stakeholder regulatory process and on its output. Arguments (such as several SRSG or business arguments, as described below) that applied an initially stabilising strategy to the deployment of system-specific logic in addressing those with whom change was desired were generally more effective in creating the ground for change, compared to statements (such as some of the EU Commission's approach with the MSF or some civil society statements, as also described below) applying de-stabilising strategies without indicating the stabilising effect for the interests of those with whom change was desired (typically companies, but sometimes authorities).

The SRSG process offers several examples of usage of stabilising arguments to smooth the ground with recipients and put an audience at ease, followed by de-stabilising arguments to articulate why change might contribute to preserving or promoting the interests at stake for the particular stakeholder group he was addressing. For instance, the SRSG would combine stabilising and de-stabilising arguments by first buying into arguments advanced by organisations opposing an institutionalisation of business responsibilities for human rights, for example by referring to the benefits that business may gain from preserving a broad measure of freedom of enterprise and not be subject to extensive and detailed regulation of their conduct. After this stabilising argument he would apply a de-stabilising argument, explaining that the possibility to preserve that freedom is enhanced if businesses accept social needs and demands on change in corporate conduct and internalise human rights as guidance.[5] As exemplified by the speech by Kofi Annan at the World 1999 Economic Forum in Davos,[6] some similar arguments were made by Global Compact architects, one of whom was the same person who was later appointed to carry out the SRSG mandate.

The Global Compact's construction of CSR normativity by applying a stabilising strategy that never questioned the voluntary character of CSR confirms how setting the ground in the already established or accepted, opened options for change within the sub-system (the economic system) with which change was intended. The MSF case study, by contrast, demonstrates that applying stabilising strategies and recipients' system-specific logic where no change is desired by the transmitter may also be an effective course to obtain that objective. This was how business organisations were able to return the Commission's demand for corporate responsibility for the benefit of public policy objectives. Business organisations shifted such demands on their own social sub-system back to authorities, effectively halting the Commissions' efforts to promote comprehensive normative change with business through the MSF process.

Observable throughout the SRSG process, the strategy of deploying a combination of stabilising and de-stabilising arguments was particularly clear towards the end of the 2005–08 term with the SRSG's clarification of the concepts of 'sphere of influence' and 'complicity'.

The SRSG process and MSF differ in the way that the construction and articulation of states' obligations evolved during the process. The SRSG initially emphasised governance gaps and states' general obligations under international human rights law. This was then cemented into

---

[5] E.g., SRSG (2005) 'Opening remarks'.
[6] K. Annan (1999) 'Address of Secretary-General Kofi Annan to the World Economic Forum in Davos'.

the state duty to protect. At the same time, the SRSG highlighted the corollary of obligations on business organisations through national law when states implement their duty to protect, and that economic risks can be expected for companies as a result of non-compliance with such law and ensuing liability. Conversely, the MSF opened with emphasis on business responsibilities, entailing the EU Commission's application of a de-stabilising strategy that presumed that companies were willing to assume enhanced responsibilities for public policy needs through the vehicle of a normative framework on CSR with a strong grounding in international instruments like the OECD Guidelines and ILO's labour standards. Due to the argumentative strategy of business organisations and their ability to use stabilising strategies when deploying system-specific logic addressing authorities, the MSF output instead emphasised authorities' legal obligations as a key issue, somewhat isolated from business responsibilities.

In launching the CSR Alliance, the Commission's argumentative approach resembled that which had been successfully applied by the Global Compact architects in obtaining initial support for the Compact initiative. This included applying a stabilising strategy and arguing for change (de-stabilisation) through system-specific language articulating a soft institutionalisation of CSR as a course to preserve both the economic opportunities of companies in a globalising world, and the core values of society as to human rights and broader social sustainability. To obtain implicit support and active participation by business in the CSR Alliance, the Commission took its ostensible point of departure in the (conservative) output of the MSF, which had basically been a preservation of status quo. The EU Commission built on this to argue for change (de-stabilisation) through system-specific logic that like the 1999 speech by Kofi Annan to the World Economic Forum had described an institutionalisation of CSR as a course to preserve the opportunities of an audience of companies.

Civil society statements that were effective in influencing outputs invoked economic or political system rationality, depending on the specific audience. Combined with calls for change invoking a limited degree of legal logic, they built an argument that targeted the audience and claimed that change (through norms on business conduct) would benefit the preservation or implementation of economic or political system interests (profit, or aspects of sustainable development from the perspective of the political economy and public policy objectives). Conversely, civil society arguments applying de-stabilising strategies calling for comprehensive change of the law (lex ferenda arguments on enforceable international law setting standards of conduct for companies) were generally not very effective. In several cases, that effect may have been enhanced by a combination of deploying a de-stabilising argument without first making a stabilising argument to explain to the audience how they may eventually gain from accepting change, as well as the generality of a proposal, which did not lend itself to direct application.

As this shows, the outputs of multi-stakeholder regulatory processes with a diverse composition representing competing or conflicting interests are not just contingent on the participation of a range of stakeholders and the procedural setting established for these to exchange expectations, needs and demands as a matter of technical information. The output is very much contingent on participants' playing on system-specific interests and their ability to articulate the interests of recipients while putting the latter at ease rather than generating defensive strategies to ward off the unknown (or change). As the case studies exemplify in various ways, addressing the interests of recipients by invoking a stabilising strategy of articulating the interests of the recipient to be preserved was the most effective way for stimulating acceptance with recipients of the specific type of outcome (change or status quo in relation to an institutionalisation of business social responsibilities) desired by the transmitter. As a result, those stakeholders who understood this strategic discursive game were in a better position to influence the output.

The subsequent section explains the discursive dynamics around the construction of normative directives or guidance in the case studies in more detail, showing how the ability of some actors to complement the deployment of recipient's system-specific logics by stabilising or de-stabilising arguments played a major part in determining the outcomes of the multi-stakeholder regulatory processes.

6.3.2 Application and Effects of Stabilising and De-stabilising Argumentative Strategies

6.3.2.1 The SRSG process on the backdrop of the Draft Norms

With the backdrop of the failure of the Draft Norms process to bring about the necessary support for the Draft Norms to become adopted into a formally agreed document, this section considers the argumentative approaches applied in SRSG process.

The SRSG process was effective in generating a shift from an antagonistic relationship with major business associations into acceptance of the significance of business organisations to understand the implications of human rights for their operations and to embrace guidance on how not to cause harm. This shift was essential in creating the support that was necessary with the private sector as well as the public actors involved to deliver a fundamentally different end outcome than that which marked the Draft Norms process. This section shows how that came about through the SRSG's application a mixture of stabilising and de-stabilising arguments to explain why at the end of the day, accepting normative change and working with it instead of against it would benefit businesses in regard to their core economic interests, for example by engaging in human rights due diligence. The argumentative strategy leading to the shift in business attitudes was complemented by statements from the SRSG that addressed public policy-makers and regulators as well as civil society. He also explained to these audiences how an acceptance of the mixed hard and soft law character of the corporate responsibility to respect would support them in responding to their own system-specific concerns and delivering results expected by their constituencies. Drawing on a different set of stabilising and de-stabilising arguments than that applied for businesses, the SRSG made it clear to public regulators that acceptance of the novel approach eventually promoted by the UN Framework and UNGPs would support them in delivering on public policy objectives of human rights protection and respect. For human rights NGOs, it was made clear that the approach would contribute to public and privately based accountability for human rights and remedy for business-related human rights abuse. In addition to Pillar 3 that is explicitly on remedy, recommendations under Pillar One and Two on human rights due diligence and reporting on human rights policies, due diligence and enterprises' actual management of human rights impacts delivers both *ex-ante* and *ex-post* accountability, thus contributing to efforts for business to avoid doing harm, and to addressing harm when it nevertheless occurs.

Following the failure of the Draft Norms, in order to gather support from the UN Commission on Human Rights, organisations opposed to the Norms combined legal system logic with a conservative stabilising strategy to refute the appropriateness and relevance of conceiving of business responsibilities for human rights. The discursive dismissal of the appropriateness of the Draft Norms, which was undertaken by ICC with IOE[7] and the US Council for International Business,[8] some other business organisations and some governments[9] deployed legal system logic

---

[7] International Chamber of Commerce and International Organisation of Employers (2003) 'Joint views of ICC and the IOE on the draft "Norms on the Responsibilities of Transnational Corporations and Other Business Enterprises with regard to Human Rights"'.

[8] B. Hearne. (2004) 'Proposed UN Norms on human rights'.

[9] United States (2005) *Explanation of no-vote, Commission on Human Rights, Item 17: Transnational Corporations*, April 20, 2005 (on file with author). Australian government statement on the draft UN Norms, late 2004, quoted in Kinley, D. *et al.* (2007) 'The politics of corporate social responsibility', at 40.

referencing general international law doctrine on states being duty bearers under international law (see Chapter 1 (section 1.3.2.2.1)) to argue that business responsibility for human rights is contrary to the idea that international obligations are held by states. These statements, which were made prior to the establishment of the SRSG mandate, addressed a wide audience among which the Commission on Human Rights and governments would be decisive for further steps. Addressing these organisations, whose tasks involve international law development and implementation, by legal system logics and a stabilising argument therefore entailed suggesting that no major change was to be initiated. The strategy was not effective in completely warding off change, but the decision by the Commission to establish the SRSG mandate and omit specific reference to the Draft Norms in the text of the mandate was a much less drastic step than a course closer to the treaty-aspirations introduced with the Draft Norms would have been.

By contrast, NGO statements such as Amnesty International's 2005 challenge of the Commission on Human Rights properly honouring its role as the 'UN's chief guarding of human rights'[10] deployed legal system language from a de-stabilising perspective to argue that non-binding initiatives, including the OECD Guidelines and the ILO Tripartite Declaration, did not sufficiently prevent human rights abuse caused by company activities or ensure corporate accountability for respect for human rights, and that more comprehensive change was needed. Along similar lines, during the first year of the SRSG mandate human rights NGOs applied legal system language to argue a de-stabilising lex ferenda course. They made the point that enforceable international rules pertaining to companies must be developed when national governance is weak. As observed, this type of argument, deployed by organisations such as ESCR-net on behalf of a larger group of NGOs[11] and ICJ,[12] was not very effective in influencing the output.

A different approach was deployed in Amnesty International's

---

[10] Amnesty International (2005) '2005 UN Commission on Human Rights: The UN's chief guardian of human rights?'.

[11] ESCR-Net Corporate Accountability Working Group (2005) *Joint NGO Submission on Human Rights and the Extractive Industry -2005* (website overview) available http://www.escr-net.org/actions_more/actions_more_show.htm?doc_id =430968 (last accessed 4 February 2013, website has been removed); ESCR-Net Corporate Accountability Working Group (2005) 'Joint NGO submission: Consultation on human rights and the extractive industry'.

[12] N. Howen (2005) 'Business, human rights and accountability', delivered at 'Business and Human Rights' conference organised by the Danish section of the ICJ, Copenhagen, 21 September 2005, available at http://www.business-human rights.org/Links/Repository/684768 (last accessed 4 February 2017).

September 2005 letter to the SRSG.[13] The argumentative style differed by combining legal system logic with economic and political system language. The combination enabled Amnesty to apply a combination of stabilising and de-stabilising arguments (calling for change, but intended to have an essentially stabilising effect on public policy objectives) to promote the implementation of human rights related public policy objectives affecting not only local communities, but also states. The reference to states' interests was that honouring their international human rights obligations is put under pressure through economic interests related to international investments. Amnesty also drew attention to the human rights implications of national level governance gaps ('where a host state is unwilling or unable to protect human rights'). Applying an even stronger combination of stabilising and de-stabilising strategies, some NGOs deployed economic and legal system language to indicate the benefits that minimum rules might present to companies.[14] Compared to some of the more general and abstractly worded lex ferenda arguments made by NGOs, some of these statements may have lent human rights 'substance' to the SRSG's political science orientated emphasis on governance gaps. Others helped demonstrate how an institutionalisation of human rights norms for business may protect business organisations against economic risks (thus, stabilising businesses' economic interests through change in norms of conduct).

As a special procedures mandate holder for the Human Rights Commission/Council, the SRSG as explained in Chapter 5 functioned as a medium for that UN human rights body and did not represent one particular system. His interest was to deliver on his mandate, and therefore to develop an output that would move the field of business responsibilities forward from the status quo stalemate that had resulted from the antagonism that marked the process of the Draft Norms and their course in the Human Rights Commission. This allowed the SRSG to be system-neutral, but pragmatically open to statements that would assist his own development of arguments towards an output that was sufficiently substantive to make a difference, yet sufficiently pragmatic to become accepted broadly among stakeholders.

It was against this background that the SRSG defined his approach to the mandate as seeking to be non-doctrinal, as for example made clear in the SRSG's 2006 report, while effectively referring to international law

---

[13] Amnesty International (2005) 'Letter to Professor John Ruggie'.
[14] E.g., Interfaith Center for Corporate Responsibility (2006) 'Letter to John Ruggie', 6 February 2006, referring to 'risks to shareholders associated with corporate violations of human rights, including litigation', and 'a minimum set of standards would reduce uncertainty and therefore be beneficial to business'.

and human rights law doctrine in a number of contexts. He did this in a series of argumentative steps. First, deploying a stabilising argument, he grounded the approach in a point that was stable or, in principle, not questioned in the debate, that is, doctrine on international obligations being state obligations. Next, he made a partly de-stabilising argument on the implications, through the state duty to protect, emphasising the horizontality aspect. Finally, he set forth the de-stabilising point for businesses to honour international law where not sufficiently implemented by states, thus moving forward to promoting change.

The SRSG's second mandate was generally marked by a continuation of the argumentative strategy developed towards the end of the first mandate term. Initially the SRSG used a stabilising strategy to ease companies' apprehension of the emergence of international law to establish business duties for human rights. Towards the end of the mandate term, he applied more de-stabilising arguments to substantiate his argument not only on states' obligations (the state duty to protect) but also the derived implications for companies (national law establishing direct obligations for companies), and how companies may benefit from legal arrangements (such a soft law) providing norms for their conduct.

During the first mandate term, the SRSG initially employed economic system logic to indicate that the tasks and objectives of companies differ from those of governments, as companies are specialised organs in society, whose tasks are mainly in the economic field. Following the acceptance created by such a stabilising argument, towards the end of the mandate term economic system logic was deployed with a more de-stabilising approach to articulate negative impact (economic risk) for business organisations that may result from their own or their sectors' disregard for human rights. The SRSG gradually built an argument in which he addressed companies through their own interests in protection against economic profit-loss and in retaining profit-enabling legal rights. This enabled the SRSG to induce business acceptance of the need to change and internalise human rights as a normative standard of conduct. That built business support for the output of the process towards the soft institutionalisation of business responsibilities for human rights.

Doctrine is per definition stabilising, because it is the theory that is currently accepted. Yet specialised doctrine (such as what may be developed in specific branches of international law, as explained in Chapter 1 (section 1.3.2.2.1)) may be turned into a de-stabilising argument when set against general and typically older or conservative doctrine. Through usage of legal system arguments based on doctrine on states as duty bearers under international law, the SRSG set a doctrinal basis for a rejection of the Draft Norms. The 2006 report's rejection of the Draft Norms as a potential regulatory instrument was accepted (albeit somewhat reluctantly among non-business stakeholders), while NGOs retained focus on the substantive content. At the same time, by rejecting the Draft Norms on grounds of institutional legal deficits resembling arguments that had been made by industry members that were sceptical of an institutionalisation of business social responsibilities, the SRSG's course earned a degree of acceptance among those members of industry.

Yet the SRSG did not reject the idea that human rights should play a direct normative role for companies' conduct. As in statements delivered when he was engaged in setting up the Global Compact, under his mandate as SRSG John Ruggie deployed a combination of legal and economic system language and stabilising and de-stabilising strategies to argue to authorities and business organisations that business respect for human rights was necessary to offset adverse social impact of business activities and balance the trade rights granted to companies by international law.[15]

Having set that stabilising context through the 2006 and 2007 reports, the basis was in place for a de-stabilising push: in the 2008 report and in statements prior to its release (for example the SRSG's October 2007 statement to the International Business Forum[16]) the SRSG applied a combination of economic and legal system logics to explain and provide examples of how companies themselves may benefit from legal institutions to avoid claims and critique of human rights abuse. At this stage of the process, the SRSG also drew attention to the obligations of states to honour their international human rights obligations within their jurisdiction. He added the human rights doctrine of the state duty to protect, and highlighted that that this means regulating and adjudicating to ensure individuals against third party human rights abuse. Recall that as a specialised doctrine, the horizontality doctrine deepens the implications of the conventional state duty under international law, with a particular regard to non-state actors acting within or from a state.

Essentially, the SRSG in this way deployed the legal doctrinal argument on obligations under international law being state obligations, which had been propounded by business organisations in the context of the Draft Norms and early in the SRSG mandate term. But by applying the more specialised horizontality doctrine and elaborating implications for companies, he enriched the point, giving it a twist to introduce the need for

---

[15] Commission on Human Rights (2006) 'Interim report of the Special Representative of the Secretary-General on the issue of human rights and transnational corporations and other business enterprises', paras 12, 15, 23.

[16] SRSG (2007) 'Remarks at plenary session on "Business and the rules of the game"'.

change, that is, a de-stabilising point. The SRSG took his point of departure in the basic doctrinal point that business organisations themselves had employed. Hence, with a stabilising strategy referring back to points made by the recipients themselves he prepared the ground for an argument that companies and their organisations would be hard put not to accept, given that the original state obligation argument had been deployed by these organisations along with statements committing to business compliance with national law. By adding human rights law doctrine to elaborate implications flowing from the basic international law doctrine on states' obligations under the specialised doctrine on the state duty to protect against violations at the horizontal level, the SRSG expanded the original point made by companies in order to transmit a message that states' obligations spill over on national law applying to business. The SRSG's arguments, therefore, did not only employ system-specific language to cause perturbation with recipients by invoking implications of doctrinal points. The argumentative strategy also re-deployed the argumentation of those (some business representatives and states) who had been making use of stabilising, conservative system-specific arguments addressing authorities in order to avert an institutionalisation of business responsibilities for human rights involving a normative change. By doing so, the SRSG made it difficult for business organisations to counter his points, because they built on or referred to points that had been made by business.

Based on the acceptance of the process as well as its emerging output that had been created through the broad stakeholder involvement and system-specific logic references in statements since 2005, the 2008 report that proposed the UN Framework extended the argument on economic risks to companies to encompass what the SRSG referred to as the 'courts of public opinion'.[17] These 'operate' in cases where companies do not live up to social expectations, even if those are not based in law applicable to companies but derive from an assumption that companies respect international human rights standards. The effect was to clarify that staying within the narrow limits of national law does not protect a company against risks to its profit-seeking interests, if applicable law is insufficient to protect social and environmental needs. Hence, the SRSG was able to argue that a de-stabilising course involving a soft institutionalisation of business responsibilities of human rights would preserve the interests of business, and therefore in essence entail a stabilisation of the overall profit-interest of business in a globalising world.

Similarly, the SRSG also employed economic system logic combined

---

[17] UN Framework, para. 54.

with legal system considerations to argue human rights due diligence as part of the corporate responsibility to respect.[18] Human rights due diligence was presented as a way out of the economic quagmire for companies seeking to navigate an unclear amalgamation of social expectations and requirements under (insufficiently implemented) national law. By making reference to due diligence, a practice well-known to company lawyers in typical profit-seeking business transactions such as mergers and acquisitions, the SRSG grounded his argument in a stabilising strategy. The strategic impact of such a combination of economic system language with an institutional legal practice intended to avoid economic risk would be to cause perturbation within company management (and their legal departments) towards the de-stabilising objective of making them accept human rights due diligence and to self-regulate, based on the normative guidance provided by the SRSG.[19]

Indeed, the special 2008 report on the concepts of 'sphere of influence' and 'complicity'[20] is perhaps the most interesting example of the SRSG's combination of legal and economic system logics and his play on stabilising and de-stabilising strategies to induce acceptance with recipients. The special report provided supportive points for the UN Framework's rejection of the 'sphere of influence' concept as unfit to be applied in a legal context, while endorsing the concept of 'complicity'. Rejection of 'sphere of influence' as imprecise in a legal context is ultimately to the benefit of companies, because the rejection helps companies avoid being caught in economically costly contractual conflicts or litigation deriving from claims that arise because of imprecise terminology. Again, the SRSG took his point of departure in a stabilising strategy to prepare the ground for acceptance of a de-stabilising action. Regarding 'complicity', the explanation of the endorsement was detailed in its examples of the significance of the concept to companies wishing to steer clear of human rights abuse. The result was that the concept of 'complicity' was presented

---

[18] Ibid., paras 56 ff.

[19] This issue, which relates to the argumentative strategy and effect on the output, differs from the discussion on whether the SRSG conflated two different forms of 'due diligence' (see J. Bonnitcha and R. McCorquodale (forthcoming) 'Is the Concept of "Due Diligence" in the Guiding Principles Coherent?'. From the perspective of the current study, the SRSG did conflate the two forms of due diligence; however, this was not due to misunderstanding the differences but, rather, for strategic argumentative reasons related to the construction and acceptance of business responsibilities for human rights and the integration of risk-based due diligence in that context.

[20] Human Rights Council (2008) 'Clarifying the concepts of "Sphere of Influence" and "Complicity"'.

as in fact benefiting companies in terms of risk management, simply by providing guidance and therefore being in their interest. Economic system arguments served to explain negative consequences for companies in terms of reputation and other risks that may cause divestment, loss of orders and other activities affecting a company's economy adversely. Similarly, as shown in Figure 6.1 below, by introducing a concept with a legal background with which companies (and particularly their corporate lawyers)

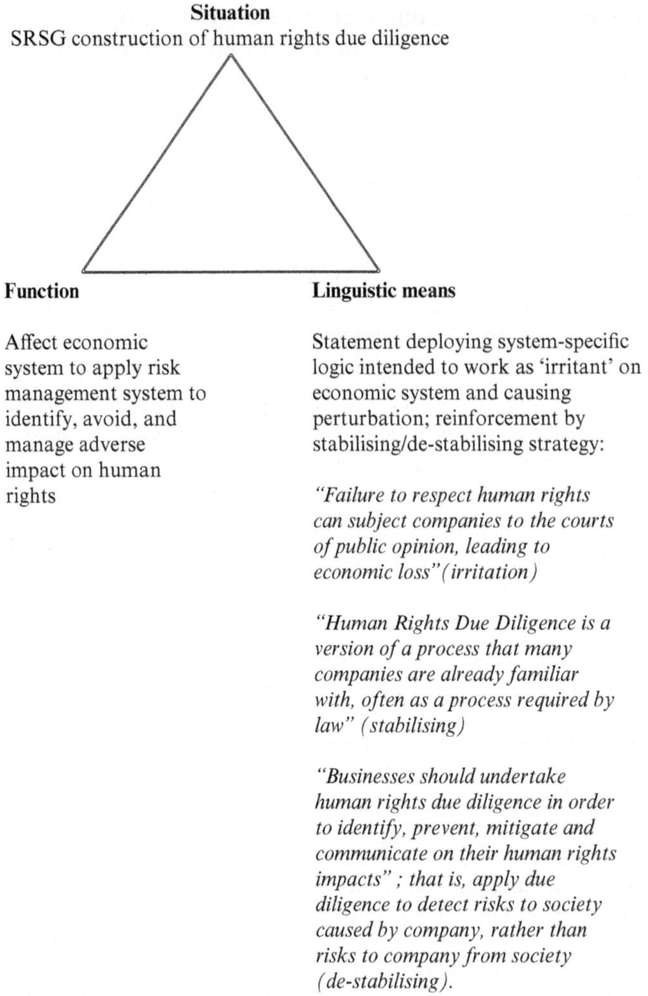

Situation
SRSG construction of human rights due diligence

Function	Linguistic means
Affect economic system to apply risk management system to identify, avoid, and manage adverse impact on human rights	Statement deploying system-specific logic intended to work as 'irritant' on economic system and causing perturbation; reinforcement by stabilising/de-stabilising strategy:
	"Failure to respect human rights can subject companies to the courts of public opinion, leading to economic loss" (irritation)
	"Human Rights Due Diligence is a version of a process that many companies are already familiar with, often as a process required by law" (stabilising)
	"Businesses should undertake human rights due diligence in order to identify, prevent, mitigate and communicate on their human rights impacts" ; that is, apply due diligence to detect risks to society caused by company, rather than risks to company from society *(de-stabilising)*.

Figure 6.1   The SRSG's argumentative strategy for human rights due diligence (company audience)

were already familiar, it argued the economic benefits for companies in conducting human rights due diligence. Applying the well-known concept as a point of departure, it was able to shift the focus from managing risk to the company on to managing risks to society. In other words, the report recommended adopting a new practice consistent with an institutionalisation of business responsibilities for human rights.

For stakeholder support for the SRSG's findings on the two complex concepts of 'complicity' and 'sphere of influence', of which the latter was dismissed in favour of human rights due diligence, the effect of the combined application of legal and economic language was to cause perturbation with the Human Rights Council as well as companies or industry organisations. As part of this, it provided clarification related to companies' conduct in practice but needing the Human Rights Council's acceptance. As a UN body concerned with human rights law, the Human Rights Council is likely to respond to messages transmitted in legal system logic. Adding economic system logic, the argument became suited to also transmit information to companies, supporting them in internalising external interests in an institutionalisation of business responsibilities for human rights but with the impetus for companies based on the economic impact. As a result, they too accepted the implications of companies' complicity in human rights abuse, the rejection of the concept of sphere of influence (still retained by the Global Compact), and the introduction of human rights due diligence. By simultaneously making an argument that would resonate directly with companies through economic system rationality, the SRSG not only prepared the ground for their appreciation of the recommendations and subsequent business willingness to self-regulate on that basis. Creating that appreciation directly rather than waiting for the Human Rights Council, the OHCHR or NGOs to 'translate' the points to companies, the SRSG also reduced the possibility (or risk) that companies and their organisations would lobby states to vote against his report.

Considering that the UN Framework was 'unanimously welcomed' by the Human Rights Council, and that this was the first time that a political UN body agreed to a formal and detailed statement on business responsibilities for human rights, the SRSG's general argumentative strategy was not only successful. It also established an agreed foundation for a change in the human rights regime to formally accept that non-state actors have duties for human rights under international law. This was a major change, even if it has not yet been transformed into international hard law. The significance was underscored by the Council's decision to immediately adopt a resolution that created the SRSG's second mandate to 'operationalise' the UN Framework, charging on the same mandate-holder, and instructing the mandate-holder in adopting a similar approach to the multi-stakeholder engagement to be undertaken under the second mandate as had been applied during the first mandate term. The Council's formal adoption in 2011 of the UNGPs further underscores that the argumentative strategy was successful and re-affirmed the basis for an emergent institutionalisation of a BHR regime.

The fact that more work was needed to specify the exact substance of the three Pillars of the UN Framework, or that the UNGPs, also limited to 30 pages, also require further elaboration (for example, for the detailed implication of human rights due diligence) do not in principle contradict possible legal relevance of the framework. Almost any early stage of international law-making would begin with ideas that need refining. This also applied to the UDHR, which began as an effort to seek to specify the general and non-detailed references to human rights in the UN Charter. Few international law scholars today argue against the legal relevance of the UDHR or its basis in the UN Charter's non-detailed provisions.

The argumentative strategy adopted by the SRSG was effective in terms of delivering an output, which in a relatively comprehensive way stated that companies may affect and should respect all internationally recognised human rights in the International Bill of Human Rights and ILO fundamental labour conventions. Its effectiveness was also proven by the fact that the output was accepted by state representatives in Human Rights Council and broadly by companies and, at least to a certain extent, by civil society as an authoritative clarification of the previously contested implications of the discourse on business and human rights. The contrast of the outputs and outcomes of the SRSG process is stark not only if compared against the Draft Norms, but also when compared with the MSF, especially with regard to the output assessed against the objective.

6.3.2.2 The process to develop the Global Compact

Statements made by UN staff and Global Compact architects to establish the Global Compact generally deployed a stabilising strategy by articulating the initiative from the perspective of voluntary business action, that is, the idea that the Global Compact did not entail new hard international law. Beginning with Kofi Annan's speech in Davos in 1999, several statements also argued with reference to the interest for business of self-regulating to reduce their adverse impact on society, because the alternative might be that governments would agree to establish more duties for businesses under international (or national) law. On that stabilising backdrop, normative guidance provided by international law instruments already adopted by the UN on human rights, labour, environment and anti-corruption were then offered as the basis for such self-regulation, thus introducing a de-stabilising element. With this point of departure, state-

Argumentative strategies 299

ments on the Global Compact suggest a strategic usage of system-specific language by UN staff addressing recipients in a manner that would cause perturbation related to their individual systemic interests in order to make them accept the Global Compact and its normative foundations.

The strategy was successful for the UN as the initiator of the process to develop the Global Compact, as the process led to the formulation of the ten principles and acceptance among companies, civil society as well as UN Members (through adoption of the General Assembly resolutions).

Statements produced by UN staff as part of the process of setting up the Global Compact, explaining the process or seeking to encourage companies to support the initiative, display a general pattern of system-specific

Situation
Arguing why commitment to Global Compact Human Rights Principles is good for business

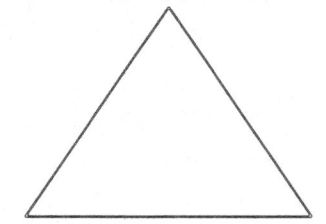

Function	**Linguistic means**
Affect economic system to adopt normativity of UN goals and UN international law instruments on human rights as guiding for their policies and activities, in order to reduce adverse human rights impact on society caused by TNCs and other business enterprises	Statement deploying system-specific logic intended to work as 'irritant' on economic system and causing perturbation; reinforcement by stabilising/de-stabilising strategy: *"Business failure to respect human rights may cause governments to strengthen duties for business under international law to balance their economic rights, possibly reducing current economic opportunities" (irritation)* *"The Global Compact is a voluntary initiative for businesses" (stabilising)* *Businesses should commit to the Global Compact Principles, including Principles 1 and 2 on human rights (de-stabilising).*

Figure 6.2   Arguing why businesses should commit to the Global Compact

logic related to the system of the recipient(s) rather than the transmitter. That is apparent through the differences between statements addressing audiences of companies, organisational or management scholars, employers' or workers' organisations, and those addressing members of the UN in the General Assembly. The statements employed political, economic and legal system references strategically in ways that had the potential to cause perturbation with a recipient system conducive to that particular recipient's acceptance of the Global Compact initiative, as well as the general idea of the UN setting normative guidance for companies, and the normative (international law) foundations of the Compact which inform the principles. As a general feature, the statements explained the benefits to a long-term stabilisation (preservation or promotion) of the interests of the specific recipient(s), ranging from economic profits and a profit-enabling international regime, to economic development and working place conditions related to the objectives of labour unions, or broader public policy objectives (such as the MDGs) related to the implementation of UN goals.

Legal system considerations were combined with economic or political logics in three differing forms relating to legal institutions. These forms comprised references to existing legal institutions related to the UN goals (such as human rights instruments); a de-stabilising argument suggesting the possibility that international society might introduce binding regulation of business conduct in order to mitigate adverse impact on social and environmental concerns; and finally a strategically stabilising articulation of the Global Compact as an instrument that differs from legal institutions and is not intended to become one. In this way, the discursive construction of the output stopped short of a hard institutionalisation of business social responsibilities, but encouraged businesses to support and adopt the Global Compact principles as a way to preserve their economic rights by taking responsibility for their impacts on society.

Through such stabilisation, which avoided kindling the debate on the voluntary or mandatory character of CSR regulation, the ground was prepared for a basically de-stabilising aim of connecting the UN Global Compact to existing normative instruments of law instruments that specifically spell out norms of conduct. The resulting de-stabilising output was brought about by combining economic system references to business interests and legal system language referring to legal institutions (international trade law) that currently protect business interests. The argument in favour of business support for the Global Compact was built by suggesting a longer term risk to the stability of business economic interests unless companies assume social responsibility through acceptance of a soft institutionalisation.

The targeted use of system-specific logic indicates that statements were developed by the UN Secretariat (and later the Global Compact Office) and other UN staff with each specific audience in mind and to particularly transmit the idea of the initiative in a way that would appeal to that particular audience. The foundational ideas and objectives are identical but different 'coating' was applied to make the unusual cooperation between an intergovernmental organisation and the private sector to jointly develop norms of conduct for business organisations based on international law instruments palatable to differing consumers of the texts.

The difference between arguments placing emphasis on economic system logic and those emphasising legal and political system logics is evident when statements made to groups outside the UN system (typically, business) are compared with the UN General Assembly Resolutions. The UN General Assembly resolutions on public-private partnerships are the main exception to the dominance of economic system language usage in the discursive construction of the Global Compact. The resolutions are dominated by references to political system considerations, in particular the UN objectives, interspersed with legal system language. This strategy, too, corresponds to the composition of the audience, which in the case of the General Assembly is made up by state representatives. As such, their main concerns, at least officially, are the public policy goals of their nation states and the implementation of the UN's objectives according to the UN Charter and other international soft and hard law instruments. Among such concerns of UN member states was also the protection of the UN against capture by external interests that would harm its integrity and potential to protect and promote human rights and other objectives stated in the UN Charter. By deploying system-specific language and setting the message into a conservative stabilising context, the resolutions' drafters were able to obtain acceptance by UN members (states participating in the annual General Assembly meetings) of engagement in a discursive construction of a role for business that at a fundamental level is de-stabilising to the UN's point of departure in conventional state-centric international law.

By abstaining from claims to change the legal status of business organisations to formal duty bearers under international law, the Global Compact architects were able to successfully invite business organisations to participate in the development of a soft institutionalisation of business social responsibilities according to which business organisations assume certain responsibilities on a voluntary basis. This functioned as a stabilising strategy that opened options for de-stabilisation. When the Global Compact architects invited business associations into the regulatory process, business was offered a formal access to rule-making processes that are normally not open to these types of organisations.

Throughout the process to construct normative guidance for business under the Global Compact process, references to the UDHR and core labour standards remained strong. This can be seen from the start with the Secretary-General's 1999 speech in Davos through the formulation of the Global Compact principles and the website. In addition, the layered construction of the Global Compact's website deepens the normative role played by international human rights from the UDHR and ILO's 1998 Declaration by providing internet links to international conventions on human rights and core labour standards. This was partly due to NGO participation in the creation of the website. But also partly based on the acceptance that the Global Compact initiative and the normative character of the principles as such had come to enjoy with the business sector. In this case, a stabilising point of departure was taken (when communicating with business) in the existing international norms already defined and (when communicating with states in the UN General Assembly) in existing but challenging public policy objectives in order to set in motion the de-stabilising process of private sector acceptance of norms of conduct extending international norms as normative sources of conduct from states to business.

The efforts taken by the UN Secretary-General and other Global Compact architects to articulate the Global Compact as distinct from binding law suggests that constructing the Global Compact as a legally binding instrument was avoided in order not to cause apprehension among some business participants and organisations. Such hesitation might have led certain stakeholders to argue against reference to detailed and hard international law instruments directly accessible from the Principles' website. The construction of the Compact as an initiative to promote business self-regulation on a voluntary basis enabled the website to provide reference to detailed hard law instruments that actually address governments, such as the ILO core labour conventions, as normative sources for CSR normativity under the Global Compact. Compared to the outcome of the Draft Norms process, this was a step forward from a situation of no UN guidance for businesses on human rights. As such, it helped develop a foundation for the specialised BHR regime.

6.3.2.3 The EU MSF and CSR Alliance

The two EU based case studies, the MSF and CSR Alliance, differ from the UN cases. That applies particularly to MSF, which was based originally in an expectation on the part of the EU Commission for the private sector to take a leading role in developing norms of conduct for business with a strong foundation in international law. Companies that were willing to work with the Commission and along its suggested substantive guidelines were simply expected to want to engage in developing normative guidelines for business self-regulation on human rights and other CSR issues.

In several instances, the Commission's strategic language usage in the 2002 and 2006 Communications[21] was caught between two conflicting sets of interests that somewhat complicated the reception of statements among the diverse group of recipients. On the one hand, the Commission as an EU institution addresses authorities. Simultaneously, the Communications also in practice address business organisations in order to seek to promote CSR from its particular public policy orientated perspective. As a result, the effect of the argumentative strategy became somewhat blurred. What was stabilising from a political system perspective (such as promoting public policy objectives) would be de-stabilising from an economic perspective (when business (self-)regulation on social responsibilities was suggested with the aim of implementing public policy objectives rather than, as was argued by the SRSG and Global Compact architects, to preserve the economic interests of business).

The 2002 Communication on CSR made it clear that the MSF was to a high degree driven by a desire to include business in the implementation of public policy interests, and that CSR was seen as an avenue for this. In this sense, the Commission employed CSR both as a paradigm that assumes (at least a degree of) business self-regulation, and a normative concept that relates to certain qualitative issues, in particular labour market, supply chain and development concerns related to labour and human rights. The Commission had already in the 2001 Green Paper[22] introduced economic system language to describe from a stabilising strategic perspective some potential benefits of CSR to companies' economic objectives. Similar to the Global Compact architects, the Commission employed legal system logic (in a binary inversion of legal = mandatory) to describe CSR as 'voluntary' and going beyond legal requirements. It employed political system language to describe the potential of business to contribute to public policy goals, rather than to argue a necessity of business to self-regulate or else become regulated. The Commission continued that argumentative strategy in the 2002 Communication while also adding de-stabilising points through legal system language that CSR 'should take international

---

[21] Commission of the European Communities (2002) Communication from the Commission concerning Corporate Social Responsibility; Commission of the European Communities (2006) Communication from the Commission to the European Parliament, the Council and the European Economic and Social Committee: Implementing the Partnership for Growth and Jobs.

[22] Commission of the European Commission (2001) Promoting a European Framework for Corporate Social Responsibility.

standards into account' and 'build on core principles laid down in international agreements'.

However, the Commission's strategy, entailing repeated references to international law as a normative source for the ambitious normative output intended by the Commission, was not very effective with regard to the formulation in the Final Report of a comprehensive framework for CSR to be based on international human rights and labour law. They were simply neutralised by business arguments, perhaps supported by internal policy conflicts within the EU Commission.

Business organisations' argumentative strategies were more effective in turning around the process towards an output that basically preserved status quo and neither delivered a comprehensive normative framework, nor constructed a European understanding of CSR as based in detailed international human rights and labour law. This was obtained by applying stabilising strategies and arguing specifically through political system language on EU and Member States' public policy objectives and legal system logic on the obligations of authorities to implement human and labour rights. Business organisations, especially those opposed to an institutionalisation of CSR and particularly of business responsibilities for human rights, were successful because they articulated their preferred output of the MSF in a manner that concretely related to existing policies and obligations of the recipients, that is, the Commission and authorities.[23] Thus, it both activated their core rationality and underscored that the tasks related to that rationality belong with the political system.

Compared with the strategies applied by the SRSG and UN Global Compact statements, the Commission's discursive strategy was less system-specifically focused on business recipients. In particular, it employed legal system language in a way that instead of being taken up by the recipients was reflected off those and returned to the Commission with the aim of emphasising authorities' own obligations.

Employers and business were successful in constructing CSR according to their interests by referring to Commission interests and former statements in a way that compelled the EU Commission to stand by its responsibilities as a public authority. Through their hegemony over the construction of CSR, established through an argumentative strategy

---

[23] EU Multistakeholder Forum on CSR (2003) High Level meetings, 13 November 2003, Address by Philippe de Buck – Secretary General UNICE; EU Multistakeholder Forum on CSR (2002) High Level meetings, 16 October 2002, Agenda, Statements, Philippe de Buck – Secretary General UNICE.

employing system-specific language and a stabilising strategy addressing authorities, employers and business preserved or enhanced their power by preserving status quo. In doing so, they at least temporarily warded off an institutionalisation (hard or soft) of CSR and business responsibilities for human rights through a detailed European normative framework. Employers and business achieved this by arguing through political system logic, referring to the political economic interests that the Commission had repeatedly highlighted, and by using legal system logic to refer to international human rights and labour law as obligations of states. Legal system logic was also used to indicate legislative tasks to promote economic interests of business. Overall, economic system logic with references to business interests per se was limited, and was used mainly to underscore points on policy interests or legal obligations that employers and business presented as Commission duties. Thus, employers and business were successful in establishing irritants on the Commission that caused perturbation within its own system on its own tasks, diverting it from action on the tasks and requirements it might make on business.

Although differing in terms of system-specific language employed, business organisations' deployment of the Commission's legal system language resembles the way in which the SRSG returned business arguments on international human rights obligations being state obligations to companies. Recall that in doing so, the SRSG explained that the state duty to protect also encompasses the horizontality doctrine, and therefore may carry along national law obligations that business must comply with. This indicates that regardless of the system of the transmitter and the recipient, strategic usage of a transmitter's own arguments may be turned to the advantage of the original recipient, if it is returned in a way that must be accepted by the original transmitter based on the original argument. Thus, system-specific arguments do have the potential to cause perturbation in a recipient system, but argumentative strength also depends on the quality and strategy of the argument.

When the EU Commission did employ economic system arguments, these generally emphasised the voluntary character of CSR. This was mainly done by the Commissioner for Enterprises, who would be working to support and stimulate business operations rather than promote corporate social responsibility (that was the task of the Commissioner for Social Affairs). Especially in later stages of the MSF, statements emphasised that the Commission did not want to complicate the exercise of business activities by establishing rules. Such statements weakened the effects of possible expectation among business that a legal basis for hard regulation might be adopted if the MSF failed to deliver a comprehensive framework on CSR. Thus, the potential of the strategic interest of business in self-regulating to pre-empt hard regulation to ensure internalisation of externalities was undermined by the Commission itself through such usage of a stabilising strategy addressing its own (law-making and political) system throughout the MSF.

At an overall level, in the 2006 Communication the Commission employed system-specific logic addressing the specific audience that for practical (if informal) purposes was targeted by the Communication proper or its Annex. The main text of the Communication addressed authorities. In the Communication proper, the Commission employed predominantly political system language, whereas in the Annex economic system language dominated. The Communication proper referred briefly and only towards the end to international law instruments (mainly the soft instruments noted in the MSF Final Report). The Annex, which sets out details on the Alliance, from the Commission's perspective for practical purposes needed to be accepted by business organisations and their members in order for these to want to join the Alliance.

By informally addressing different audiences and applying different arguments in the Communication proper and the Annex, the 2006 Communication navigated more systematically between system-specific arguments addressing diverse recipients than had been the case in the 2002 Communication. As a result, it avoided the blurring of recipients' understanding of arguments as stabilising or de-stabilising that marked (and marred) the effectiveness of the 2002 Communication with regard to influencing recipients towards the output desired by the Commission.

6.3.2.4 Summing up

In all of the case studies, the articulation of system-specific interests was influential in argumentative strategy and outputs in relation to construction of CSR normativity and resulting institutionalising of business social responsibilities. The Draft Norms and the SRSG process represent the two extremes. Due to business participants' argumentative strategy of referring from a stabilising perspective to authorities' obligations and articulating public policy implementation as calling for public authority actions, the Draft Norms were rejected by the Commission on Human Rights. The impact is highlighted by the MSF, in which a similar argumentative strategy by business associations resulted in an output that – when compared against the other case studies – was the least specific in terms of the normative role given to international human rights law. It preserved CSR as voluntary without setting substantive content, and blocked the Commission's ambitious goal of a normative framework on CSR. The SRSG output, by contrast, was the most far-reaching, with much of the output building on the argumentative strategy of articulating social actors' interests and developing further-ranging arguments on the basis of what had already been accepted.

In contrast to the other initiatives, the SRSG applied international human rights theory on states' obligations to ensure a national legal order that lives up to each government's international obligations. He drew on this to establish both the state duty to protect against human rights violations at the horizontal level, and to make the point that companies have duties under national law in their countries of operation. This, of course, should be no surprise to the UN Human Rights Council, at least in principle. To make the point, the SRSG first drew on international law theory and a stabilising argumentative strategy to highlight state obligations, a point that could hardly be countered (and was not countered) by the Council. Yet by invoking specialised international human rights theory, he also established de-stabilising elements by requiring action of governments to protect against horizontal level human rights violations. That point made, the SRSG was able to buy into the argument that some business associations had raised already from the time of the Draft Norms in stating that human rights obligations are state obligations, and that companies already have obligations to abide by national law in their countries of operation. Building on that same argument, the SRSG constructed a strongly law-informed concept of business responsibilities for human rights applying not only to states, but also to companies. By turning an argument around to the original transmitters, which had been made by those with the stabilising objective of diverting an institutionalisation of business responsibilities for human rights, the SRSG changed a stabilising argument into a de-stabilising one. The latter encompassed not only the obligation to comply with national law, but also to internalise social expectations that business organisations respect international law standards of conduct when these are not sufficiently implemented or enforced in national law.

In the MSF process, business organisations, in particular those opposed to an institutionalisation of CSR, were more influential on the output of the process than NGOs. The outcome of the Drafts Norms process suggests that a similar dynamic was at play, which came to overrule the influence of civil society organisations on the text of the Draft Norms because they were never formally adopted. In the MSF, business and employers' organisations opposed to an institutionalisation of CSR along the lines suggested by the Commission at the launch of the MSF were able to ward off a hard as well as a soft institutionalisation of CSR in terms of form as well as normative substance. These organisations employed an argumentative strategy that reasoned through the interests of recipients and invoked a stabilising strategy by referring to existing obligations or tasks.

Thus, the argumentative strategy provided perturbation within recipients to internalise and accommodate the interests of the transmitting business associations. The discursive impact evident in the MSF output was also carried over into the CSR Alliance 'toolbox' from 2008 in that the latter does not make explicit reference to specific international law standards as defined in international conventions or declaration.

Comparison between the UN and EU initiatives suggests that in a multi-stakeholder regulatory process comprising representations of different social sub-systems, discursive hegemony may be obtained through use of an argumentative strategy that addresses the system-specific interests of the recipient, and enhances this through a tailored combination of stabilising and de-stabilising arguments. This is an argumentative strategy that employs ('mimics') the system-specific logic of recipient social sub-systems, and does so in a way that deploys stabilising and de-stabilising arguments very strategically. Where change was delivered – with business – the most comprehensive institutionalisation of business social responsibilities was obtained by authorities or the SRSG noting a stabilising point of departure in terms of business rights under the legal system and the economic impact of this (benefits to companies), and gradually building a de-stabilising argument by explaining with reference to system-specific interests of business how change may serve to preserve or protect their economic interests in a manner consistent with societal needs. Where change was not desired – by business – a conservative stabilising strategy invoking *lex lata* with regard to authorities was effective, as shown by the Draft Norms and the MSF. The SRSG processes and the EU Commission's argumentative approach to set up the CSR Alliance showed that if met by a strategy as that set out in the preceding sections on those processes, such status quo as resulted from the Draft Norms and MSF processes may be avoided.

In particular, the SRSG process and Global Compact argumentative style demonstrate that a transmitter's deployment of system-specific arguments to bring forth the system-specific interests of a recipient may serve to prepare the recipient for accepting or actively engaging with a discourse or discursive process of constructing a normative concept towards an output that internalises competing or conflicting interests.

The effect of a system-specific interest-based argument can be further advanced by a strategic deployment of stabilising and de-stabilising arguments devised in such a way as to first activate the system-specific logic of an audience, which the audience may see as being under threat, in a manner that eases such fears; and next arguing that a change of norms or conduct is the longer-term solution to avert the threat and therefore in the interest of the audience. As the SRSG's introduction of human rights due diligence as part of Pillar Two shows, such a strategy may even lead to an audience accepting a practice that is based in the logic of another subsystem, if it can be explained as a solution to the risk to the core concern related to the rationality of the audience. Human rights due diligence came across as a corporate risk management approach, even though it is intended to prevent risk to society caused by the company, rather than risk to the company caused by its environment. Of course, if done well, human rights due diligence may also prevent reputational damage or other economic harm to the company.

6.4 SPECIFICITY

It was indicated above that stakeholder arguments or proposals presented in brief and operational terms were particularly influential on the SRSG outputs. This applied both to civil society business and business statements.

During the first years of the SRSG mandate, NGO arguments (generally relating to the politics of law (*lex ferenda*) by arguing in favour of a change of international law to provide for obligations and accountability of companies under international law) were neither very specific, nor generally particularly effective in terms of impact on the SRSG's reports or statements. NGO statements differed from those of the SRSG by not taking their point of departure in the 'stable' (that is, a stabilising argument aimed at putting the concerns of recipients at ease as a point of departure for later perturbation), but going straight to the de-stabilising objective. Made towards the end of the mandate term, the proposal made by the Clean Clothes Campaign[24] and CIDSE[25] on the establishment of a Global Ombudsman was an exception to this: that proposal was made in more operational terms, and did make its way into the SRSG's 2008 report (albeit with points on complexities to be considered in establishing such an institution). Quite specific statements from some NGOs[26] and governments following the 2007 report, recommending that the SRSG give increased attention to the situation of victims, had an impact on the

---

[24] Clean Clothes Campaign (2007) 'Letter to John Ruggie', Amsterdam, 23 March 2007.
[25] CIDSE – Développement et la Solidarité (2008) 'CIDSE submission to the Special Representative of the United Nations Secretary-General on Business and Human Rights'.
[26] E.g., International Network for Economic, Social & Cultural Rights (2007) 'Letter to John Ruggie; Joint NGO letter on work of the mandate', 10 October 2007.

2008 report, especially obvious in the third Pillar (access to remedy) and arguments informing that principle.[27] This underscores that in addition to the way in which statements lent themselves to incorporation by the SRSG in his own arguments, concreteness of stakeholder statements and proposals was significant for the SRSG's adoption of those.

Whereas NGO statements did not generally deploy stabilising arguments and mainly offered suggestions for change, some did refer to legal doctrine, that is, something already existing. Arguments referring to lex lata were more influential in terms of impact on the SRSG than lex ferenda arguments. This suggests that legal doctrine was readily adopted by the SRSG, because established legal doctrine is a strong argument that would support the acceptance of the SRSG's output. That by itself created a challenge for those stakeholders – mainly NGOs, but also some states – who desired a change of doctrine to specifically provide for human rights obligations for companies under international law. Also in this context, the impact of lex ferenda arguments mirrors the concreteness of the argument. Lex lata arguments were adopted more readily by the SRSG when the points they made were aligned with the SRSG's preference for grounding arguments in the stable (established or non-threatening) in order to promote change. With their point of departure in the already established, substantiating a lex lata argument (typically a stabilising argument) is relatively simple compared to lex ferenda arguments (typically de-stabilising) of which many may compete to become adopted. The strength of lex lata arguments is apparent for example in the emphasis given from the early stage of the mandate term to international criminal law's recognition of individual accountability, the SRSG's gradual shift during the mandate to explicitly recognising the horizontality doctrine under international human rights law (the state duty to protect) in response to expert advice on that specialised doctrine, and finally in the SRSG's introduction of the right to remedy and focus on the rights of victims during the last year of the mandate term. The right to remedy is an established part of international human rights law, just like consideration of the situation of victims is at the core of human rights through ex-ante prevention of harm and ex-post remedy. The few examples of lex ferenda proposals that were accepted more or less directly by the SRSG were characterised by concrete proposals, such as that on a Global Ombudsman.

---

[27] See for example para. 9, which notes that the principle of access to remedy is 'an essential component of the framework' 'because even the most concerted efforts cannot prevent all abuse, while access to judicial redress is often problematic, and non-judicial means are limited in number, scope and effectiveness'.

Civil society arguments in the MSF generally also applied legal and political system language presented through de-stabilising strategies. This might have been effective if the EU Commission had had a stronger role in the MSF to promote its fundamentally de-stabilising aim of a soft or even hard institutionalisation of business social responsibilities. However, with business organisations as strong players in the MSF and the Commission having only a coordinating role, civil society organisations' de-stabilising arguments had little influence on the MSF output. Limited specificity and operational quality of arguments combined with the lack of system-specific focus on business recipients to deliver limited effects. Compared with those civil society arguments that had the strongest influence on the SRSG output, civil society arguments in the MSF were less specific. In the MSF, civil society arguments were frequently structured in terms of ideals for future binding regulation on business conduct under EU law, that is, lex ferenda.[28] The Commission had specifically noted that a legal basis for binding regulation was not in place and that it had launched the MSF as a soft alternative to hard regulation. Civil society arguments presuming a legal basis for coercive regulation or further calling for it to be established expressed a situation that was simply off the course set out by the Commission. When not explicitly de-stabilising, legal system arguments were made by civil society in a way that in practice focused on the doctrinal elements of international law in terms of state duties, rather than the state duty to protect. As a result, in the MSF such arguments came to underscore the duties of authorities, especially – given the concern with international human rights and labour law – of Member States, rather than the Commission and companies. Thus, such lex lata arguments had a stabilising effect that unintentionally supported business arguments on human rights being state duties. In the MSF debate such arguments undermined the Commission's efforts to make business self-regulate in order to contribute to implementing states' obligations under international human rights or labour law, or implementing public policy interests that are often related to social and economic human rights. The point to be taken from this is that argumentative strategies and their deployment of stabilising or de-stabilising strategies need to be carefully considered, taking the particular audience, its interests and tasks into consideration.

---

[28] E.g., European Multistakeholder Forum on CSR (2002) High Level meetings, 16 October 2002, Agenda, Statements, Anne-Sophie Parent; EU Multistakeholder Forum on CSR (2002) High Level meetings, 16 October 2002, Agenda, Statements, Tony Long – Director, WWF European Policy Office, http://circa.europa.eu/irc/empl/csr_eu_multi_stakeholder_forum/info/data/en/CSR%20Forum%20021016%20statements%20G8.htm (last accessed 15 February 2013 – website has been removed).

Civil society in the MSF deployed economic system arguments sparingly and therefore did not activate the rationality of companies in a way that might have caused the latter to internalise social expectations on international law as a normative source for CSR towards reducing economic risks (such as loss deriving from losing customers or investors, reputational damage or recruitment problems). Some civil society statements during the MSF that partly conformed to EU Commission objectives also went beyond those in relating to international law, making lex ferenda proposals, but also provided limited specific proposals for how to proceed.

In sum, the analysis suggests that an argument that contains specific proposals for solutions to problems or ways forward may combine with system-specific interest-based arguments towards becoming accepted. The two sets of argumentative dynamics combine to cause perturbation with particular recipients by speaking to their interest and becoming adopted, and because the proposal lends itself to immediate or easily adaptable application in the output. The effect can be furthered by stabilising and de-stabilising arguments as explained in section 6.3.

6.5 TOWARDS THE BHR REGIME

By contrast to the Global Compact and the EU case studies, the SRSG process from the outset was delimited to human rights, although it was partly spurred by the general CSR discourse. The SRSG reports did not generally refer to the concept of CSR, except to provide the general context for the mandate's work on business responsibilities for human rights. During the six mandate years, the work of the SRSG progressively strengthened the emphasis on states' obligations. It developed that emphasis from the original reference to 'governance gaps' and the general international law doctrine's 'state duty' to the 2008 UN Framework's human rights law doctrine-informed 'duty to protect' and the 2011 UNGP's operationalisation of all three Pillars. The emphasis on the state duty to protect against violations by third parties, such as companies, is consistent with international human rights law and its horizontality doctrine. Through emphasis on the established human rights law concept of the state duty to protect, the SRSG built a bridge to the concern with governance gaps, which inspired his approach as an academic, even before he became SRSG.[29] He also both eased business concerns with govern-

---

[29] E.g., J. G. Ruggie, (2004) 'Reconstituting the global public domain – issues, actors and practices'.

ment obligations being shifted to business and human rights advocates' concerns that such a shift might 'let governments off the hook' with regard to state obligations. By use of legal and economic system logic he made it clear at the same time to governments as well as companies that the state duty to protect entails for governments to regulate, adjudicate and in other relevant ways turn their international obligations into national law applying to companies. This results in obligations for companies, with which they must comply under national law. That point is more clearly set out in the UN Framework[30] than in the UNGPs.

The informing role of international law augmented during the two mandate terms. Initially, references were limited. One of the striking parts of the UN Framework compared with the Global Compact Principles and the EU CSR Alliance and even the MSF process and its output, is that the informing role of international human rights law is less pronounced in terms of specific substance, and more in terms of application of theory. The SRSG's 2008 report did not list specific human rights, but observed that all human rights may be affected by companies, and referred broadly to the International Bill of Human Rights and fundamental ILO conventions as providing the substantive content of the due diligence process. The UNGPs re-affirmed that these constitute the minimum base line for the corporate responsibility to respect.

Eventually, the concept of social responsibilities for business in regard to human rights, which was constructed through the first SRSG term and reinforced with the second term, stands apart from CSR. The conceptual understanding, which resulted from the SRSG's discursive and often strategically chosen blend of legal, economic and political language, observations and considerations during the mandate years, its reports and many meetings and statements, differs from the concept of CSR in crucial ways. First, it connects state obligations and company obligations and responsibilities. Second, it is clearly bound up on law, in that it pinpoints states' duty to implement international human rights in a relevant way to regulate and adjudicate company conduct, and that it pinpoints companies' legal obligations under national law to respect human rights. For these reasons, the conceptual understanding constructed by the SRSG is a different one than CSR. It is not simply a sub-set of corporate social responsibility, but essentially a distinct discourse with normative implication – a discourse on business responsibilities for human rights, which has come to be referred to as *Business and Human Rights* (or *BHR*). The final part – the responsibility to respect which is based on the social expectation

---

[30] See the UN Framework, para. 54.

that companies conduct themselves in such a way as not to cause human rights abuse by benefitting from weak governance – is the part of the BHR concept that is the most closely related to CSR. In this way, going beyond what is required by law, it differs from the simple legal obligation. Still, it differs from CSR because it does not leave companies leeway with regard to human rights, as the International Bill of Human Rights and ILO fundamental conventions are defined as the minimum baseline for corporate conduct. All human rights may be subject to abuse by companies, directly or through complicity, and all human rights are therefore subject to the social expectation that they be respected by company conduct. For companies, BHR entails both the legal obligation to respect seen in relation to the state's obligation to protect, and the business responsibility to respect social expectations, which include not to abuse weak governance.

As a result, international human rights law has a very strong normative role for the BHR concept constructed through the SRSG process.

The emerging distinction between CSR and BHR is significant because of the differentiation in focusing on state and corporate legal obligations and societal expectations; and because more emphasis on the obligations or responsibilities of one type of actor may decrease legal pressure or social expectations on the other. The distinction is important also because the BHR discourse as developed by the SRSG has become highly informed by legal theory and terminology of obligations, compliance and liability, whereas the CSR discourse continues along a path informed by 'softer' forms of responsibility, self-regulation, 'voluntary action', and sustainability. This is not to say there are no overlaps: As the 2007 and 2008 reports of the SRSG indicate, social expectations are perceived as an important link to emerging soft law, which may in due time lead to harder national or international law.[31] The BHR discourse originated as a sub-set of the CSR discourse, but through its emphasis on state duties and formal public law has arguably solidified into an independent strain during the SRSG's first mandate. With the Human Rights Council's adoption of the second mandate and of the UNGPs that resulted from that mandate, BHR was clearly emerging as a regime that differs from the conventional state-oriented international human rights law regime, and also from the CSR discourse.

---

[31] Compare also the discussion on blurring boundaries between hard law, soft law, morals and social discourse in Shelton, D. (2000) Introduction, at 10–17, esp. 12.

7. Conclusion

Chapter 7 concludes the analysis by drawing up the main findings, explaining their significance and future use, and developing implications for theory and practice. Section 7.1 sums up the analysis and findings with a basis in the theoretical framework applied for the analysis of the five multi-stakeholder processes that form the case studies. Section 7.2 concludes on the emergence of the BHR regime. With a comparison against the other case studies, it describes how the argumentative strategy applied in the SRSG process led to an internationally agreed normative framework on business and human rights, adopted by the UN and recognising business enterprises as having responsibilities for human rights. Section 7.3 elaborates on the implications of the BHR regime and the insights on argumentative strategies for future multi-stakeholder development of norms of conduct to address sustainability-related concerns, and for their implementation. Section 7.4 draws up theoretical implications for socio-legal and organisational scholarship concerned with promoting sustainability through communication, focusing on system-specific interest-based communication, stabilising and de-stabilising arguments, and specificity. It also discusses implications for social autopoiesis and reflexive law. Section 7.5 sets forth guidance for practitioners, such as civil society, governments, intergovernmental organisations and companies with a sustainability commitment.

7.1 SUMMING UP ON ANALYSIS AND FINDINGS

This book opened by observing that current concerns with sustainability as a global problem lead to increasing attention being paid to how non-state actors like business enterprises can complement the role of states and intergovernmental organisations in regard to tasks that at a fundamental level are public policy objectives or governmental obligations. It also noted that while some such processes in recent decades have been a success, a diversity of public intergovernmental or public-private efforts to develop norms for the private sector or other societal actors in regard to societal sustainability have faltered or failed due to insufficient political will among states or lack of support among non-state actors. A diversity of interests at stake often complicates the process of developing norms and reaching agreement. Against that backdrop it was observed that there is a need to understand *how* norms on sustainability issues are negotiated and how stalemates that impede such efforts from becoming successful can be broken. Finally, it was highlighted that in the longer term, an expanded recognition of the private sector having international responsibilities could have highly interesting potential for involving companies more actively in responding to transnational sustainability challenges. This underscores the importance of understanding and learning from the discursive process that led to a breakthrough in the BHR field, a social sustainability field which until the early 2000s was marked by a stalemate.

To develop such insight five multi-stakeholder processes of developing normative guidance for businesses with regard to human rights were analysed. With a theoretical point of departure in socio-legal pragmatism, the emphasis was on the discursive process that led to the results (referred to as outputs) of each of the processes, with the SRSG process serving as the main case, and the processes towards the Draft Norms, the UN Global Compact, the EU's MSF and the CSR Alliance serving to provide perspectives. The discourse analysis was based on a large body of text, comprising statements and official reports by public organisations, business and civil society during each of the processes as well as their normative outputs. Emphasis was given to analysis of arguments on defining or 'fixing' CSR and business responsibilities for human rights as floating signifiers, particularly in terms of the form of regulation and the role to be played by international human rights law as a normative source. Struggles for hegemony or winning the discursive battle of influence on the outputs were fuelled by the concerns and interests of participants with preserving or advancing their situation or benefits, both within their functional sub-system (e.g., other companies or other civil society organisations) and vis-à-vis other functions. Businesses were concerned with staying in business, expanding their business and reducing risks, for example through reputational damage that might lead to financial loss. This corresponds to the system-specific logic of profit/loss of the economic sub-system. Policy-makers were concerned with the power implications of being able to, or perceived to, deliver on public policy objectives, such as the provision of employment or occupational health and safety and the promotion and respect for human and labour rights. This translates into the logic of power/weakness or the risk of loss of power if policy-makers are unable to deliver, even if the inability is caused by or reinforced by business activities. Civil society organisations, too, were concerned with power or loss of power in terms of being perceived by their constituencies to influence normative processes in which they are involved.

With a focus on communication as a core element in developing norms, social autopoiesis, which as described in Chapter 3 is a key element in the socio-legal reflexive law theory in regard to what makes communication successful in generating acceptance of normative change, served as the theoretical foundation for identifying the use of argumentative strategies among stakeholders. Autopoiesis allowed for analysis of statements and argumentative strategies in terms of system-specific communication as representative of different sub-systems' discursive struggles.

The analysis considered whether stakeholders sought to activate the rationality of those with whom they desired a normative change to take place by addressing them in the system-specific logic connected to the core function of the audience (recipients), or whether they used the logic of their own rationality. It analysed the impact of both and found that communication in the logic of the recipient was more effective in stimulating change. Adding the linguistic communication perspective of stabilising and de-stabilising argumentative strategies, the analysis found that the effect can be reinforced by a strategic play on the concern of the audience with preserving or promoting its core interests, and the change that is necessary for that to take place. This entails that the transmitter of a statement strategically articulates the audience's concerns in regard to its function and system-specific interests and does so in a manner that advances acceptance of the change desired by the transmitter. Finally, it found that in complex negotiations on normative issues at a high level of abstraction, a proposal for change is more likely to be adopted if it is specific and presented in a manner that lends itself to direct integration as part of the output being negotiated.

Bringing a systems-thinking perspective to the analysis, autopoiesis considers societal actors not in terms of institutions (such as parliaments or the UN Human Rights Council that are law-makers by preparing drafts and/or adopting them; or the UN Secretary-General or the EU Commission that are policy-makers or executives; or civil society organisations, which for the purposes of this analysis were also parts of the political system given their concerns and the significance of political power in regard to their constituencies or competitors; or the IOE or a particular company, which are market actors). Rather, what is significant is the societal function, which determines the rationality and therefore core concerns (or logic), e.g., as concerned with whether something is legal or not, whether it brings or reinforces power or not, or whether it means making money or suffering an economic loss.

More specifically, the analysis found that to motivate companies or business associations (organisations for companies or employers) to accept and adopt new norms of conduct in order for them to reduce their adverse societal impact, the economic logic of profit/loss or related distinctions is more effective than the legal system logic of legal/illegal or mandatory/voluntary, or the political system logic of power/no power or power/opposition. Similarly, to induce change or obtain a particular position with other functional sub-systems, communication in their logic is the key. Chapters 4 and 5 provided examples of both, as well as examples showing that communication in the logic of the speaker (transmitter) was not very effective in generating change or acceptance of new norms with the audience, if the basic societal function and therefore logic of the audience differed from that of the speaker.

It may seem intuitive that in order to make somebody, such as a business manager or CEO, adopt a particular position, communication should be such as to address the manager in a manner that activates her/his core concerns. However, this only becomes obvious through the theory perspective of social autopoiesis. If it were truly intuitive, the practice of communicating in the system-specific interests-based logic of the audience would be much more outspoken. Examples from the case studies showed that this is not the case; and also confirmed that in several instances, the practice of not communicating in the logic of the recipient caused resistance that eventually upset or contributed to upsetting the successful outcome or acceptance of the normative output. Arguments in the process leading to the Draft Norms created opposition with business by invoking the legal logic of legal/illegal rather than the economic logic of profit/loss. Similarly, arguments made by the EU Commission or civil society in the EU MSF process also created opposition with business. This opposition occurred in response to arguments that predominantly referred to legal instruments and normative sources in ways that were perceived as constraints to business, rather than to the benefits that businesses may gain by internalising societal expectations to reduce their adverse impacts on society and avoiding reputational crises and costly market-based reactions.

The multi-stakeholder regulatory initiatives that form the case studies present a diversity of levels of success in generating or stimulating acceptance of business responsibilities for their social impact in principle, and of such responsibilities being normatively grounded in international human rights law. The level of success was relative to the outputs, with the SRSG process delivering the most comprehensive and normatively solid output. The processes of the Global Compact, the MSF and the CSR Alliance delivered some, but less comprehensive results in terms of CSR and business responsibilities for human rights. While a comprehensive normative product, the Draft Norms lacked the support necessary for a formal acceptance. The degree of institutionalisation of business social responsibilities varied, with the SRSG process delivering the most comprehensive change, and the MSF process' output close to a status quo rather than change.

The finding on the significance of communicating in the system-specific logic of the audience in order to induce change with business does not mean that the economic logic is to be dominant, or that civil society, politicians, academics or others must change their *modus operandi* to the logic of the market. Quite the opposite: deploying the economic system's logic is the key to prompting companies to internalise the needs and expectations of society, and therefore promote their consideration of social, environmental and other sustainability objectives harboured by actors in their environment. Understanding and being able to apply the logic of the market is therefore a way for civil society, politicians or law-makers to induce change and acceptance with market actors of the priorities of political, legal and other functional sub-systems with regard to sustainability.

The analysis of the development of normative guidance on business responsibilities for human rights at the backdrop of societal concerns with adverse business impact on society confirms that a diversity of competing and often conflicting interests may be highly significant for the normative substance of the output of process or its adoption. Yet it also shows that stalemates may be broken, and that this may done in ways that change actors' stances from opposition to support. It showed that the discursive construction of the UN Framework led to a breakthrough in terms of acceptance that businesses have responsibilities in international law for their impacts on society. This was reinforced by the soft law UNGPs, which elaborated the UN Framework with a view to an operationalisation for states and businesses within each of the three Pillars of the State Duty to Protect, the Corporate Responsibility to Respect, and Access to Remedy.

This breakthrough not only established a solid basis for the emergent BHR regime, a basis that was anchored in the political, legal and even economic functional sub-systems as further discussed in section 7.2. Offering potentially wide-ranging perspectives, it also brought recognition that new norms of conduct for non-state actors can come about that contribute to balancing the extensive economic rights that businesses enjoy in international law (under international economic and trade law) by increased duties recognised in an international law context. Even if, as in the case of the BHR regime, these duties are so far recognised only on a soft law basis, this does not devoid them of political, legal or even economic relevance. With businesses, being non-state actors, traditionally not seen to have a place in international law, it is a major step forward for a more balanced division of international rights and obligations that an international instrument adopted by as high-level international organisation as the Human Rights Council now recognises that business have responsibilities to meet international law standards (*in casu*, international human rights law with the International Bill of Human Rights and ILO's core labour rights as the minimum baseline). It is also a major step forward that the UN Framework and UNGPs make it explicit that the corporate responsibility to respect applies to all businesses, regardless of form, size or sector. Finally, the breakthrough that led to emergent BHR regime showed that such new norms of conduct for business organisations in general or within a sector may be communicated (talked, written, etc.) into acceptance by applying a relevant argumentative strategy targeting the audience in question by explaining how it may serve its own best interest by adapting its conduct to the needs and demands of society, as elaborated for theory perspectives in section 7.4 and for advice for practitioners in section 7.5.

7.2 THE EMERGENCE OF THE BHR REGIME: BACKGROUND, INSTITUTIONALISATION, AND BREAK-THROUGH

Partly with a point of departure within the context of CSR that had evolved within civil society during the twentieth century, partly with efforts by intergovernmental organisations to develop norms for business to take responsibility for their social impacts, the SRSG process undertaken under the UN between 2005 and 2011 resulted in the evolution of what is emerging as an autonomous regime within the greater international law regime. BHR differs from the conventional state-centrist regime of international human rights law by formally recognising that business organisations have responsibilities in regard to standards of conduct developed under international law. This is a major novelty and confirms the significance of the process that lead to that result, so that future multi-stakeholder processes may benefit from the experience.

It was noted in Chapter 1 that regimes are forms of cooperation that exist despite the restrictions that they place on involved actors, and that convergence on a regime is attractive despite such restrictions because it offers order in place of anarchy.

The BHR regime is not yet fully-fledged; however, the discursive construction that evolved with the UN Framework and UNGPs demonstrates that companies and business associations came to support the idea that businesses have responsibilities for human rights, despite the restrictions that this places on their exercise, from a narrow and short-termist perspective, of their economic functions. The explicit elaboration of the implications of the state duty to protect with regard to the extent and variety of state bodies to which the duty applies and the diversity of ways in which they may or should act to implement that duty also places a restriction on states. Yet states also supported the UN Framework and UNGPs. In both cases, however, in the longer term, business responsibilities and states' duties to protect will lead to less anarchy and therefore was the more ideal alternative than no normative directives for businesses and states for business responsibilities for human rights. For example, for business enterprises anarchy is reduced through a 'level playing field' and simply knowing what is expected of the company and its managers. For governments, anarchy is reduced through lower risks of business-related human rights abuse and its disruptive impacts on individuals, communities and society in general. For businesses as well as states, the discursive construction of BHR and the argumentative strategies deployed by the SRSG convinced them that supporting the emergent formalisation of the corporate responsibility to respect and the state duty to protect was the better alternative to the status quo, that is, the situation that was in place after the failure of the Draft Norms to become adopted by the Commission of Human Rights and obtain formal status.

The normativity for businesses that has come to be recognised with the UN Framework and UNGPs set a policy and soft law basis that is currently (2017) subject to negotiations towards a possible hard law elaboration through a treaty, which is a binding instrument. A treaty, which may have a state-centric focus in terms of duties (to be implemented by states with regard to certain companies operating in or out of their territories or jurisdictions) rather than establish duties for businesses under international law, will not necessarily contribute to a strengthening or enhanced institutionalisation of the BHR regime. However, the UNGPs may co-exist alongside a treaty, complementing it by more ambitious goals than those set by the treaty, and providing normative guidance and norms of conduct (e.g., on due diligence and remedy) for companies that are not covered by the treaty. As the treaty currently looks set to apply only to TNCs, the continued relevance of the UNGPs is considerable.

Based on the theoretical framework set out in Chapter 3, Chapters 4–6 analysed the discourse that took place through the SRSG multi-stakeholder process leading to the UN Framework and UNGPs, and compared this against four other multi-stakeholder processes launched by intergovernmental organisations, either the UN or the EU. According to the UN Charter, the UN is charged with promoting socio-economic growth, peace, and the promotion and protection of human rights. The

EU is a regional organisation established around economic collaboration, and as such has a strong focus on businesses, even as it has evolved to consider human rights and labour in internal as well as external affairs of the EU and its Member States. The four processes were launched and developed their outputs in the years just before and around the same time as the SRSG process was launched and developed its first normative output, the UN Framework. The processes towards the Draft Norms, the UN Global Compact, the EU MSF and CSR Alliance were initiated to develop normative guidance on business responsibilities for human rights or on CSR with a strong human rights element.

The analysis demonstrates that up to 2004, intergovernmental efforts to develop normative guidance with an explicit focus on human rights encountered opposition that impeded the development or adoption of strong normative instruments. The Draft Norms failed to obtain recognition by the Commission on Human Rights, and statements from governments demonstrated that the idea of businesses being recognised as duty-holders – even on a policy or soft law basis – upset state support. Statements also demonstrate that certain, few but large and influential, business associations held similar conceptions. The statements also indicate that understanding or recognition of the specialised horizontality doctrine under international human rights law was originally limited. Set within a more general CSR context, the EU's MSF also failed to develop a strong normative framework, with the analysis indicating that business opposition was a major factor. Whereas some business associations felt excluded from the process of negotiating the Draft Norms, at least during the start of the process, business associations were fully integrated participants in the EU MSF. Yet many of the substantive arguments point to similar reasons for opposition, based in conceptions of shifting state obligations on to the private sector.

The analysis also shows that the process towards the UN Global Compact was set on a different course from the outset. In this case, businesses supported the idea of normative guidance for their impact on human rights as well as labour, environment and from 2004 corruption and bribery. From the very beginning, the discursive construction of the UN Global Compact focused on 'what was in it' for business, or for other audiences that the Global Compact architects were addressing. As a result of such system-specific interest-based communication, which explained the economic advantages to businesses of internalising social expectations and developing their policies and actions so as to support and respect human rights and avoid contributing to human rights abuse committed by other organisations, business associations and individual CEOs (managers) supported the initiative. The wording and adoption of the Global Compact's Principles 1 and 2 on human rights, and Principles 3–6 on (core) labour rights, helped form a normative foundation that the SRSG process was able to build on. It therefore also contributed to an early foundation for the emergent BHR regime. Notably, during the early years the Global Compact was consistently described by its architects and staff of the Global Compact Office as not being a regulatory instrument. Despite its obvious normative ambitions, this ensured that the on-going construction and elaboration of the Compact discursively activated the economic rationality of companies, and perhaps even more importantly, reduced or avoided disturbing noise which might have resulted in companies perceiving the initiative as having coercive effects. This point reconfirms the significance of system-specific interest-based communication. For those that have an understanding of the international legal system the wording of the principles and the non-enforceable character in the commitment, with reputational damage as the main sanction, the Global Compact does not differ much from the way the international human rights law regime works for states. Yet by explicitly avoiding legal system logics when addressing businesses, or doing so only in a manner that underscored the voluntary character of the Compact, the activation of businesses' economic logic was not disturbed by concerns that the Compact or commitment to the principles might cause economic losses. As a result, and in accordance with the theory of autopoiesis, their appreciation of the needs and demands of their environment, that is, the UN, governments, civil society and academics, became stimulated and prompted support for the initiative and the Compact principles. Legal logic was introduced when the Compact had gained some maturity and a committed group of participants, and the need to avoid a legitimacy crisis due to risks of 'blue-washing' became imminent. At this time, for businesses the policies of de-listing, which later came to be referred to as 'expulsion' and a 'sanction', of participants not submitting their annual Communication of Progress reports, served to enhance trust in their own commitment and therefore protect them against reputational damage and other events that might be economically costly.

The initiative to establish the Global Compact was successful in terms of setting up a new type of intergovernmental mode for regulating companies and their transnational operations. That is especially so given the fact that it was established within an organisation which is a conventional state-centrist oriented international organisation, and that it was based on international instruments that address states as duty bearers. The Global Compact initiative was originally met with considerable hesitation among states (whose representatives make up the UN General Assembly), civil society, the international labour movement and parts of industry. In view of this, the argumentative strategy was successful in convincing stakeholders of the approach and its linkages to international law, including human rights law. The analysis suggests that the strategy of appealing to recipients by arguing the benefits of the Global Compact precisely in terms of the interests of each specific audience played a part.

The EU Commission's 2006 Communication that led to the launch of the CSR Alliance also displays a clear distinction of arguments addressing the system-specific interests of governments, and those of businesses. This may have been by accident, or it may suggest that it was becoming increasingly obvious to those paying attention to the field of developing CSR normativity in public-private initiatives that activating the core rationality of any particular audience was an effective way to stimulate change.

This, too, became the approach adopted by the SRSG. However, it was not until some time into the first mandate term that system-specific arguments became a clear strategy for arguments. As the process matured, the precision of addressing audiences in their logics and activating their rationality by clearly explaining 'what was in it for them' became evident. As it matured further, it also became more specific and less abstract, developing explanations to businesses on the practical implications of their adverse impacts on human rights in economic terms supported by examples of economic risks or losses. As it matured even further, the combination of stabilising arguments and de-stabilising arguments became superimposed on the system-specific interest-based argument, creating reinforcement. By invoking the core rationality that might be feared by the audience to be at risk, but doing it in such a way as to ease the fear, the SRSG was able to obtain a basis for a constructive 'digestion' of the de-stabilising or more challenging arguments, which explained that change was the solution to preserve the system-specific core interest in a highly dynamic world with new demands on companies.

The analysis demonstrates that the SRSG's combination of the three argumentative strategies (system-specific, stabilising/de-stabilising, and specificity) set the SRSG process apart from each of the four other multi-stakeholder processes that form the case studies. In none of the others did the organisation in charge apply the combination of argumentative strategies as targeted to specific audiences as in the SRSG process. In particular, the system-specific interest-based communication and the stabilising and de-stabilising argumentative strategy combined to result in an output that was ground-breaking. It broke the previous stalemate in terms of the UN not only developing, but also adopting normative guidance for business responsibilities for human rights. And it set the formal foundation for the emergent BHR regime in two texts that became accepted or formally adopted by the Human Rights Council.

The institutionalisation of the BHR regime with the UN Framework and UNGPs has shown its significance through spilling over into the 2011 revision of the OECD Guidelines applying to the full range of matters covered by the OECD instrument, and the EU's revision of its CSR definition in the 2011 Communication. Similarly, the strength of the regime to even influence CSR normativity is evidenced by the adoption by the OECD Guidelines and ISO 26000 of the risk-based due diligence approach promoted within the UN Framework and UNGPs, and their application of risk-based due diligence beyond human rights to broader CSR issues.

It is important to remember in this context that the current study does not assess the effects that the normative guidance developed through any of these transnational business governance instruments have on business. The analysis in here is concerned with how the norms are developed and agreed to through communication, not their implementation. Future research on implementation may yield interesting findings to complement the current study. It may be assumed that the deployment of argumentative strategies – system-specific, stabilising and de-stabilising, and specificity – may also be valuable in communication processes for implementation.

7.3 PERSPECTIVES FOR THE FUTURE EVOLUTION OF SUSTAINABILITY NORMS

Whereas CSR originated as corporate self-regulation independent of public regulation, governmental and intergovernmental organisations have begun to establish processes aiming at shaping business action through various modalities for stimulating adaptation to societal demands. Concerns with the environment, climate change, and impacts on individuals and communities of action or non-action of public and private organisations means that sustainability concerns us all. Sustainability challenges are highly dynamic as the world evolves and changes, and as information on the implications of practices become known. The shift in CSR focus from inclusive labour markets in a national context and concern with working conditions in supply chains in the 1990s, to climate change mitigation in the 2010s, is a case in point. The challenges that the world, or more precisely the UN and governments encountered in developing and agreeing on what eventually became the Paris Climate Change Accord, underscores the fragility of the current international political and legal set-up for dealing with pressing sustainability concerns. The fact that many of the important actions required to mitigate climate change must be taken by companies underscores the inadequacy of the current set-up. It is naïve to think that sustainability concerns are now fully taken care of with the adoption of the Paris Accord, the SDGs, and the UNGPs. More challenges will follow, and even for those norms or agreements currently adopted, implementation remains a challenge that requires further negotiations between public and private actors who will often have divergent, sometimes conflicting, interests. The duration in years and the many meetings to develop the Paris Accord is a luxury that the world probably was not actually able to afford, and a luxury that cannot be counted on for future sustainability concerns. Recent history, especially around climate change, has shown that such concerns may emerge and grow fast. Time, therefore, is of essence.

Against that backdrop, the evolution of the BHR regime offers crucial lessons for world leaders, policy-makers, regulators, civil society, academics, individual citizens in whatever capacity, and of course businesses with a commitment to sustainability (including economic sustainability, which is increasingly recognised to be compromised by short-termism that does not consider social and environmental sustainability). It brings knowledge of how new sustainability-related norms may be argued into existence and acceptance. The diversity of the case studies in terms of argumentative strategies and outputs demonstrates the importance of awareness of the core interests of those with whom change is sought, and of communicating the needs and demands of society in their logic or logics.

As noted above, this does not mean that all will function according to the logic of those with whom change is sought, for example, business. What it does mean is that putting oneself in their place can be part of the key to being able to communicate in a manner that induces irritation, which according to the theory of social autopoiesis is a condition for the internal perturbation that supports the process of acceptance of new norms and the need for change. As the SRSG's articulation of the benefits to companies of accepting a due diligence process shows, once the foundation is made by communicating in a manner that shows recognition of the interests at stake, the basis for understanding and agreement grows, and as part of this, the willingness to work constructively with approaches that are well-known in other functional sub-systems.

Finally, in revising or updating the conception of relevant actors to include businesses, and elaborating on their roles in terms of both output and process, the discursive construction of business responsibilities for human rights offers potential for other emergent issue-specific regimes that relate to the division of rights and obligations in a global world with increased competition for resources and increased awareness of the consequences of such competition.

7.4 THEORY IMPLICATIONS

The analysis has shown that the outputs of multi-stakeholder regulatory processes with a diverse composition representing competing or conflicting interests are not just contingent on the participation of a range of stakeholders and the procedural setting established for these to exchange expectations, needs and demands as a matter of technical information. The output is highly contingent on participants playing on system-specific interests and their ability to articulate the interests of recipients while putting the latter at ease rather than generating defensive strategies to ward off the unknown (or change).

As the case studies demonstrate, addressing the interests of recipients was the most effective way for stimulating acceptance of change. As they also show, invoking a stabilising strategy of articulating the interests of the recipient to be preserved, enhanced acceptance of the change desired. It might also (as in the case of the Draft Norms and MSF) stifle action with authorities. As a result, those stakeholders who understood this strategic discursive game were in a better position to influence the output.

From this emerge three major theoretical implications for socio-legal theories on instrumental regulation, particularly those concerned with communication. Studies related to responsive or pro-active law and the 'nudging' approach, all of which build on communication, will be able to apply this to strengthen their contributions on how to advance uptake of sustainability-related norms. Given the role played by communication, these theoretical implications can also benefit other academic disciplines concerned with communication, particularly in regard to sustainability and organisational change.

The first theoretical implication to be drawn from this study is the confirmation of the assumption inherent in social autopoiesis theory of the importance of system-specific communication. The case studies have clearly demonstrated that communication that activates the system-specific rationality of the audience stands a better change of acceptance and therefore of stimulating internalisation of external needs and demands, compared to arguments that build on the logic of the transmitter. This is also a confirmation of reflexive law theory's assumption that, in principle, establishing physical or virtual forums bringing stakeholders together in a way that enables them to exchange needs and demands may cause irritation to be followed by perturbation and change. The discourse analysis demonstrates that the dynamics in interests-based communication build on the recognition of struggles for hegemony that are inherent in the process of fixing normative concepts whose meaning has not been finally settled, such as in the study here with CSR, business responsibilities for human rights, or in another context a future novel sustainability-related normative concept.

However, the study here, especially on the EU's MSF, highlights that simply bringing stakeholders representing diverse interests together does not necessarily generate irritation, perturbation or change. That only comes about when autopoiesis occurs. For that to occur, participants must have awareness, at a conscious or sub-conscious level, of the interests and rationality of others. They must also have the ability to distinguish between arguments that reflect their own interests, and those seeking to activate those of others. Previous studies show that efforts aiming at promoting organisational change through activating the rationality of recipients is sometimes reflexive-law type regulation by 'accident' rather than theory-based, and therefore not fully effective. Some of the critique of reflexive law as being lofty may be moderated by recognition of the need for an adequate knowledge of the theory-basis with organisers, and to ensure that participants have the necessary awareness of system-specific interests. Such insights are equally valuable for other academic approaches to stimulating self-regulation, as well as communication and organisation studies concerned with advancing CSR or sustainability in organisations.

The second major theoretical implication relates to the use of stabilising and de-stabilising arguments. Drawing on linguistic studies, this adds to autopoiesis by offering insights on how system-specific communication can be strengthened to achieve the desired effect. The analysis here shows that system-specific communication does not deliver change by default. As in the case of the Draft Norms or the EU's MSF, it may also stifle change, even with those who originated the process towards change. The analysis of the SRSG process shows that a strategic and targeted deployment of stabilising and de-stabilising arguments that play on the interests at stake can prepare the ground, so that subsequent more demanding arguments for normative change will be successful.

Finally, in terms of discursive construction of sustainability-related normative concepts and guidance, the study demonstrates that specificity of an argument matters, especially when it advances a proposal or new idea in a context of many competing views and proposals. This may appear as intuitive, like the idea of system-specific communication in order to stimulate change, but here too, reality tells a story of less of an intuitive issue. If it were intuitive for participants in multi-stakeholder processes aiming at developing norms of conduct, for example on business responsibilities for human rights, to deliver specific proposals that lend themselves to easy integration into other statements, more would do so. The analysis of the MSF as well as the SRSG process displays uneven patterns among participants in terms of being specific when addressing and seeking to promote normative change in a highly abstract field. Particularly, civil society organisations' influence was the greatest when they delivered proposals that would advance the objective through steps explained in practical and concrete terms, or when they voiced their concerns by reference to specific incidents. This was evidenced through the SRSG's adoption in his 2008 report of the proposal for a Global Ombudsman, and in his adoption of Access to Remedy as Pillar Three upon civil society organisations' highlighting the plights of victims (supported by observations and listening to victims of such plights).

Charged with the process set up under the mandate resolution, the SRSG was not himself part of a functional system in that function, but rather acted as a medium for the Commission on Human Rights and later the Human Rights Council. This meant that his interest was not a particular version of business responsibilities for human rights, but rather to deliver on his task under the mandate, and therefore to forge agreement among the involved functional sub-systems on as advanced a normative instrument on corporate responsibilities for human rights as he considered to be feasible.

Among the case studies, most can be defined as examples of reflexive law either due to their explicit organisation (the Global Compact Process, the EU's MSF and CSR Alliance) or due to the way in which they came to operate (the SRSG process). However, the theory of autopoiesis and the role played by system-specific rationality in arguments contributes also to understanding argumentative strategies that were decisive for the outcome of the process towards the Draft Norms, which was neither set up or effectively operated as reflexive law. The analysis in here has demonstrated that the use of autopoiesis offers a basis for understanding how an argument may promote acceptance of normative change with other participants in a regulatory process.

7.5 IMPLICATIONS FOR PRACTITIONERS

This study has considered argumentative strategies used by participants in five case studies. It analysed how particular types of arguments can promote or inhibit acceptance of normative change with other participants by either speaking to the interests and logic of those participants, or not doing so. This knowledge can help participants in future processes of developing, negotiating and agreeing on normative guidance in the broad sustainability field to develop convincing arguments and effective argumentative strategies. Regardless of whether such processes occur at the international, national or local level or aim at developing public, private or public-private (hybrid) norms, this knowledge is of benefit to civil society organisations, businesses, governments, intergovernmental organisations or other parties with an interest in sustainability.

In the early twenty-first century, neither TNCs nor SMEs function independently of political and economic developments surrounding them. Nor are they independent of social expectations. To many individuals ranging from consumers to investors and politicians, it does not seem to matter that formally, international human and labour rights law does not address companies directly as duty-bearers. Many individuals simply expect companies to respect those rights, regardless of their formal legal duties. Social expectations of business have generated increasing pressure on intergovernmental organisations to develop normative framework transforming social expectations into binding rules or at least non-binding formal guidance. Such processes are likely to continue. The analysis in here delivers three main points for civil society, regulators, policy-makers and others involved as participants in efforts to develop norms of conduct for sustainability:

(A) Pay attention to the core concerns of those with whom changed norms or actions are desired. The logic of social autopoiesis means that companies, which are part of the functional sub-system of the economy, will respond to communication that activates their system-specific rationality or code of profit/non-profit, risk (of loss)/no risk etc. The political sub-system will react to communication that activates its rationality of power/no power, and the legal sub-system to the rationality of legal/not legal or related distinctions, such as mandatory/voluntary.

Organisers of multi-stakeholder processes or other communicative processes for advancing norms on sustainability may consider the process as one in which needs or demands of stakeholders belonging to different social sub-systems work as 'irritants' on each other with the capacity to induce change or adaptation of norms. Interaction between stakeholders is not just a way of involving stakeholders, but also of making them consider and integrate societal demands or expectations (e.g., on inclusive recruitment practices or ensuring they do not employ child labour). It is also useful to consider that the process works through participants' juggling for discursive power in influencing the output of the regulatory process, so as to preserve or advance their own situation and benefits. That will often cause them to pay more attention to their own interests than those of others.

(B) Think about the possible effects of stabilising and de-stabilising arguments. Stabilising arguments can help ease concerns with other participants and therefore make them more willing to consider changes. But they may also have the unintended effect of freezing a current situation, for example, on the provision of public goods or human rights fulfilment being only tasks of governments. In the MSF such arguments came to underscore the human rights duties of authorities rather than the contributions of companies. Deployment of stabilising or de-stabilising strategies can be very strong in reinforcing an argument made in system-specific logic. It must be carefully considered, taking the particular audience, its interests and tasks into consideration.

(C) Be specific: give examples of how the impacts you seek to change are causing harm, or the benefits that they could have. When making proposals for change, offer specific examples for steps that are feasible and could be implemented to advance that change. The analysis of stakeholder statements in the SRSG and MSF processes and outputs indicates that concretely formulated recommendations from stakeholders were more strongly integrated than more open-ended or programmatic recommendations.

The emergence of the BHR regime demonstrates that by carefully combining these communicative approaches, organisations, groups and individuals may contribute to shaping new sustainability norms and promote their acceptance in a dynamic and complex context of competing and often conflicting interests.

Bibliography

Abbott, K. W. (2014) 'Strengthening the transnational regime complex for climate change', 3(1) Transnational Environmental Law pp. 1–32.

Adams, C. A. (2002) 'Internal organisational factors influencing corporate social and ethical reporting beyond current theorising', 15 Accounting Auditing & Accountability Journal pp. 223–50.

Aguilera, R. V., D. E. Rupp, C. A. Williams and J. Ganapathi (2007) 'Putting the S back in corporate social responsibility: A multilevel theory of social change in organisations', 32(2) Academy of Management Review pp. 836–63.

Andersen, N. Å. (2003) Discursive Analytical Strategies – Understanding Foucault, Koselleck, Laclau, Luhmann, Bristol: Policy Press.

Angel, D. P. and M. T. Rock (2004) 'Global standards and the environmental performance of industry', WPG 04-13, Oxford: Oxford University, School of Geography and the Environment, pp. 19–24.

Arthurs, H. (2008) 'Corporate self-regulation: political economy, state regulation and reflexive labour law'. In B. Bercusson and C. Estlund (eds) Regulating Labour in the Wake of Globalisation, Oxford and Portland, Oregon: Hart, pp. 19–35.

Arts, B. (2001/2003) 'The impact of environmental NGOs in international conventions'. In B. Arts, M. Noortmann and B. Reinalda (eds) Non-state Actors in International Relations, Hants: Ashgate, pp. 195–210.

Arts, B. (1998) The Political Influence of Global NGOs: Case Studies on the Climate and Biodiversity Conventions, Utrecht: International Books.

Ayres, I. and J. Braithwaite (1992) Responsive Regulation: Transcending the Deregulation Debate, New York: Oxford University Press.

Backer, L. C. (2014) 'The guiding principles of Business and Human Rights at a crossroads: The state, the enterprise, and the spectre of a treaty to bind them all', Coalition for Peace & Ethics, Working Paper, Vol. 7, No. 1 (July 2014).

Backer, L. C. (2006) 'Multinational corporations, transnational law: The United Nations' Norms on the Responsibilities of Transnational Corporations as a harbinger of Corporate Social Responsibility in international law', 37(Winter) Columbia Human Rights Law Review pp. 287–389.

Barnett, M. L. (2007) 'Stakeholder influence capacity and the variability of financial returns to corporate social responsibility', 32(3) Academy of Management Review pp. 794–816.
Bendell, J. (2005) 'Making business work for development: Rethinking corporate social responsibility', 54 Id21 insights April 2005.
Bendell, J. (2004) 'Barricades and boardrooms: A contemporary history of the corporate accountability movement'. Technology, Business and Society Programme Paper Number 13. United Nations Research Institute for Social Development.
Berger-Walliser, G. and P. Shrivastava (2015) 'Beyond compliance: Sustainable development, business, and pro-active law', 46(2) Georgia International Law Journal pp. 417–75.
Berle, A.A., Jr. (1931) 'Corporate powers as powers in trust', 44(7) Harvard Law Review pp. 1049–74.
Beveridge, F. and S. Nott (1998) 'A hard look at soft law'. In P. Craig and C. Harlow (eds) Lawmaking in the European Union, London: Kluwer Law International, pp. 285–309.
Bilchitz, D. (2013) 'A chasm between "is" and "ought"? A critique of the normative foundations of the SRSG's Framework and the Guiding Principles'. In S. Deva and D. Bilchitz (eds) Human Rights Obligations of Business, Cambridge University Press, pp. 107–37.
Blommaert, J. and C. Bulcaen (2000) 'Critical Discourse Analysis', 29 Annual Review of Anthropology pp. 447–66.
Blowfield, M. (2003) 'Corporate Social Responsibility in international development: an overview and critique', 10(3) Corporate Social Responsibility and Environmental Management pp. 115–28.
Blowfield, M. and J. G. Frynas (2005) 'Setting new agendas: critical perspectives on Corporate Social Responsibility in the developing world', 81(3) International Affairs pp. 499–513.
Bonnitcha, J. and R. McCorquedale (forthcoming) 'Is the concept of "due diligence" in the Guiding Principles coherent?', European Journal of International Law, available at SSRN http://papers.ssrn.com/sol3/papers.cfm?abstract_id=2208588.
Bowen, H. (1953) Social Responsibilities of the Businessman. New York: Harper & Row.
Boyle, A. (2006) 'Soft law in international law-making'. In M. D. Evans (ed.) International Law, 2nd ed., Oxford: Oxford University Press, pp. 141–58.
Brejning, J. (2012) Corporate Social Responsibility and the Welfare State: The Historical and Contemporary Role of CSR in the Mixed Economy of Welfare, Farnham: Ashgate.
Buhmann, K. (2018) Power, Procedure, Participation and Legitimacy In

Global Sustainability Norms: A Theory of Collaboratory Regulation, Routledge.

Buhmann, K. (forthcoming) 'Social transformation and normative change through CSR standards? China's engagement with international labour law in guidance for firms' social impact', NAVEIN REET: Nordic Journal of Law and Social Research.

Buhmann, K. (2016) 'Juridifying corporate social responsibility through public law: assessing coherence and inconsistencies against UN guidance on Business and Human Rights', 11(3) International and Comparative Corporate Law Journal pp. 194–228.

Buhmann, K. (2016) 'Public regulators and CSR: The "Social Licence to Operate" in recent United Nations instruments on Business and Human Rights and the juridification of CSR', 136(4) Journal of Business Ethics pp. 699–714.

Buhmann, K. (2015) 'Defying territorial limitations: Regulating business conduct extraterritorially through establishing obligations in EU law and national law'. In J. L. Cernic and T. Van Ho (eds) Human Rights and Business: Direct Corporate Accountability for Human Rights. The Hague: Wolf Legal Publishers, pp. 179–228.

Buhmann, K. (2014) Normative Discourses and Public-Private Regulatory Strategies for Construction of CSR Normativity: Towards a Method for Above-National Public-Private Regulation of Business Social Responsibilities. Copenhagen: Multivers.

Buhmann, K. (2013) 'Recognising a "Government case for CSR": Public policy objectives' impact on Global Governance through institutionalisation of CSR and business access to rule-making at intergovernmental level'. In S. D. Benedetto, and S. Marra (eds.) Legitimacy and Efficiency in Global Economic Governance, Cambridge Scholars Publishing, pp. 210–37.

Buhmann, K. (2013) 'The Danish CSR reporting requirement as reflexive law: Employing CSR as a modality to promote public policy', 24(2) European Business Law Review pp. 187–216.

Buhmann, K. (2012) 'Reflexive regulation of CSR: A case study of public-policy interests in EU public-private regulation of CSR', International and Comparative Corporate Law Journal, pp. 38–76.

Buhmann, K. (2012) 'The Development of the "UN Framework": A pragmatic process towards a pragmatic output'. In R. Mares (ed.) The UN Guiding Principles on Business and Human Rights: Foundations and Implementation. Martinus Nijhoff Publishers, pp. 85–105.

Buhmann, K. (2011) 'Integrating human rights in emerging regulation of Corporate Social Responsibility: The EU case', 7(2) International Journal of Law in Context pp. 139–79.

Buhmann, K. (2010) 'CSR-rapportering som refleksiv ret: Årsregnskabslovens CSR-redegørelseskrav som typeeksempel', 92(4) *Juristen* pp. 10413.

Buhmann, K. (2009) 'Regulating Corporate Social and Human Rights Responsibilities at the UN plane: Institutionalising new forms of law and law-making approaches?', 7891) *Nordic Journal of International Law* pp. 1–52.

Buhmann, K. (2007) Vestlig dobbeltmoral i Kina, Politiken, 7 July 2007.

Buhmann, K. (2006) 'Corporate social responsibility: What role for law? Some aspects of law and CSR', 6(2) Corporate Governance: The International Journal of Business in Society pp. 188–202.

Buhmann, K. and I. Nathan (2013) 'Plentiful forests, happy people? The EU's FLEGT approach and its impact on human rights and private forestry sustainability schemes', 4(2) Nordic Environmental Law Journal pp. 53–82.

Buhmann, K., L. Roseberry and M. Morsing (2011) 'Introduction'. In K. Buhmann, L. Roseberry and M. Morsing (eds) Corporate Social and Human Rights Responsibilities: Global Legal and Management Perspectives, London: Palgrave Macmillan, pp. 1–22.

Burke, L. and J. M. Logsdon (1996) 'How Corporate Social Responsibility pays off', 29(4) Long Range Planning pp. 495–502.

Cafaggi, F. and A. Renna (2012) 'Public and private regulation: Mapping the labyrinth'. CEPS Working Document No. 370, October 2012.

Calliari, E., A. D'Aprile and M. Davide (2016) 'Paris Agreement: Strengths and weaknesses behind a diplomatic success', Review of Environment, Energy and Economics, May 2016.

Carroll, A. B. (1999) 'Corporate Social Responsibility: Evolution of a definitional construct', 39(3) Business & Society Review pp. 264–95.

Carroll, A. B. (1991) 'The Pyramid of Corporate Social Responsibility: Toward the moral management of organizational stakeholder', Business Horizons, July/August, pp. 39–48.

Carroll, A. B. (1979) 'A three-dimensional conceptual model of corporate performance', 4(4) The Academy of Management Review pp. 497–505.

Casey, R. (2006) Meaningful Change: Raising the Bar in the Supply Chain Workplace Standards, Friedrich Ebert Stiftung & Harvard University John F. Kennedy School of Government.

Cassese, A. (2005) International Law, Oxford: Oxford University Press.

Chandler, G. (2008) 'Business and human rights – A personal Account from the front line', Ethical Corporation, 11 February 2008.

Charney, J. L. (2000) 'Commentary: Compliance with international soft law'. In D. Shelton (ed.) Commitment and Compliance: The Role of

Non-binding Norms in the International Legal System, Oxford: Oxford University Press, pp. 115–18.

Charney, J. I. (1983) 'Transnational corporations and developing public international law', 32 Duke Law Journal pp. 748–88.

Charnovitz, S. (1997) 'Two centuries of participation: NGOs and international governance', 18(2) Michigan Journal of International Law pp. 183–286.

Chilton, P. and C. Schäffner (1997) 'Discourse and politics'. In T. A. van Dijk (ed.) Discourse as Social Interaction, London: Sage Publications, pp. 206–30.

Chinkin, C. (2000) 'Normative development in the international legal system'. In D. Shelton (ed.). Commitment and Compliance: The Role of Non-Binding Norms in The International Legal System, Oxford: Oxford University Press, pp. 21–42.

Chouliaraki, L. (2001) 'Refleksivitet og senmoderne identitet: et studie i mediediskurs'. In T. B. Dyrberg, A. D. Hansen and J. Torfing (eds) Diskursteorien på arbejde, Frederiksberg: Roskilde Universitetsforlag, pp. 247–78.

Clapham, A. (2006) Human Rights Obligations of Non-State Actors, New York: Oxford University Press.

Collin, F. (2004) Konstruktivisme, Frederiksberg: Samfundslitteratur – Roskilde Universitetsforlag.

Conley, J. M. and C. A. Williams (2005) 'Engage, embed and embellish: Theory versus practice in the Corporate Social Responsibility Movement', 31(1) Journal of Corporation Law pp. 1–38.

Crane, A., D. Matten and L. J. Spence (2008) Corporate Social Responsibility, New York: Routledge.

Crane, A., A. McWilliams, D. Matten, J. Moon and D. Siegel (2008) 'The Corporate Social Responsibility agenda'. In A. Crane, A. McWilliams, D. Matten, J. Moon and D. Siegel (eds.) The Oxford Handbook of Corporate Social Responsibility, Oxford: Oxford University Press, pp. 3–18.

Cuganesan, S., C. Boedker and J. Guthrie (2007) 'Enrolling discourse consumers to affect material intellectual capital practice', 20(6) Accounting, Auditing and Accountability Journal pp. 883–911.

Dalberg-Larsen, J. (2008) Selvregulering og miljøret. In Miljøretlige emner: Festskrift til Ellen Margrethe Basse, Copenhagen: Jurist- og Økonomforbundets Forlag, pp. 297–313.

Dalberg-Larsen, J. (2001) Pragmatisk retsteori, Copenhagen: Jurist- og Økonomforbundets Forlag.

Dalberg-Larsen, J. (1991) Ret, styring og selvforvaltning. Aarhus: Juridisk Bogformidling.

Danwatch (2016), 'Maersk scraps ships at dangerous shipyards in India', 13 October 2016, retrieved from https://www.danwatch.dk/en/nyhed/maersk-scraps-ships-at-dangerous-shipyards-in-india/ (9 January 2017).

David, G. F. M. V. N. Whitman and M. N. Zald (2006) 'The responsibility paradox: Multinational firms and global Corporate Social Responsibility', University of Michigan, Michigan Ross School of Business Working Paper Series, Working Paper No. 1031, April 2006.

Davis, K. (1960) 'Can business afford to ignore social responsibilities?', 2(3) California Management Review, Spring, pp. 70–76.

De Bakker, F. G. A., P. Groenewegen and F. Den Hond (2005) 'A bibliometric analysis of 30 years of research and theory on Corporate Social Responsibility and Corporate Social Performance', 44(3) Business and Society pp. 283–316.

De Schutter, O. (2013) 'Foreword'. In S. Deva and D. Bilchitz (eds) *Human Rights Obligations of Business: Beyond the Corporate Responsibility to Respect?*, Cambridge University Press, pp. xv–xxii.

De Schutter, O. (2006) *Extraterritorial Jurisdiction as a Tool for improving the Human Rights Accountability of Transnational Corporations*, Belgium: Louvain, December 2006.

De Schutter, O. (2006) 'The challenge of imposing human rights norms on corporate actors'. In O. De Schutter (ed.) *Transnational Corporations and Human Rights*, Oxford: Hart, pp. 1–40.

Deakin, S. and R. Hobbs (2007) 'False dawn for CSR? Shifts in regulatory policy and the response of the corporate and financial sectors in Britain', 15(1) *Corporate Governance* pp. 68–76.

Deakin, S. (2005) 'Social rights in a globalised economy'. In P. Alston (ed.) *Labour Rights as Human Rights*, New York: Oxford University Press, pp. 25–60.

Deitelhoff, N. (2009) 'The discursive process of legalization: Charting islands of persuasion in the ICC case', 63(Winter) *International Organization* pp. 33–65.

Deva, S. (2013) 'Treating human rights lightly: a critique of the consensus rhetoric and the language employed by the Guiding Principles'. In S. Deva and D. Bilchitz (eds) *Human Rights Obligations of Business: Beyond the Corporate Responsibility to Respect?*, Cambridge University Press, pp. 78–104.

Deva, S. (2011) '"Protect, respect and remedy": a critique of the SRSG's framework for business and human rights.' In K. Buhmann, L. Roseberry, and M. Morsing (eds) *Corporate Social and Human Rights Responsibilities: Global Legal and Management Perspectives*, Houndmills, Basingstoke, Hampshire New York: Palgrave Macmillan, pp. 108–28.

Devinney, T. (2009) 'Is the socially responsible corporate a myth? The good, the bad, and the ugly of Corporate Social Responsibility', *Academy of Management Perspectives*, May 2009, pp. 44–56.

Ditlevsen, M. G., J. Engberg, P. Kastberg and M. Nielsen (2007) *Sprog på arbejde: Kommunikation i faglige tekster*. Frederiksberg: Forlaget Samfundslitteratur.

Dodd, E. M. Jr. (1932) 'For whom are corporate managers trustees?', 45(7) *Harvard Law Review*, pp. 1145–63.

Elkington, J. (1998) *Cannibals with Forks: The Triple Bottom Line of 21st Century Business*, Gabriola Island BC: New Society Publishers.

Epstein, E. M. (1998) 'Business ethics and Corporate Social Policy', 37(1) *Business & Society Review* pp. 7–39.

Epstein, E. M. (1989) 'Business ethics, corporate good citizenship and the corporate social policy process: A view from the United States', 8(8) *Journal of Business Ethics* pp. 583–95.

Fairbrass, J. (2011) 'Exploring corporate social responsibility policy in the European Union: A discursive institutionalist analysis' 49(5) *JCMS: Journal of Common Market Studies* pp. 949–70.

Fairclough, N. (2003) *Analysing Discourse: Textual Analysis for Social Research*. New York: Routledge.

Fairclough, N. (2001) 'Critical discourse analysis as a method in social scientific research'. In R. Wodak and M. Meyer (eds) *Methods of Critical Discourse Analysis*. London: Sage Publications, pp. 121–38.

Fairclough, N. (1995) *Critical Discourse Analysis: The Critical Study of Language*, London [u.a.] Longman.

Fairclough, N. (1992) *Discourse and Social Change,* Cambridge: Polity Press.

Fairclough, N. and R. Wodak (1997) 'Critical discourse analysis'. In van T. A. Dijk (ed.) *Discourse as Social Interaction*, London: Sage, pp. 285–312.

Farmer, L. and G. Teubner (1994) 'Ecological self-organization'. In G. Teubner, L. Farmer and D. Murphy (eds) *Environmental Law and Ecological Responsibility: The Concept And Practice of Ecological Self-Organisation*, Chichester: John Wiley & Sons, pp. 3–13.

Fox, T. (2004) 'Corporate Social Responsibility and development: In search of an agenda', 47(3) *Development* pp. 29–36.

Franck, T. M. (1990) *The Power of Legitimacy Among Nations,* Oxford: Oxford University Press.

Friedmann, W. (1964) *The Changing Structure of International Law,* London: Stevens & Sons.

GES Investment Services (2005) *Nordic Sustainability Index II*, Copenhagen: Nordic Council of Ministers: TemaNord 2005.

Gjølberg, M. (2010) 'Varieties of corporate social responsibility (CSR): CSR meets the "Nordic Model"', 4 *Regulation & Governance* pp. 203–29.

Gjølberg, M. (2009) 'The origin of corporate social responsibility: Global forces or national legacies?', 4(4) *Socio-Economic Review* pp. 605–37.

Glinski, C. (2008) 'Bridging the gap: The legal potential of private regulation'. In O. Dilling, M. Herberg and G. Winter (eds) *Responsible Business: Self-governance and Law In Transnational Economic Transactions*, Oxford and Portland Oregon: Hart, pp. 41–66.

Gond, J.-P., N. Kang and J. Moon (2011) 'The government of self-regulation: on the comparative dynamics of corporate social responsibility', 40(4) *Economy and Society* pp. 640–71.

Goyder, G. (1961) *The Responsible Company*, Oxford: Blackwell.

Habermas, J. (1996) *Between Facts and Norms: Contributions to a Discourse Theory of Law and Democracy*, translated by William Rehg. Cambridge: Polity Press/Blackwell, translated from (1992) *Faktizität und Geltung*, Frankfurt am Main: Suhrkamp.

Habermas, J. (1981) *Theorie des kommunikatives Handelns*, Frankfurt am Main: Suhrkamp.

Hajer, M. A. (1995) The Politics of Environmental Discourse: Ecological Modernization and the Policy Process, New York: Clarendon Press – Oxford.

Halter, M. and M. Arruda (2009) 'Inverting the pyramid of values? Trends in less-developed countries', 90(Supp. 3) Journal of Business Ethics pp. 267–75.

Hannum, H. (1995) 'Human Rights'. In O. Schachter and C.C. Joyner (eds) United Nations Legal Order, Vol I. Cambridge: Cambridge University Press, pp. 319–48.

Hansen, A. D. (2001) 'Lokaludvalg som konstruktion af lokale politiske fællesskaber'. In T. B. Dyrberg, A. D. Hansen and J. Torfing (eds) Diskursteorien på arbejde, Frederiksberg: Roskilde Universitetsforlag, pp. 131–60.

Hart, H. L. A. (1961) The Concept of Laws, Oxford: Oxford University Press.

Hasenclever, A., P. Mayer and V. Rittberger (1997) Theories of International Regimes, Cambridge: Cambridge University Press.

Haufler, V. (2001) A Public Role for the Private Sector: Industry Self-regulation in A Global Economy, Washington D.C.: Carnegie Endowment for International Peace.

Hearne, B. (2004) 'Proposed UN Norms on human rights: Is business opposition justified?', Ethical Corporation, 22 March 2004.

Hearne, B. (2004) 'Analysis: Proposed UN Norms on human rights shelved in favor of more study', Ethical Corporation, 3 May 2004.

Henkin, L. (1999) 'The Universal Declaration at 50 and the challenge of global markets', 25 Brooklyn Journal of International Law pp. 17–25.

Hepker, J. and A. Newton (eds) (2004) 'The Business and Human Rights Management Report: A study of eight companies and their approaches to human rights policy and management system development'. Ethical Corporation, November.

Héritier, A. and D. Lehmkuhl (2008) 'The shadow of hierarchy and new modes of governance: Sectoral governance and democratic government', 28(1) Journal of Public Policy pp. 1–17.

Hernandez, M. (2004) 'Institutionalising global standards of responsible corporate citizenship: Assessing the role of the UN Global Compact'. In M. McIntosh, S. Waddock and G. Kell (eds) Learning to Talk: Corporate Citizenship and the Development of the UN Global Compact, Sheffield: Greenleaf Publishing, pp. 114–28.

Hess, D. (1999) 'Social Reporting: A reflexive law approach to corporate social responsiveness', 25(1) Journal of Corporation Law pp. 41–84.

Hess, D. and D. E. Warren (2008) 'The meaning and meaningfulness of corporate social initiatives', 113(2) Business and Society Review pp. 163–97.

Hillemans, C. F. (2003) 'UN Norms on the responsibilities of transnational corporations and other business enterprises with regard to human rights', 4(10) German Law Journal pp.1065–80.

Holdgaard, R. (2005) 'Classic external relations law of the European Community: doctrines and discourses'. Ph.D. thesis, 1 edn, Museum Tuscul

Hopkins, M. (2006) 'Commentary: What is Corporate Social Responsibility all about?', 6 Journal of Public Affairs August–November, pp. 298–306.

Jäger, S. (2001) 'Discourse and knowledge: theoretical and methodological aspects of a critical discourse and dispositive analysis'. In R. Wodak, and M. Meyer (eds) Methods of Critical Discourse Analysis, London: Sage Publications, pp. 32–62.

Jägers, N. (2002) Corporate Human Rights Obligations: In Search of Accountability. Antwerp: Intersentia.

Jeppesen, S. and P. Lund-Thomsen (2010) 'Introduction', 93(Supp. 2) Journal of Business Ethics pp. 139–42.

Jørgensen, M. W. and L. Phillips (1999) Diskursanalyse som teori og metode. Frederiksberg: Samfundslitteratur/Roskilde University Press.

Kaysen, C. (1957) 'The social significance of the modern corporation', 47(2) American Economic Review (Papers and proceedings) pp. 311–19.

Kell, G. and D. Levin (2002) The evolution of the Global Compact Network: an historic experiment in learning and action, paper presented at The Academy of Management Annual Conference "Building Effective

Networks", Denver, August 11–14, 2002, http://www.unglobalcompact.org/docs/news_events/9.5/denver.pdf (last accessed 22 January 2017).

Kennedy, D. (1987) 'The sources of international law', 2(1) American University Journal of Law & Policy, pp. 1–96.

Khalifa, R., N. Sharma, C. Humphrey and K. Robson (2007) 'Discourse and audit change: Transformations in methodology in the professional audit field', 20(6) Accounting, Auditing and Accountability Journal pp. 825–54.

Kimathi, W. (2010) 'Corporate Social Responsibility in Africa: A fig leaf or a new development path worth pursuing?'. In K. Buhmann, L. Roseberry and M. Morsing (eds) Corporate Social and Human Rights Responsibilities: Global Legal and Management Perspectives, London: Palgrave Macmillan, pp. 129–43.

Kinderman, D. (2016) 'Time for a reality check: is business willing to support a smart mix of complementary regulation in private governance?', 35(1) Policy and Society pp. 29–41.

Kinderman, D. (2013) 'Corporate social responsibility in the EU, 1993–2013: Institutional ambiguity, economic crises, business legitimacy and bureaucratic politics', 51(4) JCMS: Journal of Common Market Studies pp. 701–20.

King, M. (1996) 'Self-producing systems: Implications and applications of autopoiesis by John Mingers (review article)', 23(4) Journal of Law and Society pp. 601–5.

Kinley, D. and R. Chambers (2006) 'The UN Human Rights Norms for corporations: The private implications of public international law', 6(3) Human Rights Law Review pp. 447–97.

Kinley, D. and J. Nolan (2008) 'Trading and aiding human rights in the global economy' 7(4) Nordic Journal of Human Rights Law pp. 353–77.

Kinley, D., J. Nolan and N. Zerial (2007) 'The politics of corporate social responsibility: Reflections on the United Nations Human Rights Norms for Corporations', 25(1) Company and Securities Law Journal pp. 30–43.

Koh, H. K. (2002) 'Opening remarks: Transnational legal process illuminated'. In M. Likosky (ed.) Transnational Legal Processes: Globalisation and Power Disparities, Colchester: Butterworths, pp. 327–32.

Koh, H. K. (1997) 'Why do nations obey international law? (Review essay)' 106(8) The Yale Law Journal pp. 2599–659.

Kolk, A. (2001/2003) 'Multinational enterprises and international climate policy'. In B. Arts, M. Noortmann and B. Reinalda (eds) Non-state actors in international relations, Hants: Ashgate, pp. 211–5.

Knox, J. H. (2008) 'Horizontal human rights law', 102 American Journal of International Law, pp. 1–47.

Krasner, S. D. (1982) 'Structural causes and regime consequences: regime as intervening variables', 36(2) *International Organization* pp. 185–205.

Laclau, E. and C. Mouffe (1985) *Hegemony and Socialist Strategy: Towards a Radical Democratic Politics*, London: Verso.

Lambooy, T. (2010) *Corporate Social Responsibility: Legal and Semi-Legal Frameworks Supporting CSR – Developments 2000–2010 and Case Studies*, Groningen: Groningen University.

Lansing, P. and A. Rosaria (1991) 'An analysis of the United Nations proposed Code of Conduct for Transnational Corporations', 14(4) *World Competition* pp. 35–50.

Lobel, O. (2005) 'The Renew Deal: The fall of regulation and the rise of governance in contemporary legal thought', 89 *Minnesota Law Review* pp. 7–27.

Luhmann, N. (1992) 'The coding of the legal system'. In G. Teubner and A. Febbrajo (eds) *European Yearbook in the Sociology of Law: State, law and economy as autopoietic systems: Regulation and autonomy in a new perspective*, Milano: Guiffre Publishers, pp. 146–86.

Luhmann, N. (1986) 'The self-reproduction of law and its limits'. In G. Teubner (ed.) *Dilemmas of Law in the Welfare State*, Berlin and New York: Walter de Gruyter, pp. 111–27.

Margolis, J. D. and J. P. Walsh (2003) 'Misery loves companies: Rethinking social initiatives by companies', 48(2) *Administrative Science Quarterly* pp. 268–305.

Margolis, J. D. and J. P. Walsh (2001) *People and Profits? – the Search for a Link Between a Company's Social and Financial Performance*, Mahwah, New Jersey: Erlbaum.

Matten, D. and J. Moon (2008) '"Implicit" and "Explicit" CSR: A conceptual framework for a comparative understanding of corporate social responsibility', 33(2) *Academy of Management Review* pp. 404–24.

Maturana, H. (1981) 'Autopoiesis'. In M. Zeleny (ed.) *Autopoiesis: A Theory of Living Organizations*, New York: North Holland.

Mayer, A. E. (2009) 'Human rights as a dimension of CSR: The blurred lines between legal and non-legal categories', 88 *Journal of Business Ethics* pp. 561–77.

McBarnet, D. (2008) 'Corporate social responsibility beyond law, through law, for law: the new corporate accountability'. In D. McBarnet, A. Voiculescu and T. Campbell (eds) *The New Corporate Accountability: Corporate Social Responsibility and the Law*, Cambridge: Cambridge University Press, pp. 9–58.

McIntosh, M., S. Waddock and G. Kell (eds.) (2004) *Learning to talk: Corporate citizenship and the development of the UN Global Compact*, Sheffield, Greenleaf Publishing.

Melish, T. J. and E. Meidinger (2012) 'Protect, Respect, Remedy and *Participate*: "New Governance" lessons for the Ruggie Framework'. In M. Radu (ed.) *The UN Guiding Principles on Business and Human Rights: Foundations and Implementation*, Martinus Nijhoff Publishers, pp. 303–36.

Meyer, M. (2001) 'Between theory, method, and politics: positioning of the approaches to CDA'. In R. Wodak, and M. Meyer (eds) *Methods of Critical Discourse Analysis*, London: Sage, pp. 14–31.

Midttun, A. (2008) 'Partnered governance: aligning Corporate Responsibility and public policy in the global economy', 8(4) Corporate Governance pp. 406–18.

Moon, J. and D. Vogel (2008) 'Corporate Social Responsibility, government, and civil society'. In A. Crane, A. McWilliams, D. Matten, J. Moon and D. S. Siegel (eds) The Oxford Handbook of Corporate Social Responsibility, Oxford: Oxford University Press, pp. 302–32.

Mutua, M. (2007) 'Standard setting in human rights: critique and prognosis', 29(3) Human Rights Quarterly pp. 547–630.

Neves, M. (2001) 'From the autopoiesis to the allopoiesis of law', 28(2) Journal of Law and Society pp. 242–64.

Newell, P. and J. G. Frynas (2007) 'Beyond CSR? Business, poverty and social justice: An introduction', 28(4) Third World Quarterly pp. 669–81.

Nolan, J. (2005) 'The United Nation's compact with business: hindering or helping the protection of human rights?' 24(2) University of Queensland Law Journal pp. 445–66.

Nonet, P. and P. Selznick (1978) Law and Society in Transition: Toward Responsive Law, New York: Harper/Colophon.

O'Brien, C. M. (2011) 'The UN Special Representative on Business and Human Rights: Re-embedding or dis-embedding transnational markets?' In C. Joerges, and J. Falke (eds) Karl Polanyi, Globalisation and the Potential of Law in Transnational Markets, Oxford: Hart, pp. 323–57.

O'Reilly, P. and S. Tickell (1999) 'TNCs and social issues in the developing world'. In M. K. Addo (ed.) Human Rights Standards and the Responsibility of Transnational Corporations, The Hague: Kluwer Law International, pp. 273–87.

Ochoa, C. (2008) 'The 2008 Ruggie Report: A framework for business and human rights', 12(12) ASIL Insight 18 June 2008.

Orlitzky, M., F. L. Schmidt and S. L. Rynes (2003) 'Corporate social and financial performance: A meta-analysis', 24(3) Organization Studies pp. 403–41.

Orts, E. W. (1995) 'A reflexive model of environmental regulation', 5(4) Business Ethics Quarterly pp. 779–94.

Orts, E. W. (1995) 'Reflexive environmental law', 89(4) Northwestern Law Review pp. 1229–340.
Parker, C. and J. Howe (2012) 'Ruggie's diplomatic project and its missing regulatory infrastructure.' In R. Mares (ed.) The UN Guiding Principles on Business and Human Rights: Foundations and Implementation, The Hague: Martinus Nijhoff Publishers, pp. 273–301.
Porter, M. and M. Kramer (2011) 'Creating Shared Value', Harvard Business Review, January/February 2011.
Prieto-Carron, M., P. Lund-Thomsen, A. Chan, A. Muro and C. Bhushan (2006) 'Critical perspectives on CSR and development: What we know, what we don't know, and what we need to know', 82(5) International Affairs pp. 977–89.
Ramasatry, A. (2015) 'Corporate Social Responsibility versus Business and Human Rights: Bridging the gap between responsibility and accountability', 14 Journal of Human Rights pp. 137–59.
Redmond, P. (2003) Transnational enterprise and human rights: Options for standard setting and compliance. 37 Int'l Lawyer, pp. 69–102.
Rees, C. (2011) Piloting Principles for Effective Company-Stakeholder Grievance Mechanisms: A Report of Lessons Learned, CSR Initiatives, Harvard Kennedy School, Cambridge.
Regil, A. J. D. (2008) 'Business and human rights: Upholding the market's social Darwinism.' In Human Rights and Sustainable Human Development, The Jus Semper Global Alliance, October 2008.
Rehbinder, E. (1992) 'Reflexive law and practice: The corporate officer for environmental protection as an example', European Yearbook in the Sociology of Law: State, law and economy as autopoietic systems: Regulation and autonomy in a new perspective, Milano: Guiffre Publisher, pp. 579–608.
Reinalda, B. (2001) 'Private in form, public in purpose: NGOs in international relations theory'. In B. Arts, M. Noortmann and B. Reinalda (eds) Non-state Actors in International Relations, Hants: Ashgate, pp. 11–40.
Reinalda, B., B. Arts and M. Noortmann (2001/2003) 'Non-state actors in international relations: Do they matter?'. In B. Arts, M. Noortmann and B. Reinalda (eds) Non-state Actors in International Relations, Hants: Ashgate, pp: 1–8.
Rendtorff, J. D. (2007) Virksomhedsetik En grundbog i organisation og ansvar, Frederiksberg: Forlaget Samfundslitteratur.
Reuters (2016) 'Maersk to scrap ships at certain Alang sites, NGO dismayed', 12 February 2016, http://in.reuters.com/article/maersk-shipping-alang-idINKCN0VL1VZ (last accessed 9 January 2017).
Roepstorff, A. (2010) CSR: Virksomheders sociale ansvar som begreb og praksis, Copenhagen: Hans Reitzels Forlag.

Rogowski, R. (2001) 'The concept of reflexive labour law: Its theoretical background and possible applications'. In J. Priban and D. Nelken (eds) Law's New Boundaries: The Consequences of Legal Autopoiesis, Aldershot: Ashgate, pp. 179–96.

Rogowski, R. (1994) 'Industrial relations, labour conflict resolution and reflexive labour law'. In R. Rogowski and T. Wilthagen (eds) Reflexive Labour Law: Studies in industrial relations and employment regulation, Deventer and Boston: Kluwer Law and Taxation Publishers, pp. 53–93.

Rogowski, R. and T. Wilthagen (eds) (1994) Reflexive Labour Law: Studies in Industrial Relations and Employment Regulation, Deventer and Boston: Kluwer Law and Taxation Publishers.

Rostgaard, M. (2000) 'Patriarkalisme og industriledelse i Danmark ca. 1880–1910'. In M. Rostgaard, and M. F. Wagner (eds) Lederskab i dansk industri og samfund 1880–1960, Aalborg: Aalborg University Press.

Rottleuthner, H. (1988) 'Biological metaphors in legal thought'. In G. Teubner (ed.) Autopoietic Law: A New Approach to Law and Society, Berlin and New York: Walter de Gruyter, pp. 97–127.

Ruggie, J. G. (2016) 'Hierarchy or ecosystem? Regulating human rights risks of Multinational Enterprises.' Forthcoming in Rodriguez-Garavito, C. (ed.) Business and Human Rights: beyond the end of the beginning, available at SSRN: http://ssrn.com/abstract=2776690 (accessed 29 September 2016).

Ruggie, J. G. (2013) Just Business: Multinational Corporations and Human Rights. New York: W. W. Norton & Company.

Ruggie, J. G. (2004) 'Reconstituting the global public domain – issues, actors and practices', 10(4) European Journal of International Relations pp. 499–531.

Ruggie, J. G. (2002) The theory and practice of learning networks. Reprinted in M. McIntosh, S. Waddock and G. Kell (eds.) Learning to Talk: Corporate Citizenship and the Development of the UN Global Compact, Sheffield, Greenleaf Publishing, pp. 32–41.

Sagafi-Nejad, T., in collaboration with J. H. Dunning (2008) The UN and Transnational Corporations: From Code of Conduct to the Global Compact, Indiana University Press.

Sand, I.-J. (1996) Styring av kompleksitet: Rettslige former for statlig rammestyring og desentralisert statsforvaltning, Bergen: Fagbokforlaget Vigmostad & Bjørke.

Sanders, A., (2015) 'The impact of the "Ruggie Framework" and the "United Nations Guiding Principles on Business and Human Rights" on transnational human rights litigation'. In J. Martin and K. E. Bravo (eds) The Business and Human Rights Landscape: Moving Forward, Looking Back. Cambridge: Cambridge University Press, pp. 288–315.

Scherer, A. G. and G. Palazzo (2011) 'The new political role of business in a globalized world – a review of a new perspective on CSR and its implications for the firm, governance, and democracy', 48(4) Journal of Management Studies pp. 899–931.

Scherer, A. G., A. Rasche, G. Palazzo and A. Spicer (2016) 'Managing for political corporate social responsibility: new challenges and directions for PCSR 2.0', 53(3) Journal of Management Studies pp. 273–98.

Scheuerman, W. E. (2001) 'Reflexive law and the challenges of globalization', 9(1) The Journal of Political Philosophy pp. 81–102.

Schoenberger, K. (2002) Levi's Children: Coming to Terms with Human Rights in The Global Market Place, New York: Atlantic Monthly Press.

Schwartz, M. S. and A. B. Carroll (2003) 'Corporate Social Responsibility: A three-domain approach', 13(4) Business Ethics Quarterly pp. 503–30.

Scott, C. D., F. Cafaggi and L. Senden (2011) 'The conceptual and constitutional challenge of transnational private regulation', 38(1) Journal of Law and Society pp. 1–19.

Selznick, P. (1992) The Moral Community: Social Theory and the Promise of Community, Berkeley: The University of California Press.

Seppala, N. (2009) 'Business and the International Human Rights Regime: A comparison of UN initiatives', 87 Journal of Business Ethics pp. 401–17.

Servais, J.-M. (2014) International Labour Law, Wolters Kluwer.

Shelton, D. L. (2014) Advanced Introduction to International Human Rights Law. Cheltenham, UK, Northampton MA, USA: Edward Elgar.

Shelton, D. (2006) International law and 'Relative Normativity'. In M. D. Evans (ed.) International Law, 2nd ed., Oxford: Oxford University Press, pp. 159–85.

Shelton, D. (2000) 'Introduction'. In D. Shelton (ed.) Commitment and Compliance: The Role of Non-binding Norms in the International Legal System, Oxford: Oxford University Press, pp. 1–18.

Sjöström, E. (2004) Investment Stewardship: Actors and Methods for Socially and Environmentally Responsible Investments, Copenhagen: The Nordic Partnership.

Snyder, F. (1994) 'Soft law and institutional practice in the European Community'. In S. D. Martin (ed.) The Construction of Europe: Essays in Honour of Emile Noël, Dordrecht: Kluwer, pp. 197–225.

Spar, D. L. and L. T. La Mure, (2003) 'The power of activism: assessing the impact of NGOs on global business', 45(3) California Management Review pp. 78–101.

Spence, C. (2007) 'Social and environmental reporting and hegemonic discourse', 20(6) Accounting, Auditing & Accountability Journal pp.855–82.

Staffe, M. -L. (2008) Retsretorik, Copenhagen: Thomson Reuters.

Szasz, P.C. (1995) 'General law-making processes'. In O. Schachter and C. C. Joyner (eds) United Nations Legal Order, Vol I., Cambridge: University Press, pp. 35–108.

Sørensen, E. (2001) 'Skolebestyrelser – i klemme mellem konkurrerende decentraliseringsstrategier'. In T. B. Dyrberg, A. D. Hansen and J. Torfing (eds) Diskursteorien på arbejde, Frederiksberg: Roskilde Universitetsforlag, pp. 105–30.

Tamanaha, B. Z. (1997) Realistic Socio-Legal Theory: Pragmatism and a Social Theory of Law, Oxford: Oxford University Press.

Teubner, G. (1993) Law as an Autopoietic System, Oxford: Blackwell.

Teubner, G. (1992) Social order from legislative noise, European Yearbook in the Sociology of Law: State, law and economy as autopoietic systems: Regulation and autonomy in a new perspective, Milano: Guiffre Publisher, pp. 609–49.

Teubner, G. (1988) 'Introduction to Autopoietic law'. In G. Teubner, (ed.) Autopoietic law: A New Approach to Law and Society, Berlin & New York: Walter de Gruyter, pp. 1–11.

Teubner, G. (1986) 'Introduction'. In G. Teubner (ed.) Dilemmas of Law in the Welfare State, Walter de Gruyter: Berlin and New York, pp. 3–11.

Teubner, G. (1986) 'After legal instrumentalism?'. In G. Teubner (ed.) Dilemmas of Law in the Welfare State, Walter de Gruyter: Berlin and New York, pp. 299–325.

Teubner, G. (ed.) (1986) Dilemmas of Law in the Welfare State, Berlin and New York: Walter de Gruyter.

Teubner, G. (1984) 'Autopoiesis in law and society: a rejoinder to Blankenburg', 18(2) Law and Society Review pp. 291–301.

Teubner, G. (1983) 'Substantive and reflective elements in modern law', 17(2) Law and Society Review pp. 239–85.

Teubner, G., R. Nobles and D. Schiff (2005) 'The autonomy of law: An introduction to legal autopoiesis'. In J. Penner, D. Schiff and R. Nobles (eds) Jurisprudence, New York: Oxford University Press, pp. 897–954.

Thiele, B. and M. Gomez (2006) 'Highlights of the fifty-eighth session of the United Nations Sub-Commission on the Promotion and Protection of Human Rights', 24(4) Netherlands Quarterly of Human Rights pp. 703–14.

Trubek, D. M. (2004) 'Human rights, transnational private law litigation and corporate accountability'. In C. Joerges, I.-J. Sand and G. Teubner (eds) Transnational Governance and Constitutionalism, Oxford: Hart, pp. 321–5.

Trubek, D. M. and L. G. Trubek (2006) 'New governance and legal regulation: complementarity, rivalry or transformation', 13 *Columbia Journal of European Law* pp. 1–26.

United Nations Intellectual History Project (2009) *The UN and Transnational Corporations*, Ralph Bunche Institute for International Studies, Briefing Note No. 17, July 2009.

Vallentin, S. (2002) *Pensionsinvesteringer, etik og offentlighed – en systemteoretisk analyse af offentlig meningsdannelse,* Copenhagen: Samfundslitteratur.

Van Dijk, T. A. (2001) 'Multidisciplinary CDA: a plea for diversity'. In R. Wodak and M. Meyer (eds) *Methods of Critical Discourse Analysis*, London: Sage, pp. 95–119.

Van Dijk, T. A. (1997) 'Discourse as interaction in society'. In T. A. van Dijk (ed.) *Discourse as Social Interaction*, London: Sage Publications, pp. 1–37.

Vogel, D. J. (2005) 'Is there a market for virtue? The business case for Corporate Social Responsibility', 47(4) *California Management Review* pp. 19–45.

Von Eyben, B. (2004) *Juridisk Ordbog*, Copenhagen: Thomson Gad Jura.

Warhurst, A. and K. Cooper in association with Amnesty International (2004) *The 'UN Human Rights Norms for Business'*, Maplecroft: United Kingdom, 26 July 2004.

Webb, T. (2005) 'Comment: Lobby groups and NGOs should rethink their approach to the UN Norms', *Ethical Corporation*, 23 April 2004.

Webb, T. (2004) Analysis: Human rights Norms at the UN, *Ethical Corporation*, 24 October 2004.

Weissbrodt, D. and M. Kruger (2005) 'Human rights responsibilities of businesses as non-state actors'. In P. Alston (ed.) *Non-State Actors and Human Rights*, New York: Oxford University Press, pp. 315–50.

Weissbrodt, D. and M. Kruger (2003) 'Norms on the Responsibilities of Transnational Corporations and Other Business Enterprises with Regard to Human Rights', 97(4) *American Journal of International Law* pp. 901–22.

Wellens, K. C. and G. M. Borchardt (1989) 'Soft law in European Community law', 14 *European Law Review* pp. 267–321.

Wettstein, F. (2015) 'Business and Human Rights: implementation challenges'. In D. Baumann-Pauly and J. Nolan (eds) *Business and Human Rights: from Principles to Practice,* Routledge, pp. 77–89.

Wettstein, F. (2015) 'Normativity, ethics, and the UN Guiding Principles on Business and Human Rights: a critical assessment', 14(2) *Journal of Human Rights* pp. 162–82.

Wettstein, F. (2013) 'Making noise about silent complicity: The moral inconsistency of the "Protect, Respect and Remedy" Framework'. In S. Deva and D. Bilchitz (eds) *Human Rights Obligations of Business*, pp. 243–68.

Wettstein, F. (2009) 'Beyond voluntariness, beyond CSR: Making a case for human rights and justice', 114(1) *Business and Society Review* pp. 125–52.

Wetzel, J. R.-M. (2015) *Human Right in Transnational Business: Translating human rights obligations into compliance procedures*, Luzern Springer.

Wilthagen, T. (1994) 'Reflexive rationality in the regulation of occupational safety and health'. In R. Rogowski and T. Wilthagen (eds) *Reflexive Labour Law: Studies in Industrial Relations and Employment Regulation,* Deventer and Boston: Kluwer Law and Taxation Publishers, pp. 345–76.

Wodak, R. (2001) 'The discourse-historical approach'. In R. Wodak and M. Meyer (eds) *Methods of Critical Discourse Analysis*, London: Sage, pp. 63–94.

Wodak, R. (2001) 'What CDA is about – a summary of its history, important concepts and its developments'. In R. Wodak and M. Meyer (eds) *Methods of Critical Discourse Analysis*, London: Sage, pp. 1–14.

Wouters, J. and A. Chané (2013) 'Multinational corporations in international law', Working Paper No. 129, Leuven: Leuven Centre for Global Governance Studies.

Wright, M. and A. Lehr (2006) 'Business recognition of human right: Global patterns, regional and sectoral variations', A study conducted under the direction of John G. Ruggie, Harvard University, UN Secretary-General's Special Representative for Business and Human Rights, 12 December 2006.

Wæver, O. (2001) 'Europæisk sikkerhed og integration: en analyse af franske og tyske diskurser om state, nation og Europa'. In T. B. Dyrberg and A. D. Hansen (eds) *Diskursteorien på arbejde*, Roskilde: Roskilde Universitetsforlag, pp. 279–317.

Zadek, S., M. Merme and R. Samans (2005) *Mainstreaming Responsible Investment,* World Economic Forum Global Corporate Citizen Initiative in cooperation with Accountability, January 2005.

Zanitelli, L. M. (2011) 'Corporations and Human Rights: The debate between voluntarists and obligationists and the undermining effect of sanctions', 8(15) *SUR International Journal on Human Rights* pp. 35–54.

Zerk, J. A. (2006) *Multinationals and Corporate Social Responsibility: Limitations and Opportunities in International Law,* Cambridge: Cambridge University Press.

Zumbansen, P. (2012) 'Transnational law, Evolving'. In J. Smits (ed.) *Elgar Encyclopedia of Comparative Law*, Cheltenham, Northampton MA: Edward Elgar, 2nd ed., pp. 898–925.

OFFICIAL INTERNATIONAL ORGANISATION DOCUMENTS

Commission of the European Communities (2006) Communication from the Commission to the European Parliament, the Council and the European Economic and Social Committee: Implementing the Partnership for Growth and Jobs: Making Europe a Pole of Excellence on CSR, COM (2006)136.final.

Commission of the European Communities (2002) Corporate Social Responsibility: A business contribution to sustainable development. COM(2002)347.

Commission of the European Communities (2001) Promoting a European Framework for Corporate Social Responsibility. COM(2001)366.

Commission on Human Rights (2006) Interim report of the Special Representative of the Secretary-General on the issue of human rights and transnational corporations and other business enterprises, UN Doc. E/CN.4/2006/97, 22 February 2006.

Commission on Human Rights (2005) Human rights and transnational corporations and other business enterprises, UN Doc. E/CN.4/2005/L.87, 15 April 2005.

Commission on Human Rights (2004) Decision 2004/116, UN Doc. E/CN.4/2004/L.73/Rev.1, 16 April 2004.

Constitution of the International Labour Organization, adopted by the Peace Conference in April of 1919, established the International Labour Organization (ILO), 15 UNTS 40.

Council of the European Union (2000) Presidency conclusions, Lisbon European Council, 23 and 24 March 2000.

Council of Europe (1996) European Social Charter (Revised), Strasbourg, ETS No. 163.

Council of Europe (1961) European Social Charter, Strasbourg, ETS No. 35.

Council Regulation (EC) No 2173/2005 of 20 December 2005 on the establishment of a FLEGT licensing scheme for imports of timber into the European Community, EU doc. OJ 2005 L 347/1.

Draft Code of Conduct on Transnational Corporations. *Development and International Economic Cooperation: Transnational Corporations*, UN Doc. E/1990/94, 12 June 1990.

Directive 2014/95/EU of the European Parliament and of the Council of 22 October 2015 amending Directive 2013/34/EU as regards disclosure of non-financial and diversity information by certain large undertakings and groups, EU doc. OJ 2014 L 330.

Directive 2013/50/EU of the European Parliament and of the Council of 22 October 2013 amending Directive 2004/109/EC of the European Parliament and of the Council on the harmonisation of transparency requirements in relation to information about issuers whose securities are admitted to trading on a regulated market, Directive 2003/71/EC of the European Parliament and of the Council on the prospectus to be published when securities are offered to the public or admitted to trading and Commission Directive 2007/14/EC laying down detailed rules for the implementation of certain provisions of Directive 2004/109/EC, EU doc. OJ 2013 L 294.

Eide, A. (2001) 'Corporations, states and human rights: A note on responsibilities and procedures for implementation and compliance', Commission on Human Rights, Sub-Commission on the Promotion and Protection of Human Rights, UN Doc. E/CN.4/Sub.2/2001/WG.2/WP.2.

European Commission (2011) *A renewed EU Strategy 2011–2014 for Corporate Social Responsibility,* Communication from the Commission to the European Parliament, the Council, the European Economic and Social Committee and the Committee of the Regions, Brussels, 25.10.2011, EU Doc. COM(2011)681.

European Parliament (1999) Resolution on EU standards for European enterprises operating in developing countries: towards a European Code of Conduct, OJ C 104/180, EP Resolution A4-0508/98, adopted on 15 January 1999.

European Parliament (1999) Resolution on the Communication from the Commission to the Council on the trading system and internationally recognised labour standards (COM(96)0402 – C4048896), A4-0423/98, adopted on 13 January 1999, OJ 1999 C104/63 14 April 1999.

European Parliament Committee on Development and Cooperation (1998) Report on EU standards for European Enterprises operating in developing countries: towards a European Code of Conduct, A4-0508/98, 17 December 1998.

European Union: Council of the European Union (2009) *Presidency Conclusions, Brussels European Council, 18–19 June 2009*, EU Doc. 7619/1/05 REV 1, 19 June 2009.

Fall, P. L. and M. M. Zahran (2010) 'United Nations corporate partnerships: The role and functioning of the Global Compact', United Nations: Joint Inspection Unit, UN doc. JIU/REP/2010/9.

Guissé, E.-H. (2001) 'The realization of economic, social and cultural rights: The question of transnational corporations', Commission on Human Rights, Sub-Commission on the Promotion and Protection of Human Rights, UN Doc. E/DN.4/Sub.2/2001/WG.2/WP.3.

Human Rights Council (2014) *Elaboration of an international legally binding instrument on transnational corporations and other business enterprises with respect to human rights*, UN Doc. A/HRC/RES/26/9, 14 July 2014.

Human Rights Council (2011) *Guiding Principles on Business and Human Rights: Implementing the United Nations 'Protect, Respect, Remedy' Framework*. Report of the Special Representative of the Secretary-General on the issue of human rights and transnational corporations and other business enterprises. UN Doc. A/HRC/17/31, 21 March 2011.

Human Rights Council (2010) 'Business and human rights: Further steps toward the operationalization of the "protect, respect and remedy" framework'. Report of the Special Representative of the Secretary-General on the issue of human rights and transnational corporations and other business enterprises, John Ruggie. UN Doc. A/HRC/14/27, 9 April 2010.

Human Rights Council (2009) 'Business and human rights: Towards operationalizing the "protect, respect and remedy" framework'. Report of the Special Representative of the Secretary-General on the issue of human rights and transnational corporations and other business enterprise. UN Doc. A/HRC/11/13, 22 April 2009.

Human Rights Council (2008) 'Clarifying the concepts of "Sphere of Influence" and "Complicity",' UN Doc. A/HRC/8/16, 15 May 2008.

Human Rights Council (2008) 'Corporations and human rights: a survey of the scope and patterns of alleged corporate-related human rights abuse', UN Doc. A/HRC/8/5/Add.2, 23 May 2008.

Human Rights Council (2008) 'Mandate of the Special Representative of the Secretary-General on the issue of human rights and transnational corporations and other business enterprises', Human Rights Council Resolution, 18 June 2008.

Human Rights Council (2008) *Protect, respect and remedy: A framework for business and human rights*, Report of the Special Representative of the Secretary-General on the issue of human rights and transnational corporations and other business enterprises, John Ruggie, UN Doc. A/HRC/8/5 7 April 2008.

Human Rights Council (2008) Summary of five multi-stakeholder consultations, UN Doc. A/HRC/8/5/Add.1, 23 April 2008.

Human Rights Council (2007) 'Business and Human Rights: Mapping international standards of responsibility and accountability for corporate acts', report of the Special Representative of the Secretary-General on the issue of human rights and transnational corporations and other business enterprises, UN Doc. A/HRC/4/35, 9 February 2007.

ILO (1998) Declaration of Fundamental Principles and Rights at Work adopted by the International Labour Conference, 86th session, Geneva,

June 1998, 37 I.L.M. 1233, http://www.ilo.org/public/english/standards/decl/declaration/text/ (last accessed 27 December 2016).

ILO (1977) Tripartite Declaration of Principles concerning Multinational Enterprises and Social Policy (MNE Declaration), originally adopted in 1977 by the ILO Governing Body, available at: http://www.ilo.org/empent/Publications/WCMS_094386/lang--en/index.htm (last accessed 27 December 2016).

ILO Convention No. 29, Forced Labour Convention (1930) 39 U.N.T.S. 55.

ILO Convention No. 87, Freedom of Association and Protection of the Right to Organise Convention (1949) 68 UNTS 17.

ILO Convention No. 98, Right to Organise and Collective Bargaining Convention (1949) 96 U.N.T.S. 257.

ILO Convention No. 100, Equal Remuneration Convention (1951) 165 U.N.T.S. 303.

ILO Convention No. 105, Abolition of Forced Labour Convention (1957) 320 U.N.T.S. 291.

ILO Convention No. 111, Discrimination (Employment and Occupation) Convention (1958) 362 U.N.T.S. 31.

ILO Convention No. 138, Minimum Age Convention (1973) 1015 U.N.T.S. 297.

ILO Convention No. 182, Worst Forms of Child Labour Convention (1999) 2133 U.N.T.S. 161.

International Covenant on Civil and Political Rights, GA res. 2200A (XXI), UN Doc. A/6316 (1966), 999 U.N.T.S. 171.

International Covenant on Economic, Social and Cultural Rights, GA res. 2200A (XXI), UN Doc. A/6316 (1966), 993 U.N.T.S. 3.

International Labour Office (2003) 'Corporate social responsibility: Myth or reality?', Geneva: ILO labour education series 2003/1.

OECD (1976) OECD Guidelines for Multinational Enterprises, Paris: OECD, available at http://search.oecd.org/officialdocuments/publicdisplaydocumentpdf/?cote=CES(2000)17&docLanguage=En (last accessed 27 December 2016).

OECD (2011) Declaration on International Investment and Multinational Enterprises, available at: http://www.oecd.org/daf/inv/investment-policy/oecddeclarationoninternationalinvestmentandmultinationalenterprises.htm (last accessed 20 November 2016).

OECD (2011) Guidelines for Multinational Enterprises, 2011 revision, Paris: OECD Publishing, available at http://www.oecd.org/daf/internationalinvestment/guidelinesformultinationalenterprises/48004323.pdf (last accessed 17 January 2013).

OHCHR (2007) 'Human rights impact of corporate activity: Request for information from Special Procedures', Geneva 1 May 2007.

OHCHR (2007) 'SRSG to meet with treaty bodies', Geneva, 5 June 2007.
Regulation (EU) 995/2010 of the European Parliament and of the Council of 20th October 2010 laying down the obligations of operators who place timber and timber products on the market, EU doc. OJ 2010 L 295/23.
Report of the sessional working group on the working methods and activities of transnational corporations, 4th session, UN Doc. E/CN.4/Sub.2/2002/13.
Report of the sessional working group on the working methods and activities of transnational corporations, 3rd session, UN Doc. E/CN.4/Sub.2/2001/9.
Report of the sessional working group on the working methods and activities of transnational corporations, 2nd session, UN Doc. E/CN.4/Sub.2/2000/12.
Report of the sessional working group on the working methods and activities of transnational corporations, 1st session, UN Doc. E/CN.4/Sub.2/1999/9.
Rome Statute of the International Criminal Court, adopted by the UN General Assembly on 17 July 1998, UN Doc. A/Conf.183/9.
Sub-Commission on Prevention of Discrimination and Protection of Minorities (1998) The realization of Economic, Social and Cultural Rights: The Question of Transnational Corporations, UN Doc. E/CN.4/Sub.2/198/6, 10 June 1998.
Sub-Commission on Prevention of Discrimination and Protection of Minorities (1996) The impact of the activities and working methods of Transnational Corporations on the full enjoyment of human rights, in particular Economic, Social and Cultural Rights and the Rights to Development, Bearing in mind existing international guidelines, rules and standards relating to the subject-matter, UN Doc. E/CN.4/Sub.2/196/12, 2 July 1996.
Sub-Commission on Prevention of Discrimination and Protection of Minorities (1995) The realization of Economic, Social and Cultural Rights: The relationship between the enjoyment of human rights, in particular, international labour and trade union rights, and the working methods and activities of transnational corporations, UN Doc. E/CN.4/Sub.2/1995/11, 24 July 1995.
Sub-Commission on the Promotion and Protection of Human Rights (2003) Commentary on the Norms on the Responsibilities of Transnational Corporations and Other Business Enterprises with Regard to Human Rights, UN Doc. E/CN.4/Sub.2/2003/38/Rev. 2.
Sub-Commission on the Promotion and Protection of Human Rights (2003) 'Norms on the Responsibilities of Transnational Corporations

and Other Business Enterprises with regard to Human Rights', UN Doc. E/CN.4/Sub.2/2003/12/Rev.2.

Sub-Commission on the Promotion and Protection of Human Rights (1998) Resolution, 1998/8, 20 August 1998.

United Nations (2005) Press Release: Commission requests Secretary-General to appoint Special Representative on Transnational Corporations. Commission on Human Rights, 20 April 2005, available at http://www.unhchr.ch/huricane/huricane.nsf/view01/F92E35AD92F360D3C1256FEA002BF653?opendocument (last accessed 19 January 2013; website has been removed).

United Nations Charter (1945), San Francisco 1945, U.N.T.S. 993.

United Nations General Assembly (2006) Convention on the Rights of Persons with Disabilities, resolution adopted by the General Assembly, UN Doc. A/RES/61/106, 13 December 2006.

United Nations General Assembly (2007) Declaration on the Rights of Indigenous Peoples: *adopted by the General Assembly,* UN Doc. A/61/L.67, 13 September 2007.

United Nations General Assembly (2005) Towards global partnerships: Resolution adopted by the General Assembly [on the report of the Second Committee (A/60/495 and Corr.1)], UN Doc. A/RES/60/215/, 29 March 2006 (passed 22 December 2005).

United Nations General Assembly (2003) Towards global partnerships: Resolution adopted by the General Assembly, UN Doc. A/RES/58/129, 19 December 2003.

United Nations General Assembly (2003) United Nations Convention against Corruption, UN Doc. A/58/422, 31 October 2003.

United Nations General Assembly (2001) Towards global partnerships: Resolution adopted by the General Assembly, UN Doc. A/RES/56/76, 11 December 2001.

United Nations General Assembly (2000) Towards global partnerships: Resolution adopted by the General Assembly, UN Doc. A/RES/55/215, 21 December 2000.

United Nations General Assembly (2000) United Nations Millennium Declaration, UN Doc. A/Res/55/2, 18 September 2000.

United Nations General Assembly (1992) Rio Declaration on Environment and Development (United Nations Conference on Environment and Development: Annex 1: Declaration on Environment and Development), UN Doc. A/CONF.151/26 (Vol. I), 12 August 1992.

United Nations General Assembly (1986) Declaration on the Right to Development: resolution adopted by the General Assembly, UN Doc. A/RES/41/218, 4 December 1986.

United Nations General Assembly (1948) Universal Declaration of

Human Rights, G.A. res. 217A (III), U.N. Doc A/810, 10 December 1948.
United Nations High Commissioner for Human Rights/Commission on Human Rights (2007) 'Report of the United Nations High Commissioner for Human Rights on the sectoral consultation entitled "Human Rights and the Financial Sector",' 16 February 2007, UN Doc. A/HRC/4/99, 6 March 2007.
United Nations High Commissioner for Human Rights/Commission on Human Rights (2005) Report of the United Nations High Commissioner for Human Rights on the sectoral consultation entitled 'Human Rights and the extractive industry', 10–11 November 2005, UN Doc. E/CN.4/2006/92, 19 December 2005.

STAKEHOLDER STATEMENTS

Alianza Social Continental et al. (2011) Statement to Delegations on the Human Rights Council 2011, 17th session, Agenda Item 3: 'Civil Society Organisations respond to Ruggie's Guiding Principles regarding human rights and transnational corporations and other business enterprises'.
Amnesty International (2006) Letter to John Ruggie, 27 April 2006.
Amnesty International (2005) Letter to Professor John Ruggie, 16 September 2005, AI ref UN 260-2005.
Amnesty International (2005) 2005 UN Commission on Human Rights: Amnesty International welcomes new UN mechanism on Business and Human Rights, Public statement, IOR 41/044/2005 (Public) 21 April 2005.
Amnesty International (2005) 2005 UN Commission on Human Rights: The UN's chief guardian of human rights?, AI Index: IOR 41/001/2005, 1 January 2005.
Annan, K. (1999) Address of Secretary-General Kofi Annan to the World Economic Forum in Davos, Switzerland, 31 January, UN Press release SG/SM/6881, 1 February 1999 (Secretary-General proposes Global Compact on human rights, labour, environment, in address to World Economic Forum in Davos), http://www.un.org/News/Press/docs/1999/19990201.sgsm6881.html (accessed 17 December 2016).
Asian civil society statement to U.N. Special Representative on transnational business and human rights at the Asia Regional Consultation, Bangkok, Thailand, 27 June 2006.
Brown, P. (2007) 'Principles that make for effective governance of multi-stakeholder initiatives: updated, final version', UN SRSG/CCC Expert workshop on improving human rights performance of business through multi-stakeholder initiatives 6–7 November 2007, December 2007.

BusinessEurope, European Alliance for CSR, available at: https://www.busi nesseurope.eu/european-alliance-csr, (last accessed 30 December 2016).
Business Leaders Initiative for Human Rights (2006) Report 3: Towards a 'Common Framework' on Business and Human Rights: Identifying Components, London, June 2006.
Chandler, G. (2007) Open letter to the signatories of the 10 October letter to the Special Representative of the UN Secretary General for Business and Human Rights, 15 October 2007.
CIDSE – Développement et la Solidarité (2008) CIDSE submission to the Special Representative of the United Nations Secretary-General on Business and Human Rights: Recommendations to reduce the risk of human rights violations and improve access to justice, February 2008.
Clean Clothes Campaign (2007) Letter to John Ruggie, Amsterdam, 23 March 2007 available at http://www.business-humanrights.org/Documents/Clean-Clothes-Campaign-letter-Ruggie-23-Mar-2007.pdf (last accessed 6 February 2017).
CSR Alliance (2008) Toolbox: Equipping companies and stakeholders for a competitive and responsible Europe, Brussels: CSR Europe.
CSR Europe at http://www.csreurope.org/pages/en/alliance.html (last accessed 12 March 2013, website has been removed).
Declaration of the Social, Non-Governmental and Union Organizations and Indigenous and Affected Communities, Bogotá, 18–19 January 2007.
ESCR-Net Corporate Accountability Working Group (2005) Joint NGO submission: Consultation on human rights and the extractive industry, final version 9 December 2005, available at http://www.escr-net.org/actions_more/actions_more_show.htm?doc_id5430968 (last accessed 4 February 2013; website has been removed).
ESCR-Net Corporate Accountability Working Group (2005) Joint NGO Submission on Human Rights and the Extractive Industry – 2005 (website overview), available http://www.escr-net.org/actions_more/actions_more_show.htm?doc_id=430968 (last accessed 4 February 2013, website has been removed).
Euractiv (2004) Corporate Responsibility: Interview news: The new Member States will bring fresh ideas and new views to the CSR debate, Euractiv, 4 May 2004.
European Commission DG Enterprise and Industry available at http://ec.europa.eu/enterprise/policies/sustainable-business/corporate-social-responsibility/european-alliance/index_en.htm (last accessed 12 March 2013, website has been removed)
European MultiStakeholder Forum on CSR (2002–2004) The EU MSF homepage through the EU Commission's website at: http://circa.europa.eu/

irc/empl/csr_eu_multi_stakeholder_forum/info/data/en/csr%20ems%20forum.htm (last accessed 12 March 2013; webpage has been removed).
European Multistakeholder Forum on CSR (2004) Final High Level meeting, 29 June 2004, Minutes, http://circa.europa.eu/irc/empl/csr_eu_multi_stakeholder_forum/info/data/en/CSR%20Forum%20040629%20minutes.htm (last accessed 12 March 2013; website has been removed).
European Multistakeholder Forum on CSR (2004) Final Results and Recommendations, 29 June 2004 (Final Report), http://forum.europa.eu.int/irc/empl/csr_eu_multi_stakeholder_forum/info/data/en/CSR%20Forum%20final%20report.pdf (last accessed 12 March 2013; website has been removed).
European Multistakeholder Forum on CSR (2004), High Level meetings, 29 July 2004, Agenda, http://circa.europa.eu/irc/empl/csr_eu_multi_stakeholder_forum/info/data/en/CSR%20Forum%20040629%20speech%20Social%20Platform.htm (last accessed 12 March 2013; website has been removed).
EU Multistakeholder Forum on CSR (2003) High Level meetings, 13 November 2003, Address by Philippe de Buck – Secretary General UNICE, http://circa.europa.eu/irc/empl/csr_eu_multi_stakeholder_forum/info/data/en/CSR%20Forum%20031113%20speech%20UNICE.htm (last accessed 12 March 2013; website has been removed).
European Multistakeholder Forum on CSR (2003) High Level meetings, 13 November 2003, Joint Proposal for a Final Report format from the Coordination Committee, http://circa.europa.eu/irc/empl/csr_eu_multi_stakeholder_forum/info/data/en/CSR%20Forum%20031113%20report%20structure.htm (last accessed 12 March 2013; website has been removed).
European Multistakeholder Forum on CSR (2002) High Level meetings, 19 December 2002, Minutes, http://circa.europa.eu/irc/empl/csr_eu_multi_stakeholder_forum/info/data/en/CSR%20Forum%20021219%20minutes.htm (last accessed 12 March 2013; website has been removed).
European Multistakeholder Forum on CSR (2002) High Level meetings, 16 October 2002, Agenda, Statements, Alain Wolf – Adviser to the Presidency, CEEP, http://circa.europa.eu/irc/empl/csr_eu_multi_stakeholder_forum/info/data/en/CSR%20Forum%20021016%20statements%20CEEP.htm (last accessed 12 March 2013; website has been removed).
European Multistakeholder Forum on CSR (2002) High Level meetings, 16 October 2002, Agenda, Statements, Anne-Sophie Parent – Member Social Platform Management Committee, http://circa.europa.eu/irc/empl/csr_eu_multi_stakeholder_forum/info/data/en/CSR%20Forum%20021016%20statements%20Social%20Platform.htm (last accessed 12 March 2013; website has been removed).

European Multistakeholder Forum on CSR (2002) High Level meetings, 16 October 2002, Agenda, Statements, Philippe de Buck – Secretary General, UNICE, http://circa.europa.eu/irc/empl/csr_eu_multi_stakeholder_forum/info/data/en/CSR%20Forum%20021016%20statements%20UNICE.htm (last accessed 12 March 2013; website has been removed).

EU Multistakeholder Forum on CSR (2002) High Level meetings, 16 October 2002, Agenda, Statements, Tony Long – Director, WWF European Policy Office, http://circa.europa.eu/irc/empl/csr_eu_multi_stakeholder_forum/info/data/en/CSR%20Forum%20021016%20statements%20G8.htm (last accessed 12 March 2013; website has been removed).

European Multistakeholder Forum on CSR (2002), High Level meetings, 16 October 2002, Agenda, Statements, Xavier R. Durieu – Secretary General, Eurocommerce, http://circa.europa.eu/irc/empl/csr_eu_multi_stakeholder_forum/info/data/en/CSR%20Forum%20021016%20statements%20CEEP.htm (last accessed 12 March 2013; website has been removed).

European Multistakeholder Forum on CSR, Composition, http://circa.europa.eu/irc/empl/csr_eu_multi_stakeholder_forum/info/data/en/CSR%20Forum%20composition.htm (last accessed 12 March 2013; website has been removed).

European Multistakeholder Forum on CSR, Home, http://circa.europa.eu/irc/empl/csr_eu_multi_stakeholder_forum/info/data/en/csr%20ems%20forum.htm (last accessed 12 March 2013; website has been removed).

European Multistakeholder Forum on CSR, Objective, composition and operational aspects, http://circa.europa.eu/irc/empl/csr_eu_multi_stakeholder_forum/info/data/en/CSR%20Forum%20Rules.htm (last accessed 12 March 2013; website has been removed).

Federation internationale des ligues des droits de l'Homme (2006) 'Position paper: Comments to the interim report of the Special Representative of the Secretary-General on the issue of Human Rights and Transnational Corporations and other business enterprises, February 22, 2006', 15 March, http://www.fidh.org/IMG/pdf/business442a.pdf (last accessed 12 March 2013; website has been removed).

FIAN International (2011) CSOs and social movements front Human Rights Council today: Ruggie's Guiding Principles unsuitable for addressing corporate human rights abuses, 31 May 2011.

Forest Peoples Programme and Tebtebba Foundation (2006) 'Indigenous Peoples' rights, extractive industries and transnational and other enterprises: A submission to the Special Representative of the Secretary-General on human rights and transnational corporations and other business enterprises', 29 December.

Howen, N. (2005) 'Business, human rights and accountability', delivered at 'Business and Human Rights' conference organised by the Danish section of the ICJ, Copenhagen, 21 September 2005, available at http://www.business-humanrights.org/Links/Repository/684768 (last accessed 4 February 2017).
Human Rights Watch (2011) UN Human Rights Council: Weak Stance on Human Rights, News release 16 June 2011.
Human Rights Watch and others (2006) 'Joint NGO letter in Response to Interim Report 1', 18 May, http://www.fidh.org/IMG/pdf/Joint_NGO_Response_to_Interim_Report.pdf (last accessed 4 February 2013).
Interfaith Center on Corporate Responsibility (2006) Letter to John Ruggie, 10 October 2006.
Interfaith Center for Corporate Responsibility (2006) Letter to John Ruggie, 6 February 2006.
International Alert (2006) 'Speech by Salil Tripathi', Johannesburg, 27–28 March 2006.
International Chamber of Commerce (2008) UN Special Representative Ruggie addresses business audience, ICC News, Paris, 27 April 2008.
International Chamber of Commerce and International Organisation of Employers (2003) 'Joint views of ICC and the IOE on the draft "Norms on the Responsibilities of Transnational Corporations and Other Business Enterprises with regard to Human Rights"' submitted to the United Nations Commission on Human Rights, 24 November 2003.
International Commission of Jurists (2005) Corporate accountability, international human rights law and the United Nations, Geneva, 9 June 2005.
International Council on Mining and Metals (2006) 'Submission to UN Secretary General's Special Representative on Human Rights and Business: Clarity and consensus on legitimate human rights responsibilities for companies could accelerate progress', March 2006.
International Council on Mining and Metals (2006) 'Second submission to UN Secretary General's Special Representative on Human Rights and Business: Mining and Human Rights: How the UN SRSG can help spread good practice and tackle critical issues', October 2006.
International Network for Economic, Social & Cultural Rights (2007) Letter to John Ruggie, 5 September 2007.
International Organisation of Employers (IOE), International Chamber of Commerce (ICC), and BIAC (2006) 'Business and human rights: The role of business in weak governance zones: Business proposals for effective ways of addressing dilemma situations in weak governance zones', Geneva, December 2006.
International Service for Human Rights (2006) Sub-Commission on the

Promotion and Protection of Human Rights, 58th session (Geneva, 7–25 August 2006) Item 4: Economic, Social and Cultural Rights, Geneva 2006.

Joint NGO letter on work of the mandate, 10 October 2007 (available at the Business & Human Rights Resource Centre SRSG portal in version dated 25 October 2007).

Mandate of the Special Representative of the Secretary-General on the Issue of Human Rights and Transnational Corporations and other Business Enterprises (2010) 'Closing governance gaps: Application of the UN "Protect, Respect, Remedy" Framework', Expert Multi-stakeholder consultation, 20 January 2010 in Berlin; hosted by the German Federal Ministry for Economic Cooperation and Development (BMZ), organised by InWEnt – Capacity Building International, Germany.

Mandate of the Special Representative of the Secretary-General on the Issue of Human Rights and Transnational Corporations and other Business Enterprises (2010) Mandate consultation outline, October 2010.

Mandate of the Special Representative of the Secretary-General on the Issue of Human Rights and Transnational Corporations and other Business Enterprises (2009) Responsible contracting, 25 and 26 June 2009 Paris, France: Summary Report.

Moody-Stuart, M. (2005) Mark Moody-Stuart on Business and Human Rights, 17 November 2005, available at http://www.unglobalcompact.org/NewsAndEvents/news_archives/2005_11_17.html (last accessed 4 February 2016).

Revenue sharing and fiscal management: Discussion paper (2006) draft for discussion 28 July 2006.

SRSG (2008) 'Statement by Prof. John Ruggie, Special Representative of the Secretary-General on human rights and transnational corporations and other business enterprises', 63rd session of the General Assembly, Third Committee, Agenda Item 64(b): "Promotion and protection of human rights: Human rights questions, including alternative approaches for improving the effective enjoyment of human rights and fundamental freedoms", New York, 27 October 2008.

SRSG (2008) Statement of the UN Secretary-General's Special Representative on Business and Human Rights, Professor John Ruggie, to the UNCITRAL Working Group II (Arbitration and Conciliation), 48th session, New York, USA, 4–8 February 2008.

SRSG (2007) Letter to Ms Julieta Rosi, 15 October 2007.

SRSG (2007) Letter to Niko Lusiani, 29 August 2007.

SRSG (2007) 'Meeting between the SRSG on Human Rights and Business and Treaty Bodies, 19/06/07', Background paper: Mapping States parties' responsibilities to regulate and adjudicate corporate activities

under the United Nations' core human rights treaties: Main trends and issues for further consideration.
SRSG (2007) 'Meeting with UN Special Procedures', Geneva, 19 June 2007.
SRSG (2007) 'Prepared remarks at Clifford Chance', London, 19 February 2007.
SRSG (2007) 'Remarks at plenary session on "Business and the rules of the game: From rule-takers to rule-makers?"', 12th International Business Forum, World Bank, Washington D.C., 8–10 October 2007.
SRSG (2007) 'Summary report: Latin America consultation: Held by the Special Representative of the Secretary-General on human rights and transnational corporations and other business enterprises', Bogotá, January 18–19.
SRSG (2006) 'Letter to Olivier de Schutter and Antoine Bernard', FIDH, 20 March 2006.
SRSG (2006) 'Remarks', delivered at forum on Corporate Social Responsibility, co-sponsored by the Fair Labor Association and the German Network of Business Ethics, Bamberg, Germany, 14 June 2006.
SRSG (2006) 'Remarks at public session', National Roundtable on Corporate Social Responsibility and the Canadian Extractive Industry in Developing Countries, Montreal, 14 November 2006.
SRSG (2006) 'Summary report: Asian regional consultation: Held by the Special Representative of the Secretary-General on human rights and transnational corporations and other business enterprises', Bangkok, June 26–27.
SRSG (2006) 'Summary report: Seminar of legal experts: extraterritorial legislation as a tool to improve the accountability of transnational corporations for human rights violations', Brussels, November 3–4, 2006.
SRSG (2006) 'Summary report: Workshop on attributing corporate responsibility for human rights under international law', NYU School of Law, Friday, November 17, 2006.
SRSG (2005) Announcement by John Ruggie, Special Representative of the UN Secretary- General on business and human rights, regarding initiative by International Organization of Employers, 21 December 2005.
SRSG (2005) 'Opening remarks', Wilton Park conference on Business and Human Rights, 10–12 October 2005.
SRSG (2005) 'Remarks', Business and Human Rights seminar, Old Billingsgate, London, 8 December 2005.
The Corporate Responsibility Coalition (2010) 'Protecting rights, repairing harm: How state-based non-judicial mechanisms can help fill gaps in existing frameworks for the protection of human rights of people affected by corporate activities', November 2010.
United States (2005) Explanation of no-vote, Commission on Human

Rights, Item 17: Transnational Corporations, April 20, 2005 (on file with author).
Weissbrodt, D. (2006) 'UN perspectives on "Business and humanitarian and human rights obligations",' ASIL Proceedings: Proceedings of the 100th Annual Meeting, March 29–April 1 2006, Washington DC.
Wilmhurst, E. (2006) Human rights and transnational corporations: Legislation and government regulation, Chatham House, 15 June 2006.

WEBSITES AND OTHERS

Business and Human Rights Resource Centre, UN Secretary-General's Special Representative on business & human rights (SRSG Portal), available at: https://business-humanrights.org/en/un-secretary-generals-special-representative-on-business-human-rights (last accessed 27 December 2016).
Business and Human Rights Resource Centre, UN Secretary-General's Special Representative on business & human rights (SRSG Portal), Multi-stakeholder consultations – 2007 Consultations, meetings & workshops at: http://www.business-humanrights.org/SpecialRepPortal/Home/Consultationsmeetingsworkshops/Multi-stakeholderconsultations/2007 (last accessed 27 December 2016).
Digges, C. (2016) 'Danish shipping giant caught beaching ships in India and Bangladesh', retrieved from http://bellona.org/news/industrial-pollution/2016-10-danish-shipping-giant-caught-beaching-ships-in-india-and-bangladesh (9 January 2017).
Equator Principles, available at: www.equator-principles.com/ (last accessed 27 December 2016).
Forest Stewardship Council, available at: https://ic.fsc.org/en (last accessed 5 January 2017).
Global Compact Critics Blog, at: http://www.globalcompactcritics.net/ (last accessed 31 January 2013; website has been closed).
Global Reporting Initiative, available at: https://www.globalreporting.org/Pages/default.aspx (last accessed 5 January 2017).
ISO (2010) ISO 26000 – Social Responsibility, http://www.iso.org/iso/iso_catalogue/management_standards/social_responsibility.htm (last accessed 5 January 2017).
Principles for Responsible Investment, available at www.unpri.org (last accessed 27 December 2016).
Programme for the Endorsement of Forest Certification, available at http://www.pefc.org/ (last accessed 5 January 2017).
Social Accountability International, SA8000, available at http://www.sa-intl.

org/_data/n_0001/resources/live/2008StdEnglishFinal.pdf (last accessed 5 January 2017).
UN Global Compact, available at http://www.unglobalcompact.org/ (last accessed 30 December 2016).
UN Global Compact, 'The ten principles of the UN Global Compact', available at https://www.unglobalcompact.org/what-is-gc/mission/principles (last accessed 5 January 2017).
UN Global Compact, The ten principles of the UN Global Compact: Principle two: Human Rights, available at https://www.unglobalcompact.org/what-is-gc/mission/principles/principle-2 (last accessed 5 January 2017).

NATIONAL LEGISLATION AND BILLS

India Companies Act 2013, The Gazette of India, New Delhi, 30 August 2013.
Proposition de loi relative au devoir de vigilance des sociétés mères et des entreprises donneuses d'ordre ('Loi Vigilance'), https://www.senat.fr/dossier-legislatif/ppl14-376.html.
United States Alien Torts Statute, 28 U.S.C. § 1350.
United States Congress, Dodd-Frank Wall Street Reform and Consumer Protection Act (2010 – H.R. 4173), available at https://www.govtrack.us/congress/bills/111/hr4173 (last accessed on 22 December 2016).
United States Lacey Act, 16 U.S.C. § 3371–3378.

Index

Abbott, K. 13
access to remedy, SRSG process 232, 234, 235, 238, 242, 254–5, 281, 309–10, 329
Adams, C. 56
Aguilera, R. 42
Amnesty International 178–80, 186–9, 198–9, 230, 247, 290–91
Andersen, N. A. 27, 87
Angel, D. 56
Annan, K. 134, 135–7, 139, 286, 287, 298
argumentative strategies, discourse and system-specific rationality, multi-stakeholder communication and discourse analysis 85–102
  BHR discourse and effects on CSR 5, 86–7, 88, 89, 93–4, 98–9, 100–101
  construction of CSR normativity and business responsibilities for human rights 96–102
  CSR and social responsibilities 86, 88–9, 90–91
  democracy as floating signifier 87–8
  dynamic nature 86–7
  and environmental concerns 80–81, 97–8, 99–100
  floating signifiers and struggles for meanings 87–9, 91, 92–3, 94
  interdiscursivity levels, effects of 91, 96–7, 100–101
  language use as social practice 90
  linguistic means of transmission 92–5, 97, 98
  and power issues 86, 87–8, 91
  regulatory processes, textual analysis of constructing normativity in 91–5, 97–8
  social expectations 83, 84, 93, 99, 100
  and societal concern with sustainable development 90–91, 97
  stabilising and de-stabilising argumentative strategies 100–102, 257
  sub-discourses 86
  supply chain responsibility example 94–5
  system-specific interests, activating 96–100
  system-specific language of recipients 100
  text as social causal event 90
  textual analysis identifying how linguistic statements influence discourse and meaning 89–91
argumentative strategies, discourse and system-specific rationality, reflexive law 79–85, 91–5, 317–18
  communication based on interaction between different societal actors 79–102, 317–18
  developing normative standards 81
  exchanges of needs and expectations 83
  legal autopoiesis 83–4, 92–3, 98–9
  multi-stakeholder strategies 81–2, 84
  national and international level context 83
  procedural theory for regulated self-regulation 80–81, 82–3
  social sub-systems 80, 84
  social sub-systems, process of developing and causing irritation in 84–5, 91, 92–5, 98–9, 100
  system-specific rationality and communication 79–85
  three levels of reflection 82–3
argumentative strategies and influence

on output of regulatory processes 269–331
  autopoietic element in reflexive law theory 273
  BHR regime, moving towards 312–14
  discursive outcomes towards BHR regime 277–82
  discursive outputs through system-specific interests in communication 282–5
  economic sub-system 273–4, 275
  floating signifiers 272, 273
  hard institutionalisation effect 273–4, 275
  international law as regulatory system 275
  multi-stakeholder regulatory processes 276–7, 287–8
  NGOs and soft institutionalisation effects 274–5
  non-binding international law effects 274–5
  power concerns with construction of norms on business responsibilities for their social impacts 271–7
  reflexive law theory 272–3
  social expectations 274, 275–6, 281, 283, 284, 294, 295
  social responsibility to observe social expectations 275–6
  soft institutionalisation effects 274–6, 283
  specificity 309–12, 328–9
  stabilising or de-stabilising strategies, application and effects 288–302
  stabilising or de-stabilising strategies and system-specific interests 272, 285–309
  state obligations to protect 276
  system-specific logics, power, discourse and communication 271–85
  UN Global Compact development process 298–302, 323–4
argumentative structure and strategy, SRSG process 176–84
Arruda, M. 64

Arthurs, H. 81
Arts, B. 76
Asian textiles market concerns 110–11
autopoiesis theory 21, 23–6, 32, 83–4, 91, 92–3, 258, 273, 284, 317, 326, 327–8, 329
  see also reflexive law; system-specific communication
Ayres, I. 80

Backer, L. 109, 118, 124, 276
Barnett, M. 59
Bendell, J. 64, 110, 112
Berger-Walliser, G. 23, 80
best practices guidance
  EU CSR Alliance 164, 166–8, 280
  EU multi-stakeholder forum on CSR 146
  SRSG process 174, 184, 189
Beveridge, F. 71
bilateral investment treaties and host government agreements, SRSG process 231–2
Bilchitz, D. 261
binding/non-binding form of regulation, debate over 70–72, 119–20
  see also hard law; individual agreements and treaties; soft law
Blommaert, J. 31
Blowfield, M. 43, 44, 46–7, 64
Bonnitcha, J. 261, 295
Borchardt, G. 70
Bowen, H. 63
boycotts 93, 110–11
  see also consumer concerns
Boyle, A. 70–71, 72
Braithwaite, J. 80
Brejning, J. 57
Brown, P. 226
Bulcaen, C. 31
Burke, L. 59
business associations opposing Draft Norms initiative 128–9, 182, 183, 191, 193, 327
business associations self-regulation practices *see* self-regulation
'business case for CSR', moving beyond 59–64, 69

business enterprises, and Draft
Norms *see* normative guidance
for business on human rights in
a CSR context, Draft Norms
on responsibilities of TNCs and
other business enterprises
business guidance on human rights *see*
normative guidance for business
on human rights in a CSR context
Business and Human Rights (BHR)
regime 4–20, 315–16
argumentative strategies 5
conduct for transnational
corporations (TNCs) 7–8, 35–6
and Corporate Social Responsibility
(CSR) 7–8, 13, 14, 18, 19, 20
emergent nature 9–13
horizontality doctrine in
international human rights law
10–12, 22–3
moving towards 312–14
pragmatic approach to study 14–19
private non-state actors, duties of 7
public policy objectives, involvement
in 11
regime theory 12
respect, protection and fulfilment of
human rights as obligations of
states 10–11, 23
significance of 6–14
sustainability policies 13–14, 15
transnationalisation of law 9–10,
12–13
and UN Framework *see* UN
Framework
and UN Guiding Principles
(UNGPs) *see* UN Guiding
principles (UNGPs)
Business and Human Rights (BHR)
regime discourse
and effects on CSR 86–7, 88, 89,
93–4, 98–9, 100–101
outcomes towards 277–82
SRSG process 261–5, 281, 289–90,
312–14, 319–25
business impact on society, developing
norms on 74–8
Business and Industry Advisory
Committee (BIAC) 193, 209–11,
250, 254, 257, 284

business interests as priority, and
SRSG process 183–4
Business Leaders Initiative for Human
Rights (BLIHR) 126
business organisation involvement, EU
multi-stakeholder forum on CSR
141–2, 144, 146, 147–8, 152, 160,
163–4, 287, 304
business responsibilities for human
rights, argumentative strategies
96–102

Cafaggi, F. 65
Calliari, E. 13
Carroll, A. 46, 54–6, 63
case studies methodology 19–20, 34–6
case selection and coding of text
34–6
multi-stakeholder regulatory
initiative 34–5
Casey, R. 202
Cassese, A. 72
Chambers, R. 71, 125
Chandler, G. 52–3, 230, 257
Chané, A. 8
Charney, J. 71, 77, 78
Charnovitz, S. 74
Chilton, P. 86
Chinkin, C. 70, 71, 74
Chouliaraki, L. 30
CIDSE development NGOs 228–9,
258, 309
civil society involvement
Corporate Social Responsibility
(CSR) 74–6
Draft Norms on responsibilities
of TNCs and other business
enterprises 124, 178–9, 327
EU multi-stakeholder forum (MSF)
on CSR 152–3, 157, 158–9, 160,
161, 163, 165, 310–12
NGO involvement 74–6, 109,
274–5
UN Global Compact 133–4, 138,
140, 142
see also consumer concerns; multi-
stakeholder involvement
Clapham, A. 204, 245
Clean Clothes Campaign, supply chain
management 227–8, 258, 309

coercion issues 51, 53–4, 62, 98–9, 190–91
Collin, F. 87
communication and argumentative strategies
　discursive outputs through system-specific interests in communication 282–5
　system-specific logics, power, discourse and communication 271–85
　system-specific rationality and communication 79–85
companies' contributions to healthcare and pensions 108
company accountability argument, SRSG process 206–7, 211
competitiveness, and labour market development 62
complicity concerns
　Draft Norms on responsibilities of TNCs and other business enterprises 123
　and SRSG process 234, 238, 241–2, 243–51, 262, 264, 295–6
　see also sphere of influence
conduct guidance, lack of precise, normative guidance for business on human rights in a CSR context, EU multi-stakeholder forum on CSR 155, 156–7, 158
conflict zones, business activities in, SRSG process 202, 210, 225, 240, 247, 250, 254
conflict zones, guidance for business activities in 202, 210, 225, 240, 247, 250, 254
　see also weak governance zones
Conley, J. 26
consumer concerns 99, 110, 121, 216
　boycotts 93, 110–11
　see also civil society involvement
Cooper, K. 125
corporate responsibility and accountability for international crimes 221, 222–3, 245, 249
corporate responsibility to respect human rights, SRSG process 234–5, 237–8, 240–41, 254–5

Corporate Social Responsibility (CSR) 4, 5, 40–78
'business case for CSR' and economic justification 59–60, 69
'business case for CSR', moving beyond 59–64
Business and Human Rights (BHR) discourse effects 86–7, 88, 89, 93–4, 98–9, 100–101
and Business and Human Rights (BHR) regime 7–8, 13, 14, 18, 19, 20
Business and Human Rights regime, influence of 40–41, 47–8, 49
business impact on society, developing norms on 74–8
civil society involvement 74–6
civil society involvement, consensus versus confrontational approach 76
definition variations 42–8, 54–5
and discourse theory and analysis 26–7, 28–9
discretionary (or volitional) responsibilities 54
due diligence guidance 57
dynamic character 45
economic responsibilities 54
and environmental concerns 42–3, 47, 60–61, 62–4, 66, 77
ethical responsibilities 54
explicit and implicit 51
governmental objectives, fulfilling 60
governmental regulation 47–8
and hard law 41, 50, 58, 67, 69, 70–72, 91, 96
harm prevention 41, 53–4, 64
and human and labour rights 41–2, 46–7, 48, 53, 60, 61–2, 63–4, 65–6, 69
and implementation of public policy objectives 41
incentives 53, 58, 61, 62, 67
international human rights law 68–70
and international law 52–3
international soft law relevance 70–73
and labour rights 41–2, 46–7, 48, 53, 56, 60, 61–2, 63–4, 65–6, 69

legal compliance 55–8
legal incentives and rewards 53, 58, 61
legal responsibilities 54–5, 60
network-based discourse and policy processes 77–8
NGO involvement 74–6
NGO involvement, consensus versus confrontational approach 76
non-coercion-based conviction 51, 53–4, 62, 98–9
opportunistic compliance 55, 56
outsourcing and low labour law standards 56
positivist approach to law 50, 51
public policy interests 59–68
public-private partnerships and work-place integration, training and education 66
public-private regulation and intergovernmental activity 61–2
and rationality of intergovernmental organisations 60–61
regional differences 44–5
risk reduction from governance gaps or weak governance 66, 69
smart regulation 57
smart-mix regulation 60–61
social or economic rights connected with public goods 69–70
and social expectations 45, 48–9, 52, 54, 55, 60, 61, 68, 76, 312, 313–14
and social sustainability 41, 42–9
soft law definition 71–2
soft law and implicit state consent 73
soft law as test for later instruments of hard international law (treaties) 71, 72–3
and spirit of the law 46
sustainable development and political coalitions 77
and TNCs 56, 61, 74, 77–8
Triple Bottom Line: People, Planet, Profit 48
voluntary nature, challenges to 44–5, 48, 89
voluntary/mandatory dichotomy 49–59
see also normative guidance for business on human rights in a CSR context
Corporate Social Responsibility (CSR) normativity, argumentative strategies 96–102
'court of public opinion' reference, SRSG process 216–17, 220–21, 237, 242, 248–9, 294
Crane, A. 42, 44, 49
crimes, corporate responsibility and accountability for international 221, 222–3, 245, 249
criminal law regime, international 22, 193, 196, 204, 205, 218, 219, 264
critical discourse analysis (CDA) school, discourse theory and analysis 28, 29, 30
Cuganesan, S. 27

Dalberg-Larsen, J. 25
David, G. 44, 108
Davis, K. 63
De Bakker, F. 43
De Schutter, O. 176, 202, 244, 245, 254
Deakin, S. 81
Deitelhoff, N. 76
democracy as floating signifier 87–8
see also floating signifiers
Denmark
Financial Statements Act and CSR 63
'flex job schemes' as CSR 57
deregulation concerns 109
Deva, S. 260
developing countries
core labour standards 165, 166
socio-economic development 182
Devinney, T. 42
Digges, C. 52
discourse
and argumentative strategies *see* argumentative strategies, discourse and system-specific rationality
evolution 134–9, 175–6
network-based discourse and policy processes 77–8
system-specific logics, power, discourse and communication, argumentative strategies

and influence on output of
regulatory processes 271–85
discourse theory and analysis 21, 26–32
and Corporate Social Responsibility
(CSR) 26–7, 28–9
critical discourse analysis (CDA)
school 28, 29, 30
French school 27–8
knowledge, power and hegemony
(dominance) 27, 28–9, 30
power as a societal constitutive
factor 28
textual analysis and linguistic
elements 29–32
discretionary responsibilities 54, 181
Ditlevsen, M., et al. 33, 34, 92, 94
Draft Norms
and normative guidance see
normative guidance for business
on human rights in a CSR
context, Draft Norms on
responsibilities of TNCs and
other business enterprises
to SRSG mandate establishment
journey 176–85
UN Global Compact, difference
from and overlaps with 132, 133
due diligence obligations
Corporate Social Responsibility
(CSR) 57
Draft Norms on responsibilities
of TNCs and other business
enterprises 122–3, 210–11
SRSG process 187, 210–11, 235, 238,
241, 248–51, 257, 281, 295–7,
298, 326
Dunning, J. 111, 112

economic, 'business case for CSR' and
economic justification, Corporate
Social Responsibility (CSR)
59–60, 69
economic responsibilities, Corporate
Social Responsibility (CSR) 54,
69–70
economic rights, and public goods
69–70
economic system interests
EU multi-stakeholder forum on CSR
147, 303, 305–6, 311–12

language and EU CSR Alliance 165,
167
and SRSG process see SRSG
process, economic system
interests
sub-system and argumentative
strategies 273–4, 275
and UN Global Compact 135, 136–7
education, workplace 66
'effective national legislation', SRSG
process 183
Eide, A. 119
Elkington, J. 48
employment see labour
enforcement by national authorities,
concerns over 123, 129, 177–8, 181
see also national authorities
environmental concerns 16–17, 26, 29,
32
and argumentative strategies 80–81,
97–8, 99–100
and Corporate Social Responsibility
(CSR) 42–3, 47, 60–61, 62–4,
66, 77
and Draft Norms 116–17, 118, 121
EU CSR Alliance 165
EU multi-stakeholder forum on CSR
144, 146, 147, 150, 151–2, 154,
158, 279
normative guidance for business on
human rights in a CSR context
109–10, 113
SRSG process 207, 222, 294
and UN Global Compact 133–4,
135–7, 139, 140, 141–2, 278,
298–9, 300, 322
see also human rights; labour rights
Epstein, E. 43, 108
EU
CSR Alliance see normative
guidance for business on human
rights in a CSR context, EU
CSR Alliance
CSR definition 45–6, 49–50, 54
FLEGT licensing scheme for
imports of timber 47
'Illegal Timber' regulation 53
Lisbon Strategy 144–6, 151, 161–2
multi-stakeholder forum on CSR see
normative guidance for business

on human rights in a CSR context, EU multi-stakeholder forum on CSR
Non-Financial Reporting Directive 211
Transparency Directive 47
European Convention on Human Rights (ECHR) 145, 155
European Social Charter (ESC) 145, 150, 155
expectations, social *see* social expectations
export credit agencies and international financial institutions 215–16, 217

Fairbrass, J. 43, 279
Fairclough, N. 29–32, 37, 89–90, 91, 93–4
Fall, P. 134
Farmer, L. 81
Federation Internationale des Ligues des Droits des l'Homme (FIDH) 203–5, 225, 246–7
financial institutions' responsibilities to human rights 215–16, 228–9, 258
floating signifiers 7, 87–9, 91, 92–3, 94, 272, 273
Forest Stewardship Council (FSC) 51–2
Franck, T. 53
French school, discourse theory and analysis 27–8
Friedmann, W. 77
Frynas, J. 42, 43, 44, 46–7
future evolution of sustainability norms 325–31
future recommendations on soft law measures, SRSG process 217, 232, 233, 237, 282

genres and subgenres of text and communication 37–8
Gjølberg, M. 45, 65
Glinski, C. 65
Global Reporting Initiative (GRI) 48, 51–2
Gomez, M. 125
Gond, J.-P. 45
'good practices', SRSG process 195, 208

governance, weak *see* weak governance zones
governance gaps, and SRSG process 188, 213, 215, 221, 312–13
Goyder, G. 63
Greene, A. 176–7
grievance and complaints mechanisms, SRSG process 228, 235, 261–2
Guissé, E.-H. 119

Habermas, J. 24
Hajer, M. 75, 77, 97–8
Halter, M. 64
Hannum, H. 74
hard law 4, 23
  and Corporate Social Responsibility (CSR) 41, 50, 58, 67, 69, 70–2, 91, 96
  and Draft Norms 120, 129, 169
  EU multi-stakeholder forum (MSF) 149, 155, 159, 179
  and SRSG process 184–5, 193, 199, 232, 258, 276, 297–8
  see also binding/non-binding form of regulation, debate over; individual agreements and treaties; soft law
harm prevention 9, 10, 15, 23, 107, 281
  Corporate Social Responsibility (CSR) 41, 53–4, 64
  and reflexive law 85
  and SRSG process 203, 235, 288–9, 310
  UN Global Compact 132
Hart, H. 53
Hasenclever, A. 11
Haufler, V. 65
healthcare, companies' contributions to healthcare 108
Hearne, B. 119, 124, 126, 176, 178, 289
Henkin, L. 10
Héritier, A. 56
Hernandez, M. 110
Hess, D. 24, 25, 56
Hillemans, C. 110, 112, 118
Hobbs, R. 81
Holdgaard, R. 26, 27, 86, 87
Hopkins, M. 42–3, 138
horizontality doctrine in international human rights law 10–12, 22–3

Howe, J. 260–61
Howen, N. 290
human rights 21, 22–3, 42
　business guidance *see* normative guidance for business on human rights in a CSR context
　Business and Human Rights (BHR) *see* Business and Human Rights (BHR) regime
　Business Leaders Initiative for Human Rights (BLIHR) 126
　business responsibilities for 96–102, 234–5, 237–8, 240–41, 254–5
　and Corporate Social Responsibility (CSR) 41–2, 46–7, 48, 53, 60, 61–2, 63–4, 65–6, 68–70
　Draft Norms on responsibilities of TNCs and other business enterprises 121–2, 128–9, 177–8
　EU CSR Alliance 165, 166, 279, 283
　EU multi-stakeholder forum (MSF) on CSR 143–5, 147, 149–50, 154, 155–6, 157, 158, 159, 160–61, 162, 165, 279, 287, 303–4
　horizontality doctrine in international human rights law 10–12, 22–3
　natural resource extraction and human rights risk 189–91, 207, 208–9, 211, 214, 215, 245, 247
　normative guidance *see* normative guidance for business on human rights in a CSR context
　sectors prone to cause adverse impact on human rights 184
　South Africa, companies acting on human rights grounds during apartheid period 206–7
　and SRSG process 188, 192, 193, 196, 197, 200, 201, 205–7, 216, 225, 232, 233, 249, 257–8, 281, 286–7, 290, 291–2, 307, 313
　standards, and SRSG process 180, 181–2, 183, 195, 197, 204, 212–13, 215–16, 280
　state duty *see* state duty to protect human rights
　'weak governance zones' focus and human rights violations 192–4, 195–6, 209–10, 211, 213, 225, 254, 291
　see also environmental concerns; labour rights

incentives
　Corporate Social Responsibility (CSR) 53, 58, 61, 62, 67
　and SRSG process 207, 216, 223, 236–7, 240, 254
India, Companies Act 45, 47
institutionalisation 273–6, 283
interdiscursivity levels, effects of 91, 96–7, 100–101
　see also argumentative strategies
Interfaith investment group 191, 212–13
intergovernmental normative guidance, initial steps towards 111–16
intergovernmental organisations, rationality of 60–61
International Alert 206–7
International Bill of Human Rights 9, 241, 261, 281, 298, 313, 320
International Business Leaders Forum 124, 293
International Chamber of Commerce (ICC) 18, 125, 128, 129, 137, 176–7, 185, 193–4, 209–11, 250, 253–4, 257, 284, 289
International Commission of Jurists (ICJ) 187, 210
International Confederation of Free Trade Unions (ICFTU) 138, 185
International Council on Mining and Metals (ICCM) 207, 208–9, 213, 224
International Covenant on Civil and Political Rights (ICCPR) 9, 143, 155, 241
International Covenant on Economic, Social and Cultural Rights (ICESCR) 9, 143, 145, 155, 241
international crimes, corporate responsibility and accountability for 221, 222–3, 245, 249
international criminal law regime 22, 193, 196, 204, 205, 218, 219, 264
International Federation of Chemical,

Energy, Mine and General
    Workers' Union (ICEM) 138
international financial institutions
    215–16, 217
international human rights *see* human
    rights
international labour movement
    involvement, UN Global Compact
    138, 140
International Labour Organisation 9,
    18, 35, 78, 137
  core labour standards 68, 99, 149,
    150, 229, 238, 241, 261, 281,
    287, 298, 320
  Declaration on Fundamental
    Principles and Rights at Work
    73, 112–14, 115, 132, 217
  Declaration on Principles
    concerning Multinational
    Enterprises (Tripartite) 73, 112,
    119, 121, 129, 143, 144, 147,
    155, 156, 188, 217, 279, 290
  see also labour rights
International Organisation of
    Employers (IOE) 125, 128, 129,
    137, 176–7, 193–4, 209–11, 250,
    254, 257, 284, 289
  see also labour rights
international trade law, and SRSG
    process 192, 199, 205, 239
irritation, social sub-systems, process
    of developing and causing
    irritation in 84–5, 91, 92–5, 98–9,
    100
ISO 26000 Social Responsibility
    Guidance Standard 41, 51–2, 325

Jäger, S. 28
Jägers, N. 22, 204
Jeppesen, S. 64
Jørgensen, M. and Phillips, L. 27, 28,
    29, 32, 87, 90, 91

Kaysen, C. 63
Kell, G. 134, 136, 137–8
Kennedy, D. 26
Khalifa, R. 27
Kimathi, W. 44, 64
Kimberley Process 217
Kinderman, D. 57, 151

King, M. 85
Kinley, D. 71, 75, 119, 125, 289
Knox, J. 10, 22, 235
Koh, H. 11
Kolk, A. 74–5, 76
Kramer, M. 59
Krasner, S. 11
Kruger, M. 118, 119, 122, 126

La Mure, L. 110
labour rights
  core labour standards, developing
    countries 165, 166
  and Corporate Social Responsibility
    (CSR) 41–2, 46–7, 48, 53, 56,
    60, 61–2, 63–4, 65–6, 69
  EU CSR Alliance 165, 166, 279,
    283
  EU multi-stakeholder forum on
    CSR 143–5, 147, 149–50,
    154–62*passim*, 165, 279, 287,
    303–4
  International Labour Organisation
    see International Labour
    Organisation
  International Organisation of
    Employers (IOE) 125, 128, 129,
    137, 176–7, 193–4, 209–11, 250,
    254, 257, 284, 289
  outsourcing and low labour law
    standards 56
  public-private partnerships and
    work-place integration, training
    and education 66
  and UN Global Compact 136–7,
    138, 140, 141–2, 278
  see also environmental concerns;
    human rights
Laclau, E. 28, 29, 30, 87, 88, 91, 271
Lambooy, T. 110
language use 29–32, 89–95, 97, 98, 243
  see also system-specific
    communication
Lansing, P. 8, 112
law-free zones, 'workable guiding
    principles' and closure of law-free
    zones 232–3
law-in-process approach, Draft Norms
    127
legal autopoiesis *see* autopoiesis theory

legal experts' workshops, influence of 223
legal incentives *see* incentives
legal perspective, SRSG process *see* SRSG process, legal perspective
legal system rationality 36, 128, 129, 157, 179, 190, 251, 256–8
Lehmkuhl, D. 56
Lehr, A. 203
Levin, D. 134, 136, 137–8
lex ferenda argument 23, 101, 197, 237, 246, 260, 272, 287, 290, 291, 309–12
Lobel, O. 65
Logsdon, J. 59
Luhmann, N. 24, 82, 83–4
Lund-Thomsen, P. 64

McBarnet, D. 49
McCorquodale, R. 261, 295
Margolis, J. 59
Matten, D. 43, 44, 50–51, 65
Maturana, H. 83, 84
Mayer, A. 112
meaning, struggles for, and floating signifiers 87–9, 91, 92–3, 94, 272, 273
media, deregulation concerns from 109
Meidinger, E. 260
Melish, T. 260
Meyer, M. 30, 89–90
Midttun, A. 65
mining, natural resource extraction and human rights risk 189–91, 207, 208–9, 211, 214, 215, 245, 247
monitoring and verification, Draft Norms 120, 125
Moody-Stuart, M. 190, 245
Moon, J. 43, 44, 49, 50–51, 65
Mouffe, C. 28, 29, 30, 87, 88, 91, 271
multi-stakeholder involvement
and argumentative strategies *see* argumentative strategies, discourse and system-specific rationality, multi-stakeholder communication and discourse analysis
argumentative strategies and reflexive law 81–2, 84
development process, UN Global Compact 133–4, 137–9, 278, 283–4
EU multi-stakeholder forum on CSR *see* normative guidance for business on human rights in a CSR context, EU multi-stakeholder forum on CSR
'nudging' approach 327
regulatory processes and argumentative strategies 276–7, 287–8
SRSG process 175, 183–4, 204, 215–27*passim*, 231–2, 234, 242, 244–5, 252–3, 258–9, 280–81, 284, 290, 294, 297–8, 308–10
stakeholder statements, SRSG process 186–91, 198–202, 203–13, 227–30, 236–7, 255–6, 309–10
system-specific communication 327–8
see also civil society involvement
Mutua, M. 127

Nathan, I. 47
national context
argumentative strategies and reflexive law 83
Draft Norms and enforcement by national authorities, concerns over 123, 129, 177–8, 181
'effective national legislation', SRSG process 183
international criminal law implementation 205
state agencies and duty to protect 235–6
state duty to protect human rights *see* state duty to protect human rights
natural resource extraction and human rights risk 189–91, 207, 208–9, 211, 214, 215, 245, 247
network-based discourse and policy processes, Corporate Social Responsibility (CSR) 77–8
Neves, M. 83
Newell, P. 42
NGO involvement 74–6, 109, 274–5
see also civil society

Nolan, J. 75, 109, 134, 180
non-attribution rule 175
Nonet, P. 63, 80
normative guidance for business on human rights in a CSR context 105–72, 316–17, 318–19
  Asian textiles market concerns 110–11
  business impact on environment and human rights violations, societal attention on 109–10
  companies' contributions to healthcare and pensions 108
  CSR history 106–10
  deregulation concerns from NGOs and media 109
  direct and indirect human rights concerns 106–11
  environmental concerns 109–10, 113
  intergovernmental normative guidance, initial steps towards 111–16
  legal regulation of companies, move towards 109
  and self-regulation 141–2, 303
  slavery ban and moral convictions 107
  socially responsible investment (SRI) 107–8
  TNCs, boycott campaigns 110–11
  TNCs, and international Codes of Conduct 111–15, 170–71
  TNCs and trade rights imbalance 109
  welfare state development 108
  see also Corporate Social Responsibility (CSR)
normative guidance for business on human rights in a CSR context, Draft Norms on responsibilities of TNCs and other business enterprises 8, 19–20, 26, 34, 42, 73, 102, 115, 116–31, 168–9, 170–71
  approval failure 130–31
  binding or non-binding form of regulation, debate over 119–20, 177
  business associations opposing initiative 128–9, 182, 183, 191, 193, 327
  business associations self-regulation practices 128–9
  civil society consultations 124, 178–9, 327
  'complicity' concerns 123
  consumer and environmental issues 121
  due diligence obligations for human rights 122–3, 210–11
  enforcement by national authorities, concerns over 123, 129, 177–8, 181
  enterprise's 'sphere of influence' concerns 121, 123, 178–9
  environmental concerns 116–17, 118, 121
  and hard law 120, 128–9, 129, 177–8, 1692
  Human Rights Commission referral 124–6
  human rights focus 117–18, 120–23, 124–5, 179
  and international human rights law 121–2, 128–9, 177–8
  law-in-process approach 127
  legally binding concerns 129, 177
  monitoring and verification 120, 125
  'Norms', adoption of term 118–19
  origin and evolution 116–27
  pilot schemes 125–6
  'sphere of influence' reference 121, 123, 178–9, 244, 245–6, 248
  SRSG mandate, lack of mention in 126, 182, 196, 200–201, 210, 273, 276, 277–8, 284, 288–98, 322
  stabilising and de-stabilising arguments 328
  system-specific communication 127–31, 319
  UDHR as common standard of achievement 121
normative guidance for business on human rights in a CSR context, EU CSR Alliance 20, 25, 35, 42, 164–8, 169–70, 279, 280, 308
  2006 Communication 165–6, 324
  best practice guidance 164, 166–8, 280
  economic system language 165, 167

environmental concerns 165
and international human rights
and labour laws 165, 166, 279,
283
public policy objectives 165–6
stabilising strategy 287
system-specific arguments 165–8,
287
voluntary nature of CSR 165
normative guidance for business on
human rights in a CSR context,
EU multi-stakeholder forum on
CSR 20, 25, 34–5, 37, 42, 50,
142–64, 169, 171, 277
best practices appeal 146
business organisation involvement
142, 144, 146, 147–8, 152, 160,
163–4, 287, 304
civil society involvement 152–3,
157, 158–9, 160, 161, 163, 165,
310–12
conduct guidance, lack of precise
155, 156–7, 158
and economic system arguments
147, 303, 305–6, 311–12
environmental concerns 144, 146,
147, 150, 151–2, 154, 158,
279
and EU employment and social
affairs policy 149–50
EU policy initiatives 143–8
Final Report 153–6, 157–9, 160–61,
209, 279, 284–5, 304, 306
Green Paper (2001) 146–8, 303
and hard law 149, 155, 159, 179
human rights elements of the Lisbon
Strategy 146
and international human rights and
labour laws 143–5, 147, 149–50,
154–62 passim, 165, 279, 287,
303–4
Lisbon Strategy 144–6, 151, 161–2
process and output 150–59
provision of procedural and
normative details (2002
Communication) 148–50
public policy objectives 146, 147,
150, 161, 163, 304, 305
social expectations 157, 164, 318
and SRSG process launch 145

stabilising and de-stabilising
strategies 286, 287, 303–4, 311,
328
system-specific communication 152,
160–64, 191, 283, 284–5, 286,
302–8, 310–12, 319, 328
and UN Global Compact 155, 156,
159, 279, 284–5
voluntary nature of CSR 147, 152–3,
159, 160–62, 163, 279, 283, 303,
306
normative guidance for business on
human rights in a CSR context,
UN Global Compact 131–42, 169,
171
business organisation involvement
141–2
civil society involvement 133–4, 138,
140, 142
and companies' economic interests
135, 136–7
difference from and overlaps with
Draft Norms 132, 133
discursive evolution and normative
guidance 134–9
environmental concerns 133–4,
135–7, 139, 140, 141–2, 278,
298–9, 300, 322
harm prevention 132
international law standards 140, 283
and labour rights 136–7, 138, 140,
141–2, 278
multi-stakeholder development
process 133–4, 137–9, 278,
283–4
official launch 139–40
originality of 131–4
Public-Private-Partnership
resolutions 133
setting up and agreement on nine
Principles 131–2, 137
social expectations 135, 322
system-specific communication
139–42, 163, 164, 283–4
UN General Assembly acceptance
132–3
normative standards, and
argumentative strategies 81, 91–5,
97–8, 271–7
Nott, S. 71

'nudging' approach, multi-stakeholder involvement 327

O'Brien, C. 260
Ochoa, C. 260
OECD Guidelines for Multinational Enterprises 35, 112–15, 119, 121, 129, 143, 144, 147, 150, 155, 156, 188, 279, 287, 290, 325
  and SRSG process 188, 211, 229, 234, 240
Office of the High Commissioner for Human Rights (OHCHR) 123, 125, 137, 189, 215
ombudsman proposal, SRSG process 228, 238, 258, 329
'operationalisation' call, SRSG process 252, 253–5, 280
opportunistic compliance, Corporate Social Responsibility (CSR) 55, 56
O'Reilly, P. 112
Orlitzky, M. 59
Orts, E. 24, 25, 81, 82
outsourcing and low labour law standards 56

Palazzo, G. 65
Paris Accord 13, 325–6
Parker, C. 260–61
pensions, companies' contributions to 108
Phillips, L. and Jørgensen, M. 27, 28, 29, 32, 87, 90, 91
pilot schemes, Draft Norms 125–6
political coalitions 77
political system considerations, SRSG process 192, 194, 199, 208, 209, 211–12, 220–21, 224, 225–6, 229–30, 255
Porter, M. 59
power concerns
  and argumentative strategies 86, 87–8, 91, 271–85
  discourse theory and analysis 27, 28–9, 30
practitioners, implication for 329–31
'predictability gaps', SRSG process 221
Prieto-Carron, M. 64
'principled pragmatism' approach, SRSG process 197–8

procedural theory for regulated self-regulation 80–81, 82–3
see also self-regulation
profits, companies' evasion of paying taxes in states where profits were made, concerns over 178
Programme for the Endorsement of Forestry Certification (PEFC) 51–2
public goods, social or economic rights connected with 69–70
public opinion, 'court of public opinion' reference, SRSG process 216–17, 220–21, 237, 242, 294
public policy objectives
  Business and Human Rights (BHR) regime 11
  Corporate Social Responsibility (CSR) 41, 59–68
  EU CSR Alliance 165–6
  EU multi-stakeholder forum on CSR 146, 147, 150, 161, 163, 304, 305
  SRSG process 181–2, 188–9, 194–5, 196, 197, 207, 236–7, 282, 289
public-private-partnerships
  UN Global Compact 133
  and work-place integration, training and education 66

Ramasatry, A. 41
Redmond, P. 112
Rees, C. 253
reflexive law
  and argumentative strategies see argumentative strategies, discourse and system-specific rationality, reflexive law
  argumentative strategies and influence on output of regulatory processes 272–3
  autopoietic element in 21, 23–6, 273, 329
  and harm prevention 85
  multi-stakeholder involvement 81–2, 84
  and self-regulation practices 80–81, 82–3
  and socio-legal theory 24–5
  see also autopoiesis theory
Regil, A. 260

regional differences, Corporate Social Responsibility (CSR) 44–5
regulation
  and argumentative strategies *see* argumentative strategies
  and influence on output of regulatory processes
  governmental regulation, Corporate Social Responsibility (CSR) 47–8
  legal regulation of companies, move towards 109
  self-regulation *see* self-regulation
  smart regulation 57
  smart-mix regulation 60–61
  textual analysis of constructing normativity in 91–5, 97–8
Rehbinder, E. 81
Reinalda, B. 74, 75
remedy access, SRSG process 232, 234, 235, 238, 242, 254–5, 281, 309–10, 329
Rendtorff, J. 55
Renna, A. 65
reputation management and risk 237–8
'responsible operation' of TNCs, SRSG process 183
Rio Declaration on Environment and Development 132
risk management
  companies disregarding human rights issues 193, 199, 201–2, 211–13, 220–21, 239–40, 242, 256–7, 259–60, 264, 292, 296–7
  natural resource extraction and human rights risk 189–91, 207, 208–9, 211, 214, 215, 245, 247
  SRSG process 237–8
  and weak governance 66, 69
Rock, M. 56
Roepstorff, A. 56, 108
Rogowski, R. 24, 81–2
Rosaria, A. 8, 112
Rostgaard, M. 108
Rottleuthner, H. 84
Ruggie, J. 9, 52, 136, 276
  as Special Representative of the UN Secretary-General on Business and Human Rights *see* SRSG process

SA8000 51–2
Sagafi-Nejad, T. 111, 112
Sand, I.-J. 24, 33
Sanders, A. 261
Schäffner, C. 86
Scherer, A. 65
Scheuerman, W. 25
Schoenberger, K. 110
Schwartz, M. 46, 55–6
Scott, C. 65
sectors prone to cause adverse impact on human rights 184
  see also human rights
self-regulation practices 128–9, 141–2, 303
  and reflexive law 80–81, 82–3
  and SRSG process 197, 210, 213, 214, 216
Selznick, P. 63, 80, 108
Seppala, N. 12
Servais, J.-M. 109
Shelton, D. 22, 71, 72
Shrivastava, P. 23, 80
Sjöström, E. 107
smart regulation 57
smart-mix regulation 60–61
Snyder, F. 71
social affairs policy, and EU employment 149–50
social autopoiesis *see* autopoiesis theory
social causal event, text as 90
social expectations 8, 15, 330
  and argumentative strategies 83, 84, 93, 99, 100, 274, 275–6, 281, 283, 284, 294, 295
  and Corporate Social Responsibility (CSR) 45, 48–9, 52, 54, 55, 60, 61, 68, 76, 312, 313–14
  and EU multi-stakeholder forum (MSF) 157, 164, 318
  and SRSG process 197, 219–21, 223, 225, 237, 240–41, 242, 261–2, 264, 307
  and UN Global Compact 135, 322
social practice, language use as 90
social responsibilities
  argumentative strategies 86, 88–9, 90–91, 275–6

CSR *see* Corporate Social Responsibilities (CSR)
government procurement policies 214
social sub-systems 80, 84–5, 91, 92–5, 98–9, 100
social sustainability, and Corporate Social Responsibility (CSR) 41, 42–9
socially responsible investment (SRI) 107–8
societal concern with sustainable development 90–91, 97
society, business impact on society, developing norms on 74–8
socio-economic development of developing countries 182
see also developing countries
soft law 4, 5, 11, 18, 23, 38, 40
and Corporate Social Responsibility (CSR) 41, 50, 58, 69, 70–73, 78, 91, 96
definition 71–2
and Draft Norms 118, 119, 127, 129, 168–9, 198
and EU multi-stakeholder forum 155
future recommendations on soft law measures, SRSG process 217, 232, 233, 237, 282
SRSG process 206, 217–19, 223, 228, 231–3, 237, 247, 255–6, 282, 289
and UN Global Compact 132
see also binding/non-binding form of regulation, debate over; hard law; individual agreements
South Africa, companies acting on human rights grounds during apartheid period 206–7
Spar, D. 110
Special Representative of the UN Secretary-General on Business and Human Rights *see* SRSG process
specificity
argumentative strategies and influence on output of regulatory processes 309–12, 328–9

Clean Clothes Campaign, supply chain management 227–8, 258, 309
see also system-specific communication
Spence, C. 26
sphere of influence concerns 205, 234, 238, 241–2, 243–51, 262, 264, 295, 297
Draft Norms 121, 123, 178–9, 244, 245–6, 248
see also complicity concerns
spirit of the law, and Corporate Social Responsibility (CSR) 46
SRSG process 6, 20, 25–6, 35–6, 37, 38, 42, 48–9, 50, 89, 101–2, 123, 173–265, 318
acceptance of output of SRSG terms 256–65
access to remedy 232, 234, 235, 238, 242, 254–5, 281, 309–10, 329
Amnesty International statement 178–80, 186–9, 198–9, 230, 247, 290–91
argumentative structure and strategy 176–84
best practices element of mandate 174, 184, 189
bilateral investment treaties and host government agreements 231–2
and business interests as priority 183–4
business responsibilities for human rights (BHR) 261–5, 281, 289–90, 312–14, 319–25
coercion issues 190–91
companies' evasion of paying taxes in states where profits were made, concerns over 178
company accountability argument 206–7, 211
and 'complicity' 234, 238, 241–2, 243–51, 262, 264, 295–6
consultation recommendations 183–4
corporate responsibility and accountability for international crimes 221, 222–3, 245, 249
corporate responsibility to respect human rights 219–21, 224,

234–5, 237–8, 240–41, 246, 254–5, 257, 293, 294–5
'court of public opinion' reference 216–17, 220–21, 237, 242, 248–9, 294
discourse evolution 175–6
diversity of states' interests 180–81
Draft Norms to mandate establishment journey 176–85
due diligence processes 187, 210–11, 235, 238, 241, 248–51, 257, 281, 295–7, 298, 326
'effective national legislation' 183
environmental concerns 207, 222, 294
Federation Internationale des Ligues des Droits des l'Homme (FIDH) report 203–5, 225, 246–7
financial institutions' responsibilities to human rights 215–16, 228–9, 258
first mandate year 186–202, 280
future recommendations on soft law measures 217, 232, 233, 237, 282
and 'good practices' 195, 208
and governance gaps 188, 213, 215, 221, 312–13
grievance and complaints mechanisms 228, 235, 261–2
guidance for business activities in conflict zones 202, 210, 225, 240, 247, 250, 254
and hard law 184–5, 193, 199, 232, 258, 276, 297–8
and harm prevention 203, 235, 288–9, 310
and human rights standards 180, 181–2, 183, 195, 197, 204, 212–13, 215–16, 280
impartiality 193
and incentives 207, 216, 223, 236–7, 240, 254
interim report (2006) 194–8, 200, 201, 204–5, 245
and international human rights law 188, 192, 193, 196, 197, 200, 201, 205–7, 216, 225, 232, 233, 249, 257–8, 281, 286–7, 290, 291–2, 307, 313
and international trade law 192, 199, 205, 239
launch 145
legal experts' workshops, influence of 223
legal system language use 243
mandate 174, 175–6, 182–4, 199–200, 221–2
mandate, lack of mention of Draft Norms 126, 182, 196, 200–201, 210, 273, 276, 277–8, 284, 288–98, 322
mandatory reporting argument 212–13
and Millennium Development Goals (MDGs) 195
multi-stakeholder involvement 175, 183–4, 204, 215–27*passim*, 231–2, 234, 242, 244–5, 252–3, 258–9, 280–81, 284, 290, 294, 297–8, 308–10
national law implementation of international criminal law 205
natural resource extraction and human rights risk 189–91, 207, 208–9, 211, 214, 215, 245, 247
and OECD Guidelines for Multinational Enterprises 188, 211, 229, 234, 240
ombudsman proposal 228, 238, 258, 329
'operationalisation' call 252, 253–5, 280
political system considerations 192, 194, 199, 208, 209, 211–12, 220–21, 224, 225–6, 229–30, 255
'predictability gaps' 221
'principled pragmatism' approach 197–8
public policy goals 188–9
public policy interests 181–2, 194–5, 196, 197, 207, 236–7, 282, 289
report (2008), Protect, Respect and Remedy 233–43, 264–5, 280
'responsible operation' of TNCs 183
risk and general reputation management 237–8

second mandate year 202–26, 280, 292, 297–8
second report (2007), 'Business and Human Rights' 218–24, 225–6
second three-year mandate term, UN Framework to UNGPs 252–6, 264–5, 280–82, 289, 298, 312–13, 319–22, 324–5
sectors prone to cause adverse impact on human rights 184
and self-regulation 197, 210, 213, 214, 216
and social expectations 197, 219, 221, 223, 225, 237, 240–41, 242, 261–2, 264, 307
social norms and expectations 219–21, 237, 242
and socio-economic development of developing countries 182
and soft law 206, 217–19, 223, 228, 231–3, 237, 247, 255–6, 282, 289
'sphere of influence' concept 205, 234, 238, 241–2, 243–51, 262, 264, 295, 297
SRSG statements 213–17, 230–33
stabilising and de-stabilising arguments 286–7, 289, 290–91, 292–5, 308–9, 310, 324, 328
stakeholder cooperation, call for 253
stakeholder statements 186–91, 198–202, 203–13, 227–30, 236–7, 255–6, 309–10
standards identification 186–7
state agencies and duty to protect 235–6
state duty to protect human rights *see* state duty to protect human rights
statements 191–4
statements and 'non-attribution rule' 175
supply chain management and Clean Clothes Campaign 227–8, 258, 309
system-specific arguments 174–5, 185, 191, 198–9, 204, 217, 224, 231–2, 243, 246, 249–51, 254–64, 284–7, 294, 308–10, 319, 324

third mandate year (2007 report to UN Framework) 226–43
TNC situation 211–12, 223
UN human rights treaty bodies involvement 234
victims, approach to 180, 193, 199, 201, 220–21, 229–30, 231, 232, 235, 258
and voluntary nature of CSR 179–81, 208–9, 217, 223, 228, 240, 286
'weak governance zones' focus and human rights violations 192–4, 195–6, 209–10, 211, 213, 225, 254, 291
'workable guiding principles' and closure of law-free zones 232–3
SRSG process, and economic system interests
Amnesty International statement 178–80, 188–9
complicity concept 248–9, 251
and Draft Norms opposition 183
export credit agencies and international financial institutions 215–16, 217
global supply chain management 194–5
human rights responsibilities of businesses 219–21, 224, 246, 293, 294–5
Interfaith statement 191
International Alert statement 206–7
and international law 192, 225, 228–9, 231–2, 258
mining sector investment 208–9
risks if companies disregard human rights issues 193, 199, 201–2, 211–13, 220–21, 239–40, 242, 256–7, 259–60, 264, 292, 296–7
social responsibility requirement in government procurement policies 214
SRSG process, legal perspective
Amnesty International statement 178–80, 186–9
complicity concept 248–9, 251
'court of public opinion' reference 216–17, 220–21, 237, 242, 248–9, 294

and 'courts of public opinion' 248–9
and Draft Norms 177, 183, 184–5,
    190–91, 200, 293–4
FIDH report 203–5, 225, 246–7
human rights responsibilities of
    businesses 219–21, 240, 241, 257
and international law 194–5, 196–7,
    198–201, 231–2
legal expert workshops 214–15
legal logic arguments 200, 204, 205,
    225, 257, 264, 284, 287, 289
legal system language use 225–6,
    254–5, 257, 259–60
legal system rationality 179, 190,
    251, 256–8
mining sector investment 208–9
'principled pragmatism' approach
    197–8
social responsibility in government
    procurement policies 214
'sphere of influence' concept 241–2
victim protection 229–31
weak governance zones 192–4, 211
stabilising and de-stabilising arguments
    21, 32, 34, 328
  Draft Norms 328
  EU CSR Alliance 287
  EU multi-stakeholder forum on CSR
    286, 287, 303–4, 311, 328
  influence on output of regulatory
    processes 272, 285–309
  multi-stakeholder communication
    and discourse analysis 100–102,
    257
  SRSG process 286–7, 289, 290–91,
    292–5, 308–9, 310, 324, 328
  system-specific communication 272,
    285–309
Staffe, M.-L. 26
stakeholder statements, SRSG process
    186–91, 198–202, 203–13, 227–30,
    236–7, 255–6, 309–10
  see also multi-stakeholder
    involvement
state agencies and duty to protect
    235–6
state consent, and soft law 73
state duty to protect human rights
    205–7, 219, 233–4, 254–5, 256–7,
    287, 291, 321

bilateral investment treaties 231–2
export credit agencies and
    international financial
    institutions 215–16, 217
FIDH comments 203–5, 225, 246–7
governance gaps 188, 213, 215, 221,
    312–13
incentive-based regulation 223
and international law 216, 222,
    235–6, 239–40, 276, 281, 292,
    293, 305
mining industry recommendations
    208–9, 215
and multi-stakeholder involvement
    204, 217
  see also human rights
supply chain management
  and Clean Clothes Campaign 227–8,
    258, 309
  economic system interests 194–5
  responsibility example 94–5
system-specific communication
  argumentative strategies and
    influence on output of
    regulatory processes 271–85
  Draft Norms 127–31, 319
  EU CSR Alliance 165–8, 287
  EU multi-stakeholder forum on CSR
    152, 160–64, 191, 283, 284–5,
    286, 302–8, 310–12, 319, 328
  multi-stakeholder involvement 327–8
  rationality and argumentative
    strategies see argumentative
    strategies, discourse and system-
    specific rationality
  SRSG process 174–5, 185, 191,
    198–9, 204, 217, 224, 231–2,
    243, 246, 249–51, 254–64,
    284–7, 294, 308–10, 319, 324
  stabilising or de-stabilising strategies
    272, 285–309
  UN Global Compact 139–42, 163,
    164, 283–4
  see also autopoiesis theory; language
    use; specificity
Szasz, P. 71

taxation, companies' evasion of paying
    taxes in states where profits were
    made 178

Teubner, G. 24, 80, 81, 82, 83, 84, 272
text as social causal event 90
textiles market concerns, Asian 110–11
textual analysis
  external and internal 33–4
  and linguistic elements 29–32
  linguistic statements influence on discourse and meaning 89–91
  regulatory processes 91–5, 97–8
Thiele, B. 125
Tickell, S. 112
transmission, linguistic means of 92–5, 97, 98
transnational corporations (TNCs)
  boycott campaigns 110–11
  Business and Human Rights (BHR) regime 7–8, 35–6
  and Corporate Social Responsibility (CSR) 56, 61, 74, 77–8
  and Draft Norms, normative guidance *see* normative guidance for business on human rights in a CSR context, Draft Norms on responsibilities of TNCs and other business enterprises
  international Codes of Conduct 111–15, 170–71
  'responsible operation' of 183
  SRSG process 183, 211–12, 223
  and trade rights imbalance 109
transnationalisation of law 9–10, 12–13
Trubek, D. 15, 65
Trubek, L. 65

UDHR *see* Universal Declaration on Human Rights (UDHR)
UN Code of Conduct on Transnational Corporations 111–12
UN Commission on International Trade Law (UNCITRAL) 233
UN Convention against Corruption 132
UN Declaration of the Right to Development 72
UN Declaration on the Rights of Disabled Persons 150
UN Declaration on the Rights of Indigenous Peoples 73

UN Environment Programme (UNEP) 137
UN Framework 6–9, 11, 12, 20, 35, 48, 53, 88, 101–2, 204, 206, 209, 213, 216, 219
  SRSG process, second three-year mandate term, UN Framework to UNGPs 252–6, 264–5, 280–82, 289, 298, 312–13, 319–22, 324–5
  SRSG process, third mandate year (2007 report to UN Framework) 226–43
UN General Assembly Resolutions on Public-Private-Partnerships 73
UN Global Compact 19, 20, 25, 34, 35, 37, 42, 51–2, 62, 73, 102, 113, 119, 123, 129, 322–4
  companies' annual Communication on Progress reports 63
  development process 298–302, 323–4
  and EU multi-stakeholder forum on CSR 155, 156, 159, 279, 284–5
  and normative guidance *see* normative guidance for business on human rights in a CSR context, UN Global Compact
  'sphere of influence' concept 244–5, 246
  stabilising strategy 286, 300, 308
UN Guiding Principles (UNGPs) 6, 8, 9, 11, 12, 20, 35, 49, 57, 88, 115, 204, 211, 237, 251
  SRSG process, second three-year mandate term, UN Framework to UNGPs 252–6, 264–5, 280–82, 289, 298, 312–13, 319–22, 324–5
UN Human Rights Council 6, 8, 20, 35, 37, 194, 199, 220, 221–2, 226, 230, 232, 234, 242–3, 247, 250–51, 255–6, 262, 264, 282, 297, 320
UN Millennium Development Goals (MDGs) 195
UN Principles for Responsible Investment (PRI) 63
UN Sustainable Development Goals (SDGs) 13
Universal Declaration on Human

Rights (UDHR) 8, 9, 10, 68, 71, 99, 121, 132, 155, 156, 195, 237, 241, 278, 302
US
  Alien Torts Claims Act 193
  Alien Torts Statute 110–11
  Council for International Business 178, 185, 289
  Dodd-Frank Wall Street Reform Act 47
  Lacey Act 47

Vallentin, S. 108
Van Dijk, T. 28, 30
victims, approach to, SRSG process 180, 193, 199, 201, 220–21, 229–30, 231, 232, 235, 258
Vogel, D. 49, 59
voluntary nature of CSR
  challenges to 44–5, 48, 49–59, 89
  and EU CSR Alliance 165
  and EU multi-stakeholder forum on CSR 147, 152–3, 159, 160–62, 163, 279, 283, 303, 306
  and SRSG process 179–81, 208–9, 217, 223, 228, 240, 286
Voluntary Principles on Business and Human Rights 217

Wæver, O. 27
Walsh, J. 59
Warhurst, A. 125
Warren, D. 56

weak governance zones 66, 69
  focus and SRSG process 192–4, 195–6, 209–10, 211, 213, 225, 254, 291
  see also conflict zones
Webb, T. 126, 127
Weissbrodt, D. 118, 119, 122, 126
Wellens, K. 70
Wettstein, F. 49, 261
Wetzel, R.-M. 276
Williams, C. 26
Wilmhurst, E. 202
Wilthagen, T. 24, 82
Wodak, R. 30
work-place integration, and public-private partnerships 66
'workable guiding principles' and closure of law-free zones 232–3
World Bank, International Forum 231, 233, 257
World Business Council for Sustainable Development 124
World Economic Forum 286, 287
World Summit on Sustainable Development 63–4
Wouters, J. 8
Wright, M. 203

Zadek, S. 107
Zahran, M. 134
Zerk, J. 47, 58–9, 111, 187
Zumbansen, P. 9–10